COMMUNICATING

A Social and Career Focus

Seventh Edition

Roy M. Berko
George Washington University

Andrew D. Wolvin
*University of Maryland
College Park and University College*

Darlyn R. Wolvin
Prince George's Community College

HOUGHTON MIFFLIN COMPANY
Boston   New York

Sponsoring Editor: George Hoffman
Associate Project Editor: Christina Lillios
Production/Design Coordinator: Jennifer Meyer Dare
Marketing Manager: Pamela J. Laskey
Manufacturing Coordinator: Marie Barnes
Editorial Assistant (Editorial): Kara Maltzahn
Editorial Assistant (Production): Joy Park

Cover design: Linda Manly Wade

Cover art: *The Circus Series of Signs and Symbols* by Silvio DelaCruz. Courtesy Silverstein Gallery, New York.

Cartoons: Bob Vojtko

Photo Credits: Page 2, Janice Fullman/The Picture Cube; page 6, Susan Ylvisaker/Jeroboam; page 12, Bob Daemmrich/The Image Works; page 23, Mike Mazzaschi/Stock Boston; page 28, Bob Daemmrich/The Image Works; page 33, Chester Higgins, Jr./Photo Researchers, Inc.; page 41, Alexander Lowry/Photo Researchers, Inc.; page 50, Hisham Youseff/The Picture Cube; page 51, Sarah Putnam/The Picture Cube; page 59, Peter Vandermark/Stock Boston; page 72, Elizabeth Crews/The Image Works; page 78, Joel Gordon; page 90, Hazel Hankin/Stock Boston; page 96, Paul Conklin; page 102, J. Moore/The Image Works; page 106, Thomas B.W. Friedman/Photo; page 117, Bob Daemmrich/The Image Works; page 125, Ira Kirshenbaum/Stock Boston; page 132, Bob Daemmrich/The Image Works; page 134, Suzanne Arms/Jeroboam; page 154, Cleo Freelance/Jeroboam; page 160, Spencer Grant/Stock Boston; page 165, David Frazier/Photo Researchers, Inc.; page 178, Dean Abramson/Stock Boston; page 185, Jane Scherr/Jeroboam; page 192, David M. Grossman/Photo Researchers, Inc.; page 200, Jim Pickerell/Stock Boston; page 204, Arvind Garg/Photo Researchers, Inc.; page 209, Harriet Gans/The Image Works; page 222, Aneal Vohra/The Picture Cube; page 226, Laimute E. Druskis/Jeroboam; page 240, Kathy Sloan/Jeroboam; page 248, Spencer Grant/The Picture Cube; page 250, Jim Smalley/The Picture Cube; page 256, Frank Siteman/Jeroboam; page 265, Nita Winter/The Image Works; page 276, Bob Daemmrich/The Image Works; page 277, Joel Gordon; page 283, Barbara Rios/Photo Researchers, Inc.; page 306, Matthew Borkoski/Stock Boston; page 311, Dion Ogust; page 318, Hazel Hazin/Stock Boston; page 326, John Coletti/The Picture Cube; page 329, Bob Daemmrich/The Image Works; page 339, John Coletti/The Picture Cube; page 354, Spencer Grant/The Picture Cube; page 359, Ken Winokur/The Picture Cube; page 361, Jeffrey Dunn/Stock Boston; page 364, Beringer/Dratch/The Image Works; page 374, AP/Wide World Photos; page 379, Topham/The Image Works; page 381, Nita Winter/The Image Works; page 391, Jean Claude Lejeune/Stock Boston.

Printed in the U.S.A.

Library of Congress Catalog Card Number: 97-72443

ISBN: 0-395-86887-4

456789-QF-01 00 99

BRIEF CONTENTS

CONTENTS

3 Listening   *50*

4 Foundations of Verbal Language   *78*

7 Interpersonal Skills   160

12 Public Speaking: Developing the Speech

PREFACE

A Message to Students

When the first edition of *Communicating: A Social and Career Focus* was published in 1977, the first paragraph of the preface read: "As you read this book, you will find that your authors are committed to the idea that effective speaking skills are crucial for all people." We went on to state that approximately 45 percent of a person's communication time is spent in listening, 30 percent in speaking, 16 percent in reading, and only 9 percent in writing. It also revealed that 50 to 80 percent of a person's workday was spent in communication, two-thirds of which was talking.

It's now twenty years later, and the premise presented way back then still holds. Recent information still informs us that the average North American spends a great deal of life in the act of communicating. The average student, for example, listens to the equivalent of a book a day and talks the equivalent of a book a week.[1] Research demonstrates that communication skills are the most important skills a person can have for entry-level jobs and for career success alike.[2] According to a study of employers, the major competencies required of people in the workforce are working in teams, teaching others, serving customers, leading, negotiating, and working well with people of culturally diverse backgrounds.[3]

Though understanding the concepts and having the necessary skills in communication are generally accepted as critical to personal and professional success, only a limited number of people are competent communicators. Twenty-five percent of the nation's people cannot adequately communicate orally.[4] Almost 63 percent of people cannot give clear oral directions.[5] About 20 percent of the children in any given school exhibit high levels of communication anxiety in most speaking situations.[6] It is estimated that 50 to 70 percent of people are apprehensive about speaking in public.[7]

Because of these findings regarding the limited nature of communication skills, the National Communication Association, the nation's largest organization of speech and communication professors, teachers, and professionals, recently published the document *Speaking, Listening, and Media Literacy Standards for K through 12 Education*.[8] That document states, "Communication shapes our sense of self and the way we interact in our environment, from gathering and presenting information to managing conflict."[9] It goes on to state, "Speaking, listening, and media literacy are fundamental to the process, purpose, and influence of interpersonal relations in the family, the workplace, and one-to-one social interactions."[10]

"Students must study and practice communication in order to achieve such competence; it does not come naturally."[11] Research shows that "there was significant behavioral change due to the [communication] training."[12]

This text gives you the opportunity to achieve communication competency, not only to gain an understanding of the communication process but also to improve the skills that will accompany you the rest of your life—understandings and skills that are most important to your success as a human being in relational, family, social, and career settings.

A Message to Instructors

Communication is an ever-expanding field. As new editions of basic course texts are published, the trend has been for books to get longer and longer, making it difficult to cover all the material in the period of time allotted a course. With this in mind, the authors have, for this edition, concentrated on stemming this tide. You will find this edition *concise, comprehensive,* and *creative.*

Conciseness   The volume, though it continues to include the newest research and approaches in contemporary and emerging communication issues, is considerably shorter than the last edition. We have continued to use examples, clarifying materials, and details but have done so in a way that has allowed for a compression of materials.

Comprehensiveness   In the last edition, a textual section was added to deal with contemporary issues. Although the response to that coverage was very positive, and many wanted to use all of the material, they found it too time-consuming. So rather than have a separate section on contemporary issues, such areas as freedom of speech, sexual harassment, Ebonics, and the English-Only/English-Plus movements have been addressed in the general textual materials. Instead of dealing with multiculturalism (racial, ethnic, gender, sexual orientation, and cultural similarities and differences) in a single section, it is incorporated throughout the book.

Creativity   Historically, students and faculty alike have praised the writing style of the book. As has been the case with previous editions, special attention again has been given to making this book readable, student-centered, and practical. Sidebars of enlightened and entertaining value are included. Custom-drawn cartoons that are relevant to the book have been included. The cartoonist, a nationally syndicated artist, a former student of one of the authors, not only is creative, but also knows the field of communication.

Other features new to this edition:

✳ Public speaking materials have been compressed so that there are only five rather than six chapters dedicated to that topic. The new approach combines planning and presenting the message as the initial exposure to the topic. This allows the student to get an entire view of speech presentation and preparation from the initial to the culminating experience before undertaking the specifics of developing the speech.

✳ The glossary of communication terms has been expanded to include all important terms in the book, not just the vocabulary terms.

✳ Chapters contain updated feature boxes that illustrate the concepts developed. These features include advice, humorous examples, poetry, visual representations, and quotes from famous people.

✳ Though gender communication similarities and differences are presented in many sections of the text, an in-depth rewritten section of female and male communication is presented in Chapter 6.

✳ An expanded discussion of ethics and the ethics of communicating are dealt with in the initial chapter.

✳ The discussion of learning/listening styles has been expanded with the addition of a revised self-study instrument.

✳ Updating has been done in all subject areas, with a special emphasis in the chapter on nonverbal communication.

✳ The material on relationships and their development has been reconfigured, as has been the section on participating in conversations.

✳ Conflict resolution has been expanded to include not only assertive communication but also negotiation, arbitration, litigation, and mediation.

✳ The material on presentation graphics has been refined.

✳ New informative and persuasive speeches are presented to show each of those processes in action.

Ancillary Materials

These support materials are available to the adopters of *Communicating*:

* *The Handbook of Instructional Options with Test Items* has been revised by Roy Berko and Joan Aitken (University of Missouri—Kansas City, and the editor of *The Speech Communication Teacher*). The manual contains suggested course syllabi and the rationale for each; an extended section on teaching tips; evaluation forms for speeches, interviews, and group discussions; transparencies; and activities and questions for each chapter.

* *Multicultural Activities Manual* by Marlene Cohen and Susan Richardson (Prince George's Community College), which contains activities that enhance student understanding of diversity and help them develop skills for living in a multicultural society, has been rewritten.

* *Speech Outlining Software* (IBM and Macintosh), a computer program especially tailored to this text, leads students through the process of outlining their own speeches. The self-directed, step-by-step program takes students through formats for each major speech design discussed in the text.

* An audiovisual order program, which allows instructors who adopt the text to obtain free videotapes, has been developed.

* Test-generating software (IBM and Macintosh) is available.

* PowerPoint slides of key concepts and figures in the text will be available on the Houghton Mifflin web site.

Acknowledgments

We wish to thank James Scruggs, for editorial assistance; George Hoffman, Sponsoring Editor, Kara Maltzahn, Editorial Assistant, and Barbara Brooks, Development Editor, all of Houghton Mifflin, for their encouragement and dedication regarding this project; Dr. Charles Buckalew, Professor of Philosophy, Lorain County Community College, for insightful advice on the subject of ethics; Helen Shepard, Associate Professor of Foreign Languages, Lorain County Community College, for expert analysis of the section on Hispanic dialect; The Reverend Ralph Hammond, for evaluation of the material on Black English.

We are indebted to those professors who have been loyal users of this book through its first six editions and hope that you will continue to use the text and to give insightful and helpful comments for future editions.

Appreciation also is extended to our professional colleagues who read and critiqued the manuscript through its development:

Nina-Jo Moore, Appalachian State University

Cheryl Mueller, Northwestern College

Michael Bruner, University of North Texas

Deborah Hefferin, Broward Community College

Carl M. Cates, Valdosta State University

Thomas Hunter, Martin Luther College

Shirlee A. Levin, Charles County Community College

Cherie C. White, Muskingum Area Technical College

 ## In Conclusion

Writing a book, whether it be a first or seventh edition, is a time-consuming and emotionally exhausting experience. The response to the prior editions of this text has been so overwhelmingly positive that both the publisher and the authors feel that the energy that we have put into the project has been rewarding. We hope that you agree, and that your communicative understandings and abilities are enhanced by having experienced what we present in this text.

COMMUNICATE COMPETENTLY!

R.M.B.
A.D.W.
D.R.W.

chapter 1

The Human Communication Process

After reading this chapter, you should be able to:

List and explain the components of human communication

Understand the relationship between communication and culture

Explain the effects of perceptions on the human communication process

Identify, define, and give examples of the noise factors that affect the human communication process

Illustrate, define, and give examples of the linear, interactional, and transactional models of communication

Understand the concept of communication as a system

Understand the role of First Amendment speech as a rhetorical tool

Explain the role of the ethical value system in communication

When confronted with the requirement of taking a communication course as part of their academic major, students sometimes ask, "Why do I need that? I know how to talk." Communication is more than talking. When you answer a question in class, receive a compliment, challenge another person's ideas, argue with a family member, touch someone, participate in a job interview, take part in a group meeting, listen to a classroom lecture, do a victorious high-five, select clothing to wear, or go through the process of buying a car, you are involved in the act of communicating! Significant friendships, successful family relationships, and academic and occupational success depend on communication abilities.

Studying communication, and learning how to be an effective communicator, is not just an academic exercise. The understanding of and ability to use communication is one of the most important skills you will learn. For example, your academic success may well be linked to your ability to communicate. "Students must have speaking, listening, classroom management, and interpersonal communication skills for successful completion of a college degree."[1] In classes, students must be able to ask and answer questions, summarize opinions, distinguish facts from opinions, and interact with their peers and instructors.[2]

Communication competency is indispensable for successful participation in the world of work. The ability to communicate effectively will often determine a person's perceived overall competency and level of success.[3] The most essential skills needed to be a competent employee are interviewing, listening, planning and conducting meetings, resolving conflicts, and public speaking.[4]

Most people are not effective communicators. Twenty percent of the nation's young people cannot accomplish any of the simplest of communication tasks,[5] almost 63 percent cannot give clear oral directions,[6] about 95 percent of the population reports some degree of anxiety about communicating with a person or in groups,[7] the apprehension level of those who fear speaking in public is estimated at 50 to 70 percent,[8] and adults listen at a 25 percent level of efficiency.[9]

Okay, so there is a need to be able to communicate, but the question still is, why do you have to take a course in communication? Though you may be able to talk, if you are typical, you still may not be able to effectively communicate. "Students must study and practice communication in order to achieve such competence, it does not come naturally."[10]

Did you know?

The average person spends 30% of his or her waking hours in conversation.

Communication Defined

Communication is a conscious or unconscious, intentional or unintentional process in which feelings and ideas are expressed as verbal and/or nonverbal messages, sent, received, and comprehended. This process can be *accidental* (having no intent), *expressive* (resulting from the emotional state of the person), or *rhetorical* (resulting from specific goals of the communicator).

Being able to effectively communicate improves your facility to maneuver ideas. Vague impressions gain reality; ideas are picked up and examined, set in categories, and eventually added to other ideas.

Human communication occurs on the intrapersonal, interpersonal, and public levels. **Intrapersonal communication** is communicating with yourself. It encompasses such activities as thought-processing, personal decision-making, listening, and determination of self-concept. **Interpersonal communication** refers to communication that takes place between two persons who establish a communicative relationship. Forms of interpersonal communication include conversations, interviews, and small-group discussions. **Public communication** is characterized by a speaker sending a message to an audience. Public communication may be direct, such as a face-to-face message delivered by a speaker to an audience, or indirect, such as a message relayed by radio or television.

A classic explanation describes communication as dynamic, continuous, irreversible, interactive, and contextual.[11] That concept is as contemporary today as when it was coined almost forty years ago.

Human communication is *dynamic* because the process is constantly in a state of change. As the attitudes, expectations, feelings, and emotions of persons who are communicating change, the nature of their communication does so as well.

Communication is *continuous* because it never stops. Whether asleep or awake, we are all processing ideas and information through our dreams, thoughts, and expressions. Our brains remain active; we are communicating.

Communication is *irreversible*. Once we send a message, we cannot undo it. Once we make a slip of the tongue, give a meaningful glance, or make an emotional outburst, we cannot erase it. Our apologies or denials cannot eradicate what has taken place.

Communication is *interactive*. We are constantly in contact with other people and with ourselves. Other people react to our speech and actions, and we react to our own speech and actions and then react to those reactions. Thus a cycle of action and reaction becomes the basis for our communication.

The highly complex process of communication is *contextual* because it is very much a part of our entire human experience. The complexity of communication dictates that we develop the awareness and the skills necessary to function effectively as communicators, and to adapt to the setting, the people present, and the purpose of the communication. A recent word-processing advertisement summarized this well when it heralded, "You don't talk to your mother the same way you talk to your buddies. (Better not, for your sake.) That nice polite talk is perfect for Sunday dinners. Or when you're asking for money. That's why you've got street talk. Small talk. Back talk. Coffee talk. Baby talk. And—even when you're not saying a word—body talk, which has absolutely no regard for syntax and grammar. Custom languages made to order. . . ."[12]

To be an effective communicator, you need to understand the relationship between communication and culture, how the communication process operates, and not only how you send and process information but also how you reason your way to conclusions and evaluate the ideas others send. In addition, good communicators know what ethical standards they use in making their decisions.

Communication and Culture

What phrase or terms immediately come to mind when you are asked, "What is your culture?"

Intercultural/Intracultural Communication

Usually, "when one speaks of culture, nationality comes to mind."[13] *Nationality* refers to the nation in which one was born, now resides, or has lived in or studied for enough time to become familiar with the customs of the area. Some nationality identifiers are Irish, Egyptian, and Korean. Nationality is only one factor of culture. Cultural group identifiers can include the region of a country (e.g., the southern part of the United States), religious orientation (e.g., Jewish), political orientation (e.g., Democrat), socioeconomic status (e.g., upper middle class), gender (e.g., female), sexual orientation (e.g., gay male), age/generation (e.g., senior citizen), vocation (e.g., executive), avocation (e.g., stamp collector), family background (e.g., Italian Catholic from a large family), marital status (e.g., married), and parental status (e.g., single father). We are each culture-filled, a combination of many cultures.

Think about your daily communication. A great deal of it centers on your cultural identifications. As a student, for example, how many times do you refer to student-oriented topics, including the institution you

A great deal of a person's daily communication centers on his or her cultural identifications.

attend and how your education will help you in the future? You probably compare and contrast your "studentness" to other students and nonstudents.

Communication and culture have a direct link. A **culture** consists of all those individuals who have a shared system of interpretation.[14] Culture is a communication phenomenon because it is passed among its adherents by communication—written and oral, verbal and nonverbal. "Culture is the software that allows the hardware (the person) to operate."[15] Your parents, schools, and the media were all influential in aiding you to develop your belief system through communication. You were spoken to and listened to, and you saw and read about the rules, customs, and habits of those with whom you lived, in your home, region of the country, and nation. This is an ongoing process; it was and is done through communication.

When you interact with those with whom you have a cultural bond, you are participating in **intracultural communication**. For example, a baseball fanatic speaking to another baseball fanatic has a cultural bond. When you speak to those with whom you have little or no cultural bond, however, it is referred to as **intercultural communication**. A Japanese citizen with little knowledge of New Zealand and a New Zealander with little knowledge of Japan or its customs who are speaking with each other are involved on an intercultural level.

Communicating Cross-Culturally

If you work with people whose native language is not your own, follow these tips to communicate instructions clearly:

✳ Avoid complicated and lengthy explanations. Keep instructions short.

✳ Make it clear that you welcome questions when something is unclear.

✳ Ask them to repeat your instructions in their own words. *Reason:* If they repeat the instructions in your words, they may have memorized the words but not the message.

SOURCE: Sondra Thiederman, Ph.D., president of Cross-Cultural Communications, cited in *Leadership for the Front Lines*, 24 Rope Ferry Road, Waterford, CT 06386.

When people from various cultures live in the same place, unique multicultural problems exist.

Multiculturalism

The term **multiculture** refers to a society consisting of varied cultural groups.[16] The United States is a multicultural country as it relates to ethnic derivation, as it is made up of hyphenatedly-identified people: African-Americans, Hispanic-Americans, Irish-Americans to name a few. It is also multicultural as it relates to the broader definition of culture since it contains such differences as women and men, homosexuals and heterosexuals, and religious believers and atheists.

Much attention has been given to **multiculturalism**, a political and attitudinal movement to ensure cultural freedom. The movement came about because "a lot of people are ignorant about people of color, gay and lesbians, or whatever [Hispanics, Spanish Americans, Asians, and people from other cultures]. These groups feel like they are marginalized."[17]

"By the year 2000, one in four Americans will be black, Hispanic, or Asian."[18] "By 2035, more than half of all Americans younger than eighteen will belong to minority groups."[19] Many of these individuals have verbal and nonverbal patterns quite different from mainstream Americans because of their cultural background, in this specific case, their ethnic group.

People from ethnic minority groups face a different and sometimes hostile and alien culture, value system, and communication system when entering such areas as schools systems and corporate, social service, and governmental environments.[20] For example, many minority students perform poorly in school classes because they lack competence in the majority culture's rules for communication.

The ethnic majority often doesn't understand or has biases against those who are culturally different, and the culturally different don't understand the motives and patterns of the mainstream.

Accepting that you are a cultural being, understanding the process you use to discuss cultural affiliations, as well as other aspects of yourself, are important parts of learning to be a competent communicator.

 ## The Components of Human Communication

As human beings, we are capable of **selective communication**. That is, from the wide repertory available to us we can choose the symbol we feel best represents the idea or concept we wish to express. We can think in abstractions, plan events in the future, and store and recall information. Selective communication allows us to combine sounds into complicated structures and, therefore, describe events and objects.

Simply put, when we communicate we **encode** (take ideas and put them into message form), send them through a channel composed of our **primary signal system** (the senses: seeing, hearing, tasting, smelling, and touching), to someone who receives them via her or his primary signal system, and **decode** (translate) the message. We express our reactions to what we have sensed by both verbal and nonverbal signs. You may say, "I heard the bell" or "It feels soft." These are examples of verbal communication that are responses to what your senses have received. You can also respond on a nonverbal level. You touch a hot stove, pull your finger away quickly, and your eyes well with tears. The pulling away and eyes welling are nonverbal communication.

In any communication process, the degree to which the communication is effective depends on the communicators' mutual understanding of the signals being used. Suppose you are about to take an examination and suddenly realize you forgot to bring a pencil to class. You ask one of your friends, "May I please borrow a pencil?" She says, "Yes," and gives you a pencil. You have just participated in an effective communication transaction. You (communicator A) encoded a message ("May I please borrow a pencil?") and sent it out over a channel (vocal tones carried on sound waves) to your friend (communicator B). Your friend received the message (by using sensory agents, ears) and decoded it (understood that you wanted a pencil). Your friend's feedback (the word *yes* and handing the pencil to you) indicated that the message was successfully received and decoded.

Now suppose that the person sitting next to you is from France and speaks no English. The symbol that he or she uses for pencil is *crayon*. Unless both of you communicate in French, that person will be unable to decode your message. Or suppose that just as you start to ask your question, the public-address system goes on and a loud screech pervades the room. In this case, the receiver may not be able to hear the question, and so no successful communication takes place.

Remember that *the act of speech is not itself communication.* Speech is only a biological act: the utterance of sounds, possibly of vocal symbols of language. Communication, however, is broader: it involves the development of a relationship among people in which there is shared meaning among the participants. That is, the intent of the message received is basically the same as the intent of the message sent.

Figure 1.1 illustrates how the components of the communication process work. The circles representing the **source** (the originator of the message) and the **receiver** (the recipient of the message) overlap as each

Figure 1.1
The Components
of Communication

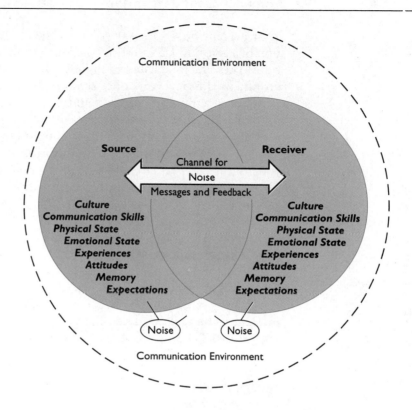

Communication Environment

Source

Receiver

Channel for

Noise

Messages and Feedback

Culture
Communication Skills
Physical State
Emotional State
Experiences
Attitudes
Memory
Expectations

Culture
Communication Skills
Physical State
Emotional State
Experiences
Attitudes
Memory
Expectations

Noise   Noise

Communication Environment

Source	Receiver
1. Senses aroused by idea or need to communicate	1. Senses aroused by stimuli or need to communicate
2. Chooses to communicate the message using language symbols (the code)	2. Receives symbols (the code) in distorted form
3. Uses memory and past experiences to find language symbols to communicate the message (encoding)	3. Uses memory and past experiences to attach meaning to symbols (decoding)
	4. Stores information
	5. Sends feedback

person sends **messages** (communication) and **feedback** (response to a message) to the other through a **frame of reference** (a perceptual screen). The overlapping circles suggest that communication is possible only when each communicator understands the other's message. The variables that affect the frame of reference make up the perceptual screen through which verbal and nonverbal messages are communicated.

Communicator Perceptions

Your **perceptions**—the way you view the world—affect your interpretation of a communication stimulus. Many factors make up your perceptual filter. These factors, listed in Figure 1.1, include your *culture* (the background world-view you hold), *communication skills* (developed from experience and training), *physical and emotional states* (how you feel at this particular time), *experiences* (your cultural background), *attitudes* (negative and positive predispositions to respond to any particular stimulus), *memory* (ability to store and recall information), and *expectations* (what you anticipate will occur). Because of our perceptual differences, two people reporting on an incident they have both seen may report their observations differently.

The Source and the Message

The communication process starts when the source is consciously or unconsciously stimulated by some event, object, or idea. A need to send a message is then followed by a memory search to find the appropriate language (verbal and/or nonverbal) in which to encode the message.

The Channel

During a communicative act, the encoded message is carried through a **channel** or channels. If the communication occurs face to face, these channels may be some or all of the five senses. Typically, we rely on sight and sound as channels in speaking and listening. Instead of communicating face to face, however, we may choose to use an electronic channel that utilizes sound (e.g., the telephone) or sight (e.g., television). In some instances, we may choose to send a message to someone by means of physical contact, such as by tapping the person on the shoulder. In this case, we utilize the touch channel.

The Receiver and the Message

At the end of the channel, the message must be decoded before communication can be accomplished. On gaining verbal and nonverbal signals, the receiver processes them through a memory search so that the signals are translated into the receiver's language system. This decoded message is not identical to the one encoded by the source because each person's symbol system is shaped by a unique set of perceptions. A chef and an amateur cook, for instance, have different concepts of what "season to taste" means in a recipe.

Feedback

Once meaning is assigned to the received message, the receiver is in a position to respond. This response, called *feedback*, can be a verbal or a nonverbal reaction to the message, or both. Feedback indicates whether the receiver understands (e.g., by nodding), misunderstands (e.g., by shrugging the shoulders and saying, "I don't understand"), encourages the source to continue (e.g., by leaning forward and saying, "Yes"), or disagrees (e.g., by pulling back and saying, "No way!"). The act of responding, by which the receiver sends feedback to the source, actually shifts the role of the receiver to that of source.

Noise

Messages are influenced not only by the interpretations of each communicator but also by **noise**, which is any internal or external interference in the communication process.[21] Noise can be caused by environmental obstacles, physiological impairment, semantic problems, syntactic problems, organizational confusion, cultural influences, or psychological problems.

Environmental Noise   **Environmental noise** comprises outside interference that prevents the receiver from gaining the message. This can happen when you are in the kitchen running water and the sound muffles your friend's voice when he asks you a question from the adjoining room.

Physiological-Impairment Noise   A physical problem can also block the effective sending or receiving of a message, thus creating **physiological-impairment noise**. For example, deaf persons do not have the sensory capabilities to receive a message in the same way as do people with normal hearing. Unless they use some mechanical device such as a hearing aid, or unless they are able to read lips, deaf people cannot receive oral messages. Similarly, a person with a speech impediment may be difficult to understand.

Semantic Noise   Problems may also arise regarding the meaning of words, or semantics, creating **semantic noise**. For example, semantic noise may result when people use language that is common only to one specific group, to a particular part of a country, to another country, or to a particular field, profession, or organization.

Environmental noise comprises outside interference that prevents the receiver from gaining the message.

Travelers frequently encounter semantic problems. The midwesterner who goes into a store in many parts of the East and asks for a *soda* will probably get a soft drink rather than a mixture of ice cream, fruit flavoring, and soda water.

Experts—professors, physicists, mechanics—sometimes forget that those who do not have as much knowledge of their field may not be familiar with its vocabulary. For example, clients often complain that lawyers fail to communicate clearly because they use confusing legal jargon.

Similarly, people sometimes use the initials of organizations, equipment, or activities rather than their full names. An agency such as the Securities and Exchange Commission is referred to as the SEC, and federal executives may forget that most Americans do not recognize this "alphabet soup." To avoid semantic problems, communicators must be aware that although they know the meanings of the words they use, those at the receiving end must assign similar meanings for a communication to be effective.

Syntactical Noise   Each language has a syntax, a customary way of putting words together in a grammatical form. Various types of **syntactical noise**, inappropriate grammatical usage, can interfere with clear communication. For example, receivers may become confused if someone changes tenses in the middle of a story ("She went down the street and says to him . . .").

The usual sequence of a grammatically correct English sentence is noun-verb-object (*I give him the book*). But other languages—Spanish, for example—do not follow this pattern. In Spanish, the same sentence reads Le doy el libro (*To him I give the book*). Thus someone who is learning a new language must master not only its vocabulary but an entirely different system of grammar. Until this new system becomes natural, the language may be quite difficult both to encode and decode.

Organizational Noise   When the source fails to realize that certain ideas are best grasped when presented in a structured order, **organizational noise** may result. One geography instructor presents ideas in a random fashion: first he talks about India, then China, then Greece, then India, and then China. After a while, his students become so confused they have absolutely no idea which country he is discussing.

Many methods of organization can provide a clear structure. In giving directions, for example, a person may set a pattern by starting at the departure point and proceeding in geographical order (e.g., *Go to the first street, turn right, proceed three blocks, and turn left*). If material is presented in a specific pattern, the receiver is likely to grasp the meaning. If the material is not organized, the receiver must not only try to figure out what is said but also sort out the information.

Cultural Noise   **Cultural noise** is preconceived, unyielding attitudes derived from a group or society about how members of that culture should act or in what they should or shouldn't believe. "Nice people don't do things like that." "That's the way it has always been, and that's the way it is always going to be." These are examples of statements made by individuals who believe in a set pattern of rules and regulations.

An instance of cultural noise is the attitude that any action by a representative of one's own group is always right, whereas the actions by a member of another group are wrong. Thus a person who has always voted for one political party may find it difficult to be open-minded when listening to information about the opposing political party's candidates.

Psychological Noise   We sometimes find ourselves in situations where **psychological noise**—stress, frustration, or irritation—causes us to either send or receive messages ineffectively. Think of what happens when you are so angry that you "can't think straight." This is a normal example of psychological noise getting in the way of effective communication.

Unfortunately, some people have severe psychological problems that cause them to communicate in unusual ways. Those afflicted with schizophrenia (a disintegration of personality) or catatonia (immobility and speechlessness) may have great difficulty communicating. Such people may talk in riddles and rhymes, make up words, switch personalities, or simply not try to communicate at all.

Dealing with Noise

Although noise interferes with communication, we must learn to adapt to and compensate for it, because it is commonly present. For example, a source should offer opportunities for feedback to make sure that a message has been received and understood. Rather than simply assuming that someone in another room has heard your message, word the statement so that it requires an answer: "The phone is for you; are you going to answer it?" Another way to compensate for noise is to define terms that might be misunderstood or that may not be part of the receiver's vocabulary. Rather than repeating exactly the same words in a message that has been misunderstood, you can change the terms or the sentence structure to aid the receiver in decoding the message. In the same way, a receiver should ask questions or repeat the message's general ideas to be sure that distractions have not interfered with comprehension.

The way a person does or does not respond may give you some clues as to how to compensate for a noise problem. For instance, consider what happens if you request a sheet of paper and the person does not do anything. Environmental noise may have stopped the message from being received, or the person may not have been paying attention because of psychological or cultural noise. Or the person may say, "I have difficulty hearing. Could you repeat it and speak up a little?" In this case, you must increase the volume level when you repeat the message. A response of "No comprende!" to the question, "Where is the Grand Hotel?" may indicate that the person to whom you asked the question does not speak English. You may then want to switch to Spanish, if you know the language, or show the person a brochure of the hotel. As a sender of messages, you must keep eyes and ears open to anticipate a problem and, if one exists, to adjust your communication accordingly.

The Context

Communication does not occur in a vacuum. It always relates to the **context**—who is present, where the communication is taking place, and the general attitude of those assembled. Where we are and who is with us affect our communication. Such factors as the size of the room, the color of the walls, and the type and placement of the furniture can all affect how we feel, the way in which we communicate, and the type of communicating we engage in. For example, placing a large number of people in a small

Speaking to Diverse Groups

Today's audiences include an increasing percentage of foreign-born people—both employees and foreigners on temporary assignments.

Speaking to these culturally diverse groups requires special preparation and understanding. Some tips:

✳ Start by finding out how many foreign-born folks will be in the audience. Ask where they are from and how well they handle the English language. Keep in mind that English taught in foreign classrooms won't qualify them to handle "words" such as, "Waddayathink?"

✳ When speaking, slow down and use natural pauses. "Speaking slower . . . with natural pauses . . . will allow everyone . . . a chance to absorb . . . your message."

✳ Avoid causing them the shame of losing face. *How:*
  —Don't call on them unless you're sure they'll understand what you'll be asking.
  —Be sure to give the instructions for an activity twice.

✳ Use as many visuals as possible.

✳ Be careful about using culturally specific examples, such as "touchdown" or "the Cosby Show." Use universal themes, such as the desire for success or the importance of good friendship.

SOURCE: *Power Speaking: How Ordinary People Can Make Extraordinary Presentations*, by Dr. Frederick Gilbert, Frederick Gilbert Associates, 1233 Harrison Ave., Redwood City, CA 94062.

work area, as is often the case with direct-phone salespeople, may bring about strained communication.

Communication as a System

Think of your daily messages, your sending and receiving. There is a *system*, a pattern, to the way you communicate with others. The pattern centers on who speaks, what the speaker says or is allowed to say, the way in which the message is sent, and where the speaker and receiver are. Specifically, the participants, the setting, the purpose, and how they interact form the basis of the **communication system**.

The flow of communication in a consistent pattern allows communication to be regular and predictable, not random, and gives everyone who participates a sense of assurance and security. Identify a communication system with which you are familiar (e.g., your family or work unit). You can probably anticipate what is going to happen and how your actions will affect others before you actually participate. Your awareness of how well your ideas will be accepted or of how much encouragement or discouragement you will receive may well dictate what you do and do not say.

The type of communication system used affects who speaks. In a strongly parent-dominated home, for example, the father may place restrictions on the type of language children may use, and the topics they can discuss. Any attempt by the children to challenge the system may be met with strongly negative reactions and may result in physical or verbal punishment.

A communication system can be shaped by the communicators' age, status, gender, attraction for each other, and cultural heritage. For example, in a family system, the rules for the male members may be different from those for female members; regulations may alter as the children get older; and favored children may be allowed more freedom. Certain families may be influenced by a historical ethnic pattern that dictates how much public display of emotion is allowable and whether opinions may be expressed. In many households, when children reach adolescence, their attempts to change the rules and not to be treated as little kids are at the core of many family conflicts.

A particular setting may encourage or discourage communication. In some settings, people may feel free to disagree, whereas in others they may feel restricted. Some instructors, for example, encourage differences of opinion in their classroom; others demand adherence to their philosophy and interpretations. Students quickly learn the rules in classrooms and conform accordingly; if not, they may be faced with lowered grades or verbal insults.

The purpose of the communicative act may also result in limits to the system. Trying to tell someone about what you believe is a different task and experience from attempting to persuade that person to take some action you desire. Parents may be more than willing to hear children talk about what curfews their friends have, but when children try to persuade their parents to extend their own curfew, the attempt usually meets with little success.

A mobile is a good analogy to a system. It swings around until, by addition, subtraction, and other alterations, it attains balance. It remains that way until something disturbs the balance. In human communication, once a system is set up and operating, any attempt to alter that system and its pattern of rules will often impair the system or cause it to stop functioning. This does not mean that all systems that are working are good ones. It merely suggests that when a system is functioning, regardless of whether the participants are happy with the pattern, at least there is a basis for understanding how the communication of the people within that system will take place. For example, if you are aware that your boss is not going to accept anyone else's ideas, you learn to live with the system or get out.

Good can result from a system not working well, because awareness of a problem may halt a negative system. For example, if a family unit has been operating under a reign of physical and verbal abuse, something happening to stop the abuse could result in a much-needed change or could bring the system to an end.

Once rules become nonexistent or fuzzy, chaos may result. The basis of good communication patterns between any two or more people is the ability to alter the system with little chaos in the process. The inability to adjust within a reasonable period of time is often the basis for arguments and conflict.

In the complex process of human communication, it is not enough simply to be able to identify the component parts and realize that communication is systematized. We must also understand how these components fit together. A useful way of doing this is to look at models of the process of communication illustrating how the various elements relate to each other.

Models of Human Communication

Any model must necessarily be a simplification; communication does not, for example, have the clear-cut beginning and end that a model suggests. Despite this limitation, models can help us to see the components of communication from a perspective that will help us to analyze and understand them.

Although there are many ways to describe the act of communication, three are used here to illustrate the process: the linear, the interactional, and the transactional.

The Linear Model of Communication

Early theoretical work concerning verbal communication evolved from ancient Greek and Roman rhetoricians who were concerned with the proper training of orators. For this reason, early theories of communication stressed the roles of the public speaker. They reflected what might be called a one-directional view of communication, according to which a person performs specific actions in a specific sequence during a speech and elicits specific desired responses from listeners. This view is called the linear model of communication (see Figure 1.2).

In the **linear model of communication**, a source encodes a message and sends it to a receiver through one or more of the sensory channels. The receiver then receives and decodes the message. For example, after you buy a computer, you listen to the tape-recorded message from the manufacturer. The tape explains how to insert the operating system disk and turn the computer on. When you follow the directions and the computer comes on, the communication has been successful.

Figure 1.2
The Linear Model
of Communication
(One-Directional
Communication)

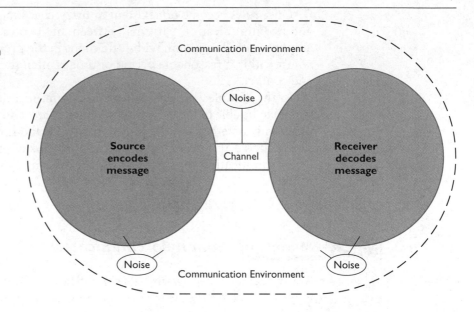

Although one-directional communication is often necessary, its effectiveness is limited. To illustrate this, let us consider an example. José (the speaker) says, "Please put the book on the table when you are done with it." He then turns and walks from the room. Brooke (the listener) has a stack of books in front of her, but she is not certain which one to place on the table. In this example, José is assuming that since he said something, this sending of a message is all there is to communicating. But this assumption ignores the important role of the receiver in responding to (and consequently affecting) the sender and/or the message by providing feedback. This feedback can enable the sender to check to see if an order is understood, a policy accepted, or a message clear.

When it is impossible to open communication for feedback, as in media newscasters, reporters must give careful consideration to figuring out the most appropriate language, clarifying examples, and structure to assist in avoiding communication noise.

The Interactional Model of Communication

The linear model of communication does not take into account all the variables in the communication process. Rather, it is a simple source-receiver model. For this reason, some early behavioral scientists, influenced by research in psychology, expanded the notion of the process to encompass greater interaction and to demonstrate the dynamic, ongoing nature of communication. The interactional model of communication is displayed in Figure 1.3.

In the **interactional model of communication**, a source encodes and sends a message to a receiver (through one or more of the sensory channels). The receiver receives and decodes the message, as in linear communication, but then encodes feedback and sends it back to the source, thus making the process two-directional. The source then decodes the feedback message. Based on the original message sent and the feedback received, the source then encodes a new message that adapts to the feedback (adaptation). For example, José says to Brooke, "Please hand me the book." Brooke looks at the pile of books in front of her and says, "Which one?" (feedback). José responds, "The red one on the top of the pile" (adaptation).

This view of communication accounts for the influence of the receiver's responses. It thus suggests a process that is somewhat circular: sending and receiving, sending and receiving, and so on.

Whenever possible, communicators should attempt to interact so that they can find out how effective their communication actually is. For example, José's analysis of the number of books available might have led him to the conclusion that he needed to be more specific, and he therefore said, "Please hand me the red book on the top of the pile." Or he might have wanted to ask, "Do you know which book I want?" Or he might have waited until Brooke put the book on the table to see whether she understood him. If not, he could then have corrected his error by being more specific in his directions.

Figure 1.3
The Interactional Model of Communication (Two-Directional Communication)

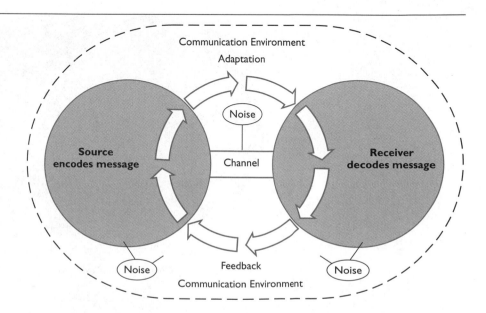

The Transactional Model of Communication

Theorists have suggested that communication may not be as simple a process of stimulus and response as the linear and interactional models suggest. This view supports the idea that communication is a transaction in which source and receiver play interchangeable roles throughout the act of communication. Thus a clear-cut model of the process is not easy to construct. Figure 1.4 illustrates the **transactional model of communication**. In this model messages are processed simultaneously by the communicators. Communicator A encodes a message and sends it. Communicator B then encodes feedback and sends it to A, who decodes it. But these steps are not mutually exclusive; encoding and decoding may occur simultaneously. Speakers may send a verbal message and at the same time receive and decode a nonverbal feedback message from listeners. Because messages can be sent and received at the same time, this model is multidirectional.

Notice that one person is not labeled the source and the other the receiver. Instead, both communicators assume the roles of encoder and decoder in the transaction, thus simultaneously communicating. Consider

Figure 1.4
The Transactional Model of Communication (Multidirectional Communication)

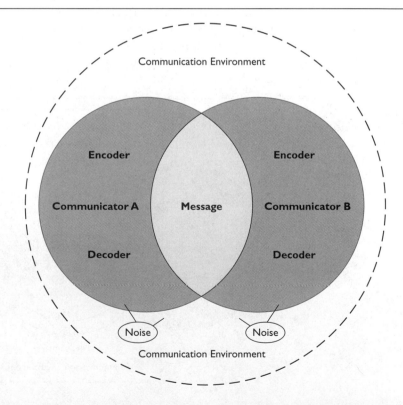

the simultaneous communication in this transaction:

Miguele (source) says, "I love you," *while*

Miguele (receiver) sees Latica walk away as he is speaking, *while*

Latica (source) walks away from Miguele, *while*

Latica (receiver) says, "I love you," *while*

Miguele (source) stops, turns, frowns, and says, "I'm not sure you mean that," *while*

Latica (receiver) sees Miguele nod his head and walk toward her as she speaks, *while*

Miguele (receiver) hears her words, *while*

Miguele (source) nods his head and walks toward Latica as she speaks.

Throughout the encounter, both Miguele and Latica are simultaneously sending and receiving (encoding and decoding) verbal and nonverbal messages.

The Models Compared

Comparing the three models in an example will give you an understanding of how each one differs from the others. Consider these scenarios.

A director of public relations of a major corporation presents a speech over closed-circuit television from the headquarters' media studio to the marketing personnel at the various district offices located throughout the country. This is an example of the *linear model of communication*.

Next the director gives the same presentation in the corporation's board room. She sticks to the manuscript she prepared, making no effort to seek feedback. Following the speech, she asks if there are any questions. A member of the board asks a question, which the director answers. The question-and-answer session demonstrates the *interactional model of communication* in which the sender encoded and sent a message, it was received and decoded, feedback was given (the question), and adaptation made (the answer).

Then the sales staff enters the room. The public relations director starts to speak. As she does so, a salesperson asks a question. While the question is being asked, the speaker nods her head. She then verbally agrees with the salesperson. While this is happening, the salesperson also nods his head, indicating that he understood what was just explained, and says, "I get it." This is an example of the *transactional model of communication*.

Besides understanding what the communication process is, it is also important to understand how, in the United States, the concept of freedom of speech affects our communication.

First Amendment Speech

The First Amendment to the Constitution bans Congress from passing laws "abridging the freedom of speech." Therefore, when confronted with the question of the meaning of **freedom of speech**, the answer tends to be that it is the protected right to speak without restrictions; to be free to say what we want. In reality, however, since it is impossible to know the specific original intent of any of the items in the Constitution or Bill of Rights, First Amendment rights have been broadly interpreted over the years to include many forms of expression.[22]

This lack of a clear definition of what is really meant by "abridging the freedom of speech" and the resulting differences of opinion in what is allowable have led to controversy and lawsuits. An examination of several cases shows the complexity of the issue of freedom of speech:

✱ A student was expelled from Brown University for shouting racist, anti-Semitic, and homophobic epithets outside a campus dormitory while in a drunken state. The decision was challenged on the grounds that his First Amendment rights were violated by the university code, which restricts actions showing flagrant disrespect for the well-being of others.[23]

✱ The Iowa Board of Regents imposed a policy that requires professors to tell state university students when they are about to see explicit representations of human sexual acts. The policy stemmed from complaints over a film that was billed as an erotic comedy and landmark in gay filmmaking. Some critics accused the regents of restricting academic freedom and taking away First Amendment rights.[24]

✱ For years, colleges and universities have had regulations regarding what speech acts and activities are acceptable and permissible on their campuses. "In June, 1993, a Supreme Court ruling dismantling a hate speech ordinance in Minnesota forced colleges and universities nationwide to rethink their hate speech policies."[25] The court made it clear that hateful speech could not be banned because of its content.

Is there justification for limitations placed on freedom of speech, or are such restrictions unacceptable?

One of the justifications offered for limitations on freedom of speech is that *words are deeds.* It contends that some symbolic behavior may be so harmful that we are justified in restraining it. A presidential assassin might plead that he or she acted for the purpose of sending a political message to the public. To regard such a claim as legitimate may blur the line we must maintain between speech and action.[26]

An argument against limitations on freedom of speech centers on the idea that *speech codes leave the judgment of whether the speech is good or*

The First Amendment to the Constitution bans Congress from passing laws "abridging the freedom of speech."

bad, to the speech code enforcer. The reason for the First Amendment, it is contended, is that "the government is neither capable nor deserving of determining what is true, benevolent or moral speech."[27]

A further contention against limitations on the freedom of speech proposes that "more often than not, *the free-speech issue becomes a weapon to fight some other cause* . . . flag burning, blocking access to abortion clinics, pornography."[28] This assertion suggests that it is not freedom of speech or the First Amendment that is being dealt with in these cases, but the causes themselves.

Also questioned is the issue of where to draw the line. "*If one speaker is banned, every speaker must be banned*, not only those who are not politically correct"[29] or with whom authorities disagree. The point can be carried to its extreme. Since almost everyone has someone who will disagree with her or him, no one would be allowed to speak.

The arguments about what freedom of speech really is and what the writers of the Constitution really meant by First Amendment rights rage on. In her U.S. Supreme Court nomination hearings, Ruth Bader Ginsburg stated, "We are a society that has given, beyond any other, maximum protection for the speech that we hate, and on the other hand, are concerned for the quality and dignity of individuals. Those two principles collide in this area [hate speech]."[30]

How might this conflict affect you on a personal level? Should your speech instructor be allowed to limit what topics you may speak about in a speech class? Should Internet providers be allowed to censor what you send? Should your collegiate organization be allowed to bring a speaker to campus who attacks others' religious or ethnic heritage? Should an instructor be allowed to lower your grade because you speak out in class in opposition to her views?

Not only what you are allowed to and not allowed to communicate is an issue, but also important is what your ethical standards are as you act as a speaker and as a listener.

Ethics

Ethics is the systematic study of what should be the grounds and principles for right and wrong human behavior.[31] Ethics is not just something practiced by individuals: it is a value shared by society as a whole. The word *ethics* comes from the Greek word *ethos*, meaning custom and character. Customs and characteristics pervade society—individuals, families, media, government, and organizations.

Your ethics are the values that have been instilled in you, that you have knowingly or unknowingly accepted, and that determine how you act. Your **ethical value system** is the basis for your decision-making and your understanding of why you will or will not take a particular stand or action. It is the basis for your communication ethics.

The Ethics of Communicating

Ethics without Borders

When ethics are in question, ask: "Would I be happy if the whole story were made public?"

SOURCE: *Solid Gold Success Strategies for Your Business*, by Don Taylor, AMACOM, 135 W. 50th St., New York, NY 10020.

Over the decades, speech communication instructors and theorists have stressed that competent speakers should, by definition, be ethical speakers. "Potential ethical issues are inherent in any instance of communication between humans to the degree that the communication can be judged on a right-wrong dimension, involves possible significant influence on other humans, and to the degree that the communicator consciously chooses specific ends sought and communicative means to achieve those ends."[32] Therefore, it is contended that speakers should give the audience assistance in making wise decisions and that speakers' decisions about what to say should be based on moral principles. It has also been stressed that, although Adolf Hitler and other hate-mongers were certainly persuasive and compelling speakers, their ultimate downfall was their lack of ethical values.

Ethical communicators are generally defined as those who conform to the moral standards a society establishes for its communicators. Although this definition seems plausible, it contains a major flaw: the words ring hollow because it is impossible to either list or gain acceptance for universal moral standards. Although some people claim they have the true answer, in reality there is no universal agreement on what exactly it means to be moral.

Since most readers of this book live in a society that stresses Western philosophy, the discussion of what it means to be an ethical communicator centers on this viewpoint, while recognizing that it may not be appropriate for all.

Accepting the limitations of culture and perspective, research in the communication field has isolated some specific traits of an ethical speaker in the United States. The premise of ethical speaking can be stated as, "You must understand that you are a moral agent, and when you communicate with others and make decisions that affect yourself and others, you have a moral responsibility because your actions have human consequences."[33] Specifically, an ethical speaker[34]

* Does not knowingly expose an audience to falsehoods or half-truths that cause significant harm.

* Does not premeditatedly alter the truth.

* Presents the truth as he or she understands it.

* Raises the listeners' level of expertise by supplying the necessary facts, definitions, descriptions, and substantiating information.

* Presents a message that is free from coercion.

* Does not invent or fabricate statistics or other information intended to serve as a basis for proof of a contention or belief.

* Gives credit to the source of information; does not pretend that information is original when it is not.

From the standpoint of the receiver, "in most public and private communication, a fundamental implied and unspoken assumption is that words can be trusted and people will be truthful."[35] This does not mean you should accept everything that is said; that would be naive. You must, to be an ethical receiver, listen carefully to the information presented and ask yourself whether the conclusions reached are reasonable and expected. In other words, can you, from the information presented, comfortably come to the conclusion that the sender presented, and does what the speaker says make sense?[36]

IN CONCLUSION → Communication is a conscious or unconscious, intentional or unintentional process in which feelings and ideas are expressed as verbal and/or nonverbal messages, sent, received, and comprehended. It can take the form of intrapersonal, interpersonal, or public messages. Three factors are present in any communicative event—the communicators, the purpose, and the setting. We communicate through our senses. The process of communication can be understood by investigating the linear, the interactional, and the transactional communication models and the various components that make up the process. Communication is directly influenced by culture. In the United States, multiculturalism is an important aspect of communication, as is freedom of speech, and an understanding of what is meant by ethical communication.

LEARN BY DOING →

1. Design a model of communication that differs from any of the three presented in this chapter, and explain it to the members of the class.

2. Identify an experience in which your attempt to communicate was a failure. Use the classification of sources of noise given in the text to label the type of interference you encountered. Why did this happen? What, if anything, could you have done to correct the interference problem?

3. Describe a context in which you find it difficult to communicate. Describe a context in which you find it easy to communicate. Why did you select each one? What implications for communication are involved in your choices?

4. Describe the system of communication by which your family operates (or operated) by investigating the patterns of communication and the rules of operation. What were the advantages and disadvantages of that system?

5. Write down one phrase or expression that is unique to your family or group of friends. It should be an expression that has meaning only for a select group, not commonly used in society as a whole. It may be an ethnic expression, an in-group reference, or some other special phrase. The other students then read the expression and try to figure out what it means. Draw inferences about semantic noise from this activity.

6. Individually each student decides on what he or she would do in each of these situations. You will then be divided into small groups to discuss your answers and report back to the class as a whole on the trends in each group.

   a. You are taking a public speaking course. The instructor requires three quoted references in the speech that you are to present in about five minutes, but you did not have time to do the necessary research. Would you make up three references, not give the speech and get a failing grade, give the speech without the references and hope for the best, or take some other action? If you would take another action, what would it be?

b. You have just finished eating in a restaurant. You check the bill and realize that the waiter has made a $10 error in your favor. The waiter sees your reaction and asks if anything is wrong. How do you respond?

c. You look up during a test and see that your best friend, who needs a passing grade in this class to get off academic probation, is using cheat notes. You think the instructor also saw the action. As you hand in your paper, the instructor says, "Remember, this class operates on the honor system. Is there anything you want to say to me?" How do you respond?

7. Your class will discuss or debate: A higher educational institution must be a platform for the debate of social issues. Therefore, it is resolved that [name of your college/university] allow, encourage, and invite *all* speakers to present their views in public forums on this campus.

8. Your class will discuss: "Is it realistically possible to be an ethical communicator?"

KEY TERMS →

communication
intrapersonal communication
interpersonal communication
public communication
culture
intracultural communication
intercultural communication
multiculture
multiculturalism
selective communication
encode
primary signal system
decode
source
receiver
freedom of speech
messages
feedback
frame of reference
perceptions

channel
noise
environmental noise
physiological-impairment noise
semantic noise
syntactical noise
organizational noise
cultural noise
psychological noise
context
communication system
linear model of communication
interactional model of
    communication
transactional model of
    communication
ethics
ethical value system
ethical communicators

chapter 2

Personal Communication

LEARNING OUTCOMES →

After reading this chapter, you should be able to:

Define and explain the concept of intrapersonal communication

State and discuss the theory of basic drive forces as they affect inner communication

Explain self-concept and its role as a guiding factor in a person's actions

Define self-talk and explain its relation to our communication accomplishments

List some options and sources for improving one's self-concept, self-confidence, and/or self-esteem

Define and explain the causes, results, and aids for communication apprehension

28

As you lie in bed at night, before you fall asleep, you may review the events of the day. As you take a test, you may carry on a conversation with yourself to arrive at the answers. In both cases, you are participating in the act of **intrapersonal communication**, internally communicating with yourself.

The basis for communication with others is the ability to communicate with oneself. Those people who tend to know who they are, what they believe in, what their attitudes are, and have a clear understanding of their beliefs, values, and expectations are much more likely to be able to communicate these ideas to others. Those people who can internally process ideas and decide how to present them can communicate that information to others.

There is disagreement about where to draw the line as to what intrapersonal communication is. For our purposes, assume that at times we talk to ourselves, such as when we debate during a test which of the multiple-choice answers is correct. Let us also assume that our bodies can "speak" nonverbally, as when muscles in the back of the neck tighten when we get emotionally upset. This nonverbal aspect of intrapersonal communication is an important aspect of the Gestalt theory of psychology, which centers on getting in touch with present-tense feelings to gain awareness of our intrapersonal messages. Also, intrapersonal communication may occur below our level of awareness, such as when we daydream or dream.

One way of understanding your intrapersonal communication and, if necessary, improving your communication skills is by understanding your self-talk.

Self-Talk

There is a saying that it is okay to talk with yourself, but when you start answering back it is time to worry! That tongue-in-cheek contention is basically incorrect. Indelible links exist between what we say to ourselves and what we accomplish. In addition, our self-talk has a powerful impact on our emotional well-being.

We all engage in **self-talk**—a nearly constant subconscious monologue or inner speech with ourselves. Sometimes we are conscious of our vocalizing aloud within our heads, but self-talk is often silent thinking, an internal whisper of which we are scarcely aware, or our automatic nonverbal reactions. Even though it may be quiet, its impact can be enormous. "Your behavior, your feelings, your self-esteem, and even your level of stress are influenced by your inner speech."[1] Everything that you do begins as self-talk. "Self-talk shapes our inner attitudes, our attitudes shape our behavior, and of course our behavior—what we do—shapes the results we get."[2]

Think of the inner struggles you often have concerning whether you believe something, will take a particular action, or will make a certain decision. Awake or asleep, you are constantly in touch with yourself. You mumble, daydream, dream, fantasize, and feel tension. These are all forms of inner speech.

The subconscious will work for or against you. It's up to you. Tell yourself you're clumsy, or aren't comfortable in social situations, and that is what you probably will be. "We have a choice each time we think, to think positively or negatively. Many of us don't believe it, but that absolutely is our choice. Once we understand that our private thoughts are ours alone to determine, we can select to program our brains with empowering, confidence-building thoughts."[3] One method to overcome negative self-talk is to (1) be aware of your negative messages; (2) collect your recycled negatives, write them down, and regularly read them to yourself; and (3) replace the negative thoughts with a positive one by flooding your brain with such statements as "I'm an effective speaker," "I'm a people person." Once you start focusing on the positives, the negatives have to go away. Negative self-talk can't survive if you don't feed it.[4]

This method has been used extensively with athletes to overcome negatives. In one study, basketball players were divided into three groups for foul-shot practice. The first group used imagery (internally picturing that they were shooting and making their shots) and negative-message elimination but did not practice shooting. The second group practiced shooting, and the third group did both corrective imaging and practicing. Although all three groups improved, the first and third groups improved by the same amount, while the second group improved less. "Positive self-talk really can turn your life around and make any life more successful."[5]

In addition to self-talk, one of the important aspects of intrapersonal communication is how we process information as we receive it.

Cognitive Dissonance

Your culture, background, family, education, and experiences all serve as the framework for shaping how you deal with incoming information and affect the way you decide on what actions to take or avoid. The act of **cognitive processing** is the comprehending, organizing, and storing of ideas. An aspect of intrapersonal communication, it is how we process information in relationship to our values, attitudes, and beliefs.

Listen to Your Inner Voice

Consider these ideas to help you think faster when you need to decide something in a hurry:

✳ **Treat so-called** gut feelings or hunches as information, not imagination. *Reason:* Your brain routinely fuses feelings, sensations, taste, sight and smell and presents them as a quick impression.

✳ **Don't ignore** a hunch that, for example, tells you that you should make that phone call now. You'll find that respecting hunches can improve your sense of timing.

✳ **Switch to** a completely different activity when you're having trouble solving a problem logically. Doing so often sparks activity in the intuitive side of your brain.

✳ **Call on** the side of your brain that receives and blends data at high speed. To do so, relax, close your eyes and breathe deeply, and then let the intuitive side of your brain take over.

✳ **Build confidence** in using your intuition by acknowledging when a hunch or gut feeling gives you the help you need.

SOURCE: *Communication Briefings,* as adapted from Laurie Nadel, writing in *The Take-Charge Assistant,* 135 W. 50th St., New York, NY 10020.

Each of us carries with us **values** (what we perceive to be of positive or negative worth), **attitudes** (our perspective and viewpoints), and **beliefs** (our convictions). Most people try to keep their actions parallel to their values, beliefs, and attitudes. If things are in balance, we feel fairly good about ourselves and the world around us. If not, we may intrapersonally become confused and frustrated, which may cause us to act negatively toward ourselves or others, maybe even blaming them for what's wrong. This imbalance happens, for example, when you know that a certain action you are about to take is wrong based on your value system. Your "internal voice" cries out, "be careful, don't do that." Before the event, you may have a sleepless night as you toss and turn with the internal voice speaking messages, or you dream about the negative things that are going to happen as a result of your taking the action.

The *imbalance* between your values, attitudes, and beliefs and your actions is called **cognitive dissonance**.[6] Cognitive dissonance often leads to what has become known as a **guilty conscience**—the real or perceived fear that we are going to get caught, get punished, or "found out." For example, an individual who believes cheating is wrong, yet does so on a test may feel cognitive dissonance following the act, no matter the grade received.

If you become aware of cognitive dissonance before you act, and decide not to do the deed, you could chalk it up to your conscience warning you and saving you from a perceived disaster. If you brood about the action afterward, then you may need to accept the fact that you did the deed,

7976

there is nothing you can do about it now, and go on from there, with the internal pledge of not doing it again. Our internal voice, through its self-talk technique, often continues to shout at us until we can put the imbalance to rest. Sometimes apologizing to someone else is in order if the action hurt someone else.

Another part of intrapersonal communication is self-concept.

Self-Concept

Your understanding of yourself is known as your **self-concept**. "Self-concept is the guiding factor in a person's actions. How a human being views oneself will determine most of his or her actions and choices in life. Essentially a person is going to choose what he or she feels he or she is worth."[7] Thus the more positively you perceive yourself, the more likely it is that you will have **self-confidence**, that is, a sense of competence and effectiveness.

Each person possesses a real self, an ideal self, and a public self. The **real self** is what you think of yourself when you are being most honest about your interests, thoughts, emotions, and needs. For many people, the real self is dynamic and changing. This accounts for why you may feel like you are in constant turmoil, searching for who and what you are, questioning your motives for doing and not doing certain things.

The **ideal self** is who you would like to be or think you should be. This is the "perfect you." It is the "perfect" you, being perceived as being "perfect" by yourself and/or others. It's often the you the significant others in your life (relatives, employers, the media, and/or advertising) have told you that you should be, or who they want you to be.

The **public self** is the one you let others know. It is the you that you have decided to let others see. It is based on the concept that "if others believe the right things about me, I can get them to like me; I can persuade them and generally get my way." It acknowledges that "if others believe the wrong things about me, I can be rejected and blocked from my goals. Not only actors and politicians shape their public selves, we all do."[8]

Recognition of the importance of self-esteem and self-concept is not a new development. American psychologists and educators have been interested in the study of the self for many years and have developed different theories about it. Communication theorists have examined the self and self-esteem based on observing and studying what we intrapersonally communicate to ourselves about ourselves, and what we communicate to others.

How to Accept a Compliment

Do you have a problem accepting compliments? Do you often answer with "Oh, it was nothing"?

Be aware that deflecting a compliment often draws unwanted attention and belittles both you and the person offering the compliment.

Instead, just say "Thank you."

You'll be pleased at how well it works.

SOURCE: *Communication Briefings,* as adapted from *The Wellness Book,* by Dr. Herbert Benson and Eileen M. Stuart, Birch Lane Press, 600 Madison Ave., New York, NY 10022.

The way a human being views himself or herself will determine most of his or her actions and choices in life.

The classic theory about the self is that it is composed of four different aspects, the spiritual, the material, the social, and the physical. The *spiritual* is what we are thinking and feeling, the *material* is represented by our possessions and physical surroundings, the *social* is represented by our interactions with others, and the *physical* is our physical being.[9] Much of our self-talk centers on how we perceive the four aspects.

Another theory stresses that the self evolves from the interactions a person has with other people and how we intrapersonally integrate these interactions into our self-thought. This evolution takes place in stages. For example, the young child aims for a sense of self as a separate person while developing gender identity; the adolescent tries to establish a stable sense of identity; the middle-age person emphasizes independence while adjusting to changes in body competence; and the elderly person seeks to come to terms with being old.[10] As we go through the various changes, our self-communication reflects the alterations that are taking place, and for this reason we experience multiple concepts, rather than a single one, of who we are. Thus at any one time in our lives we may perceive ourselves to be a different person than at another time. You are probably not the same person today that you were five years ago, and you are not the same person today that you will perceive yourself to be five years from now.

Likewise, self-concept seems to be situational. Who you are with one person or in one place may not be the same as who you are with someone else or in a different place. In one relationship you may take on the role of student, yet in another the role of friend. At work you may be the leader, and at home, the follower. Many of these role-plays are based on our intrapersonal perception of who we should or need to be with these people, in this environment.

It is important that you understand yourself and your perceptions of yourself. This is the basis of self-awareness, which, again, is the basis for much of your self-talk.

Are Your Sabotaging Yourself?

Check off the statements that apply to you

1. _____ My life often seems to be out of my control.

2. _____ Much of my life is spent on other people's goals or problems.

3. _____ I often get into trouble by assuming I know something when I don't.

4. _____ I have a tendency to expect the worst.

5. _____ I often find myself saying "I don't feel up to it."

6. _____ The fear of appearing stupid often prevents me from asking questions or offering my opinion.

7. _____ I have trouble taking criticism, even from my friends.

8. _____ If I'm not perfect, I often feel worthless.

9. _____ I have trouble focusing on what's really important to me.

10. _____ I often wish I were someone else.

11. _____ I often feel irritable and moody.

12. _____ I find that when I really want something, I'll act impulsively to get it.

13. _____ I waste a lot of time.

14. _____ I often do not live up to my potential because I put things off to the last minute.

15. _____ I spend time with people who belittle me or put down my thoughts or ideas.

Total number of statements checked: _____

0–2: You are not likely to be sabotaging your life.

3–5: Like most people, you're doing some things that may be holding you back. A little effort at self-improvement will do wonders for you.

6–11: You may be undermining your life in a major way. Begin now to identify and remove your barriers.

12–15: Warning! Sabotage may be everywhere. Sustained effort may be needed to break down the walls of self-sabotage.

SOURCE: From "The Sabotage Factor" course by Daniel G. Amen, M.D., author of *Don't Shoot Yourself in the Foot* (Warner, 1992). Reprinted by permission of the author.

Understanding Yourself

Most people have only a general idea of who they are and what they really believe in. This explains why many of us don't understand why we think the thoughts we do and are intrapersonally motivated to act in particular ways.

It is often of great personal value to attempt to discover the you who is within you, the you who carries on your self-talk, cognitively processes, and acts on her/his self-concept.

Here is an activity to get you started in investigating your motives and beliefs and your self-concept. Complete these statements:

I am

I would like to be

I like to

I believe that

I have been

I wouldn't want to

The quality I possess that I am most proud of is

My biggest flaw is

Something that I would prefer others not know about me is

Now that you are finished responding to these items, go back over your list of answers and write a two-sentence description of yourself based just on the answers to the statements.

It has been said that you are what you are based on your verb *to be*.[11] What you have done in the activity you just completed is to describe yourself based on your perceived verb *to be*. You have used your intrapersonally stored data to examine your past experiences (*I have been/ done*), present attitudes and actions (*I am*), and future expectations or hopes (*I would like to be/do*). If you were honest and revealed what you really think and feel, you have just gained a glimpse at your perceived self.

Another way of looking at yourself is through the model known as the **Johari window,**[12] which allows you to ascertain your willingness to disclose who you are and allow others to disclose to you (see Figure 2.1). From an intrapersonal perspective, the Johari window helps you understand a great deal about yourself and some of cultural underpinnings of your self-thinking.

In the Johari window, area I, the *free area,* includes everything you know and understand about yourself and that all other people know and understand about you—your values, personality characteristics, and perceptions. For example, you may enjoy wearing nice clothes and so you

Figure 2.1
The Johari Window

	Known to Self	Not Known to Self
Known to Others	I. Free Area	II. Blind Area
Not Known to Others	III. Hidden Area	IV. Unknown Area

SOURCE: From *Group Processes: An Introduction to Group Dynamics,* 3rd edition by Joseph Luft, 1984, Mayfield Publishing Company. Reprinted by permission of the author.

spend time selecting a wardrobe. This is communicated to others through the clothes you wear. Others, in turn, are aware of your enjoyment of wearing nice clothing because they observe what you wear and the care you take in selecting it.

The *blind area*, area II, represents all those things about you that others recognize but that you do not see in yourself. You may, for example, make a poor first impression on certain people because you are boisterous. Unless this behavior is pointed out, it will remain in the blind area. Information in the blind area is revealed only when you have the opportunity to investigate other people's perceptions of you.

In the *hidden area*, area III, you recognize something about yourself but choose not to share it with others. If you are a man, for example, you may have learned not to show certain types of emotions, such as crying; yet you sometimes face situations in which tears would express your true feelings. No one knows about your emotional feelings since you hide them from view.

The *unknown area*, area IV, represents all those things that neither you nor others know about you. Often these aspects are so well concealed that they never even surface. Since you don't reveal them, these traits remain unknown not only to you but also to everyone else. For example, in therapy a person may suddenly remember that he was sexually abused as a child, which may explain his strong aversion to being touched.

This activity will help you chart your Johari window:[13]

Before each item in Part I, place a number from 1 to 6 to indicate how much you are *willing to reveal*. A 1 indicates that you are willing to self-disclose nothing or almost nothing, and a 6 indicates that you are willing to reveal everything or almost everything. Use the values 2, 3, 4, and 5 to represent the points between these extremes.

Before each item in Part II, place a number from 1 to 6 to indicate how *willing you are to receive feedback* about what you self-disclose. A 1 indicates that you refuse or resist feedback, and a 6 indicates that you consistently encourage feedback. Use the values 2, 3, 4, and 5 to represent the points between these extremes.

PART I: Extent to which I am willing to self-disclose my

_____   1. goals

_____   2. strengths

_____   3 weaknesses

_____   4. positive feelings

_____   5. negative feelings

_____   6. values

_____   7. ideas

_____   8. beliefs

_____   9. fears and insecurities

_____   10. mistakes

_____   Total

PART II: Extent to which I am willing to receive feedback about my

_____   1. goals

_____   2. strengths

_____   3. weaknesses

_____   4. positive feelings

_____   5. negative feelings

_____   6. values

_____   7. ideas

_____   8. beliefs

_____   9. fears and insecurities

_____   10. mistakes

_____   Total

Figure 2.2
Your Johari
Window

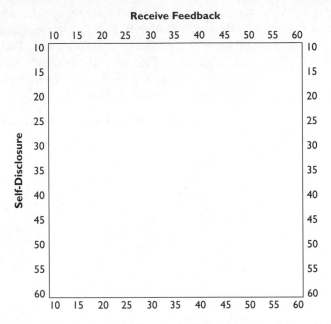

SOURCE: Based on "Relational Disclosure," an unpublished paper by Lawrence Rosenfeld. Reprinted by permission of the author.

Use Figure 2.2 to plot your scores. Circle the number on the top line of the square, designated "receive feedback," that corresponds to your score on Part II of the activity. Circle the same number on the bottom line of the square. Connect the two circles with a straight line.

Then circle the number on the left side line of the square, designated "self-disclosure," that corresponds to your score on Part I of the activity. Circle the same number on the right side line of the square. Connect the two circles with a straight line.

You now have the four "panes" of your Johari window. Color in the four-sided figure in the upper left-hand side of the square as illustrated in Figure 2.3. Compare your pattern to those in the figure to ascertain your self-disclosure/receive-feedback style.

Style I people spend little time disclosing or giving feedback. They tend to be perceived as good listeners and fairly shy or quiet, sometimes labeled as introverts.

Style II people spend a great deal of time listening and not much time sending out personal information. After being with this type of person for a while, they tend to know a great deal about you but you don't know much about them. This is also a style of introverts.

Figure 2.3
Sample Johari
Window

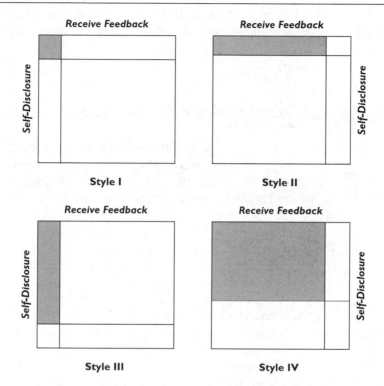

SOURCE: From *Interplay: The Process of Interpersonal Communication,* Fifth Edition by Ronald B. Adler, Lawrence B. Rosenfeld, and Neil Towne, copyright © 1992 by Holt, Rinehart and Winston, Inc. Reproduced by permission of the publisher.

Style III people give a great deal of feedback but don't like to disclose very much. They are the kind of person who tells you about themselves. They are often perceived as great talkers but not very good listeners. You tend to know a great deal about them, but they don't know much about you.

Style IV people like to both give and get information. People who are very open and easily share themselves with others normally have a large free area and smaller blind, hidden, and unknown areas. Because these kinds of people share, they are known to themselves and to others. They are often referred to as extroverts, as they are outgoing and interactive.

If your four-sided figures are approximately the same size, you do not have a predominant self-disclosure/receive-feedback style.

What you hopefully gained is an understanding of not only your perception of yourself, and how it affects your intrapersonal communication, but also how others may perceive you based on your willingness or unwillingness to both disclose and receive disclosure.

Let us now turn to a theory relating to intrapersonal communication, a concept that is so important that some colleges and universities are using the theory's principles as the basis for developing their entire communication curriculum.[14]

Need Drives Affecting Communication

We are each born with certain biological tools that allow us to communicate—a brain, sound-producing organs (mouth, tongue, larynx), and a receiving apparatus (ears, eyes). We also, according to **ethnographers**—researchers who study cultures—are born with need drives that must be satisfied. Some communication theorists feel that these intrapersonal drives are the bases for our communication—what we think, what we express, what inspires us to act the way we do, and how we react to the way others express and use their drives. This concept explains why we commnicate in ways that go beyond our usual understanding of communication.[15]

The basic forces that determine human behavior are survival of the species, pleasure-seeking, security, and territoriality.[16] These drives are not manifested equally by every person. One person may have a pleasure need that is stronger than any of the other forces, whereas another may have strong needs for both security and territoriality. This view offers a contrast to theories that posit a hierarchy of needs, each of which must be satisfied before a person can move on to the next.

Survival

A person who is threatened screams out for help; when a pebble flies against the windshield of your moving car, you duck. These are examples of attempts to ensure survival. These are reflexive—inborn reactions—that we use to communicate our fear of a possible ending of our survival.

Our ability to communicate selectively gives us a distinct survival advantage. We can call for help, plead, explain our need for food, or try to convince attackers that their action is unwise. In addition, we are aware of our own evolution, an awareness that is probably not found in other animals. Because of this, we can communicate about how we reproduce, what causes us to die, and how we can attempt to alter conditions to prolong our lives and those of our descendants. We have been able to communicate these ideas from person to person and thus to build on the experience of the past in developing intrapersonal understanding.

We are basically pleasure-seeking and need-satisfying beings.

Pleasure-Seeking

We are basically *pleasure-seeking* and need-satisfying beings. A good part of our lives is devoted to communicating our pleasure or lack of pleasure as we exploit our conquests, stress our influences, and reinforce our accomplishments. We create awards, citations, and grades to communicate to others that we have succeeded, thus satisfying our intrapersonal messages.

People find different events pleasurable, and each of us may find both pleasure and pain in a single event. Moreover, we may find pleasure in satisfying not only our own needs but also the needs of others, or in fulfilling long-term goals as well as immediate desires. What pleases one person may well torture another. One person happily gives a speech before a large audience; another is petrified by any speaking situation.

Communicatively, if given the opportunity, we choose to communicate in those situations in which we perceive we will get pleasure. You raise your hand to answer a question in class if you think you know the right answer. Unless forced to do so, individuals who fear public speaking avoid putting themselves in a position of giving a speech. But a speaker who has received positive reactions from an audience is much more likely to try the experience again. We are constantly sending ourselves intrapersonal messages relating to whether some experience was or was not pleasurable, or whether a perceived activity will render pleasure.

Security

You enter a classroom for the first meeting of a class. You see a place that is unfamiliar, people you do not know, a professor who is an unknown entity. You feel insecure. Your desire to participate and your comfort in this situation can be affected directly by the messages you send yourself.

Security is a basic human need. Because of it, we seek equilibrium, a keeping of balance. When security is absent, when we feel a lack of control, most of us are uneasy, overly cautious, uncertain.

Our concept of ourselves in situations of security or insecurity motivates our verbal and nonverbal communication. Fear causes the vocal pitch to rise, the body to shake, and the stomach to churn. We find ourselves afraid to speak, or speaking incessantly, or stammering. But as we become more comfortable in a situation, as we learn the rules of the game, we find ourselves acting quite differently because we send ourselves positive messages. The first day of class, for instance, you may not say a word. But later, as you acclimate yourself to the situation, you may feel relaxed enough to participate.

Hearing intrapersonal messages of fear of the unknown explains why some people will not wander down the unmapped paths of life . . . the messages they send themselves center on the words "beware of the unknown, the uncomfortable."

Territoriality

We intrapersonally define a particular *territory*, whether physical or perceptual, and then feel secure within that territory. We defend it from invasion and use it for protection. We mark off land by defining it precisely with a deed indicating length, width, and location. We also mark our territory with fences, signs, and numbers that specifically say "This belongs to me." We feel secure when we are in our own territory, and we often identify ourselves by our hometown, our school, and our social groups, all of which are territorial markers.

We act differently in different territories. When friends come to visit you, conditions are not the same as when you go to visit them. The friend you invite over for dinner does not act the same at your house as when you go to his or her house for dinner. In the same way, there is a definite difference between playing an athletic game at home and playing it on the road The home team is estimated to have an advantage of about one touchdown in football and ten points in basketball.

In addition to physical territory, we also have ideas and areas of exper-

We mark off territory by specifically saying, "This belongs to me!"

tise that we identify as ours. Inventors obtain patents to protect their inventions; writers copyright their books. Both are attempts to establish a territory and to communicate this to others.

Have you ever raised your hand in class and asked your instructor a question he or she could not answer? You might have been surprised when the instructor became irritated? Think about it. The reaction could have occurred because you invaded the person's territorial area of expertise, thereby causing a defensive response.

The more insecure a person is within a territory, the greater is that person's intrapersonal fear of losing the territory. Once people have defined something as theirs, they will tend to defend it. Thus an invasion of someone else's territory is likely to invite a counterattack.

Clearly, one's basic drives have a significant influence on intrapersonal communication.

The field of communication generally uses information from psychology, sociology, and anthropology to develop many of its concepts. One area related to intrapersonal communication is exclusively the property of the communication field . . . communication apprehension.

Anxiety: Communication Apprehension

Anxiety—excessive worry or concern—is an important variable that may affect our perceptions and performance. Anxiety is based on negative intrapersonal messages as they specifically relate to pleasure and security. Although many think of communication anxiety only in regard to public speaking, it is much broader.[17] Worries, concerns, and fears interfere with efficient listening, communicating in groups, talking in class and on the telephone, and verbalizing during interviews. Anxiety can make us so preoccupied that we do not get the message being communicated, or we become incapable of sending the message.

Communication Anxiety Defined

In the field of communication, the term used for speech anxiety is **communication apprehension**. The communicatively anxious person is aware of the anxiety because intrapersonal messages clearly warn of the fear. The messages warn of unfavorable outcomes and the person experiences a sense of impending doom. These messages result in a wide variety of behaviors, including preperformance fears such as excessive worry, and can bring on such things as sleeplessness, headaches, and upset stomachs. During the performance, such manifestations as a dry mouth, shaking knees, and facial flushing may be present. The anxiety often reflects in negative feelings about oneself.

"Shy people have inaccurate self-concepts."[18] They often believe that they are inadequate when they are not. "They tend to blame themselves for failure and credit others for success. They tend to erase themselves: They avoid eye contact, speak softly or less than others, and rarely take a strong position on a topic."[19] People who experience speech anxiety think poorly of themselves, feel fearful, and perform in an inadequate fashion.[20]

Almost 95 percent of the population reports having apprehension about communicating with some person or group in their lives.[21] Communication apprehension may be situation specific, or general. For example, some people only feel fear when confronted with giving a speech. A recent survey indicates that 40.6 percent identified their major fear to be speaking before groups, exceeding fear of heights, death, and loneliness![22] On the other hand, some people report perceived discomfort only in one-on-one conversations, or in groups. Others indicate anxiety in any speaking situation. To find out if you are situationally or generally apprehensive do Learn by Doing activity 6 at the end of this chapter.

Revised Cheek and Buss Shyness Scale

Instructions: For each statement, rate yourself on this scale:
1 = very uncharacteristic or untrue, 2 = uncharacteristic, 3 = neutral, 4 = characteristic, 5 = very characteristic or true.

_____ 1. I'm tense when I'm with people I don't know well.

_____ 2. It's difficult for me to ask other people for information.

_____ 3. I'm often uncomfortable at parties and other social functions.

_____ 4. When I'm in a group of people, I have trouble thinking of the right things to say.

_____ 5. It takes me a long time to overcome my shyness in new situations.

_____ 6. It's hard for me to act natural when I'm meeting new people.

_____ 7. I'm nervous when speaking to someone in authority.

_____ 8. I have doubts about my social competence.

_____ 9. I have trouble looking someone right in the eye.

_____ 10. I'm inhibited in social situations.

_____ 11. I do find it hard to talk to strangers.

_____ 12. I am more shy with members of the opposite sex.

_____ Total score

Ratings: Over 45 points, very shy; 31 to 45, somewhat shy; below 31, probably not shy, although you may feel shy in some situations.

SOURCE: Jonathan M. Cheek and Bronwen Cheek, *Conquering Shyness.* Dell Trade Paperback Edition, 1990. © 1989 by J. M. Cheek and B. Cheek. Reprinted by permission of the authors.

The Causes of Communication Apprehension

Communication apprehension can result from heredity; some people have a natural predisposition to be shy and uncomfortable with others. Estimates are that 10 to 15 percent of babies studied were born apprehensive, as demonstrated by their crying when being exposed to unfamiliar things. Tests on children progressing from two weeks of life to 7 years indicated that at 21 months they clung to their caretakers in new situations and hesitated before interacting with new persons; at 4 years they remained quiet in the presence of an unknown adult, and at 7 years they exhibited a greater degree of reaction to imagined threats than other children.[23] Biologically, shy children react more intensely to the stimuli around them than other children do, as exhibited by racing hearts, widening pupils, and vocal cord tenseness.

Communication apprehension can also spring from social conditioning. Children may imitate or model such behaviors as observed in others.

Apprehensive parents often have apprehensive children. Another potential cause includes having been brought up in environments where perfection was stressed, often causing the person to fear being evaluated, which is a major fear of many communicatively anxious people.[24] In addition, a person may be reinforced in anxiousness by the negative feedback received because of avoidance of communicative activities.[25]

Help for Communication Apprehension

Communication apprehension is not a mental disorder.[26] Since, except for those born with the anxiety, communication apprehension is a title given to the person by himself or herself, it can be removed. The most simplistic way, of course, is simply for the person to declare that he or she doesn't want or need the title. This is very difficult for many to do, so be reassured that aid is available to help rid those who want to rid themselves of the title. Such actions as skill training, systematic desensitization, and cognitive modification are forms of aid.

Skill Training   One of the factors that is perceived to be a problem among communicatively anxious people is their lack of oral communication skills. Not knowing how to structure or organize a speech, how to start and continue a conversation, or how to participate in a group can manifest itself into triggering the negative aspect of two of the basic human needs—security and pleasure.

By learning the skills needed to be an effective communicator, security is present and pleasure is anticipated. Many of the theories and skills stressed in this book, and taught in other communication classes, can teach a person the necessary skills.

Systematic Desensitization   People's fear of humiliation and embarrassment when they are around unfamiliar people, or being evaluated negatively by others, are other major apprehension inducers.[27] Through systematic desensitization, people are taught to recognize tension in their bodies and then how to relax.[28] As many as 80 or 90 percent of the people treated professionally by this system report the complete elimination of their apprehension.[29] Nevertheless, such a program works only if the person wants to change and has the skills to modify his or her behavior. If the individual does not have the necessary abilities, then skill training must precede systematic desensitization.

Cognitive Modification   The basic concept behind cognitive modification is that people have learned to think negatively and must be retaught to think positively. The first step in this process is for people to learn how to

What to Do If You're Shy

To overcome your shyness:

✳ **Write down** what you want to say when you have something important to discuss with someone. Rehearse it aloud to yourself and then to a close friend.

✳ **Force yourself** to smile and make eye contact. Practice first on a friend, then acquaintances, and finally strangers.

✳ **Watch others** who—without being obnoxious—assert themselves and get what they want. Model their behavior.

SOURCE: *Communication Briefings,* as adapted from *Men's Fitness,* 21100 Erwin St., Woodland Hills, CA 91367.

recognize when they are thinking negatively and to identify their own negative statements about their communication. Then they learn to replace negative statements with positive ones. Rather than saying, for example, "I really say stupid things," they may substitute "I can present clear ideas; it isn't that hard." The last stage of the training is to practice substituting positive statements for negative ones. This may sound very theoretical, but in reality, it works. The success of this technique is quite high.[30]

IN CONCLUSION →

The basis for communication with others is the ability to communicate with oneself. The internal messages that we send to ourselves are called intrapersonal communication. Each person's culture, background, family, education, and experiences serve as the framework for shaping how you deal with incoming information and affect the way you decide on what actions to take or avoid. How a human being views oneself will determine most of his or her actions and choices in life; however, most people have only a general idea of who they are and what they really believe in. Some communication theorists feel that the intrapersonal drives we are born with are the bases for our communication—what we think, what we express, what inspires us to act the way we do, and how we react to the way others express and use their drives. Most people possess some form of communication apprehension.

LEARN BY DOING →

1. Prepare a list of ten questions an interviewer should ask to get an accurate picture of who you really are. These questions should allow the interviewer to understand your personal history, beliefs, and future plans. Phrase the questions so that they require more than a one- or two-word reply. Your instructor will then match you with another member of the class. You will interview each other using the questions that each of you has prepared. Then introduce each other in a two- to three-minute presentation to the class. After the class presentation, answer the following questions:

   a. What did it feel like to reveal yourself to a stranger?

   b. Did you conceal things about yourself during the interview? If so, why?

   c. How did you feel and what did you do while your partner was introducing you to the class?

2. Bring to class a painting, poem, or piece of music you like. Share it with the class or a small group and indicate why you have positive feelings about it. What does your choice indicate about you?

3. State whether you agree or disagree with these statements: A person is

changeable and can alter behavior patterns if she or he really wants to do so. No one can change anyone; only the individual can change himself or herself. Explain the reasons for your answers.

4. Fill out your Johari window. Get one of your friends to fill in the Known-to-Others part of the window about you. Compare that person's answers with yours. What did you learn about yourself from this activity?

5. Make a shieldlike coat of arms out of a piece of cardboard large enough for the class to see. Draw or cut out and paste at least four pictures, symbols, or words on the coat of arms that represent you—your beliefs, attitudes, bodily image, hobbies, future plans, past successes or failures. The class will be broken into groups. Each person is to explain his or her coat of arms and why you have selected these things to represent you.

6. Personal Report of Communication Apprehension (PRCA-24)[31] directions: This instrument is composed of twenty-four statements concerning feelings about communicating with other people. Please indicate the degree to which each statement applies to you by marking whether you (1) strongly agree, (2) agree, (3) are undecided, (4) disagree, or (5) strongly disagree. Record your first impression.

_____ 1. I dislike participating in group discussions.

_____ 2. Generally, I am comfortable while participating in a group discussion.

_____ 3. I am tense and nervous while participating in group discussions.

_____ 4. I like to get involved in group discussions.

_____ 5. Engaging in a group discussion with new people makes me tense and nervous.

_____ 6. I am calm and relaxed while participating in group discussions.

_____ 7. Generally, I am nervous when I have to participate in a meeting.

_____ 8. Usually I am calm and relaxed while participating in meetings.

_____ 9. I am very calm and relaxed when I am called upon to express an opinion at a meeting.

_____ 10. I am afraid to express myself at meetings.

_____ 11. Communicating at meetings usually makes me uncomfortable.

_____ 12. I am very relaxed when answering questions at a meeting.

_____ 13. While participating in a conversation with a new acquaintance, I feel very nervous.

_____ 14. I have no fear of speaking up in conversations.

_____ 15. Ordinarily I am very tense and nervous in conversations.

_____ 16. Ordinarily I am very calm and relaxed in conversations.

_____ 17. While conversing with a new acquaintance, I feel very relaxed.

_____ 18. I'm afraid to speak up in conversations.

_____ 19. I have no fear of giving a speech.

_____ 20. Certain parts of my body feel very tense and rigid while giving a speech.

_____ 21. I feel relaxed while giving a speech.

_____ 22. My thoughts become confused and jumbled when I am giving a speech.

_____ 23. I face the prospect of giving a speech with confidence.

_____ 24. While giving a speech, I get so nervous I forget facts I really know.

Scoring:

18+ scores for items 2, 4, 6; minus the scores for items 1, 3, 5 =

_____ Group discussion score

18+ scores for 8, 9, 12; minus the scores for 7, 10, 11 =

_____ Meetings score

18+ scores for 14, 16, 17; minus the scores for 13, 15, 18 =

_____ Interpersonal conversations score

18+ scores for 19, 21, 23; minus the scores for 20, 22, 24 =

_____ Public speaking score

Add group, meetings, interpersonal, and public speaking scores =

_____ Total score

Your score should range between 24 and 120. If your score is below 24 or above 120, you have made a mistake in computing the score. (Your instructor will use the _Instructor's Manual_ for this textbook to tell you the meaning of your scores.)

KEY TERMS →

intrapersonal communication
self-talk
cognitive processing
values
attitudes
beliefs
cognitive dissonance
guilty conscience
self-concept

self-confidence
real self
ideal self
public self
Johari window
ethnographers
anxiety
communication apprehension

chapter 3

Listening

LEARNING OUTCOMES →

After reading this chapter, you should be able to:

Explain the importance of listening in daily communication

Contrast hearing and listening

Define and state the role of reception, perception, attention, the assignment of meaning, and response as they relate to the listening process

List and explain some of the listening influencers

Define discriminative, comprehensive, therapeutic, critical, and appreciative listening

Identify and explain some of the techniques available for improving personal listening

I f you are fairly typical, you have had little if any training as a listener. Most schools operate on the assumption that you don't know how to read or write when you come to school, so they teach you how to perform those skills. They also assume that since you can talk and hear, you can communicate and listen. This assumption is incorrect. Talking and hearing are biological functions. Listening and communicating, like reading and writing, are learned skills.

How effective a listener do you think you are? How much of your time do you spend listening?

The average American spends 50 to 80 percent of her or his day listening but actively hears only half of what is said,[1] understands only a quarter of that, and remembers even less. Most people use only 25 percent of their innate ability to listen.[2]

The Importance of Listening

Listening is an important skill we use daily. Your academic success, employment achievement, and personal happiness often depend on your ability to listen efficiently.

Listening is an important means for learning at the college level.

Listening is an important means for learning at the college level. In fact, listening is the most used academic skill. "Students listen to the equivalent of a book a day; talk the equivalent of a book a week; read the equivalent of a book a month; and write the equivalent of a book a year."[3] In fact, listening has been found to be more critical to academic success than reading or academic aptitude.[4]

Several years ago, the Sperry Corporation (which has since become part of Unisys) launched a major advertising campaign to point out how important it is to listen effectively both in our personal lives and in our careers. Like many other American corporations, Unisys has instituted training programs to prepare its executives, managers, and employees to be better listeners. Control Data, 3M, and Ford are just a few other major companies that provide training in listening.

As an educated person, you have an obligation to strive to be an effective listener. And to be a responsible listener, you must know what the process is about, what it takes to be an effective listener, how to evaluate your own listening, and how to work toward improving your weaknesses while retaining your strengths.

The Listening Process

Many people assume that hearing and listening are the same, but they are not. **Hearing** is a biological activity that involves reception of a message through sensory channels. Hearing is only one part of listening. **Listening** is a process that involves reception, perception, attention, the assignment of meaning, and response by the listener to the message presented.

Reception

The initial step in the listening process is the **reception** of a stimulus or message, which includes both the auditory message and the visual message. The hearing process is based on a complex set of physical interactions between the ear and the brain. Proper care of the ear is important because auditory acuity enhances the ability to listen efficiently. It is estimated that approximately 28 million Americans (more than one out of every twenty) are deaf or hard-of-hearing.[5] To keep these statistics from rising, people who work near loud machinery are now required to wear ear protectors. But the workplace is not the only source of potential danger. For example, individuals who expose themselves to loud music or lis-

Why We Don't Hear Others

If you want to listen so you really hear what others say, make sure you're not a:

* **Mind reader.** You'll hear little or nothing as you think, "What is this person really thinking or feeling?"

* **Rehearser.** Your mental tryouts for "Here's what I'll say next" tune out the speaker.

* **Filterer.** Some call this selective listening—hearing only what you want to hear.

* **Dreamer.** Drifting off during a face-to-face conversation can lead to an embarrassing "What did you say?" or "Could you repeat that?"

* **Identifier.** If you refer everything you hear to your experience, you probably didn't really hear what was said.

* **Comparer.** When you get sidetracked assessing the messenger, you're sure to miss the message.

* **Derailer.** Changing the subject too quickly soon tells others you're not interested in anything they have to say.

* **Sparrer.** You hear what's said but quickly belittle it or discount it. That puts you in the same class as the derailer.

* **Placater.** Agreeing with everything you hear just to be nice or to avoid conflict does not mean you're a good listener.

SOURCE: *Communication Briefings*, as adapted from *The Writing Lab*, Department of English, Purdue University, 1356 Heavilon Hall, West Lafayette, IN 47907.

---

ten to music through earphones should be aware that they can damage their hearing mechanism. Indeed, the use of earphones to listen to music is considered the source of much of the hearing damage suffered by Americans.[6] An audiologist warns that, "As you enjoy the blaring music in your car, home, or your headsets, or at a concert, be aware that you can be permanently damaging one of your most important biological tools . . . your hearing mechanism."[7]

In addition to using the hearing mechanism, people listen through their visual system. People listen through the eyes to observe a person's facial expression, posture, movement, and appearance, which all provide important cues that may not be obvious merely by listening to the verbal part of the message.

Receiving the message through the visual and the auditory channels is but one part of the listening process. The listener also must attend to the message.

Attention

Once the stimulus—the word and/or visual symbol—is received it reaches the attention stage of the human processing system.

Attention represents the focus on a specific stimuli selected from all the stimuli received at any given moment.

The Role of Attention   In listening, **attention** represents the focus on a specific stimulus selected from all the stimuli received at any given moment. In this phase, the other stimuli recede so that we can concentrate on a specific heard word or visual symbol. Normally your attention is divided between what you are attempting to listen to, what is currently happening in the rest of the environment, and what else is going on in your mind. Consider, for example, what happens if you are attending a movie. Perhaps the person in front of you is constantly whispering to the person next to him, there is a buzz in the sound system, and you are worried because you left your car in a no-parking zone. Your attention is being pulled in several directions. But if the film is interesting enough, you will focus on what is being portrayed and the other factors will be relegated to the back of your consciousness.

Attention to a stimulus occurs in a person's short-term memory system. The capacity of the short-term memory—our **attention span**—rarely lasts more than forty-five seconds at any one time.[8] Thus, the ability of the listener to focus attention is limited. In fact, teachers have observed that students cannot handle much beyond a fifteen-minute time frame at best. The reasons for this are not yet fully understood, although experts have suggested that "it's entirely possible that our capacity for sustained attention and deliberate thought is being altered by television viewing."[9] Most of us who have been raised on television have come to expect a seven- to ten-minute viewing format followed by a commercial break.

The Role of Concentration   Undoubtedly one of the most difficult tasks we have to perform as listeners is concentration. Motivation plays an important role in activating this skill. For example, if you really want to listen to a speaker, this desire will put you in a better frame of mind for concentrating than anticipating that she will be boring.

Two other factors that affect listening concentration are interest level and difficulty of the message. Some messages may be boring, but if you need to get the information, careful concentration is imperative. For example, you may not find the chemistry professor's ideas fascinating, but if you do not listen effectively, you will probably fail the next test. You may also find the information so difficult that you turn it off. Again, if it is imperative for you to understand the ideas, then you have to force yourself to figure out what you do not understand and find a way of grasping the meaning.

We can think three to four times faster than the normal conversation rate of 125 to 150 words per minute.[10] And because we can receive messages much more quickly than the other person can talk, we tend to tune in and tune out throughout a message. The mind can absorb only so much material. Indeed, the brain operates much like a computer: it turns off, recycles itself, and turns back on to avoid information overload.[11] It is no wonder, then, that our attention fluctuates even when we are actively involved as listeners. Think back to the class you attended. Do you recall a slight gap in your listening at times? This is a natural part of the listening process. When you turn off, the major danger is that you may daydream rather than quickly turn back to the message. But by taking notes and/or forcing yourself to paraphrase, you can avoid this difficulty.

Research with compressed speech illustrates the human capacity for efficient listening. In this technique, taped material is speeded up mechanically to more than three hundred words per minute. Incredibly, there is no loss of comprehension at this faster rate. Tests even reveal increased comprehension, much as the tests given to people who have been taught to speed-read show an increase in their retention of information. Because of the rapid speeds, the test participants anticipated retention problems and thus forced themselves to listen more attentively and concentrate more fully than they would otherwise have done.

Concentration also requires the listener to control for distractions. As a listener, you probably have a whole list of things that you have to attend to in addition to the speaker's message. Rather than attempting to dismiss them, control your concentration by mentally setting these other issues aside for the moment to give the speaker your full attention. It takes mental and physical energy to do this, but concentration is the key to successful listening.

The Role of Paraphrasing   Paraphrasing—making a summary of the ideas you have just received—will provide you with a concise restatement of what has been presented. It will also allow you to determine whether you understand the material. If you cannot repeat or write down a summary of what was said, then you probably did not get the whole message, or did not understand it. Keep this in mind when you are listening to an instructor and taking notes. Try to paraphrase the material instead of writing down direct quotes. If you cannot do so, it is a clue that you should ask for clarification or make a note to look up that particular material later on.

Try verbally paraphrasing the next time you are involved in a demanding conversation, such as when you are receiving directions. Repeat back to the speaker what you think she or he just said in order to check whether you both received and understood the same things. One of the benefits of paraphrasing is that it eliminates the common complaint that you weren't listening. Giving people back the ideas they have just presented makes it impossible for them to support the claim that you were not paying attention.

Perception

After the message is received and attended to, the listener's perceptions come into play. Perceiving is an active process. During the act of **perception** a person takes the material received and attempts to evaluate what has been input. The act of perceiving might be compared to a chef straining ingredients in order to filter what she wants from what she is not interested in using; for example, separating pasta from the water in which it was cooked by passing it through a strainer. The strainer can be compared to your **perceptual filter**, which strains the stimuli you receive and separates what makes sense from what doesn't. As you listen to information, your perceptual filter strains the information to which you are listening through your background, culture, experience, role, mental and physical state, beliefs, attitudes, and values.

The process of narrowing your attention to specific bits or pieces of information is referred to as **selective perception**. An idea's distinctiveness or the satisfaction of your needs is often the basis for why you will pay attention to a particular stimulus. The more relevant, the more novel the stimuli, the more likely they are to be perceived by the listener.

Perceptual Differences of Women and Men

	Women	Men
Love:	A feeling	A ritual (evidenced by actions: send flowers, dinners, etc.)
Friendship:	Verbally intimate: Express oneself	Buddy No self-exposure
Commitment:	A relationship to be nurtured, supported over time	Loss of freedom
Leadership:	Facilitative	Directive
Communication:	To understand and be understood	To win, outsmart; one-upmanship
Intimacy:	Sharing and discussing innermost thoughts and feelings	Physically close

SOURCE: From "Sex Stereotypes and Expectations: Classroom and Campus Strategies for Change," by Linda A. M. Perry, Phil Backlund, and Lisa Merrill, a short course at the Speech Communication Association Convention, October 29–November 1, 1992, Chicago, IL. Used by permission of the National Communication Association.

The Assignment of Meaning

Once you have paid attention to the material presented, the next stage in the listening process is to categorize the message so as to assign meanings to its verbal and nonverbal stimuli.

The Role of Assigning Meaning   The **assignment of meaning**—the process of putting the stimulus into some predetermined category—develops as we acquire our language system. We develop mental categories for interpreting the messages we receive. For instance, our categorizing system for the word *cheese* may include such factors as food, dairy products, taste, and nourishment, all of which help us to relate the word *cheese* to the context in which it is used.

The categorical assignment of meaning creates **schema**—scripts for processing information. The mental representations that we carry in our brains—**schemata**—are shaped by the language categories and by the way our brains process information. An individual's culture, background, family, education, and experience all serve as the framework for creating the schema that enable us, then, to deal with incoming information. The cognitive process draws on all of a person's schemata for the purpose of interpretation, and these schemata provide the mental links for understanding and creating meaning from the verbal and the nonverbal stimuli we receive.[12] Understanding a discussion of some of the customs and traditions on a college campus, for example, may be difficult for freshmen because they do not have the cognitive schema to relate to the information.

The Role of Global/Linear Thinking/Listening   We are unique in the way we listen and learn. Part of the differences among us is based on the way our brain works. The human brain is divided into two hemispheres, and research shows that some people are prone to use one side of the brain more than the other. This **brain dominance** accounts for learning and listening in patterned ways.[13]

The left hemisphere of the brain is most responsible for rational, logical, sequential, linear, and abstract thinking. People who tend to be left-brain dominant listen and learn best when materials are presented in structured ways. They tend to prefer specifics and logic-based arguments. Because they tend to take information at face value, abstractions and generalizations don't add much to their learning. Because they are so straight-line in their learning preferences, they are often referred to as **linear learners/listeners**.

The right hemisphere of the brain is responsible for intuitive, spatial, visual, and concrete matters. It is from the right side of the brain that we are able to visualize. Those with this listening/learning dominance prefer examples rather than technical explanations. They prefer knowing the information can be useful and applied. The right-brain dominant person tends to be creative and rely on intuitive thinking, can follow visual/pictographic rather than written instructions, likes to explore information without necessarily coming to a conclusion, and enjoys interaction rather than lecturing. Because of their preference for a generalized rather than specific description, right-brain dominant persons are often labeled as **global listeners/learners**. Many global learners find much of the traditional lecture method of teaching in U.S. schools and universities, a linear methodology, to be dull and frustrating.

Most people are a combination of global and linear learner/listeners. If you fall into this classification, you can be more flexible in how you listen and learn than those with extreme style preferences.

It is important for you to recognize your listening/learning style; it can make a difference in the way you approach the listening/learning environments. If you know that you need examples and the speaker is not giving them, you should ask for them. If the speaker is not drawing specific conclusions and not speaking in a structured format, and these are necessary for your understanding, then you must probe for information that will allow you to organize the ideas. Don't assume that the speaker knows how you need to receive information; he or she doesn't. Many classroom instructors teach based on their own listening/learning style, forgetting that all students don't learn that way. If you are a global listener/learner, this

The right-brain dominant person tends to be creative and rely on intuitive thinking, can follow visual/pictographic rather than written instructions, likes to explore information without necessarily coming to a conclusion, and enjoys interaction rather than lecturing.

may account for why you had trouble with some math or science classes. On the other hand, if you are a linear listener/learner, literature and poetry classes may have been difficult for you.

If you are interested in finding out your learner/listener style based on the hemispheres of your brain, complete Activity 7 in the Learn by Doing section at the end of this chapter.

The Role of Culture in Listening   Like brain dominance, a person's culture also influences listening/learning abilities. Some cultures, such as many in Asia, stress good listening by being a silent communicator in order to receive messages.[14] People in Japan, for example, are more likely to spend less time talking on the job than do Northern Americans, stressing instead the listening aspect of communication. In addition, some cultures stress concentration resulting in longer attention spans. Buddhism, for instance, has a notion called "being mindful." This means giving whatever you are doing your complete and full attention. Training to have long attention spans starts in childhood. To those raised in a typical North American environment, these listening enhancing concepts are not part of the background.[15]

A Comparison of Left-Mode and Right-Mode Characteristics

L-Mode

Verbal: Using words to name, describe, define.

Analytic: Figuring things out step-by-step and part-by-part.

Symbolic: Using a symbol to *stand for* something. For example, the drawn form ◉ stands for eye, the sign + stands for the process of addition.

Abstract: Taking out a small bit of information and using it to represent the whole thing.

Temporal: Keeping track of time, sequencing one thing after another: Doing first things first, second things second, etc.

Rational: Drawing conclusions based on *reason* and *facts*.

Digital: Using numbers as in counting.

Logical: Drawing conclusions based on logic: one thing following another in logical order—for example, a mathematical theorem or a well-stated argument.

Linear: Thinking in terms of linked ideas, one thought directly following another, often leading to a convergent conclusion.

R-Mode

Nonverbal: Awareness of things, but minimal connection with words.

Synthetic: Putting things together to form wholes.

Concrete: Relating to things as they are, at the present moment.

Analogic: Seeing likenesses between things; understanding metaphoric relationships.

Nontemporal: Without a sense of time.

Nonrational: Not requiring a basis of reason or facts; willingness to suspend judgment.

Spatial: Seeing where things are in relation to other things, and how parts go together to form a whole.

Intuitive: Making leaps of insight, often based on incomplete patterns, hunches, feelings, or visual images.

Holistic: Seeing whole things all at once; perceiving the overall patterns and structures, often leading to divergent conclusions.

SOURCE: From *Drawing on the Right Side of the Brain* by Betty Edwards, p. 40. Copyright © 1979, 1989 by Betty Edwards. Reprinted by permission of The Putnam Publishing Group/Jeremy P. Tarcher, Inc.

An investigation into the learning/listening style of the Navajos, a Native American tribe, demonstrates cultural effects. The Navajo listening/learning process has four components: observe, think, understand/feel, and act. This is in contrast to the "Anglo [white North American] process of act, observe/think/clarify, understand."[16] Anglos tend to learn from examining components in relationship to the whole. Native Americans spend much more time watching and listening and less time talking.[17] In an academic learning situation, this may result in "Anglo teachers seeing Native Americans as inattentive, laconic and dull-witted, while students see their teachers as directive and bossy."[18]

The Role of Evaluation   One of the greatest barriers to effective listening is our tendency to evaluate the stimuli we receive, regardless of whether they are relevant to the message. In fact, this tendency is thought to be the most persistent barrier to communication we have to overcome.[19] Although assigning meaning to stimuli often requires a quick evaluation, listeners should attempt to avoid instant judgments based primarily on superficial factors. Sometimes, if you feel you don't have enough information, or need to study the information, it may be better for you not to come to a conclusion.

A strategy useful to listeners in assigning meaning to messages is to differentiate factual statements (those based on observable phenomena or common acceptance) from opinions (inferences or judgments made by the speaker).

Likewise, it is helpful for the listener to sift through verbal obscurities and work for clarification of meanings. Unclear terms and phrases, euphemisms, and evasive language make interpretation difficult. The effective listener, however, asks questions and seeks clarification from speakers and the contextual cues in their messages.

Listeners also benefit from recognizing what their emotional biases are and how they affect interpretations of messages. One way to discover such biases is to draw up a list of terms and phrases that serve as "red flags" triggering particular emotional responses. Recognition of such emotional barriers is a good first step toward compensating for the knee-jerk reactions that effectively tune out the speaker. Some people have strong reactions, for example, to such words and concepts as skinheads, gay rights, taxes, abortion, and, yes, even homework.

The assignment of meaning is a complex process involving categorizing, evaluating, filtering through verbal obscurity, and recognizing emotional biases.

Response

Once we have assigned meaning to a message, we continue the information-processing with an **internal or external response**—intellectual or emotional reaction—to the message. It is hypothesized that every stimulus we receive is stored somewhere in our brain.

The Role of Memory Techniques   Many people find remembering names a problem. In some cases, it may be that you don't remember because you don't listen when the name is said, or you don't immediately repeat the name to entrench it in your memory. "Thirty to 40 percent of people are unable to remember names because they don't hear the name in the first place. Most of us are so focused on ourselves in social situations that we fail to give any real attention to the other person."[20] But there are techniques that can be learned to improve memory, including name recall. For example, when you are introduced to someone, you must first decide that you want to remember this person's name and then get ready to remember it. If you tend to remember things by pictures, you should picture the person in a particular setting, perhaps the location where you are meeting him or her. You can remember the person either with a sign across his or her chest, emblazoned with a name, or you can tie the person's name to some picture. (This is a good technique for right-brained people who tend to remember pictures, not words.) If you tend to remember words better than pictures, concentrate on the name and repeat it several times to yourself, or select a familiar word with which the name rhymes (a good technique for left-brained people, since words, rather than pictures, are generally their way of remembering). Finally, repeat the name several times as you speak to the person. If you carry through on this process, the odds of your remembering the name increase greatly.

The Role of Questions   One area of response that can assist the listener in storing information in long-term memory, and at the same time provide meaningful feedback to the speaker, is asking questions. This enables the listener to ensure that the message he or she has received and interpreted is consistent with the original intent of the speaker.

To be effective, however, questions must be relevant to the message presented by the speaker. When asking questions, try to figure out what you don't understand. Most commonly, difficulties in perceiving information center on a lack of understanding of vocabulary, a need for clarifying examples, or a need for the material to be presented in a different format or order. For example, you are taking notes in class and can't paraphrase the instructor's ideas so that you can write them down. One of the mistakes students often make is not to say anything. If it is important for you to gain the information, you must probe for meaning. If an opportunity is available, such as when a teacher indicates that questions are welcome, use that invitation to your advantage. When asking for information, don't say, "I don't understand." The instructor won't be able to clarify; you haven't given him or her the clues needed to be of help. It is common in certain academic subjects for the vocabulary to be new and unusual. If you don't understand the terms being used ask, "Would you please define (fill in the term)?" Or, if you vaguely understand but need something more, you could state, "Would you please give us several examples to illustrate (insert the specific topic)?" (This is often what is needed for right-brained people to grasp the idea because they need examples they can picture, rather than terms.) Or, if you don't understand the concept, you could state, "Could you restate the concept of (fill in the topic) in a step-by-step process?" (This is a technique needed by left-brained people, who need the structure to understand what may be confusing because it was not put in a patterned manner.) In each case you are specifically centering on what needs to be done to help you gain the information. The same techniques work on the job and in other situations where gaining information is important.

The Role of Feedback   Good listeners are conscious of the role of feedback cues; they recognize the importance of giving the speaker an understanding of whether the message was received. Asking questions, nodding or shaking your head, smiling or frowning, verbalization such as "uh-huh" or "um?" are all forms of listener feedback. Feedback responses can be either verbal or nonverbal, and they should function to further enhance and/or reinforce the communication.

Effective feedback should be readily perceptible to the speaker. Listeners must take a major responsibility for the outcome of the communication. Rather than enter into the listening process passively, assume an active, energetic role as a listening communicator. Assume responsibility for the outcome of the communication. Take seriously your part in sending feedback that will support the speaker's goals and further the communication, for this feedback plays a critical role in creating and maintaining the communication climate for listener and speaker alike.

Listening Influencers

The process of listening, through which the listener receives, attends to, perceives, assigns meaning to, and responds to messages, is a complex process. To be effective, the listener must be actively involved throughout and work to overcome barriers that may arise. Certain key influencers can facilitate or hinder the process.[21]

The Role of the Speaker   The speaker's credibility—that is, the listener's perception of the speaker's trustworthiness, competence, and dynamism—can lead the listener to accept or reject a message. Unfortunately, some listeners are so in awe of a particular speaker that they may lose all objectivity in analyzing the person's message. For example, if the speaker is a Hollywood celebrity, the listener may overlook that she or he is not an expert on the specific subject in question. If the listener accepts the speaker's message simply because he or she is a celebrity, the receiver may be overlooking the logical weaknesses of the presentation.

The speaker's physical presentation—animation, appearance, clothing—can have an instantaneous effect on listener attention. A speaker who is dynamic and humorous may be able to get past the critical listening abilities of certain listeners. To be a discerning listener, it is important to listen to the message, not just the reputation or presentational style of the speaker.

The Role of the Message   Another major influencer is the message itself. If its presentation is not clearly organized—if the arguments are not well ordered—the listener may have difficulty concentrating on and staying tuned in to the message.

Likewise, the tone and the treatment of the message can affect a person's listening abilities. Some religious speakers, for example, are known for their ability to put fear into the minds of their listeners when they prophesize eternal damnation. Listeners must ascertain whether the message is appropriate for them, and whether they believe in the prophecies presented.

The Role of the Channel   The communication channel also can influence listening ability. Some people are more auditory, and some are more visual in orientation. The public speaker, for example, who couples the message with clear visual aids may assist listeners in comprehending the material. Electronic channels versus face-to-face presence can also have an effect. Television, for example, has changed the whole nature of political campaigning. Historically, a candidate had to appear in person before an audience, where listeners could have some physical contact with him or her. Now, sound bites, thirty-second spots, videotaped messages, and debates in which listeners can't directly participate in the listening experience have made for drastic differences.

Students have reacted both positively and negatively to the concept of distant learning in which television sets replace a live instructor. Some like the fact that the instructor cannot call upon the listener, that the message can be viewed whenever the receiver wants to listen/watch, and that they can replay the material for reinforcement. On the other hand, there are those who feel that the separation between listener and speaker causes a sterile environment and eliminates the feedback needed for effective communication.

The Role of External and Internal Variables   Noise (any sort of interference) in the communication channel can diminish the effectiveness of the listener. Static on the telephone or distortions on the television screen can interrupt good listening. Noise from the environment also affects listeners. If the lighting is poor or the room temperature is too cold, the listener has greater difficulty attending to the speaker's message. Control of or adjustment for the distraction may be necessary; for example, by moving to a different spot so that you can see or hear the speaker more readily, adjusting the auditory or visual channel in some way, or negotiating with the speaker to move to a better environment.

It should be recognized that listeners are influenced not only by a vast array of external factors but also internal ones. Receivers are affected by their physical state (general health, gender, age), experiences (background, life history, training), culture, attitudes (predispositions), memory, and expectations.[22] The listener's culture, can also be influential. People from different cultures have different ways of attending to each other as indicated by the amount of eye contact, distance between each other, and amount of patience. For example, in some South American cultures, it is perceived bad manners to look directly in the eyes of a speaker, especially if the presenter is an authority figure. Some Arabic and Asian cultures stress standing very close to people while conversing, which makes many North Americans uncomfortable, thus making concentration difficult.

The positive or negative attitude the listener carries into a listening situation (in conjunction with expectations of the experience) is important. A listener who goes to a training session, for example, convinced beforehand that it will be a waste of time will probably carry that negative attitude into the session and refuse to suspend judgment and listen comprehensively.

The listener's positive or negative attitude extends to himself or herself as a listener. Just as speakers have self-concepts, so too do listeners. Most people have had very little praise or external reward for good listening but have probably heard lots of negative messages: "Keep quiet and listen." "Why don't you ever listen to me?" These negative messages, which are received from a very early age, can create a negative attitude in listeners about their own listening abilities.

The Role of Memory and Time   Throughout the entire process of listening, memory plays an important role. The listener must be willing to hold the message received in short-term memory long enough to perceive, attend to, and assign meaning to it. This activity requires sufficient auditory and visual memory to maintain focus long enough to process the message.

Coupled with the influence of memory is the influence of time. The listener has to have the time, and be willing to take the time, to listen with discrimination and comprehension. People lead busy lives and frequently have little time to engage in actively listening to another person. Well-intentioned listeners find it useful to recognize that they are busy. Be willing, however, to mentally set aside or "bracket" the other internal factors competing for your attention ("Yes, I do have to finish that memo") and focus on the speaker and his or her message at the moment.

Purposes of Listening

We listen on a number of levels, for a variety of purposes. We listen to distinguish among sounds, gain ideas, discriminate among ideas, aid others, and appreciate sounds or symbols. Awareness of the purposes of listening sometimes aids a listener to select the listening techniques that best fit the desired outcome.[23]

Discriminative Listening

In **discriminative listening**, we attempt to distinguish among auditory and visual stimuli. Distinctions are at the base of the listening we do. Through discrimination we can come to understand differences in verbal sounds (dialects, pronunciation) and nonverbal behavior (gestures, facial reactions). By understanding such differences, we gain sensitivity to the sights and sounds of our world. You can then determine, for example, whether a person is being sarcastic, cautious, negative, or uncooperative because you realize that the same set of words can be taken in a variety of ways.

Discriminative listening is also important when you come in contact with some of the nonhuman features of our everyday lives. You may listen, for instance, to household appliances to determine whether they are functioning properly. People in certain professions, such as doctors and repairpersons, sometimes find discrimination to be their most important listening skill.

Comprehension Listening

In **comprehension listening**, the objective is to recognize and retain the information in a message. To comprehend a message, the listener must first discriminate the message to recognize its auditory and visual components. But listening for comprehension goes beyond the objective of discriminating a message. At this point in the process, heightened concentration is needed. In academia, comprehension is vital. "The classroom consists of the verbal and nonverbal transactions between teacher and students and among students the ability to learn in a world of expanding information and cultural diversity demands competence in communication [listening]."[24]

Some techniques have been found to enhance listening comprehension. One strategy is to concentrate on getting the main points of a message rather than all the supporting details. That is, a student listening to an instructor should focus on the main point rather than on the elaboration and details. Even when taking notes, it is wise to sort the main points and the supporting details. This can be done, for example, by drawing a vertical line down the middle of the paper, putting the main points in the left-hand column, and noting the supporting ideas in the right-hand column. Abbreviation of commonly used words saves time in writing, which allows for more listening time. For instance, if this chapter were given as a lecture, the notes for it thus far might look like those in Figure 3.1.

The student whose notes are shown in Figure 3.1 obviously felt there were sufficient cues for understanding the material so that examples were

Figure 3.1
Note-taking Format

Lstng
Lstng Process

Hearing – biological process
Lstng – active processing of
   info heard
Reception – get message
Attention
   focus on ideas
   anticipate next point
   paraphrase – restate in
     own words
   get ready to lstn rapidly
Perception – screen info
Assignment of meaning –
   categorize symbols
Response – info storage
   choose to remember
   visualize what is to
     be remembered
   associate info
   practice material

Purposes of Lstng

Lstng Influencers
   speaker
   message
   channel
   noise
   internal variables
   attitude
   memory
   time
Discrimination
Comprehension

SOURCE: This is a sample Figure source note

not essential. Nevertheless, many note-takers like to provide examples to help clarify material. Each note-taker has to determine for her- or himself how much detail and how much reinforcement are necessary.

Some communication experts recommend a technique called *clarifying and confirming* to enhance concentration. This strategy calls for the listener to ask for additional information or explanation. This system works well when added to a technique known as *acknowledging or bridging*—relating one part of the message to another. Good radio and television talk-show hosts use this system when interviewing guests. Public radio's award-winning interviewer Terri Gross is excellent at using paraphrasing (repeating ideas), verbal feedback ("uh-huh" and "that's an interesting idea"), internal summaries (summarizing one topic before going on to the next), and bridging (indicating what topic or idea she'd like to talk about next by referring to a quote in a book or one just made by the speaker). The abilities of clarifying, confirming, acknowledging, and bridging are necessities for individuals going into listening professions such as counseling, social work, police work, newscasting, and reporting.

Remembering the main points at a later time may also require the development of a number of memory techniques. Some research indicates that a person can lose as much as half of any given information after the first day unless she or he takes notes and reviews them. Because it is so easy to lose information in memory storage, the good listener will work to gain the information presented. Some students have found, for example, that they retain ideas best if they review the information immediately after it is presented and then go over it daily, rather than waiting until the night before an examination to cram.

People listen for special purposes: to provide a therapeutic setting for a person to talk through a problem, critically evaluate a persuasive message, or appreciate aspects of a particular message.

Therapeutic Listening

Listening at the therapeutic level is important for those in such fields as psychology, social work, speech therapy, and counseling. **Therapeutic listening** requires a listener to learn when to ask questions, when to stimulate further discussion, and when, if ever, to give advice.

Therapeutic listening is not restricted to professional counselors. In daily life people often need a listener when dealing with a problem. The listener can help the speaker talk through the situation. To be effective in this role, the therapeutic listener must have empathy for the other person—the ability to understand that person's problem from their perspective by momentarily putting yourself into his or her shoes and attempting to see the world as the other person sees it. This is difficult for many people to do, as there is a tendency to want to solve the other person's problem and rid them of pain.

How can a person learn to be an effective therapeutic listener? The empathic training given to hotline volunteers includes teaching them to resist the temptation to jump in with statements such as "The same thing happened to me" or "If I were you, I would. . . ." In addition, remember that there is nothing wrong with silence. Often we want the other person to keep talking. Listen patiently. The person in pain may need time to feel the pain and get in touch with her or his thoughts and feelings. The listener can help the speaker generate a list of possible alternatives from which that person may choose; then he or she will have some commitment to carrying it out. Another technique taught is not to diminish the person's feeling to pain. They feel pain, they know it. Saying, "that's no big problem," doesn't help diminish the hurt.

Critical Listening

Critical listening centers on the listener comprehending and evaluating the message that has been received. A critical listener assesses the arguments and the appeals in a message and then decides whether to accept or reject them.

An understanding of both the tools of persuasion and the process of logic and reasoning enables critical listeners to make judgments about the merits of the messages they receive. Judgments should take into account such factors as

1. *The personal appeal of the speaker.* The speaker's credibility, stems from the position held (e.g., sports celebrity), expertise, trustworthiness, and dynamism. The critical listener needs to recognize how much this credibility is influencing how the message is being understood and analyzed.

2. *The speaker's arguments and evidence.* Does the speaker present a logical argument supported by substantive and relevant data?

3. *The speaker's motivational appeals.* How is the speaker attempting to get the listener involved in the message? What appeals to the listener's needs are utilized to get the listener to respond to a persuasive message?

4. *Assumptions on the part of the speaker.* Does the speaker assume that something is a fact before it has been established as such? Just because someone says, "It is readily apparent that . . ." doesn't make it so.

5. *What is not said.* In some cases, the speaker implies, rather than states, his or her ideas, so the listener is forced to read between the lines to supply the message. "You know what I mean" is a remark to which the listener should be alert. What do you really know from what was said?

The critical listener should be aware of these factors and assess the merits of a particular message. Sales pitches, advertising messages, campaign speeches, and persuasive briefings all require critical analysis.

As a speech student, you probably will be called on to critique the speeches of fellow students. In this mode of critical listening, your role is to provide information to help the speaker improve his or her work. Offer comments on what the speaker does effectively as well as what the speaker needs to improve. Deal with content—topic choice, structure, supporting materials, clarity, and interest—and with delivery—animation, vocal dynamics, eye contact.

Appreciative Listening

Appreciative listening takes place when a person engages in enjoyment or sensory stimulation of a message, such as listening to humorous speakers, comedians, or music videos. Appreciation is a highly individual matter. Some people believe that the more knowledge they have about a particular subject, the more they can appreciate it. Others feel, however, that the more they know about something, the more they lose their ability to appreciate all but the best.

Improving Your Listening

Effective listening is a complex, involved, and involving process requiring a great deal of commitment on the part of the listener. Despite its complexities, you can do a great deal to improve your skill as a listener.

Improvement of listening skill requires breaking old habits, putting new strategies in their place, and practicing these new skills until they feel comfortable and are part of your listening repertoire.

Here are some suggestions to help listeners develop greater skill in the process.

1 *Recognize that both the sender and receiver share responsibility for effective communication.* If you are sending a message, define your terms, structure your message clearly, and give your receiver the necessary background to respond effectively. As a receiver, you should ask questions and provide feedback if you cannot understand the speaker's point. If possible, repeat the major ideas so that the speaker can check to be sure you have grasped his or her meaning.

2 *Suspend judgment.* One of the greatest barriers to human communication is the tendency to form instant judgments about almost everything we encounter. As listeners, we are prone to assess speakers prematurely, before we have even comprehended the entire message. Statements such as "I don't like his voice" and "This is a boring lecture"

set up barriers to effective listening. Good listening involves setting aside these judgments and listening for the message.

3 *Be a patient listener.* Avoid interrupting or tuning out until the entire message has been communicated. We often find ourselves beginning to act before we have totally understood what is being said. This is especially true of global listeners who intuitively act on perceived information.

Think about how difficult it is to assemble a new product until you thoroughly comprehend the instructions. Or remember the times you filled out a form, only to realize later that you put down your first name when the directions said your last name should have come first. Patience in listening will help you avoid having to go back over messages you missed the first time around, or did not understand because you did not let the whole message come through.

4 *Avoid egospeak.* **Egospeak** is the "art of boosting our own ego by speaking only about what we want to talk about, and not giving a hoot in hell about what the [other] person is speaking about."[25] When you jump into a conversation and speak your piece without noticing what the other person is trying to communicate, or listen only to the beginning of another's sentence before saying, "Yes, but . . . ," you are engaging in egospeak. As a result, you do not receive the whole message because you are so busy thinking of what you want to say or saying it. Although egospeak is a very natural human temptation, it can easily become a real barrier to communication.

Several techniques can be used to control egospeaking. First, monitor your body. Individuals who are about to interrupt have a tendency to lean forward as if to jump into the conversation, and poise an arm and hand so that they can thrust them forward to cut in. If you feel your body taking these actions, be aware that you are about to egospeak—and don't.

Another way to deter yourself from egospeaking is to intentionally repeat the ideas of the speaker before you give your point of view. Be aware that if you can't summarize, you didn't listen long enough to gain the message. In future conversations, see if you can repeat the message of the speaker to yourself before you jump in.

5 *Be careful with emotional responses to words.* Inciting words are those that trigger strong feelings within us, either positive or negative. How do you react to the words *child abuser, rapist,* and *income tax?* Words like these often send us off on tangents. In an everyday situation, you may tighten up and block out the rest of the message when your friend mentions the name of a person with whom you have just had an argument. Or you might start daydreaming about the beach

Be aware that your posture affects your listening.

when your instructor uses the word *sunshine*. Speakers should be aware that listeners can be sent off on tangents by certain words, resulting in interference with the effort to communicate. As receivers, we should be aware that we can be led astray and lose our concentration through our emotional responses.

There is no quick way to prevent yourself from reacting to inciting words. By monitoring your body, however, you might catch yourself physically pulling in, feel yourself flushing as you become upset, or catch yourself daydreaming. These responses are typical of the emotional triggers that set us off while listening.

6 *Be aware that your posture affects your listening.* When you listen to an exciting lecture, how do you sit? Usually you lean slightly forward, with your feet on the floor, and look directly at the presenter. On the other hand, if you slump down and stare out the window, it's unlikely that you're actively participating in the communication act taking place.

Have you ever left a classroom and felt totally exhausted? You may have been concentrating so hard that you became physically tired. After all, good listening is hard work. An effective listener learns when it is necessary to listen in a totally active way and when it is possible to relax. An analogy can explain the concept. When you're driving a car with an automatic transmission, the car shifts gears when it needs more or less power. Unfortunately, people don't come equipped with automatic transmissions; we have to shift gears for ourselves. When you need to concentrate, you shift into your active listening position—feet on the floor, posture erect, looking directly at the speaker to pick up any necessary nonverbal clues. Once you feel that you understand the point being made (a test for this would be the ability to paraphrase what has been said), you may want to shift your posture to a more comfortable position. When a new subject arises, or when you hear transitional words or phrases such as *therefore* or *in summary*, then you shift back into your active listening position.

7 *Control distractions.* All of us are surrounded by noise. Such factors as the sound of machinery, people talking, and music playing can interfere with efficient listening. If the message is important to you, try to adjust the interference or control it. If possible, turn off the machinery or move away from it. Tell someone who is speaking to you while you are talking on the telephone that you cannot listen to both people at the same time. Turn off the radio or raise your voice so that others can hear you over the sound. Remember that there is little point in continuing the communication if you cannot hear the other person or that person cannot hear you.

8 *Tune in to the speaker's cues.* An effective speaker provides the listener with verbal and nonverbal cues. You should recognize transitions (words indicating a change of idea or topic: *therefore, finally*), forecasts of ideas (statements that show a series of ideas: "there are three ideas that . . .," "the next point is . . ."), and internal summaries (restatements of ideas that have just been explained: "and so we have seen that . . ."). These are all vehicles for furthering your grasp of the major points the speaker is presenting.

The rate, volume, pitch, and pauses used by the speaker can also help you to understand the points being developed. By stressing words, pausing before an idea, or increasing the volume of a phrase, the speaker is telling you that something is important, or significant.

The speaker's physical movements can also carry a meaning that may reinforce or contradict a verbal message. For example, a speaker who uses a forceful gesture, or enumerates points with the fingers, can assist listeners in following the main points. We often have to listen with our eyes as well as our ears to pick up all the cues to help us understand the real message.

9 *Paraphrase.* Paraphrasing can be one of the most effective ways to sharpen concentration, because to do so requires careful focus and

storage in short-term memory. By repeating the ideas in your answer, you let the speaker know what you have received. Then if the paraphrase is not correct, the speaker can clarify and make you understand what was really intended. The use of active feedback allows both of you to be sure that the message sent was the message received.

10 *Visualize.* To engage in a communication, a good technique, especially for global learning/listening, is to visualize the speaker's points or what he or she is doing when certain concepts are presented. Visual associations are a useful way to enhance storage and retrieval in the long-term memory. For example, a student told one of the authors, who was her former instructor, that even today when she hears topics discussed many years ago, she visualizes where the instructor stood in class and can remember what he said.

IN CONCLUSION → Listening is an important part of the communication process. Listening is a process of receiving, perceiving, attending to, assigning meaning, and responding to messages. We listen to discriminate among auditory and visual stimuli; comprehend information; provide therapeutic support to other communicators; critically evaluate messages; and appreciate messages.

Various strategies can be undertaken to improve a person's listening skills, including awareness that both the sender and the receiver share responsibility for effective communication; suspending judgment and being a patient listener; avoiding egospeaking; being careful with emotional responses to words; being aware that your posture affects your listening; making a conscious effort to listen; controlling distractions; tuning in to the speaker's cues; learning how to use paraphrasing; and using visualization.

LEARN BY DOING →
1. Contrast hearing and listening. Draw a verbal analogy between listening and reading.

2. Analyze your own listening. Name one listening behavior you have that does not match the characteristics of a good listener as described in this chapter. Consider how you can change this listening behavior to be more effective.

3. Now that you are aware of some of the principles of effective listening, put them into practice. At the next speech or lecture you attend, sit up, concentrate on what the speaker is saying, and focus all your attention and energy on comprehending the material. Make internal summaries and paraphrase to assist yourself. After the session is over, analyze your listening behavior and determine what you can still do to improve your comprehension.

4. Critically analyze an editorial on television. Listen for the arguments and appeals, and determine how those persuasive elements were arranged to get a positive response from you, the listener.

5. Make a list of your "red flags." Go back and review these terms. Why do you think they incite you? If class time is available, your instructor will divide the class into groups of four to six students. Discuss your "red flags" and what implications they have for your communication.

6. a. Indicate whether you thoroughly agree (TA), agree (A), disagree (D), or thoroughly disagree (TD) with each of these statements:

   (1) Prayer should be allowed in the public schools.

   (2) Children who contract AIDS should not be allowed to attend public schools.

   (3) Homosexual marriages should be legally sanctioned.

   (4) College students should not have required courses outside of their major area of concentration.

   b. Your class is divided into groups of four to six students. Your task is to get everyone in the group to accept one of the attitudes (TA, A, D, or TD) for each of the preceding statements. You must paraphrase during the entire discussion. You may not give your opinion until you have summarized the statement of the person who preceded you. One member of the group acts as referee and says, "Foul" if anyone speaks without summarizing. (If time does not allow for a discussion of all four questions, your instructor will randomly select one for discussion.)

   c. Now make a list of the positive aspects of paraphrasing as a listening technique, then frustrations it causes.

7. Left/Right, Linear/Global Dominance.[26] Answer all of these questions quickly; do not stop to analyze them. When you have no clear preference, choose the one that most closely represents your attitudes or behavior.

   1. When I buy a new product, I

      A. _____ usually read the directions and carefully follow them.

      B. _____ refer to the directions, but really try and figure out how the thing operates or is put together on my own.

   2. Which of these words best describes the way I perceive myself in dealing with others?

      A. _____ Structured/Rigid

      B. _____ Flexible/Open-minded

3. Concerning hunches:

   A. _____ I generally would not rely on hunches to help me make decisions.

   B. _____ I have hunches and follow many of them.

4. I make decisions mainly based on

   A. _____ what experts say will work.

   B. _____ a willingness to try things that I think might work.

5. In traveling or going to a destination, I prefer

   A. _____ to read and follow a map.

   B. _____ get directions and map things out "my" way.

6. In school, I preferred

   A. _____ geometry.

   B. _____ algebra.

7. When I read a play or novel, I

   A. _____ see the play or novel in my head as if it were a movie/TV show.

   B. _____ read the words to obtain information.

8. When I want to remember directions, a name, or a news item, I

   A. _____ visualize the information, or write notes that help me create a picture, maybe even draw the directions.

   B. _____ write structured and detailed notes.

9. I prefer to be in the class of a teacher who

   A. _____ has the class do activities and encourages class participation and discussions.

   B. _____ primarily lectures.

10. In writing, speaking, and problem solving, I am

    A. _____ usually creative, preferring to try new things.

    B. _____ seldom creative, preferring traditional solutions.

Scoring and interpretation:

Give yourself one point for each question you answered b on items 1 to 5 and a on 6 to 10. This total is your score. To assess your degree of left- or right-brain preference, locate your final score on this continuum:

Left _____ Right

      1   2   3   4   5   6   7   8   9   10

The lower the score, the more left-brained tendency you have. People with a score of 1 or 2 are considered highly linear. Scores of 3 and possibly 4 show a left-brained tendency.

The higher the score, the more right-brained tendency you have. People with scores of 9 or 10 are considered highly global. Scores of 7 and possibly 6 indicate a right-brained tendency.

If you scored between 4 and 7 you have indicated you probably do not tend to favor either brain and are probably flexible in your learning and listening style.

Please bear in mind that neither preference is superior to the other. If you are extremely left- or right-dominant, it is possible to develop some of the traits associated with the other hemisphere, or you may already have them.

8. The text mentions public radio's Terri Gross as an excellent interviewer/listener. Listen to a radio or watch a television interview and critique the listening, feedback, and follow-up skills of the person. Be prepared to discuss the person and specifically what she or he did to either enhance or distract from the quality of the interview.

KEY TERMS →

hearing
listening
reception
attention
attention span
paraphrasing
perception
perceptual filter
selective perception
assignment of meaning
schema

schemata
brain dominance
linear learners/listeners
global listeners/learners
internal or external response
discriminative listening
comprehension listening
therapeutic listening
critical listening
appreciative listening
egospeak

chapter 4

Foundations of Verbal Language

LEARNING OUTCOMES →

After reading this chapter, you should be able to:

Name and describe several theories of the origins of human language

Explain and illustrate how people select, process, use, and learn symbols

Identify the features common to all languages

Define and illustrate the emotive, phatic, cognitive, rhetorical, and identifying functions of language

Explain the roles of ambiguity, vagueness, inferences, and message adjustment in relation to language distortion

Define and contrast standard versus nonstandard dialects, and relate the effects of speaking a nonstandard dialect

Analyze slang as it relates to standard dialects

Understand the English-Only and English-Plus movements

Each speech community conveys to its children a value system. These assumptions are reflected and reinforced in language, and language thus creates or re-creates a social reality. Language is a giant, hidden structure that permeates life.[1] Those who study language and its effects have long contended that there is a connection between language and self-perception and self-esteem as well as between language and behavior.[2] Language reflects our attitudes. Words can create categories and expectations so deep-seated that only such devices as affirmative action plans and antihate laws can force individuals to act differently than their language seems to allow them.

What is **language**? It is "a system of human communication based on speech sounds used as arbitrary symbols."[3] It provides one of the means for encoding messages. The *study of language* involves the study of meaning,[4] meaning based on words, the way the words are placed together, and the backgrounds and experiences of the communicators.

The channel by which the words are conveyed help create their meaning. When they appear on a printed page, words are one-dimensional; the meaning is based on what the reader thinks the words mean, with no other clues for interpretation. But the words pick up additional dimensions when they are spoken, as the rate, pitch, pause, and volume of the spoken words help us to further figure out the meaning of the words and the intent of the sender. Even more dimensions are available when the receiver can see the speaker and note facial expressions, gesture patterns, and body positions.

Origins of Human Language

Although there is no one accepted theory of the origins of human language, researchers generally agree that people first relied on gestures to communicate and later developed a code by which to communicate orally.[5] To account for the shift to vocal language, explanations center on the probable linking of sounds with gestures because the lips, tongue, and mouth "imitate" hand movements (e.g., sticking one's tongue out when threading a needle).[6] Then, because gestural language can develop only limited messages, whereas sounds can be altered to form many additional ideas, vocal language must have increased in use. Much later, the need for an additional way to convey messages brought about a written code.

Language does not remain static; it is constantly changing. These changes reflect changes in technology, lifestyles, and social attitudes. For example, the new edition of a much-used dictionary has 16,000 new entries.[7] Among them are *buck up*, meaning to turn on (based on the computer usage); *internet*, meaning to connect together (based on electronic-highway advances); and *womyn*, the plural for *woman* (a variant that avoids the sexism perceived in wo*men*).

Selecting Symbols

How are we are able to select the symbols we want to use at the split second when the need arises to use them? The process can be clarified with an example. If I hold up a cylindrical piece of graphite about one-eighth of an inch in diameter, covered with wood, painted a yellowish gold, with an eraser on one end and a sharpened point on the other and ask you what the object is, you will probably answer, "A pencil."

Look at your surroundings, focus on an object, and identify it. Did you respond quickly with a word for the object? Now think back to the experience. Did you (as we did with *pencil*) think of all the parts that describe the object you just named? Probably not. Instead, you looked at the object, recognized it, assigned the symbol to it if you could, and then spoke or thought the relevant word.

Try another experiment. Picture these objects: *pen*, *apple*, *glass of milk*. You probably had little trouble "seeing" these objects. This means that you have been exposed to the objects and their symbols can be identified. Try the experiment again: *finger*, *book*, *jerboa*. The first two words in the series were probably familiar, but what about the third? *Jerboa?* A jerboa is a mouselike rodent found in North Africa and Asia that has long hind legs for jumping and looks a little like a miniature kangaroo with the head of a mouse. You had no trouble with the words *finger* and *book* because you have already come in contact with these objects and have been told what to call them. But few Americans—with the exception of those who have traveled or lived in Asia or Africa or who have stumbled on a book or a television show that included information about this type of rodent— have had any exposure to the word *jerboa*.

Processing Symbols

A second question now emerges: how do we remember what we have been exposed to in our environment? In the human brain, the area that allows us to communicate selectively is the cortex. It is the center for memory and other activities necessary for communicating. The primary language areas of most human brains are thought to be located in the left hemisphere of the cortex because only rarely does damage to the right hemisphere, for example when one has a stroke, cause language disorders.[8]

Figure 4.1
The Cybernetic
Process

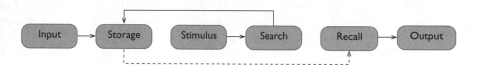

Our senses continuously bombard us with signals that are begging to be interpreted and stored in our information bank. In response, the cortex stores, computes, and eventually processes some of these incoming signals and puts forth the necessary information. This operation, called the **cybernetic process,** functions much like a computer. It is schematized in Figure 4.1.

By investigating the process you used to identify the pencil, you can gain understanding of the operation of the cybernetic process. You have been taught the word *pencil* (*input*), and it has been placed (*stored*) in your cortex. Thus when you see an object made of graphite, wood, and an eraser, the sight of the object (*stimulus*) activates your storage system to sort through its stored visual signals (*search*), find the symbol that represents the image (*recall*), and allows you to identify the combination of the stored term and the object and you say, "pencil" (*output*). You have just experienced the cybernetic process in action.

A mathematician and logician who played an important role in the development of high-speed computers coined the term *cybernetics.*[9] It comes from the Greek word for "steersman." The originator noted that the means for internal control and communication in an animal—its nervous system—are similar to those of self-regulating machines such as furnaces with thermostats. In each one, a measuring device feeds back information about performance. In human beings, the input comes in the form of a sense image (*taste, smell, sight, sound, touch*) that is tested against stored material (*symbols, images*); the output (*feedback*) represents the symbol or image. The major difference between human and machine communication is that "[human] communication is imperfect. You can program a computer to send and receive the messages exactly the way you intended, but this is not the case with human beings."[10] This error factor accounts for some of our language problems, such as why you sometimes can't remember the information when you take a test, even though you studied. Sometimes the stored information is incorrect. Sometimes not enough information has been stored. Sometimes an overload occurs. Just as machines trip circuit breakers because the demand placed on their circuitry is too great, so too can you trip psychological breakers from too much pressure. It is possible to get so upset that you block messages from coming forth. But when the emotional pressure is removed, the normal flow returns. That is why experts advise people taking a test or under stress to "turn off" every so often and then return to their work—look out the window, put your head down, walk around, sing a song to yourself to break the tension.

Cybernetic processing starts to develop in humans at about the third month after birth. It does not become fully operative, however, until a child is capable of processing the image-symbol relationship and selecting symbols.

Learning Symbols

Two views of how we acquire our unique language as well as beliefs, values, and attitudes are the Language-Explosion Theory and Significant-Other Theory.

Language-Explosion Theory   The **Language-Explosion Theory** proposes that we build communication skills from the core of language we develop early in life. If you were asked to name the one person who had the most influence on your ability to communicate, what would your answer be? You would probably name an immediate family member, probably your mother. In some instances the mother-infant **dyad** (pair) is replaced by a father-infant, sibling-infant, or grandparent-infant dyad. And in still other situations, the day care center or a baby sitter may replace the family member. It all depends on who spoke to the child the most. Adults with a weak language base are often children who were not spoken or read to much as youngsters.

Whatever the child's primary influence, his or her circles of influence quickly expand to include the communication patterns of many other people. The child's neighborhood, area of the country in which he or she lives, and schools attended all influence overall ability to communicate, as does exposure to the media.

Significant-Other Theory   When we are young, our influences are all of the sources around us. At a certain stage in our lives, we start selecting specific people or groups whose language, ideals, and beliefs we allow to influence us. These people become the significant others in our lives, and their effect is great. Indeed, social psychologists contend that we have no identity whatsoever except in relationship to others. This view is called the Significant-Other Theory.[11]

The **Significant-Other Theory** centers on the principle that our understanding of self is built by those who react to and comment on our language, actions, ideas, beliefs, and mannerisms. Thus if we respect someone, we are likely to adjust our behavior and our messages to derive the most encouraging evaluation from that person. We may be influenced by their messages because of the position they hold, as is the case with politicians, sports heroes, or movie stars, or the control they have over us, as is true of a boss, teacher, or parent.

We are constantly coming into contact with people who have the potential to be significant others in our lives. If you think about who you are today and compare your present language, beliefs, values, and attitudes with those you held five years ago, you will probably find some noticeable differences. These very likely were brought about by your acceptance of someone else's influence. No one can change you except you, but the significant others in your life can alert you to new concepts and help lay the foundation for the changes that come when you accept them.

The Concept of Meaning

Understanding what language is, and how we acquire and access it, gives us an important basis for understanding how meaning results. The study of the structure of human language is called **linguistics**. It tells us that certain features are common to all languages. Among these are:

Languages are based on a set of symbols, both verbal and nonverbal. We use the letters s-c-i-s-s-o-r-s, for example, to represent the instrument that is used for cutting. Or, we form a circle with our thumb and index finger and extend the other three fingers to signify that everything is "okay."

Languages that are alphabetically based recognize the differences between vowels and consonants. In English, the vowel sounds are represented by the letters *a, e, i, o,* and *u,* singly or in combination. The consonants are such letters as *b, c, r,* and *m.* Be aware that not all languages use an alphabet. Some languages are pictographical, for example, Chinese. A symbol represents a single word and is not made up of letters, as is the case with such languages as Danish, Greek, and Hebrew.

Languages have ordered structural categories, such as verbs, noun phrases, and objects. Our language is symbolic as we use words to represent objects and ideas. The sentence "The car is beautiful" designates the object (*car*) and expresses the idea about the car (*is beautiful*).

Words in and of themselves are not inherently meaningful. The meaning derived from our language stems from how we interpret the symbols used in that language. Because words carry no meaning as such, we derive our meaning for the symbols through our own backgrounds, experiences, and perceptions. This is well illustrated in the comic strip "Calvin and Hobbes." The boy Calvin says to his father, "The meaning of words isn't a fixed thing! Any word can mean anything! By giving words new meanings, ordinary English can become an exclusionary code! Two generations can be divided by the same language." Father to Calvin: "Marvy, Fab, Far out."[12]

Because we interpret symbols, we assign meaning to them according to our **frame of reference**—our backgrounds, experiences, and perceptions. Since each of our frames of reference are so different, our interpretation may be very far from the intent of the sender. To make matters even more confusing, all meanings for symbols are not easily definable. Symbols can carry both denotative and connotative meanings.

We give words **denotative meanings**—direct, explicit meanings—when we want to categorize them. For instance, the **denotative word** *dog* carries the denotative meaning of a "four-legged, furry animal, canine." This denotation enables you to classify the animal and to understand the literal characteristics of the term. In contrast, **connotative words** have an implied or suggested meaning. Words such as *good, pretty,* and *nice* have connotative meanings. It is difficult for people to agree on exactly what these words mean.

Our language is filled with connotative meanings that derive from denotative words. **Connotative meanings** are those that we associate with certain words or to which we attach particular implications. Thus, the denotative word *dog* may carry pleasant connotations such as *lovable, friendly,* and *warm* if we have had pleasant associations with these animals. Postal carriers, however, may find that the word has negative connotations; to them *dog* may carry the connotative meaning of *mean, snarling, biting animal.*

Besides connotative problems, people who study **semantics**—the relationship of language and meaning—warn us to avoid a rigid orientation that sees everything as falling into one of two categories of value: good or bad, right or wrong. Instead of approaching the world with this either/or, **two-valued orientation**, we can remember that life is multidimensional and that meanings vary as the backgrounds and experiences of the communicators differ. (To test your two-valued orientation do Activity 6 in the Learn by Doing section at the end of this chapter.)

Instructors who say, "Alex is a good student" or, "Manuel is a poor student" reflect a two-valued orientation because such statements do not allow for other dimensions of a student's performance. Perhaps, for example, Alex is strong in some subjects but weak in others. Or perhaps Manuel has not been motivated to work in school but does have considerable academic ability.

A sender should attempt to use language as precisely as possible to reduce misunderstanding and thus avoid semantic noise. The use of definitions, examples, synonyms, and explanations can serve to clarify terminology. Consider these examples: A dentist says to an assistant, "Hand me the instrument." The assistant looks at a tray of fifteen different instruments and responds, "Which one?" Obviously, the word *instrument* was so imprecise in this situation that the assistant was unable to determine the intended meaning. Or suppose a friend says to you, "Take the communication theory course from Professor Riley. She's great!" What does "great" mean in this context? Does she give all As? Assign no homework? Cover the material thoroughly? If your friend had said, "Take the communication theory course from Professor Riley. She's great because she'll tutor you individually if you don't understand the material," the message would have been clear.

Remember that not only the source has a responsibility, but the receiver is also an active participant in the transaction. Giving feedback, such as by asking questions and repeating the message, can aid in clarifying the meaning in a communication transaction. Feedback can also eliminate organizational noise (if you ask the person to structure his or her ideas in a different way) or semantic noise (if you state that the words of the message need defining).

The Functions of Language

The way in which a person uses language is affected not only by the vocabulary available but also by the functions of language.[13] These functions are generally classified into five categories: emotive, phatic, cognitive, rhetorical, and identifying.

Emotive language is used to express the feelings, attitudes, and emotions of the speaker. Emotive language employs emotional connotative words. In discussing a movie, for example, a person who says that it is *riveting* and *gripping* is using emotive language.

Phatic language is used to reinforce the relationship between the participants in a communicative exchange. Language functions such as greetings, farewells, and small-talk exchanges are phatic aspects of language. The traditional "Hello, how are you?" and "Have a nice day" are examples of phatic language.

The function of **cognitive language** is to convey information. Cognitive language tends to be denotative. This section on the functions of language is an example of cognitive language.

Word Power

Language is a powerful tool for reinforcing aims and values. *Examples:* Disneyland calls its staff "cast members" and customers "guests" to remind employees that their aim is "to make people happy." Many therapists use the term "client" rather than "patient" to clarify their role as consultants. A quality-award-winning asphalt company calls employees "Granite Rock People."

SOURCE: Bruce W. Woolpert, CEO, Granite Rock Company, Box 50001, Watsonville, California 95077.

The purpose of **rhetorical language** is to influence thoughts and behaviors. The speaker employs connotative terms to create persuasion by using emotionally vivid pictures and drawing implications while developing logical appeals. Advertisements to sell products, or a speech supporting organ donations that uses examples of people who died because organs weren't available, are examples of the rhetorical function of language.

The role of **identifying language** centers on naming things, thus being able to clarify exactly what we are speaking about; for example, "Ming went to Midway Mall." Using the name *Ming*, rather than *she* or *someone,* is identifying language.

But identification also carries implications beyond just hanging a name on something. In Sanskrit, the word for name is derived from "gna," meaning "to know."[14] Naming defines people and influences communication responses. In the Bible, Genesis tells that Adam's dominion over animals was demonstrated by his being given the *power* to name them. "The North American Indian regards his [her] name as a distinct part of his [her] personality, just as much as his [her] eyes or teeth."[15]

To be unnamed is to be unknown, to have no identity, such as the "Unknown Soldier." Names can be positive, for example, elevating the "ingroup" with positive terms, or negative, stigmatizing the "outgroup." The outgroup is generally dehumanized and this justifies oppression and/or extermination. Hitler used this technique before and during World War II to attack the Jews by labeling them "enemies of the country" and by taking away their name identities and branding them with numbers, making them no better than cattle. Native Americans were debased when they were given the names "savages" and "primitives," thus implying they were less than civilized, less than human. For years, male terms for females included demeaning names such as "chicks" (dumb fowl) and "dolls" (a toy to be played with). To avoid the results of negative labels, some groups have changed their names. For example, in the 1960s civil rights leaders rejected the terms "Negro" and "colored" as historical terms that identified a weak and controlled people, and labeled themselves "black" as a clear identifier of their individuality, their skin color. Later, believing a name should connect the people to their country of origin, the name changed to "African American."[16]

Much of what is called hate speech falls within the realm of identification. People use those images to construct their social reality, and the group being oppressed then starts to be a group at risk. The labels become the identification that demoralizes the recipient, and a tool to be used as the reason for psychological and/or physical destruction. From this perspective, it is acceptable to bash a "faggot," burn down the store of a "rice-eater," or sexually abuse a "broad."

Doublespeak is grossly deceptive, evasive, euphemistic, confusing, and self-contradictory language.

Language Distortion

Words stand for different meanings, people intentionally or unintentionally distort information as they process it, and people intentionally or unintentionally use language that is unclear. These factors lead to **language distortion,** which is caused by ambiguity, vagueness, inferences, and/or message adjustment.[17]

Ambiguity can be present when a word has more than one interpretation. For example, does the word *hog* mean a *fat pig, someone who eats too much, a person who controls others' attention, a large car,* or *a motorcycle?* All these definitions are appropriate depending on the context. Fortunately, ambiguity can often be overcome if the listener refers to the word's context to determine whether it describes an overindulging dinner guest or the purchase of a Harley cycle, or the sender defines the term when used.

Vagueness results from words or sentences lacking clarity. Use of words such as *they, he,* and *things like that* are vague unless we specifically know who or what is being referred to by the speaker. Many connotative words, because they have no specific definition, are vague.

A special form of vagueness that is deceptive, evasive, and/or confusing is **doublespeak**.[18] Examples of doublespeak abound. There are no *potholes* in the streets of some cities, just "pavement deficiencies." There are no longer any *street people*, just "non-goal-oriented members of society." Americans are not paying any *taxes*; they are just being subjected to "revenue enhancements" and "user fees." Patients do not die due to *malpractice*; "a diagnostic misadventure of a high magnitude" occurs. And some colleges are no longer administering *tests*; instead, students participate in "educational opportunities."[19]

Doublespeak is a conscious use of language as a weapon or tool by those in power to achieve their ends at the expense of others. Some doublespeak is funny, but much of it is frightening. It can be a weapon of power, exploitation, manipulation, and oppression.[20]

Inferences result when we interpret beyond available information, or jump to conclusions without using all of the information available. Because communicating is a creative process, inferences are an inevitable part of processing information. If we do not have enough material, we just complete an idea with what seems logical to us, what we have experienced in the past, or what we hope or fear is the potential outcome. Read the following sentence quickly:

The cow jump over
over thee noon.

Did you see "jump," or did you read it as "jumped"? What about the first and the second "over," or "thee" and "noon"? Many people simply see the first couple of words and, based on their past experience, instinctively infer the nursery rhyme statement "The cow jumped over the moon."

The Languages We Use

Language, like chemical compounds, has a structure. There is a limited set of elements—vowels and consonants—and these are combined to produce words, which in turn compound into sentences.[21] It is the responsibility of a **linguist**—a social scientist who studies the structures of various languages—to provide concepts that describe languages.

"Systematic and rule-governed differences exist between languages,"[22] reported one linguist. "Each language is a collection of similar dialects. Dialects, like languages, differ from each other in terms of pronunciation, vocabulary, grammar, and prosody [accent or tone.]"[23]

There are significant variations in language within this country based on region, social class, religious and ethnic group, gender, and age. The same item may carry different word identifiers according to the region of the country. Philadelphia's "hoagie" is a "bomber" in upstate New York, "wedge" in New York City, "grinder" in Boston, "Cuban sandwich" in Miami, and an "Italian" in Kansas City.[24]

The dialects of the English language have more similarities than differences. For this reason, speakers of different English dialects can communicate with relative ease, though at some times, an **accent**—the pronunciation and intonation used by a person—may cause some difficulty in understanding. Southerners, for example, often are difficult for Northerners to understand, and the "New York–New Jersey" sound is clearly identifiable, yet often not always understood by those outside that area.

Each speaker of a language speaks some dialect of it, or a combination of dialects. A common mistake is to view one dialect as best. No single dialect of a language is *the* language. But in every language there is a continuum of prestige dialects from the lowest to the highest. High-prestige dialects are called **standard dialects**, and low-prestige dialects are **nonstandard dialects**. The dialects of those who are in power, have influence, and are educated become the standard dialects of a language; and the literature, science, and official records are written using the vocabulary and grammar that approximate the standard dialects.[25] "Powerful groups have held nonstandard speech against its speakers because it was a way of bonding their own social identity and of manifesting their social status."[26]

Not only do dialects and accents create some difficulties, but the choice of which should be used can create controversy.

English-Only Movement

The United States has been described as a great melting pot. Others view it as a linguistic gumbo because many people who live in the United States do not speak English, so they do not "blend in."[27] This country's citizens communicate in 329 different languages. The most common language is English, followed by Spanish, spoken by more than 17 million people. The other top non-English spoken languages are French, German, Italian, and Chinese. About 335,000 speak Native American languages.[28]

A real challenge to the American society is the continued low status of many minority groups. Historically, those non-English-speaking immigrant groups who have gained the most status are those who were able to most closely approximate the Anglo mode,[29] that is, those who have learned the language and corresponding cultural patterns, such as second-generation Jews and Asians, while those who have retained their native language exclusively have remained on the societal fringes.

English-Plus laws protect the use of languages other than English.

Some believe that one of the glues that holds a society together is the ability of the citizenry to interact with each other. They believe that, historically, English has been the language of this country and that, for a person to be fully accepted into society, he or she must be able to participate in the mainstream language.[30] A survey indicates that 78 percent of the people think English should be the official language of the government. These attitudes brought forth the **English-Only Movement**, whose advocates sponsored a constitutional amendment to make English the official language of the country. Although the amendment had not been passed as this book went to press, English has been voted the official language in eighteen states.[31]

In opposition to this trend, some states have passed **English-Plus laws**, which protect the use of languages other than English and encourage the study of foreign languages. "Such laws are in effect in New Mexico, Washington and Oregon, and Hawaii and Louisiana have official policies aimed at preserving languages and cultures."[32] Critics of English-Only indicate that it is unnecessary, since past immigrants learned English within a generation without laws compelling them to do so, and so too will the present immigrants. They further state that the English-Only concept is unrealistic, it is educationally unsound, it is unfair, it is invasive since it denies people the right to choose the language they wish to use, and it is unconstitutional because the First Amendment guarantees freedom of speech.[33]

Accepting that there is controversy over the exclusive use of English, let us examine what is meant by "English" as we refer to it in this country.

Standard American English

Standard American English is the language generally recognized by linguists as representative of the general population of the United States.[34] It is the oral form usually spoken by national news personalities and generally characterized by the oral sounds of the residents of the Middle West (Midwest) and West. The pronunciation is identified by articulating the final *r* (*father* versus *fa'da*) and the *r* before consonants in words (as in *park* versus *pok*). In these and other respects, Standard American English differs from the dialects spoken in the other principal regional-pronunciation areas—the Midland, New England, and the South (see Figure 4.2). In New England and the Midland, the *a* in such words as *fast* is generally pronounced like the *a* in *father*, and the *r* is not pronounced when it is a final consonant or precedes a final consonant. In the South, the *r* is not pronounced after vowels (*for* becomes *fo*), and simple stressed

Figure 4.2
Principal Regional
Pronunciation
Areas

SOURCE: From Wilbur Zelinsky, *The Cultural Geography of the United States*, A Revised Edition, ©1992, p. 118. Adapted by permission of Prentice Hall, Englewood Cliffs, New Jersey.

vowels are dipthonged (*him* becomes *he-im*). Out-of-the mainstream pronunciation often is used as a source of humor. Entertainers Rosie O'Donnell and Penny Marshall, for example, have made their accents one of the focal points of their careers.

Although there may not be one "best" way of pronunciation, some standards of American pronunciation are generally accepted. The words *pitcher* and *picture* do not have the same meaning and are not pronounced the same way. Such words as "hunderd" (*hundred*), "liberry" (*library*), "secatary" (*secretary*), and "alls" (*all*) linguistically do not exist. Words ending with *ing*, such as *going* and *coming* are not generally pronounced "goin" and "comin." Saying "jeet yit?" is not a substitute for *Did you eat yet? Many* isn't "minnie," and *didn't* is not "dint."

The Standard American words and grammatical forms are those of nationally published magazines (such as *Time* and *Newsweek*) and newspapers (*USA Today* and the *New York Times*). These words tend to represent the vocabulary of the West, the Midwest, the Midland, and the southern section of New England. Notice, for example, that though New Yorkers tend to have their own pronunciation patterns, these do not carry over into their grammatical usage or word selection.

Some linguists contend that as long as no single pattern of language has been officially declared, there can be no such thing as a standard by which American English can be judged.

In addition to dialects and accents, slang plays a role in language.

Slang

The English language is comprised of somewhere between 600,000 and 1 million words (see Figure 4.3). But the average American's vocabulary consists of only about 20,000 words, 2,000 of which may be slang.[35]

Slang denotes words that are related to a specific activity or incident and are immediately understood by members of a particular group. "Groups create their own language within a language. Peers recognize each other through its use. It's a way of belonging."[36] According to slang theory, "any group that wishes to bond together develops slang.[37] Slang knows no color, class, or boundary."[38]

Types of Slang   Slang may come from anywhere. All it needs is a group of people who use and understand it. Computer users have developed *technobabble*, which is computer language used for other meanings. Technobabblers *interface with each other* and *debug their relationships*.[39] Because of the prevalence of computers in our society, technobabble is becoming a permanent part of Standard American English, thus it may lose

Figure 4.3
The Average
American's
Vocabulary

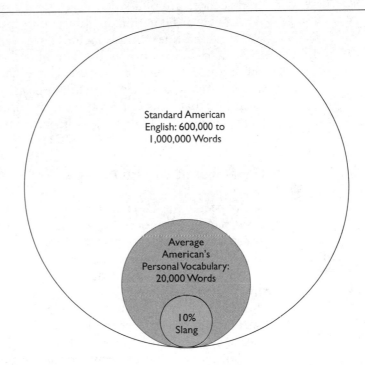

its status as slang. Once slang becomes mainstream language, it is no longer slang as it gets included in dictionaries, the chronicles of the language.

There is also regional slang. In New England, a *flatlander* is anybody who does not live in Vermont, New Hampshire, or Massachusetts. People in the Midwest refer to a brown paperbag as a *sack*, whereas in some parts of the South the same item is referred to as a *poke*. Among some southern Florida college students, *maxin'* means relaxing; *tossin' chow*, eating quickly; *shootin' the gift*, having a conversation; *jam*, partying; *phat flavor*, good music; *pop duke*, father; and *blaze*, leave. So in that environment it would make perfectly good sense to say, "We were maxin', tossin' chow, shootin' the gift, and listening to phat flavor at the jam, when the pop duke told us to blaze."[40]

Inarticulates

Inarticulates are uttered sounds, words, or phrases that have no meaning or do not help the listener gain a clear understanding of the message.

Inarticulates are fillers that cover up the speaker's inability to think of what to say or fill in thinking time, or are bad vocal habits.

Vocalized filler sounds include "um," "and-uh," and "well-uh." Common inarticulate phrases are "you know" and "stuff like that." None of these sounds or phrases aids the listener's understanding. If the receiver already knew, the speaker would not have to say "you know." And what is "stuff like that"? A speaker who uses inarticulates is often considered lacking in language skills or being deliberately evasive.

Nonstandard English Dialects

Many people in this country speak languages and/or dialects that differ from Standard American English. Some of these speakers use a recognizable alternative language form such as Spanish, French, Chinese, or one of the Native American tongues. In some cases, speakers present their ideas in identifiable dialects of Standard American English, such as Spanglish. Still others speak a separate but definite rule-based communication system called Ebonics, which fulfills the definition of language because it has a distinct grammatical and symbolic system; but because it has so many similarities to Standard American English, it is considered by some to be a dialect.

One of the major problems confronting today's schools is how to handle non-Standard American English speakers. Most schools adopted the attitude that "We accept the language the students bring from home, but we teach them that Standard English is a tool they must have. They may not use it all the time, but when you need it, you need it."[41]

Any discussion of dialects must recognize that "there are many dialects and some get a lot of respect and some don't get any. In some cases, the respect given to the dialect is in the same amount that is given to the people who speak it."[42] A brief examination of Black English, Spanglish, Asian-American English, and Native American languages may lead to some understanding of their nature, their history, the speakers who use them, and the perceived effects of speaking an alternative language or dialect.

Ebonics/Black English   On December 19, 1996, "the Oakland, California school board voted to recognize **Ebonics** (Ebony phonics), sometimes referred to as **Black English**, as the primary language of many black students and use it as a starting point to teaching Standard English."[43] At that time the school board stated that Black English was recognized by many linguists as a legitimate language form with a unique and logical syntax, semantic system, and grammar.[44]

A recent publication indicated that "Vernacular Black English [Ebonics] is the most common dialect used by African Americans. This is not street talk; it is not broken English; and it is not slang."[45] It is "a private vocabulary of Black people which serves the users as a powerful medium."[46] "Moreover, Black English is not a regional dialect. It reflects the common national culture of the American black community. The grammar used by many black adults in Los Angeles in their home setting is virtually the same as that used by adolescent groups in New York. As a famous black novelist stated, 'Black English is a vivid and crucial key to black identity.'"[47]

There is controversy as to the historical development of Ebonics. One theory states, "Black English is rooted in a historical past that spans Africa, the Caribbean, the Creole heritage, the South, and now the northern U.S. cities."[48] Another proposes that "Africans came to the United States with no knowledge of English and developed the dialect [language]."[49] Still another version is that "It is a creole language formed out of mainstream American English and native African languages evolving from largely West African pidgin forms."[50]

Whatever its roots, linguists cite fifty characteristics of Black English that differentiate it from Standard English, many of which have parallels with the linguistic structure of West African languages.[51] Among the most common speech markers is the use of the "invariant be" to denote an ongoing action ("He be going to work"). This usage is not present in Standard English grammar but is parallel to the indefinite or habitual tense of languages such as French and Spanish.

"The distinctiveness of African American speech style has been problematic for group members [with mainstream speakers and in commerce]. On the one hand, speech that marks the individual as a member of the group can be important for ingroup acceptance."[52] The other is that "children don't learn standard dialect so that they will be able to assimilate and demonstrate marketable skills in mainstream society."[53] Based on the latter viewpoint, some community leaders have encouraged African Americans to learn Standard American English and become **code switchers**—"selectively use Black English and mainstream American English depending on the situation."[54]

Spanglish   A significant group of Americans speaks a dialect referred to as **Spanglish**.[55] It is common linguistic currency wherever concentrations of Spanish Americans or Hispanics are found. Spanglish takes a variety of forms, from *hasta la bye-bye* to *lonche* (a quick lunch rather than a leisurely one), the description of a group of *los teenagers*, and the almost universally used *no problema*. Spanglish sentences are mostly

Spanglish is mostly Spanish, with a quick detour for a few English words and some fractured syntax.

Spanish, with a quick detour for a few English words and some fractured syntax.[56]

A professor of linguistics who speaks Spanglish with relatives and neighbors said, "Among Latinos, Spanglish conversations often flow easily from Spanish into several sentences of English and back again. It's unconscious. I couldn't even tell you minutes later if I said something in Spanglish, Spanish, or English."[57]

Asian-American Dialect   The last several decades have seen a large immigration of Asian-Pacific language speakers into the United States. People have come from such countries as Vietnam, China, Korea, Taiwan, Japan, and Cambodia. They bring with them languages that differ from English, and often from each other.

As with Spanish speakers, when Asian-Pacific speakers develop an Asian-American dialect by adapting their language to English, both vocabulary and pronunciation are major stumbling blocks.

Aside from the vocabulary and pronunciation, Asian-Pacifics confronted by English often have difficulty in developing arguments. "English is a language whose relative preciseness encourages not just argumentation and debate, but detailed analysis, Western logic, and thorough explanations."[58] This is not true of such languages as Chinese and Japanese, which are pictographic. In these languages, "precision is cumbersome and inelegant. Ordinary speech is necessarily vague and depends heavily on the cooperative imagination and sympathy of the listener."[59]

Native American Languages   Controversy surrounds any attempt to discuss Native American or American Indian language. This centers on what constitutes "Indian-ness" and therefore their language(s). Indian identity is not the same as tribal identity, as all tribes have differing languages and customs.[60]

Research in Native American language and customs has resulted in seven prominent modes of communication behavior: "(a) reticence with regard to interaction with strangers, (b) the acceptance of obligations, (c) razzing, (d) attaining harmony in face-to-face interactions, (e) modesty and doing one's part, (f) taking on familial relations, (g) permissible and required silence, and (h) a unique style of public speaking."[61] Since permissible and required silence are encouraged, many Native Americans are labeled as communicative apprehensive.

Two ways of regarding Native American language and usage is to examine a traditional pattern and present-day usage: Navaho, the most prominently spoken tribal language, and razzing.

The idea of harmony pervades the Navaho belief system of what things are and what they ought to be. "Rhetoric in such a universe has as its primary function not in discovery but in use, and its uses are carefully prescribed, sanctioned by ancestral tradition, and functional in maintaining the world as it ought to be."[62] The basic concepts are that talking it over is a way to straighten things out; talking is the most important means of persuasion; speaking and thinking are ways to energize and secure knowledge. Decisions must be discussed with all who happen to be around, which accounts for the importance of family councils.[63]

The use of razzing is a communication format unique to Native Americans. "**Razzing** is a collective form of storytelling in which participants take some episode, humorous or not, from a present or past experience and relate it humorously to the others in attendance. The story, which is often lengthy, is then characteristically embellished and altered by others who are present."[64] Razzing serves as a method to "determine cultural competency, identify ingroup and outgroup members, and as a form of instruction."[65]

A difficulty some Native Americans encounter in speaking with Standard English speakers centers on the use of narration. Traditionally, Native Americans have relied on razzing and telling historical or experiential stories to clarify their points. Often the tales only allude to the point being made rather than directly relating to the specific issue. It is called the **spiral structure of argument**. This is similar to the narrative communication patterns of many Hispanics and Arabs and strikes many Standard American English speakers as abstract and imprecise since it does not set up a clear purpose and use evidence to clarify and prove.

The Effects of Speaking a Dialect or Nonstandard English   Recent studies have reinforced the concept that speaking a nonstandard dialect rather than Standard American English can be detrimental to a person's educational and economic health. Children entering schools with weak Standard English skills are at a definite disadvantage.[66] Since they don't know the alphabet, or have the vocabulary, learning to read and understanding class discussions become extremely difficult. They often quickly turn off and eventually drop out.

In economic terms, nonstandard speakers are given shorter interviews and fewer job offers than Standard English speakers. When job offers are presented, nonstandard speakers are offered positions paying as much as 35 percent less than Standard English speakers.[67]

In social terms, speakers of nonstandard dialects often are confronted with mistaken, negative assumptions concerning their intelligence, dependability, and creativity. Standard English even contains prejudicial terms to describe those who speak non-Standard English (e.g., *hillbillies* and *crackers*).

People speaking dialects should be aware that in some instances, education and speech therapy can make alterations in their vocabulary and speaking patterns if they desire change. That desire is usually based on a person's awareness that her or his career and social goals include particular language requirements which the person does not possess.[68]

IN CONCLUSION  In this chapter, the foundations of verbal language were discussed. The important concepts concluded that there is no one accepted theory of the origins of human language. The processing of language can be explained by the cybernetic process. We acquire our language, beliefs, values, and attitudes from people and influences surrounding us. Languages are based on a set of symbols, both verbal and nonverbal. Successful communication takes place when the sender adapts the message to the background and knowledge of the particular person or audience being addressed. A dialect is used by people from the same geographical region, occupational group, or social or educational class.

Standard American English is the language usually recognized by linguists as being representative of the general society of the United States. Aspects of language are slang, inarticulates, and dialects.

LEARN BY DOING →

1. A major controversy was ignited when the Oakland, California, school district recognized Ebonics as a language. Research the topic and have a class discussion or debate that agrees or disagrees with the newspaper headline "Black English, white flag. Oakland schools' sell-out to street slang abandons good sense and kids' future."[69]

2. Find an example of doublespeak in a speech, a letter to the editor, or a newspaper or magazine article. Bring the material to class. Discuss what you feel the speaker was trying to hide or manipulate by using doublespeak.

3. Write down one phrase or expression that has meaning only for a select group. It may be an ethnic expression or an ingroup reference. The other students then read the expression and try to figure out what it means.

4. Make a list of five people who have had a significant effect on your present language. Identify which of these people was the most influential.

5. List five words that have different meanings depending on the people who use them or the place in which they are used. See how many different definitions you can develop for each word.

6. This activity is geared at ascertaining your two-valued orientation. Read each statement and indicate if it is *T* (true or is proven accurate by information provided in the story); *F* (false or is proven inaccurate by the information provided in the story); or *I* (inconclusive or can-

not be proven accurate or inaccurate because the story does not indicate whether the information is true or false). [Your instructor will find the answers in the instructor's manual that accompanies this book.]

Dale went to a travel agency to arrange some plane reservations. When Dale arrived in St. Louis, it was only two days before the wedding. After the wedding, the bride and groom took a trip to Hawaii.

a. Dale arrived in St. Louis two days before the wedding.

b. Dale got married in St. Louis.

c. Dale went to a travel agency.

d. The plane reservation to get to the wedding in St. Louis was made by a travel agent.

e. Dale went to Hawaii on her honeymoon.

7. Identify someone who speaks a nonstandard dialect. Write down some examples of her or his pronunciation and language selections. Share the information with the class. (You are trying to learn about nonstandard dialects, not to belittle the user.)

8. Are you in favor of or against the English-Only Movement? Be prepared to defend your view.

9. Your class will debate or discuss: "Resolved: all states should pass English-Plus laws."

KEY TERMS →

language	emotive language
cybernetic process	phatic language
Language-Explosion Theory	cognitive language
dyad	rhetorical language
Significant-Other Theory	identifying language
linguistics	language distortion
frame of reference	ambiguity
denotative meanings	vagueness
denotative words	doublespeak
connotative words	inferences
connotative meanings	linguist
semantics	accent
two-valued orientation	standard dialects

nonstandard dialects   Black English
English-Only Movement   Ebonics
English-Plus laws   code switchers
Standard American English   Spanglish
slang   razzing
inarticulates   spiral structure of argument

Nonverbal Communication

Do you believe that while communicating with another person your *words* carry the majority of the meaning of the message? If you answered yes, you are mistaken. There has long been an awareness that it is possible to communicate a great deal without using verbal language. We are also aware that nonverbal acts are symbolic acts closely connected to any talk in progress. They don't merely reveal information, they represent meaning.[1] "Nonverbal communication is a major force in our lives."[2] Nonverbal behaviors such as smiling, crying, pointing, caressing, and staring appear to be used and understood the world over.[3]

Nonverbal communication is "all those messages that people exchange beyond the words themselves."[4] We have interpreted body talk, perhaps without knowing we were doing so, but only in recent years have attempts been made to analyze and explain nonverbal communication in a scientific manner.

Research has established that nonverbal language is an important means of expression. Experts in the field have identified patterns of body language usage through the study of films and videotapes and direct observation. Nonverbal acts seem to have three key characteristics: they are sensitive to the relationship between the sender and receiver, they have meaning based on their context (the communicators, the setting, and the purpose of the communication), and they are part of, not a separate entity from, verbal communication.[5]

Because the study of nonverbal communication is newer than the study of verbal communication, we do not, as yet, have a dictionary of its terms or a thorough understanding of the process involved. But attempts are already being made to apply the information that has been collected. One such attempt, known as **neurolinguistic programming**, has been developed to codify and synthesize research on nonverbal communication with that of other fields of communication, including cybernetics (the study of how the human brain processes information) and language study.

Traditionally, experts tend to agree that nonverbal communication itself carries the impact of a message. "The figure most cited to support this claim is the estimate that 93 percent of all meaning in a social situation comes from nonverbal information, while only 7 percent comes from verbal information."[6] The figure is deceiving, however.[7] It is based on two 1976 studies that compared vocal cues with facial cues.[8] Other studies have not supported the 93 percent, but it is agreed that both children and adults rely more on nonverbal cues than on verbal cues in determining social meaning.[9]

In attempting to read nonverbal communication, we must remember that no one signal carries much meaning. Instead, such factors as gestures, posture, eye contact, clothing styles, and movement must all be regarded together. This grouping of factors is called a **cluster.**

We must also remember that, just as in verbal communication, non-verbal signs can have many different meanings. For example, crossing the arms over the chest may suggest that a person is cold. But crossed arms accompanied by erect posture, tightened body muscles, setting of the jaw, and narrowing of the eyes would likely indicate anger.

A person's background and past pattern of behavior must also be considered when we analyze nonverbal communication. The relationship between present and past patterns of behavior, as well as the harmony between verbal and nonverbal communication, is termed **congruency**. When you say to a friend, "You don't look well today," you are basing your statement on an evaluation of present appearance compared with past appearance. In other words, something has changed, and you have become aware of a difference. If you did not have past experience to draw on, you would not have noticed the change.

 ## Sources of Nonverbal Signs

We learn to read words through a step-by-step process in which we are taught to use our written form of communication. But how do we acquire nonverbal signs? There are two basic sources: innate neurological programs, and behavior common to a culture or a family.

Neurological Programs

Innate neurological programs are those automatic nonverbal reactions to stimuli with which we are born. These nonverbal "automatic reactions" are **reflexive** because of neurological drives. These reflexive drives seem to be tied to our need drives (see Chapter 2). For example, we blink our eyes automatically when we hear a loud noise (survival drive) or when a pebble hits the windshield of the car we are driving (survival and territorial drive). Our stomach muscles tighten and our hands sweat when we feel insecure (security drive).

That we are born with some of our nonverbal tendencies is clearly illustrated by the fact that "people born blind move their hands when they talk, although they've never seen anyone do it."[10]

Cultural/Intercultural Behavior

Some nonverbal behavior is learned in the same way as spoken language. As children, we observe and imitate people around us, thus we learn not

On Nonverbal Communication

Here is a quiz, based on solid research, that will test your knowledge of nonverbal communication. Just answer "true" or "false."

1. Women are more sensitive to nonverbal cues—especially facial cues—and they transmit more accurate nonverbal cues to others.

2. When contradictory messages are sent through both verbal and nonverbal channels, most adults see the nonverbal message as more accurate.

3. People with low self-esteem use more eye contact when receiving negative messages than when receiving positive ones, while those with high self-esteem do just the opposite in each case.

4. When people are conjuring up a lie, their pupils tend to become smaller. However, when they tell the lie, their pupils tend to dilate.

5. The three nonverbal cues an interviewer remembers most about a job applicant are gestures, posture, and handshake.

Answers: 1. true, 2. true, 3. true, 4. true, 5. false—interviewers remember eye contact, appearance, and facial expressions.

SOURCE: *NVC: Nonverbal Communication Studies and Applications*, by Mark L. Hickson III and Don W. Stacks, Wm. C. Brown Communications Inc., 2460 Kerper Blvd., Dubuque, IA 52001.

only to speak but to behave as they do. Every culture has its own body language, and the young learn its patterns along with those of spoken language. As a research anthropologist indicated, "The important thing to remember is that culture is very persistent. In this country, we've noted the existence of culture patterns that determine [physical] distance between people in the third and fourth generations of some families, despite their prolonged contact with people of very different cultural heritages."[11] These cultural patterns are readily identifiable. Italians, for example, are noted for using their hands when they speak. In contrast, the British are noted for controlling their gestures.

A person who uses more than one language gestures according to the language he or she is speaking. Fiorello LaGuardia, New York City's mayor in the 1930s and early 1940s, carried on his political campaigns in English, Italian, and Yiddish—the languages of the major voting blocs in the city. He used one set of gestures for speaking English, another for Italian, and still another for Yiddish.

Nonverbal gestures and behaviors convey different messages throughout the world. An Arabic male, for example, commonly strokes his chin to show appreciation for a woman, whereas a Portuguese man does it by pulling his ear. But in Italy a similar kind of ear tugging is a deliberate insult.

In communicating nonverbally, people also operate on different action chains. "An **action chain** is a behavioral sequence with two or more participating organisms, in which there are standard steps for reaching a goal.

Every culture has its own body language.

If an individual leaves out a step, the chain gets broken, and you have to start all over again."[12] Different cultures operate under different action chains. For example, to an American, being on time normally means making contact within five minutes or so of a designated hour. To a Mexican, however, being on time often means within a reasonable time. An American businessperson, having been kept waiting for twenty minutes in a Mexico City client's office, may decide to leave the office, feeling that she or he is being ignored and that the client's lateness is a sign of lack of interest in the business deal. But the Mexican client may not consider himself or herself at all tardy and may be totally confused by the American's quick exit.

Americans engaged in business dealings with Arabs, for example, should understand and adhere to their customs of hospitality so as to be successful. The initial meeting with an Arab businessperson is typically devoted to fact-finding. No commitments are implied or made, but the initial session is usually lengthy and thorough. Based on their pattern of working quickly so as not to waste time, Americans often feel that the process is tedious. The next meeting is taken up with additional rituals. It is not unusual, then, for a business deal to take as long as thirty days to complete.

Gesture patterns, which have verbal meanings, also vary. For instance, the thumb-and-forefinger-in-a-circle gesture means "okay" in the United States. In France or Belgium, however, it means the recipient is worth zero.

The same gesture in Greece and Turkey is a sexual invitation. Similarly, an index finger tapping to the temple with the other fingers curled against the palm usually means "He is smart" in the United States, whereas it communicates "He's stupid" in most of Europe."[13]

The use of space also varies widely around the world. Arabs, South Americans, and Eastern Europeans generally favor close conversational encounters, which may make Americans feel somewhat uncomfortable, and Germans and Scandinavians totally uncomfortable.

We tend to read nonverbal signs on the basis of our own personal background and experiences and we assume that others share the same interpretations. But this assumption can be misleading, even dangerous. We must remember that in all forms of communication, an understanding of the receiver is necessary. And, as if matters were not complicated enough, we must also be aware that although cultural patterns are reported to be persistent, not all the people within a given culture share identical patterns.

Emotional Influences on Nonverbal Communication

Emotions have a direct effect on the size of people's personal territory and their resulting nonverbal responses. When people are insecure, they tend to avoid closeness. People who are emotionally upset may even become violent if someone invades their territory. Again, these are representative of the basic human needs and what happens when they are not being satisfied.

When people are upset, their bodies may become rigid. For example, many people who are nervous about public speaking report that their throats tighten and their stomach muscles contract when they must present a speech. Under great tension, the pitch of the voice also rises because vocal cords tighten.

Those who attempt to mask their emotional upsets may become physically ill. The body must release its pent-up feelings. Suppressed emotions must get out somehow, and the result may be a headache or an upset stomach.

People under stress also find that other people loom larger and closer than they actually are. To a frightened child, an adult can seem like a giant. Because of this, in dealing with crying or hysterical children, adults should kneel to talk with them. By the same token, police interrogators and trial lawyers know that moving in close to an interviewee may cause him or her to get upset and say something that would be controlled under normal conditions. This emotional pressure may result in the breaking down of defenses.

Sometimes nonverbal patterns change because of outside influences. For instance, a vast difference exists between normal nonverbal communication and deviant communication such as that caused by drugs, alcohol, or shock. Patterns change as people lose control of their ability to make decisions and value judgments. A person under the influence of alcohol or drugs does not walk, talk, or have the same bodily controls as when that person is sober. This has resulted in the development of drunk-driver-walking-a-straight-line and touching-the-nose tests, with the assumption being that a sober person can perform these acts, while a drunk person can't.

Verbal and Nonverbal Relationships

Obviously, a link exists between verbal and nonverbal communication. Because they are so tightly interwoven, it is necessary to identify, analyze, and understand their various relationships. The main relationships of nonverbal to verbal communication can be described as substituting, complementing, conflicting, and accenting.[14]

The Substituting Relationship

Suppose someone asks you a question. Instead of answering verbally, you nod your head vertically—up and down. In doing so, you have used the **substituting relationship**, replacing the action meaning "yes" for the word *yes*.

The Complementing Relationship

Body language can complement a verbal message. For example, shaking your head horizontally from side to side while saying *no* reinforces the negative verbalization. This saying and doing creates a nonverbal **complementing relationship**, in which a nonverbal message accompanies a verbal message and adds further dimension to communication.

The Conflicting Relationship

A person's physical movements sometimes can conflict with his or her verbal message. For example, suppose a professor is confronted by a student after a class session. The student asks, "May I speak with you?" The professor says, "Sure, I have lots of time." While making this reply, however, the professor is packing books, glancing at the clock, and taking several steps away. A conflict exists between the verbal and nonverbal messages.

When actions conflict with verbal messages, thus forming a **conflicting relationship** between the verbal and nonverbal, as a receiver you should rely more on the nonverbal aspect of communication. Nonverbal clues are often more difficult to fake than verbal ones. When you were young, you might have been surprised to find that your parents knew when you were not telling the truth. There you stood, looking at the floor, twisting your hands, with a flushed face, as you insisted, "I didn't do it." The father of the modern psychology movement said, "He that has eyes to see and ears to hear may convince himself that no mortal can keep a secret. If his lips are silent he chatters with his fingertips; betrayal oozes out of him at every pore."[15]

Lie detectors read the body's nonverbal reactions by measuring changes in blood pressure, respiration, and skin response—in other words, by attempting to detect a conflicting relationship between the verbal and the nonverbal. This is accomplished by hooking up a meter to the fingers, measuring perspiration, or checking heart rate on an electrocardiograph machine. "The polygraph is not infallible," claims one source, "but it could be as high as 90 percent accurate in the hands of a good examiner."[16] Other estimates range from 50 to 70 percent accuracy.

The Accenting Relationship

Nonverbal behavior may accent parts of a verbal message, much as underlining or italicizing emphasizes written language. In the **accenting relationship**, the nonverbal message stresses the verbal one. Jabbing someone's shoulder with a finger as you turn the person to look at you while commanding, "When I speak to you, look at me!" obviously accents the verbal message with nonverbal signs.

 ## Categories of Nonverbal Communcation

Nonverbal channels can be divided into many categories. Eight of them are: kinesics (body language), paravocalics (vocal sounds), proxemics (space), chronemics (time), olfactics (smell), aesthetics (music and color), physical characteristics (body shape and size, skin color), and artifacts (clothes, makeup, eyeglasses, jewelry).[17] (See Figure 5.1.)

Figure 5.1
Categories of
Nonverbal
Communication

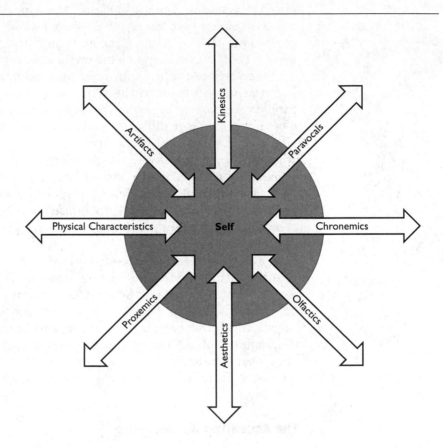

Kinesics

Kinesics is the study of communication through body movement. We communicate through the gestures we use, the way we walk and stand, the expressions on our faces and in our eyes, and how we combine these variables to open or close channels.

Gestures   As people attempt to communicate, they make gestures. These gestures may be classified as speech independent and speech related. **Speech-independent gestures** are not tied to speech. These gestures are referred to as emblems.[18] **Speech-related gestures** are directly tied to, or accompany, speech.[19] These gestures are illustrators, affect displays, regulators, and adaptors.

Emblems   **Emblems** are nonverbal acts that have a direct verbal translation or dictionary definition, which usually consist of a word or two.[20] The sign language of the deaf, gestures used by behind-the-scenes television personnel, and signals between two underwater swimmers are all examples of the use of emblems. It is important to realize that not all emblems are universal. In fact, they tend to be *culture-specific*, meaning that an emblem's meaning in one culture may not be the same as that same emblem's meaning in another. For example, in Hong Kong, signaling a waiter for the check is done by making a writing motion with both hands. Extending the index finger and motioning toward yourself, as is done for calling a waiter in many parts of the United States, is used only for calling animals.[21]

Illustrators   **Illustrators** are "kinesic acts accompanying speech that are used to aid in the description of what is being said or trace the direction of speech."[22] They are used to sketch a path, point to an object, or show spatial relationships. Saying "*Josh, please stand up* (point at Josh and bring your hand upward), *go out the door* (point at the door), *turn to the left* (point to the left), and *walk straight ahead* (point straight ahead)" is an example of a cluster of illustrators.

Affect Displays   **Affect displays** are facial gestures that show emotions and feelings such as sadness or happiness. Pouting, winking, and raising or lowering the eyelids and eyebrows are examples of affect displays. Different people and cultures tend to use facial expressions in different ways. For example, North American white males frequently mask and internalize their facial expressions because they have been taught that to show emotion is not manly; however, Italian males express their emotions outwardly.[23]

Regulators   **Regulators** are nonverbal acts that maintain and control the back-and-forth nature of speaking and listening between two or more people. Nods of the head, eye movements, and body shifts are all regulators used to encourage or discourage conversation. Imagine, for example, a conversation between a department manager and an employee who has asked for a raise. The manager glances at her watch, her fingers fidget with the telephone, and she glances through some materials on the desk. The manager's regulator signs indicate that for her the transaction is completed.

Adaptors   **Adaptors** are movements that accompany boredom, show internal feelings, or regulate a situation. For example, those who are bored often tap their fingers on a table or bounce a crossed leg. Consider the typical situation in which a person is waiting on a street corner for someone who is late: he or she often stands with arms crossed, fingers tapping on upper arms, foot tapping the pavement, checking the time every few seconds.

Posture, Walk, and Stance   Does a person's posture, walk, the way the person stands, say something about him or her? Research indicates that it most decidedly does.[24] A person's walk can give us clues about his or her status, mood, ethnic and cultural affiliation, and self-perception.

Detectives and airline-security personnel are trained to pick out suspicious people by the way they walk. Walking even follows cultural patterns: Europeans, Americans, and Asians have different walks. Europeans coming to the United States often ask why Americans are in such a hurry, an impression that comes from the quick pace at which Americans walk.

In general, the way you walk and stand tells more about you than you probably realize. When someone enters a room, you instantly form conclusions about that person. Some people walk with confidence, and stand with head high, shoulders back, jaw set. Others walk slowly with a stance of sloping shoulders, eyes down, withdrawing within their bodies. This posture may indicate lack of confidence.

The Face and Eyes   A number of nonverbal studies have concentrated solely on the face and the eyes.[25] Indeed, we have more data about these features than about any other physical nonverbal communication tool.[26]

The eye, unlike other organs of the body, is an extension of the brain.[27] Because of this, it is almost impossible for an individual to disguise eye meaning from someone who is a member of the same culture. Sayings such as, "Look at the sparkle in her eye," and "He couldn't look me straight in the eye," have meaning. Of all our features, our eyes are the most revealing. Often they communicate without our even knowing it. For example, when the pupils of our eyes are dilated, we may appear friendlier, warmer, and more attractive.

A theory known as **pupilometrics** indicates that pupils dilate when the eyes are focused on a pleasurable object, and contract when focused on an unpleasurable one.[28] Enlarged pupils signify interest and contracted pupils reflect boredom. Thus knowledgeable teachers often watch the pupils of their students' eyes to ascertain their interest in a particular lesson. The idea of wide-eyed wonder and interest is not new. In Napoleon's (late eighteenth century) time, European women placed a drug called belladonna in their eyes to keep their pupils large and make them look both interested and interesting.

An astute observer can ascertain what a person is doing by watching his or her eyes.

Members of different social classes, generations, ethnic groups, and cultures use their eyes differently to express messages. Americans often complain when they feel foreigners stare at them too intensely or hold a glance too long. This is because a gaze of longer than ten seconds is likely to induce discomfort in an American.

But lengthy eye contact may be comfortable as long as the communicating people have sufficient distance between them. As you walk down a corridor, notice that you can look at someone for a long period of time until you suddenly feel uncomfortable and glance away. This usually happens at a distance of about ten feet.

When individuals in Western cultures are intent on hiding an inner feeling, they may try to avoid eye contact. Thus the child who has eaten forbidden candy will not look at a questioning parent during the interrogation. Remember when you were told, "Look me in the eye and say that"?

People in many cultures are very aware of the part played by eyes in communicating. This awareness has led some to try to mask their eyes.

"Since people can't control the responses of their eyes," reported one source, "many Arabs wear dark glasses, even indoors."[29] This is especially true if they are negotiating.

Thus, in addition to watching a person's actions, an astute observer can ascertain what that person is doing by watching his or her eyes. For example, when 90 percent of people look up and to the left, they are recalling a memory. Eyes up and to the right register a future thought.[30]

Open and Closed Channels   Few of us realize how much we depend on nonverbal communication to encourage and discourage conversations and transactions. For instance, we consciously wave at waiters, and raise our hands to get a teacher's attention. Much of our opening and closing of channels, however, occurs without our consciously realizing it.

If you observe people conversing, you notice that they may indicate they are listening by moving their heads. If they agree with what is said, they may nod affirmatively. They may also smile to show pleasure or agreement. If, however, they glance several times at their watch, divert their gaze from the speaker, cross and uncross their legs, and stand up, they are probably signaling that they have closed the channel and wish to end the transaction.

Paravocalics

All the vocal effects we make to accompany words, such as tone of voice—but not the words themselves—are called **paravocalics**.[31] Vocal quality communicates nonverbally to the listening ear. The rate (speed), volume (power), pitch (such as soprano or bass), pause (stopping), and stress (intensity) of sounds all have particular meanings. These paravocal tools are often referred to as vocal cues.

Often we can use vocal cues to determine the sex, age, and status of a speaker. We can also make some pretty accurate judgments about the emotions and feelings of the people with whom we communicate by their paralinguistic presentation. If you are very angry, the pitch of your voice often goes up. And when you are very, very angry, you sometimes say words slowly and distinctly, pausing after each word for special effect.

Research indicates that the voice also may be important in some aspects of persuasion.[32] A faster rate of speech, more intonation, greater volume, and a less halting manner seem to be related to successful attempts at persuasion. If a person sounds assured, the receiver credits him or her with a higher degree of credibility. Network television anchors, for example, work to cultivate an assured voice in their news broadcasts.

Vocal cues can provide much information about a speaker, and our overall reaction to another person is colored at least somewhat by our reactions to these cues. Our perceptions of vocal cues, combined with other verbal and nonverbal stimuli, mold the conceptions we use as bases for communicating.[33]

Proxemics

A basic difference among people can be seen in how they operate within the space around them—how they use their territory. The study of how people use and perceive their social and personal space is called **proxemics**. Much of what is known about this field is based on anthropological research.

Every person is surrounded by a psychological bubble of space. This bubble contracts and expands depending on the person's cultural background, emotional state, and the activity in which he or she is participating. Northern Europeans—English, Scandinavians, and Germans—tend to have a larger zone of personal space and often avoid touching and close contact. They require more room around them and structure their lifestyles to meet the need for this room. Thus the English are stereotyped as being distant and impersonal, not showing great emotion through hugging, kissing, and touching. This stereotype derives from the respect they exhibit for each other's territory. In contrast, Italians, Russians, Spaniards, Latin Americans, Middle Easterners, and the French generally tend to like close personal contact.

Some marriage counselors believe that a major cause of marital conflict in the United States is the lack of spatial and emotional compatibility between spouses. Consider, for example, what happens when a woman from a family with an English heritage marries a man with an Italian background. If they follow stereotypical patterns, she is physically and emotionally controlled, whereas he wants to touch and invade her territory. He expects her to kiss and hug, soothe him after a hard day, sit close to him, and show outward emotion. She does not understand the "loud" voices and "exaggerated" gestures of his family. And he cannot understand why members of her family never touch each other. Thus a conflict can result from differences in these two partners' proxemic patterns and expectations.

Personal space is important to us because we feel that if someone touches our body, he or she is attacking us because we are our body.[34] Many of us do not like to be touched but do not really know why. This dislike may stem, not from something unique to us, but from cultural training. When someone who does not like to be fondled meets a toucher, the situation can be quite uncomfortable. If the toucher places a hand on the arm of the nontoucher and he or she jerks away, the toucher may well get the idea that a rejection has taken place when in fact it is the touch, not them, that has been spurned.

Space Distances   Most middle-class Americans maintain four principal distances in their business and social relationships. These distances are classified as intimate, personal, social, and public.[35]

Intimate distance covers a space varying from direct physical contact with another person to a distance of eighteen inches. It is used for our most private activities—caressing, making love, and sharing intimate ideas and emotions. We can often get clues about a relationship by noticing whether the other person allows us to use his or her intimate space. For example, if you have been on a hand-holding/physically touching basis with someone, and suddenly he or she will not let you near, or pulls away when you get very close, based on congruency patterns a change in the relationship may have occurred. If the other person suddenly encourages close body proximity, this may also indicate a change in attitude.

Personal distance, eighteen inches to four feet, is sometimes called the *comfort bubble.* Most North Americans feel most comfortable keeping at this distance when talking with others, and invasion of this personal territory will cause us to back away. If we are backed into a corner, sitting in a chair, or somehow trapped, we will lean away, pull in, and tense up. To avoid invasion of our territory, we might place a leg on the rung of a chair or on a stair. Some of us even arrange our furniture so that our territory cannot be invaded. For example, businesspeople may place their desks so that employees must sit on one side and the boss on the other. In contrast, interviewers have reported a completely different atmosphere when talking to job applicants if the two chairs are placed facing each other about three to four feet apart instead of on opposite sides of the desk.

Social distance covers a four- to twelve-foot zone that is used during business transactions and casual social exchanges. Also part of social distance is the **standing-seated interaction**, in which the person in control stands and the other person sits. Standing-seated positions occur, among others, in teacher-pupil and police officer–arrestee transactions.

Public distance may dictate a separation of as little as twelve feet, but it is usually more than twenty-five. It is used by teachers in lecture rooms and speakers at public gatherings as well as by public figures who wish to place a barrier between themselves and their audiences.

Cultures and Space   When people from different cultural backgrounds come into contact, they often assume they have the same concept of space.

We can often get clues about a relationship by noticing whether the person allows us to use his or her intimate space.

This, of course, is not true. In fact, "cultures can be distinguished by the distances at which members interact and how frequently members touch."[36] It has been proposed that there are **contact cultures**—those characterized by tactile modes of communication (e.g., Latin Americans, Mediterraneans, French, Arabs) and **noncontact cultures** (Germans, English, North Americans).[37] Though heterosexual men in the United States or England rarely touch other men, except in times of great emotion (such as athletic game victories), or for shaking hands when welcoming or meeting someone, arm linking between two men is common in many Latin countries.[38]

Even within our own culture, the space bubble varies according to our emotional state and the activity being performed. Although Americans usually keep well beyond the three-foot personal circle of space, this can change very quickly. If you are on a crowded bus and someone presses against you, you may tolerate it. If, however, you are standing at a bus stop and someone presses against you, you will probably object. This situation brings into play your idea of public distance.

Your emotional state can also change your idea of space. For instance, when some people are angry, they may grab someone by the front of the shirt, step in close, get "nose to nose," and shout.

Touch   **Touch** is the physical entering of another person's territory. This may be done with or without permission. Your skin is a receiver of communication: pats, pinches, strokes, slaps, punches, shakes, and kisses all convey meaning. A doctor touches your body to ascertain sensitivity and possible illness. You shake hands to satisfy social and business welcoming needs. You intimately touch through kisses and use sexually arousing touch in the act of lovemaking. The messages that touch communicates depend on how, where, and by whom you are touched.

The importance of touch is well documented. Many people find that when they are upset, they rub their hands together or stroke a part of their body such as the arm. We reassure others by touching them on the shoulder or patting them on the arm. "Touched and massaged babies gain weight much faster than unmassaged babies. They are more active, alert, responsive, better able to tolerate noise, and emotionally are more in control."[39]

Most people—except those who have been abused, raped, or brought up in a low- or no-touch family or society—associate appropriate touching with positive messages.[40] Those whose bodies have been invaded without permission, however, as in the case of sexual abuse, often pull back or feel uncomfortable being touched. In fact, touch avoidance is one of the signs counselors sometimes use to identify those who have been physically or sexually abused.[41]

If you have ever wondered why you felt comfortable, or uncomfortable, when you were touched, it could well have to do with your upbringing. Different cultures regard touch in different ways. Some avoid touch, while others encourage touch. The same is true within families. For example, in the United States, which is a moderate-touch society, "it is not unusual for an adult to pat the head of a small child who has been introduced by his or her parents. In Malaysia, and other Asian Pacific countries, touching anyone's head—especially a child's—is improper and considered an indignity because the head is regarded as the home of the soul."[42] In the United States, a handshake is appropriate as a business greeting, a bow fulfills the same purpose in Japan, and kissing on both cheeks is the French custom.

Touch is not only culture-specific but gender-specific. Women in the North American culture tend to engage in more intimate same-sex touch than do men. Female pairs are more likely to exchange touches (e.g., hugs, kisses, touching on the arm or back) and to do so for longer durations than are male pairs.[43] Men touch one another using only narrowly circumscribed behaviors such as handshaking, or in instances of extreme emotion (e.g., athletic accomplishments), in such actions as hugging, butt slapping, or kissing. The acceptability of showing physical affection by women may be one of the reasons lesbians may be less discriminated against than gay men.[44] When physical displays between women take place, there is less attention drawn, and less reaction to it, than to similar actions between men. This is not true in other countries where men holding hands or kissing is an acceptable action. In the United States, when men touch, kiss, or hug each other, attention is drawn to the activity, and since it is not generally part of the cultural norm, it is perceived by some in negative ways.

Permission to touch tends to follow an action chain sequence. If you have ever wondered why someone with whom you'd like to be intimate pulls away or gets rigid when you or the other person is touched, it may well be that you have jumped forward in the sequence too quickly. For a person brought up in a moderate-to-low-touch society, there is an appropriate time to not touch, then to touch, to kiss, and then to fondle. If one person feels he or she is at the no-touch stage, and the partner acts at the fondle stage, strong negative verbal and physical reactions may follow, including screaming, slapping, or physical fleeing.

If you would like to measure your touch/touch avoidance, fill out the scale in Figure 5.2.

Small-Group Ecology   The physical placement of members of small groups in relation to one another has an effect on their behavior. This **small-group ecology**, which includes the placement of chairs, the placement of the person conducting a meeting, and the setting for a small-group encounter, clearly influences the group's operation.

If, for example, people are seated in a tight circle, they will probably feel more comfortable and interact more than they would if they were sitting in straight rows. They will be able to see each other's nonverbal reactions, and because there is no inhibiting physical distance, they will lose their self-consciousness as they become members of the group.

Business organizations make considerable use of such nonverbal strategies in small-scale conferences. One technique is to seat key members of the group in prominent positions, to stimulate discussion or even direct it.

Chronemics

You communicate to yourself and others by the way you use time. The way people handle and structure their time is known as **chronemics**. "Each of us is born into and raised in a particular time world—an environment with its own rhythm to which we entrain ourselves."[45] Time, as a communication tool, is sometimes greatly misunderstood. Only within certain societies, for example, is precise time of great significance. Some cultures

Figure 5.2
The Touch
Avoidance Scale

The Touch Avoidance Scale

Directions: This instrument is composed of 18 statements concerning feelings about touching other people and being touched. Please indicate the degree to which each statement applies to you by circling whether you (1) Strongly Disagree, (2) Disagree, (3) Are Undecided, (4) Agree, or (5) Strongly Agree with each statement. While some of these statements may seem repetitious, take your time and try to be as honest as possible.

1. A hug from a same-sex friend is a true sign of friendship	1	2	3	4	5
2. Opposite-sex friends enjoy it when I touch them.	1	2	3	4	5
3. I often put my arm around friends of the same sex.	1	2	3	4	5
4. When I see two people of the same sex hugging, it revolts me.	1	2	3	4	5
5. I like it when members of the opposite sex touch me.	1	2	3	4	5
6. People shouldn't be so uptight about touching persons of the same sex.	1	2	3	4	5
7. I think it is vulgar when members of the opposite sex touch me.	1	2	3	4	5
8. When a member of the opposite sex touches me, I find it unpleasant.	1	2	3	4	5
9. I wish I were free to show emotions by touching members of the same sex.	1	2	3	4	5
10. I'd enjoy giving a massage to an opposite-sex friend.	1	2	3	4	5
11. I enjoy kissing persons of the same sex.	1	2	3	4	5
12. I like to touch friends that are the same sex as I am.	1	2	3	4	5
13. Touching a friend of the same sex does not make me uncomfortable.	1	2	3	4	5
14. I find it enjoyable when a close opposite-sex friend and I embrace.	1	2	3	4	5
15. I enjoy getting a back rub from a member of the opposite sex.	1	2	3	4	5
16. I dislike kissing relatives of the same sex.	1	2	3	4	5
17. Intimate touching with members of the opposite sex is pleasurable.	1	2	3	4	5
18. I find it difficult to be touched by a member of my own sex.	1	2	3	4	5

Directions for scoring:

A. Add up the circled numbers for items 1, 2, 3, 5, 6, 9, 10, 11, 12, 13, 14, 15, and 17:   _____

B. Score items 4, 7, 8, 16, and 18 in reverse, so a circled 1 is scored as 5, 2 as 4, 3 as 3, 4 as 2, and 5 as 1, and add them up: _____

C. Add up items (A) and (B) above to get your score: _____

A score of 70 or higher indicates a very strong motivation to touch. Less than 14% (about one-seventh) of the population scores this high. If your score is right around 60, your motivation is about average, but still generally positive, since the midpoint between positive and negative on the scale is 54. A score of 50 or lower would place you approximately in the lower 14% in terms of motivation for touch.

Note: Item 15 from the original scale (Andersen & Leibowitz, 1978) has been altered from "when my date and I embrace" to "when a close opposite-sex friend and I embrace." Also, the scoring has been reversed from the original, so that a higher score indicates a more positive attitude toward touch.

SOURCE: From *Environmental Psychology and Nonverbal Behavior, 3,* Human Sciences Press, Inc. Reprinted by permission of Plenum Publishing Corporation.

relate to time as a *circular phenomenon* in which there is no pressure or anxiety about the future. Existence follows the cycle of the seasons of planting and harvesting, the daily rising and setting of the sun, birth and death. In **circular time**, there is no pressing need to achieve or create newness, or to produce more than is needed to survive. Additionally, there is no fear of death. Such societies have successfully integrated the past and future into a peaceful sense of the present.[46] Many Native Americans have been raised with this cultural attitude toward time.

Other societies operate on **linear time**, which is concerned primarily with the future. These societies focus on the factual and technical information needed to fulfill impending demands. In most of Western Europe, North America, and Japan, punctuality is a part of good manners. Thus tardiness can be a sign that a person wants to avoid something or that the activity or person to be met is not important enough to warrant the effort to be on time. Procrastinators are not valued.

Another way of viewing time is to understand its technical, formal, and informal uses. **Technical time** is precise time, as in the way some scientists look at how things happen in milliseconds. Few of us continually come in contact with this usage. On the other hand, **formal time** is the way in which a culture defines its time, and it plays a daily role in most of our lives. It refers to centuries, years, months, weeks, days, hours, and minutes. As a student you may think in terms of semesters or terms.

Informal time refers to a rather flexible use of time such as "soon," or "right away." These terms often cause communicative difficulty because they are arbitrary and mean different things to different people. For example, how long is "pretty soon"?

Time has become a critical factor in the American workplace. Throughout a person's career, punctuality is often used as a measure of effectiveness. A person who arrives late for a job interview probably will have difficulty overcoming such a negative first impression, and employees who arrive late or leave early may be reprimanded and even dismissed.

Time is culture based. Euro-Americans, North Americans and western Europeans, in general, are clock bound; African, Latin American, and some Asian-Pacific cultures are not clock bound. Time is based on personal systems.[47] Americans traveling abroad often are irritated by the seeming lack of concern for time commitments among residents of some countries. In Mexico and Central America, tours may be late; guides fail to indicate the correct arrival and departure times. Yet in other places, such as Switzerland, a traveler can set her or his watch by the promptness of the trains. Businesspeople may get confused over what "on time" means as they meet those from other cultures. "In Britain and North America one may be 5 minutes late for a business appointment, but not 15 minutes and certainly not 30 minutes late, which is perfectly normal in Arab countries."[48] In Latin America one is expected to arrive late to an appointment. This same tardiness for Germans or North Americans would be perceived as rudeness.[49]

The differences in the use of time have been noted in regard to college students and when they arrive for classes and turn in assignments. Brazilian students showed few signs of concern for lateness, arriving as much as an hour late for a two-hour class, but also feeling comfortable to ask questions long after the class had officially ended.[50] One of the authors of this book, who used to teach at a school that had a very large Puerto Rican and Mexican population, had to announce at the start of each semester that class starting time and assignment due dates were based on "gringo time"—North American white people's time—or students would wander in at will and turn in assignments whenever. Some cultures, such as gays and Hispanics, often are amused by their use of time and even have names that refer to the habitual lateness such as *gay-late* and *mañana time.*

In cultures that value promptness, one of the questions often raised about time centers on the person who is constantly late. What does habitual tardiness reveal about the person? Chronic lateness is deeply rooted in a person's psyche. Compulsive tardiness is rewarding on some level. A key emotional conflict for the chronically late person involves his or her need to feel special. Such a person may not gain enough recognition in other ways; people must be special in some way, so the person is special by being late. Other reasons include needs for punishment, power, or as an expression of hostility.[51]

Olfactics

Olfactics is the study of smell. We communicate through our smells.

Our sense of smell is extraordinarily precise. Growing evidence also suggests that we remember what we smell longer than what we see and hear.[52] Our sense of smell is very selective and helps us reach conclusions. We are attracted by the scents of certain colognes and repulsed by others. Some people find certain body odors offensive. This is especially true in a country such as the United States where we have been taught by advertisers and medical people to wash off natural odors and replace them by neutral, fragrance-free, or substitute smells. This is not the case in other cultures, causing North Americans to think of people with natural body smells as being dirty.

We often make decisions without realizing that these decisions are based on odors. Several phenomena provide insight into how smell serves as a nonverbal communication tool: smell blindness, smell adaptation, smell memory, smell overload, and smell discrimination.[53]

Smell Blindness   Each person is unique in his or her ability to identify and distinguish smells. **Smell blindness** occurs when a person is unable to detect smells. It parallels color blindness or deafness because it is a physiological blockage. It accounts for the fact that some people do not smell their own or others' body odors or detect the differences in the odors of various foods. Because smell and taste are so closely aligned, this can explain why people who are smell-blind may also have taste-identification difficulties.

Smell Adaptation   **Smell adaptation** occurs when we gradually lose the distinctiveness of a particular smell through repeated contact with it. When you walk into a bakery, you may be aware of the wonderful odors. The clerk, however, may have become so used to the odors that he or she is not aware of them. The speed at which the odor message is adapted to depends on the strength of the odor and the length of time we are in contact with it.

Smell Memory   If as a child your grandmother baked your favorite dessert, walking into someone's home years later and smelling that same odor may cause you to flash back to memories of your grandmother. This ability to recall previous situations when encountering a particular smell associated with them is **smell memory**. Smelling a crayon may trigger experiences of kindergarten, the odors of a dentist's office may cause your teeth to ache, or passing a perfume counter with samples of a cologne a former lover wore may trigger intrapersonal smell memories.

Smell Overload   Have you ever entered an elevator and been bombarded by the heavy dose of perfume of another passenger? Onions in a salad are fine, but slicing several at the sink may cause you to cry. These are both examples of smell overload. **Smell overload** takes place when an exceptionally large number of odors or one extremely strong odor overpowers you. Walking down a detergent aisle in a supermarket or standing in a small room with several people who are smoking can trigger smell overload.

Smell Discrimination   The ability to identify people, places, and things on the basis of their smell is **smell discrimination**. We can detect more than ten thousand different odors.[54] You may have been able to distinguish someone who comes up behind you undetected by the smell of her or his hair. The identification takes place through smell discrimination, which allows us to tell the difference between cinnamon and garlic, bananas and oranges, and one person and another.

Aesthetics

The communication of a message or mood through color or music is called **aesthetics**. As you stroll through the supermarket, you may not even be aware that this principle is in force. During a nine-week test, the music in one supermarket was randomly played at a slow 60 beats a minute on some days and at 108 beats a minute on others. Not surprisingly, on slow-tempo days the store's gross receipts were 38.2 percent higher.[55]

Effects like this can be observed in many situations. For example, when you are driving a car, the type of music on the radio affects your driving, alertness, and concentration. And the music in an elevator is almost never loud and pulsating because such strong sounds would be too emotionally stressful for a small contained area. A study on the impact of rock music tested more than twenty thousand records for their effect on muscle strength. (This sort of activity is part of a science entitled **behavioral kinesiology**,[56] which holds that particular kinds of food, clothes, thoughts, and music strengthen or weaken the muscles of the body.) According to a behavioral kinesiological study, "listening to rock music frequently causes all the muscles in the body to go weak."[57] This relationship may well account for the drugged and dreamlike feelings of some people who attend rock concerts. It is theorized that some rock music has a stopped quality that is not present in other types of music, that is, the beat is stopped at the end of each bar or measure. Because the music stops and then must start again, the listener subconsciously comes to a halt at the end of each measure; this may tire out the listener.

Other studies indicate that music's effect is also based on tempo, rhythm, and instrumentation. Music can heighten a person's attention or induce boredom, thereby creating a nonverbal language that can change or stimulate various activities.[58] These effects, combined with the behavioral kinesiology studies, suggest that music can serve as a type of drug in regulating behavior. Music, for example, has been credited with easing pain and a type of music therapy is being used in hospices in working with dying patients.

Colors also affect people, and many institutions are putting into practice this awareness. For example, hospitals are experimenting with using

Double Standards

"Despite the great strides women have made in the workplace, a woman's image still appears to be more crucial to her career—and more carefully scrutinized—than a man's. Part of the reason is the uniform nature of men's suits. For example, it may be perfectly acceptable for a man to wear the same suit two days in a row, provided he changes his shirt and tie. But if a woman wears the same outfit two days in a row, it may raise the question of whether she went home the night before."

SOURCE: *National Institute of Business Management Inc.* Courtesy of B. Shackman & Co., NY, NY

What it means to be attractive differs from culture to culture.

various colors for their rooms in hopes that the colors may motivate sick people to get well or ease pain. Fewer hospital rooms are being painted green, because green is often associated with sickness and nausea. Hospitals also are painting large pieces of equipment, such as x-ray machines, the same color as the background walls so they do not appear as frightening to patients. Sheets and blankets are now made in softer colors—pinks, blues, and pastels—rather than sterile, cold white. Prisons also are using pale pink shades because it is the most calming of colors. Similarly, bright colors are being added to classrooms to make students feel alert, but not in such amounts that the colors become overpowering.

Physical Characteristics

General attractiveness and height are all nonverbal communication signs.

Attractiveness   We often are drawn to or repulsed by people according to how they appear physically. The prejudice against unattractive people is deeply ingrained in North American society. This attitude may, in part, be the result of the emphasis projected by the advertising industry on attractiveness in their magazine, newspaper, and television ads, and the depiction of what makes for attractive people, whether men, women, or children.

Attractiveness is in the eye of the beholder. What it means to be attractive differs from culture to culture. For example, judges at international beauty contests have difficulty judging who the winner is because of the vast physical differences between the contestants and the lack of a universal definition for beauty. And, though thinness for women might be the in-beauty thing in the white North American culture, that is not necessarily true with African Americans. In a study of teenage girls, white girls painted attractiveness as "5' 7", between 100 and 110 pounds, with blue eyes and long flowing hair."[59] The black girls in the study named full hips and large thighs as the signs of attractiveness.[60]

A jury's decision can be affected by both the plaintiff's and the defendant's physical appearances. In one study, participants in an automobile-negligence trial heard tape-recorded testimony. The first set of jurors was shown photographs of an attractive male plaintiff and an unattractive male defendant; the second set of jurors saw the reverse. A third panel saw no pictures but heard the testimony. The results: the attractive plaintiff received a 49 percent positive vote from the first jury, the unattractive plaintiff got only a 17 percent positive vote from the second jury, and 41 percent of the third group, which did not see any pictures, ruled for the plaintiff.[61]

Even salary can be affected by attractiveness. A study indicates that male attorneys who are attractive earn more money than their counterparts who are plain-looking. [62]

Height   It should not be surprising that height can be a communicator. Men often are judged purely by their physical presence. "Size can affect a man's life. Short men are discriminated against."[63] Men under 5' 6" are considered short. People regard them as having less power. Short men are referred to as *submissive* and *weak*, tall men garner such titles as *mature* and *respected*. Even elementary students are aware of the height prejudice.[64]

A comparison of starting pay of business school graduates indicates that tall males received $600 per inch more in yearly salary.[65] What are the implications? Short men need to be better prepared, be aware that they must exceed in grades and talent, sell themselves during job interviews. Success is not impossible; for example, two-term Clinton cabinet member Robert Reich is less than 5 feet tall, President James Madison was 5' 4", Attila the Hun, 5'; and, of course, there was Napoleon.

Although American society seems to show a preference for taller men, "tall women often are labeled 'ungainly'; short businesswomen, in fact, may have an advantage in not acquiring whatever threatening overtones may attend to increasing height."[66] Oprah Winfrey is just five feet tall, as is Mother Teresa.[67]

Artifacts

A person's clothing, makeup, eyeglasses, and jewelry carry distinct messages. These items are classified as **artifacts**.

Clothing is probably the most obvious of the artifact communicators. It is almost like a substitute body, telling an observer something about who you are. Because you have made a choice about what to wear, it follows that this is the image you want to portray, this is the attitude you want to present about the type of person you are, and this is the way you want others to perceive you. Wearing something out of the mainstream can influence reactions to you. For example, in the 1997 era of youngsters having vividly dyed spiked hair, wearing dog collars and black leather clothing, and possessing a pierced body part often resulted in their being labeled as *drug users* and *deviants* by mainstream people.

For those interested in climbing the business ladder, the corporate uniform is still in for interviews. "A job interview is like any other ceremony that requires a costume."[68] "For women a dark blue suit, cream-colored shirt, hems on skirts should be at the knees, and no pants."[69] "For men, dark blue suit, white shirt and red tie is the way to go."[70]

In spite of the emphasis on corporate clothing for interviews, there have been some major changes in daily wear. Originally started in California's Silicon Valley at such companies as Apple Computers, this trend has resulted in a major change in dressing at work. Seventy-four percent of companies allow casual dress, with *casual Fridays* as a popular policy.[71] This trend allows or even encourages employees to wear casual clothing on Friday. Even IBM, which had a notoriously stiff dress code, has eliminated its restriction. "Here's stuffy IBM losing millions, and Microsoft, where the employees wear jeans and T-shirts, making millions. The irony is not lost on anyone."[72]

Though most companies don't allow blue jeans, sneakers, and sweats, loafers, sweaters, and chinos are in vogue. The guideline? Dress "the way men and women would dress to go to a singles bar Friday nights."[73] Many clothing manufacturers have developed whole lines of casual work clothing.[74]

Another new trend is workplace uniforms. They are seen not only at fast-food restaurants, but on bank officers, travel agents, runners at the stock exchange, and employees at funeral homes. The trend, which started with the Century 21 gold-blazered real estate brokers, has expanded.[75]

Be aware, however, that casualness is not universal. Companies dealing in foreign markets know that the business suit, which originally rose in nineteenth-century Europe as a costume to make managerial workers stand out from production workers, is still very much the business garb.

In countries like Japan, England and Germany, casual is definitely not the in thing.

Legal professionals also are aware of the effect of clothing for themselves and their clients. If you are to appear in a courtroom, attending to your appearance can prove beneficial. As someone being tried, if you have a beard or a mustache, think seriously about shaving it off. Dress conservatively but appropriately for your age and social standing. And do not wear sunglasses.

IN CONCLUSION → Nonverbal communication is communication through all external stimuli other than spoken or written words. It includes body motion, characteristics of appearance, characteristics of voice, and use of space and distance. Experts tend to agree that nonverbal communication carries the impact of a message. Nonverbal signs can be caused either by innate neurological programs or by learned behavior common to a culture. Each culture has its own body language. There is a vast difference between normal nonverbal communication and deviant communication such as that caused by drugs, alcohol, or shock. The channels of nonverbal communication are kinesics, paravocalics, proxemics, chronemics, olfactics, aesthetics, physical characteristics, and artifacts.

LEARN BY DOING →

1. Research one of these topics or people and be prepared to give a two-minute speech on what you have learned regarding the topic and nonverbal communication: neurolinguistic programming, Ray Birdwhistell, Albert Mehrabian, Edward Hall, pupilometrics, biorhythms, Muzak, behavioral kinesiology.

2. Give examples of your own recent use of substituting, complementing, conflicting, and accenting.

3. Carefully observe members of your family or think of the nonverbal patterns they display. Can you find any similarities between their patterns and your own?

4. Identify a culture-specific nonverbal trait and describe it to the class.

5. Make a list of five emblems used in North America. Be prepared to demonstrate them. Compare your explanations of what they mean with those of your classmates.

6. Carry on a conversation with a person outside your classroom. As you speak, slowly move closer to him or her. Continue to move in on

the person gradually. Observe his or her reaction. Did the person back up? Cross his or her arms? Report to the class on the results of this experiment.

KEY TERMS ➤

nonverbal communication
neurolinguistic programming
cluster
congruency
innate neurological programs
reflexive
action chain
substituting relationship
complementing relationship
conflicting relationship
accenting relationship
speech-independent gestures
speech-related gestures
emblems
illustrators
affect displays
regulators
adaptors
pupilometrics
paravocalics
proxemics
intimate distance

personal distance
social distance
standing-seated interaction
public distance
contact cultures
noncontact cultures
touch
small-group ecology
chronemics
circular time
linear time
technical time
formal time
informal time
olfactics
smell blindness
smell adaptation
smell memory
smell overload
smell discrimination
aesthetics
behavioral kinesiology

PART two

Personal Communication

131

chapter **6**

The Theory of
Interpersonal
Communication

LEARNING OUTCOMES →

After reading this chapter, you should be able to:

Illustrate how self-disclosure plays a role in both self-understanding and understanding of another person

Explain the roles of trust, approval-seeking, emotions, and power as they relate to interpersonal communication

Explain the similarities and differences in the communication of males and females and their effect on interpersonal communication

Define what relationships are and demonstrate how they develop, continue, and end

The concept of interpersonal communication developed in the early 1950s.[1] As a result of research on the subject, the field of speech expanded from the study of mainly public speaking into a new field entitled communication, encompassing such areas as self-disclosure, approval-seeking, relational communication, family communication, conversational communication, and conflict resolution.

The term **interpersonal communication** has been assigned the definition of "communication that is based on communicators' recognition of each other's uniqueness and the development of messages that reflect that recognition."[2] It can also be described as an interactional process in which two people send and receive messages. Two primary themes underlie this process: communication necessitates give and take, and communication involves relationships and information.

As there can be no communication unless the communicators give and take information, the basis for interpersonal transactions is the sending and receiving of messages in such a way that they are successfully encoded and decoded. The more experiences the communicators have in common and the more openness they have between them, the more likely it is that their communication will be successful.

Our interpersonal relationships bring together the most important people, roles, contexts, and energies we experience. Interpersonal communication functions to combat loneliness, shape self-concepts, confirm experiences, renew personal and intrapersonal growth, and aid us in understanding who we are and how we relate to others.

Basic Concepts of Interpersonal Communication

As you read about interpersonal communication, keep some basic concepts in mind:

1 *Communication takes place within a system.* As we enter into communicative relationships with others, we set a pattern by which we will interact. For example, in a family, there are flow patterns of message sending and receiving: who speaks to who, who controls the interactions, who has the power to praise and punish, who can encourage or stop the message flow. If you examine any relationship you are in, you will recognize patterns by which the communication flows.

A change in the system results in a change of the communication. If someone in the system changes roles (e.g., teenager leaves for college), or outside factors change the system (grandma gets sick and moves in), that changes the communicative system.

The effectiveness of any one-on-one communication depends greatly on the relationship between the people involved.

There may be resistance to changing the system because this may involve a shift in the power structure. If your boss, spouse, lover, or friend likes being in control and you are proposing a change, problems may arise. At the other extreme, there also may be situations in which the system requires adjustment so that a person is forced to assume responsibility after having been dependent on someone else. Whatever happens, the communication system remains unchanged as long as the status quo is maintained.

2 *We teach others how to treat us.* The system in which communication takes place needs to be structured. In developing a system, each person plays a role; if that role is accepted by the other person, then that becomes part of the system. If it is rejected, then it does not become a system rule. Often we wonder why people treat us like they do. In many instances it is because when they treat us in a particular way, we don't object; therefore, it becomes the pattern. For example, habitual physical abusers at one point hit a person, and the person didn't object or didn't feel that he or she had the power to defend themselves. Therefore, the next time the abuser got angry, he or she repeated the action. The cycle is set!

3 We *communicate what and who we are.* Every time we communicate, we tell a great deal about ourselves. Our selection of words, the tone of our voice, and the gestures we use combine to give a picture of our values, likes and dislikes, and self-perceptions. We give clues of our

background by the pronunciation patterns we produce, and the attitudes we express. As receivers, we form conclusions about senders and react to these conclusions based on our own culture—background, experiences, and beliefs.

4 *Much of our interpersonal communication centers on our wanting others to act or think or feel as we do; in other words, much of it is an attempt at persuasion.* In our interpersonal relations with parents, children, and friends, we often attempt to alter or reinforce behavior, give advice, or elicit some type of action.

5 *Meaning is in people, not in words.* The meaning of a word only has that meaning by virtue of the meaning people give to that word. In communicating with others, we must be aware that what a particular symbol means to us is not necessarily what it means to them. A homeowner hearing the word *grass* may think of the *lawn.* A drug counselor probably thinks of *marijuana.* Unless some basis for understanding exists, ineffective communication may be the result. Thus, we must define terms and give examples, keeping our audience in mind and adjusting our messages accordingly.

6 *We cannot not communicate.* Communication does not necessarily stop simply because people stop talking and listening. Suppose you do not answer a question your instructor has asked. Or suppose you sit quietly at the dinner table instead of joining in the conversation. In these cases, you are still sending messages, although your lips are silent. Remember that much of our communicating is done below the verbal level. You may think that if you do not actively participate, you are not sending messages—but you are! In many instances your body is communicating nonverbally, and the very fact that you are not saying something may be interpreted as if you were telling the other person that you are not interested, don't care, or disagree.

7 *People react to our actions.* We are constantly demonstrating the **action-reaction principle.** When we smile, others are likely to smile back; when we display anger, others tend to do the same. Try an experiment. The next time you walk down a hallway or a sidewalk, smile as others come toward you. You will probably find that the people you pass smile back, often saying *hello*—action-reaction. Think back to the last time you had an argument. If you raised your voice, what did the other person do? No doubt that person also raised his or her voice—action-reaction.

8 *We do what we do because in the end we expect to achieve happiness.* When we choose to enter into communication, we do so hoping to gain from the experience, but certainly to be in no worse psychological

Figure 6.1
Commonality of
Experience
Between Two
Persons

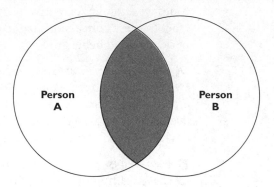

shape than when we entered. Consequently, many people try to avoid any situation in which they feel they may get negative feedback or be unsuccessful in communicating their ideas.

9 *We cannot always have the same understandings and feelings as others.* As we communicate, we must recognize that because of differences in our cultures, the only areas we share are those in which we have a common experiential background. To illustrate this, let us assume that all our knowledge and experience is contained within one circle and that all the knowledge and experience of the person with whom we are communicating is contained within another circle. The only commonality, the only place where our ideas, concepts, beliefs, and vocabulary will overlap, is where we have had similar exposure. Figure 6.1 illustrates this idea. Only in the area where the circles overlap are there any common unities.

If we add a third person to the conversation, the problem becomes even greater, as Figure 6.2 illustrates. Here, many areas of overlap exist between persons A and B, between persons A and C, and between persons B and C. But notice the small area of overlap among all three. The difficulty of communicating with large groups of people can be easily demonstrated when this process of drawing representative circles is continued.

Self-Disclosure

The starting point of any interpersonal communication is **self-talk**— intrapersonally communicating within one's self. The self-talk often triggers confidences and inquiries we have about ourself, which then affects

Figure 6.2
Commonality of
Experience Among
Three Persons

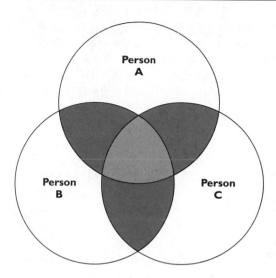

our interpersonal communication decisions. The view you have of yourself, your **self-concept**, determines what you will say and to whom you will say it. For example, if we perceive ourself to be a good communicator, then we are likely to feel confident in our communication. But if we label ourself as shy or apprehensive, then we may find it difficult to express ourself. At the heart of this dynamic process is the premise that if we do not accept ourself, probably no one else will either; our lack of confidence is easily caught by those with whom we interact.

Some of us worry about appearing too self-confident and being thought a braggart. Nevertheless, accepting yourself as a worthy person does not necessarily mean you are boasting. Sometimes you have to "blow your own horn" because no one else knows how to play the tune. You know yourself better than others and know more about yourself and your skills and talents than others do. There is a difference, however, between tooting your own horn and playing a symphony (e.g., sharing with others your accomplishments, and going on and on about them or exaggerating). In this vein, consider this advice.

Self-love means accepting yourself as a worthy person because you choose to do so. Self-love has nothing to do with the sort of behavior characterized by telling everyone how wonderful you are. Self-love means to love yourself; it doesn't demand the love of others. Self-love is the basis for accepting who and what you are and realizing that if others can't accept you as you are, that is their problem and not yours. This is not to say that you can't listen to the input of others and attempt to make changes in

Make Eye Contact

Try this simple tip to help you project a good first impression: Notice the color of a person's eyes as you shake hands. *Why it works:* You'll gain strong eye contact in a way that shows you care.

SOURCE: *Communication Briefings,* as adapted from *Secrets of Power Persuasion*, by Roger Dawson, Prentice Hall, Englewood Cliffs, NJ 07632.

yourself, but the bottom line is your ability to accept yourself as a viable human being. This, does not, of course, allow you to physically, sexually, or psychologically aggress against others.

Self-disclosure is "intentionally letting the other person know who you are by communicating self-revealing information."[3] This revealing can be done through verbal or nonverbal messages.

Whether the atmosphere is supportive or defensive is a large factor in determining how much will be revealed and how vulnerable we will allow ourselves to become. The amount and type of disclosure will also be based on the relationship between the people involved. The deepest level of self-disclosure occurs when two people open themselves in such a way that each can be hurt by the other's actions.

Self-disclosure allows others to understand us as well as allows us to understand ourself. As we talk about ourself, not only the other person is exposed to us; we may learn something about ourself. One of the activities in psychotherapy, for example, is to get a client to talk about herself or himself in order to talk out what is thought and felt, with the intent of having the patient learn who she or he really is.

The Self and Others

Your image of yourself may be referred to as your "I."[4] The **self-perceived I** is the image you project, the way you perceive yourself. It is sent out through the words, ideas, actions, clothing, and lifestyle you choose. All of these communicate your "I" to others.

Those with whom you come into contact also build their own images of you for themselves, and they sometimes communicate this image to you. For example, friends comment about what they like and dislike about you; teachers and parents praise and criticize; significant others and bosses evaluate. These collective judgments by significant others develop into a "Me." The **other-perceived Me** is the person that others perceive you to be. It may be the same or different from your self-perceived I.

One of the best ways to understand how the I-Me dichotomy affects your communication is to examine the entire process as a mathematical formula. Under ideal conditions, we come as close to I = Me (I equals Me) as we can. Just as in algebra, when the equation balances, there is no basic error. If your perception of self (I) and the perception of you held by significant others (Me) are basically the same—if these perceptions balance—then you maintain your equilibrium and continue to function as before. As a result, you continue to communicate in the same manner as previously.

When the I and the Me are not in balance, you have four options for how to react:

1. *You can alter your communication actions.* In doing so, you are attempting to make the specific changes the significant other has indicated. For example, in the play *Our Town*, George, one of the play's young lovers, must decide whether to alter his behavior as a result of a conversation with his girlfriend, Emily. She tells George that he is spending all his time playing baseball and that he has become stuck-up and conceited. As the conversation continues, George offers to buy Emily an ice cream soda to celebrate not only their recent election as class officers but also his good fortune in having a friend who tells him what he should be told. The scene ends with George's promise to take Emily's advice and change his ways.

   We can change on our own or get help from mental health professionals, friends, or relatives. You have probably known someone whose personality changed suddenly, or even over a period of time, because of an alteration of attitudes and ideas as expressed through verbal and nonverbal communication.

2. *You can accept an evaluation by acknowledging that it exists, but for some reason you feel the recommended change is not desirable.* Consequently, you accept the evaluation but do not change. For example, a group member may take the leadership role after a group makes no progress toward accomplishing its goal. Another group member may accuse the newly emerged leader of exerting too much power. Because the group made no previous progress, and is now well on its way to fulfilling its goal, the newly emerged leader may decide to accept the evaluation but not make any changes in her behavior pattern.

3. *You completely reject the input.* You consider the information, decide it is not true, and do nothing about making any changes. This happens, for example, when a student in a speech class, rather than accepting comments about his presentation, refuses to consider any suggestions.

4. *You can ignore any evaluation.* You don't seek out criticism and, if someone attempts to give it, you refuse to even listen to what is said. Ignorers use statements such as "Don't even bother to tell me what you think. I'm not interested." Sometimes you block out all criticism because you find it so self-defeating. Think, for example, of people who adopt the attitude: "I am what I am, and I'll be that way no matter what you say!"

Seeking Approval

A great deal of our interpersonal communication often is spent on trying to get the approval of others. In some instances, people seek approval at the expense of diminishing their self-worth. Some people are so controlled by others, and the fear that others won't like them, or that relatives/friends/employers won't like them that they almost become immobile. Thus, not being able to make decisions for themselves, they turn over their destiny to others.

If you want to eliminate approval-seeking behavior as a major need in your life, keep the following guidelines in mind:

If you think someone else is trying to control you by withholding approval, say so.

When you are faced with disapproval, ask yourself, "If they agreed with me, would I be better off?"

Accept that some will never understand you and that this situation is perfectly acceptable.

You can refuse to argue or try convincing anyone of the rightness of your stance and still simply believe it.

Trust yourself.

Stop verifying your ideas by having them substantiated by others.

Work at eliminating the apologies you make even when you are not wrong or sorry for what you have said or done.

The **self-fulfilled person**—the person who confidently chooses what to reveal and to whom—is not intimidated into a negative self-concept and realizes that there will always be problems, frustrations, and failures in life. He or she has learned to be happy and is, therefore, confident of his or her ability in interpersonal communication.

Emotions

A theory that relates to how the brain works indicates that in the process of human development two brains developed. These parallel to the right and left lobes of the brain. The first brain to develop was the emotional brain (the right lobe), and, therefore, it triggers first. Then the second brain, the logical brain, is triggered.[5] The logical brain contains the information we are taught . . . our reasoning patterns, the rules of civilized behavior, and cultural rules. This also parallels the concept that we instinctively act, then we logically reason to conclusions. It has been estimated that 90 percent of our actions are emotional, and only 10 percent intellectual. It can be said, then, that we make decisions emotionally, not intellectually.[6]

Any message we communicate, therefore, is made up of both logic and emotion. Emotional states include fear, anger, disgust, grief, joy, surprise, and yearning. You probably have grown up believing that you can control your emotions, that anger, fear, and hate, as well as love, ecstasy, and joy are things that happen to you but can be stuffed—held inside, especially if you are a typical North American white male. If you were brought up to believe that it is good to control your emotions, whether they are love or hate; that nice people do not display their emotions; or that big boys do not cry; then this statement may startle you: *there is nothing wrong in expressing your feelings!*

Let us examine one of the most feared interpersonal displays of emotion, that of anger. Anger is a natural, normal emotion. To react with anger to a given situation or set of events is not bad. Anger serves as an emotional defense mechanism to relieve the stress of an overstressful situation. Suppressed anger leads to ill health, emotional disturbance, and a general feeling of unhappiness.[7] Expressions of anger, however, can be constructive or destructive. Letting out your anger by saying how you feel while not verbally or physically attacking another person can be a positive outlet. But physically or verbally abusing a person is not a positive way of showing emotions. If we use someone as a scapegoat, blaming him or her for our own shortcomings, we are not being fair to ourself or to the other person. Each of us must assume responsibility for our feelings and for our reactions to them.

Power

"**Power** is the ability to control what happens—to cause things you want to happen and to block things you don't want to happen."[8]

The hierarchy of power may determine the message sent and received and the effect of that message. Thus people in positions of power—parents, judges, police officers, bosses—are often able to obtain a desired response because of the position they hold. After all, a judge can confine a prisoner; a boss can fire an employee. When these symbols and controls are held over the "victim," the weakness of his or her position becomes obvious.

When we are involved in interpersonal communication, we must recognize that we can lose a great deal by failing to realize the consequences

"Speak when you are angry and you will make the best speech you will ever regret."

Ambrose Bierce on Anger

of what we say and to whom. If a person has the power to control us, we must be willing to pay the price for any show of strength we may make; the price can include losing a job, failing a class, or getting a traffic ticket. If, however, we are in a position of power, we can, if we so desire, demand obedience based purely on our ability to manipulate, reward, and control.

Ideally, the use of power is controlled to the extent that it becomes a tool of cooperation rather than a weapon of punishment. A Hindu proverb should be kept in mind: "There is nothing noble in being superior to another man; true nobility is in being superior to your former self." Realistically, however, we must recognize that many people do not hold this attitude, and we should take this into consideration in our dealings with others.

Your gender is an important aspect of how you perceive and react to anger, power, trust, and self-confidence. Gender considerations are at the base of much of our interpersonal communication.

Male-Female Communication

It is always dangerous to generalize to conclusions. Saying, for example, men are more task-oriented in their communication, while women are more supportive, opens any theorist up to attack. However, much research seems to support that, yes, men and women have differences in the ways in which they communicate, but they also have some similarities. It is also dangerous to say "women," which is taken to mean "all women." Again, research recognizes this. Social science researchers recognizes that not "all" perform exactly in the same way, but that there is a general tendency for the "group" to act that way. For this discussion on male-female communication, you will have to put aside the fact that you, or people you know, don't all act in a particular way, and just go with the communication research trends.

Much attention has been given through the media and pop-psych books to the communication of men and women. Whether examining the play *Return of the Caveman* or the bestseller *Men Are from Mars, Women Are from Venus,* the thesis is the same—men and women communicate differently.

Male and female communication can be examined by looking at sex and gender, how men and women communicate differently, and working toward change in male-female communication differences.

Sex and Gender

"Sex refers to one's biological or physical self while gender refers to one's psychological, social, and interactive characteristics."[9] Recent biological research has "produced a body of findings which paints a remarkably consistent picture of sexual asymmetry. The sexes are different because the brain, the chief administrative and emotional organ of life, is differently constructed in men and in women. It processes information in a different way, which results in different perceptions, priorities and behavior."[10]

These biological underpinnings can have a profound effect on communicating. For example, scientists suggest that the differences in emotional response between men and women can be explained by the differences in the structure and organization of the brain. Because the two halves of a man's brain are connected by a smaller number of fibers than a woman's, the flow of information between one side of the brain and the other is more restricted. It is proposed, therefore, that a woman can express her emotions better in words because what she feels has been transmitted more effectively to the verbal side of her brain.[11]

Parallel to this view are findings about gender. This research shows that "gender is socially constructed. Because the lessons we learn about ourselves and our world are often gender-specific lessons, women and men develop differently. As children and later as adults, females and males are treated differently, so it is hardly surprising that our ways of knowing and ways of being are distinct."[12] "From infancy on, males generally learn masculine traits-independence, self-absorption, competition, aggression."[13] "Men value power, competency, efficiency, and achievement. They are more interested in objects and things than people and feelings."[14] "Females learn feminine traits—dependence, other-absorption, nurturance, sensitivity."[15]

How Men and Women Communicate Differently

"Some people become angry at the mere suggestion that women and men are different."[16] "Recent decades have witnessed two contradictory processes: the development of scientific research into the differences between sexes, and the political denial that such differences exist."[17] In spite of the latter wishes that it isn't so, "research has shown that men and women in our culture use distinctive styles of speech and also tend to play different roles when talking with one another."[18] Therefore, communication theorists have laid to rest the debated question of whether men and women speak differently in the North American culture with the conclusive, "Yes, they do."[19] With this in mind, let us now examine the communication differences.

Communication between men and women is, essentially, cross-cultural communication, sometimes as confusion-ridden as talk between people from two different countries. Because men and women approach one another from distinct worlds, the simplest phrase can carry separate, sometimes conflicting meanings to members of the opposite sex. Men and women use language to contrary purposes and effect. "Men use speech to report, to compete, to gain attention, and to maintain their positions in a social hierarchy. Women use speech to gain rapport, maintain relationships, and reflect a sense of community."[20] Women tend to use language to create intimacy and connection, and men tend to use language to preserve their independence and negotiate their status.

How do these differences develop? Girls and boys grow up in different worlds of words. Boys and girls have very different ways of talking to their friends. Boys tend to play in large groups that are hierarchically structured; there is a leader and/or a competition for leadership; there are winners and losers in the games they play, as well as complex rules. The emphasis is on skill and who is best. Girls tend to play in small groups or pairs and usually have a best friend, intimacy is the key, everyone gets a turn, there are usually no winners and losers, and girls are not expected to boast about their successes. Girls don't generally give orders; they express their preferences as suggestions. Boys say, "Gimme that!" and "Get out of here!" Girls say, "Can we do this?" and "How about doing that?" Gender differences in language can be observed in children as young as age three.[21]

Both male and female styles are valid in their own ways. Misunderstandings arise because the styles are different.

There are general patterns of communication that are identifiably male and female. For example, which of the following are true?

* Women use more words to make their point.

* Men are more competitive in their speaking.

* Men tend to be more task-oriented.

* Women are more supportive conversationalists.

* Men are more direct in their communication.

* Women disclose more personal information to others than men do.

* Women have larger vocabularies for describing emotions and aesthetics.

Yes, *women do use more words to make their point*. Much of this centers on their desire to fill in details and to explain more fully. They tend to be more sensitive to the needs of the listener. Men tend to say what they have to say, assume that the message is clear, and proceed from that point. Therefore, men may believe that women are wasting time, talking too much, or not getting to the point because of the additional effort women spend in clarifying and enlarging.[22]

Yes, *men are more competitive in their speaking.* They have been socialized to "take charge" and get things done. Typically men engage in **competitive turn-taking**, or grabbing the floor by interrupting another speaker. Women have been conditioned from childhood to believe that to interrupt is impolite. Indeed, research on male-female communication patterns found that 96 percent of the interruptions and 100 percent of the overlaps in mixed pairs in daily conversations were performed by men.[23]

Yes, *men do tend to be more task-oriented; women tend to be more maintenance-oriented.* Men tend to want results at any cost. Women are usually more concerned about the process used, about keeping things going smoothly, and about doing business in the least disruptive manner. Women characteristically use tentative phrases such as "I guess," and turn direct statements into indirect ones. For example, a woman may say, "Don't you think it would be better to send that report first?" A man will typically say, "Send the report."[24] Men will say, "What's next on the agenda?" and "What's the bottom line?" Women tend to ask, "You haven't spoken; what do you think?" or "How does everyone feel about this?"

Yes, *women are more supportive conversationalists.* They are much more likely to check the connection of conversations. Women tend to ask more questions and work harder than men do to keep the conversational ball rolling. In fact, women ask questions three times as often as men. Women often feel that it is their role to make sure that the conversation goes well, and they assume that if it is not proceeding well, they have to do something to remedy the situation.

Yes, *men are more direct.* When men want something, they ask for it directly; women tend to be more indirect.[25] A man may ask a woman, "Will you please go to the store?" He wants something; he feels that he has the status to ask for it and get it. But a woman asking a man may say, "Gee, I really need a few things from the store, but I'm so tired." Often she speaks this way because she feels in a low-status position that does not include the right to make a request.[26] A man may well describe the manner in which a woman makes a request as "beating around the bush," and he may ask, "Why, if you want something, don't you just ask for it?" Women also tend to use more **tag questions**, question added onto the end of statements, such as "That movie was terrific, don't you think?" The intent is to get the partner to enter the conversation. Men sometimes construct the tag question as just continuing what has already been discussed.

Yes, findings indicate that *women disclose more personal information than men do.* In their vocabulary selections, females tend to be people-oriented and concerned with internal psychological and emotional states, whereas men are self-oriented and concerned with action.

Yes, *women have larger vocabularies for describing emotions and aesthetics.* Women have been taught to express their feelings, men to hide or disregard theirs. Therefore, women have a larger repertoire of words to describe what they are feeling. Women also have broader vocabularies that can finitely separate aesthetics such as colors. Men, for example, will describe the color as red; women describe specific shadings such as ruby, magenta, and rose. In addition, there may also be some physiological reasons based on brain function that account for females being able to express their emotions and differentiate finite colors.

Other factors that seem to be present in male-female patterns are:

When a man resists a woman's suggestion she feels as though he doesn't care; she feels her needs are not being respected. As a result, she may feel unsupported and stops trusting him.[27] "When a woman resists a man's solutions he feels his competence is being questioned. As a result he feels mistrusted, unappreciated, and stops caring. His willingness to listen understandably lessens."[28]

The most frequently expressed complaint women have about men is that they don't listen. Underlying this is that she wants empathy, yet he thinks she wants solution; she thinks she's nurturing him, while he feels he's being controlled.[29]

"Men are more interested in visual stimulation, physical details. Women are more interested in tactile sensations, emotional overtones, and intimacy."[30]

Additional differences include:[31]

Men offer solutions and invalidate feelings, while women offer unsolicited advice and direction.

Men tend to pull away and silently think about what's bothering them; women feel an instinctive need to talk about what's bothering them.

Men are motivated when they feel needed, while women are motivated when they feel cherished.

Men primarily need a kind of love that is trusting, accepting, and appreciative. Women primarily need a kind of love that is caring, understanding, and respectful.

For the past decade, some people have believed that men need to change, since it is perceived that women are more effective communicators and more sensitive to human needs. In fact, a review of communication books leads to the conclusion that feminine patterns of being supportive, talking through issues, not interrupting, are positive; however, the task orientation, the directness, and the lack of tentativeness of males also gains points.

Some staunch and outspoken feminists have felt that men are taking too long to change, and that women have to take matters into their own hands and be more forceful.[32] Men are accused by some women of making them live in fear, being angry tyrants, focusing only on sex, not feeling, not relating to children, and not understanding a word women say.[33] Men find themselves under scrutiny—if not outright attack through what has been labeled "men bashing."

What could or should be done regarding the cultural differences in male and female communication?

Working Toward Change in Male-Female Communication Differences

What are the implications of these differences in male and female speech and communication needs? One implication is that the divide between the species must be crossed, and the women's movement has looked to androgyny as one solution. **Androgyny** is the internalization of both masculine and feminine language and characteristics so that both men's and women's speech falls further from sex-type extremes and closer to some ground in between.

Another suggestion is to use **genderflex**, which is to "temporarily use communication behaviors typical of the other gender."[34] Genderflex helps each gender increase its potential for influence. It is based on the premise that men and women have different communication styles, structures, and content and both are acceptable.

Here are some suggestions of how to put genderflex into action for men speaking to women:[35]

✳ Use examples that stress people, feelings, and relationships.

✳ Avoid a lecture style. Women, in particular, feel more comfortable with an interactive approach.

✳ Use anecdotes about successful women, as well as successful men.

✳ Don't offer unwanted solutions.

✳ When a woman rejects your ideas, understand that your timing and/or delivery are being rejected, not your solution. Don't take it personally.

Suggestions of how to put genderflex into action for women speaking to men include:

✳ Use more humor—but never the self-effacing type. Use anecdotes, stories, and jokes.

✳ Avoid disclaimers, apologies, and qualifiers.

✳ Use power words and phrases when appropriate.

✳ Don't reject him or his ideas just because he is a "man."

Although those interested in gender communication want to believe there have been drastic changes in male-female relationships based on communication style changes, little conclusive research exists to demonstrate that a true elimination of sex-role communication differences has occurred.[36] Our behavioral choices continue to be limited by sex stereotypes—how males and females are "supposed" to be and behave.

Accepting the theory that men and women live in different worlds, even under the same roof, means that to understand and accept each other, both must try to take the other on their own terms rather than applying the standards of one group to the language usage of the other.

Habitual ways of talking are hard to change. Learning to respect others' ways of talking may be a bit easier. Mutual acceptance will at least prevent the pain of being told you are doing something wrong when you are only doing things your way.[37]

 ## Sexual Harassment

"Human communication performs a central yet complex role in sexual harassment. Communication is the primary medium through which sexual harassment is expressed; it is the means by which those who are harassed respond to harassment, and it is also the primary means by which policies for eliminating sexual harassment can be implemented.[38] **Sexual harassment** may be described as "generalized sexist remarks or behavior; inappropriate and offensive, but essentially sanction-free, sexual advances; solicitation of sexual activity or other sex-linked behavior by promise of rewards; coercion of sexual activity by threat of punishment; and assaults."[39] It also includes "unwanted and unwelcome sexual actions in work and educational contexts."[40]

The effect of sexual harassment, as a communicative event, was summarized by writer Toni Morrison in her 1993 acceptance speech for the Nobel Prize for literature when she stated, "Oppressive language does more than violence . . . it is violence."[41]

Sexual harassment is a serious and pervasive problem in modern organizational life, with both the targets and those accused (falsely or not)

A Sexual Harassment Quiz

Here are some questions, based on court rulings in sexual harassment cases. Answer "true" or "false."

1. A single incident or statement does not normally constitute sexual harassment.

2. If a person participates voluntarily in an unwelcome sexual relationship, sexual harassment is not an issue.

3. The courts recognize that fear of retaliation can prevent a victim from communicating that a harasser's conduct is unwelcome—even though the victim is expected to communicate this fact.

4. For vulgar language or sexual flirtation to be considered as creating a hostile environment, behavior has to adversely affect the working environment—in the judgment of a reasonable person.

5. If a sexual harassment problem is common knowledge at work, the employer is presumed to know about it.

6. Displaying "girlie" pictures can constitute a hostile work environment—even though some workers think they are harmless.

Answers: 1. True. Usually a sustained pattern is necessary—unless the incident was severe or physical. 2. False. The Supreme Court has ruled that voluntariness is not a defense. 3. True. 4. True. 5. True. 6. True.

SOURCE: *Communication Briefings,* as adapted from *Working Together,* by Andrea P. Baridon and David R. Eyler, McGraw-Hill Inc., 1221 Avenue of the Americas, New York, NY 10020.

suffering personal anguish and dehumanization.[42] A survey of female employees found that 43 percent had experienced sexual harassment.[43]

Sexual harassment takes place not only in the workplace but on college campuses. Students at one university report that as many as 89 percent of women experienced sexual harassment at least once, and that many experienced it more than once.[44]

"Sexual harassment is experienced primarily by women."[45] This does not mean that men are not also victims. However, in our society, where men may perceive a come-on as positive, women perceive the same advances as negative. Men, therefore, instead of feeling like victims, may perceive harassment as an ego booster, a cause for bragging.

Men's perceptions of what their behavior means are vastly different from women's. The harasser may see himself as intending to exercise his power over women, protect his professional turf, enhance his macho self-image, and demonstrate his friendliness and helpfulness. The harassed may want to stop the harassment; deter future incidents; preserve her reputation; avoid retaliation; maintain rapport; and preserve self-respect, physical safety, and psychological well-being.[46]

Sexual harassment has not changed over the years. "What has changed is that people now are more willing to label these behaviors as being sexual harassment, people are more willing to talk about it, and people are more angry about it."[47]

Responding to Sexual Harassment

One of the questions often asked regarding sexual harassment is, "What should I do if I were a recipient of unwelcome behavior? In general, if you question a person's actions as being inappropriate:[48]

✳ *Trust your instincts.*

✳ *Don't blame yourself.* You are the victim, not the perpetrator. A common ploy by harassers is to intimate that the victim brought it on, encouraged the actions/advances by the type of clothing she or he wore, the way the person looked at them, the type of language the person used. In almost all instances, this is a ploy to turn the innocent person into the guilty party. Those people with weak self-concepts often fall for this ploy.

✳ *Get emotional support.* Turn to a mental health professional, an expert in harassment, or a support telephone service/line that deals with harassment.

✳ *Say no clearly and early to the individual whose behavior and/or comments make you uncomfortable.* Don't allow the person to continue with the harassing actions or verbalizations. Call a halt to it immediately by saying emphatically, "I will not (allow you to speak to me like that), or (put up with that type of talk), or (allow you to touch me)."

✳ *Document every incident in detail.* Keep a record. Write down everything that happened including exactly what was said/done, with dates and times, and any other supporting evidence. Share the information with another person to verify the acts have taken place. If possible, get a witness to attest to the action(s).

✳ *Find a way to speak out.* Make a statement to someone in the personnel or human resources department of your organization, alert your supervisor, confront the perpetrator.

✳ *Seek out supportive individuals.* More and more businesses and institutions are designating safe zones. A safe zone is a person or department responsible for providing resources for persons who perceive that they have been harassed.

✳ *Seek out institutional and company channels and use them.*

✳ *File a charge with a local, state, or federal antidiscrimination agency if necessary.* As with any legal action, it will be your responsibility to prove the harassing actions/verbalizations. Be sure you can document the accusations.

If a friend shares that he or she has been or is being harassed, you should:

✳ *Listen without judging.*

✳ *Validate that sexual harassment is wrong.*

✳ *Offer to help explore resources and support the recipient's efforts to seek help.*

✳ *Be prepared for displaced anger as the recipient may not be able to channel it appropriately.* In some instances, when a person is feeling stressed, she or he will attack the nearest source. So, don't be surprised if the victim turns her or his wrath on you, even if you are trying to be helpful. The person is not really attacking you, just acting out of frustration.

✳ *Offer affirmation to the recipient that whatever feelings are being expressed are his/her right to have.* Victims sometimes are confused and don't trust their own judgment. They need affirmation as to their rights and responsibilities.

✳ *Reassure the recipient that you care and are there to be supportive.* Offer to be of assistance in whatever way you can, but be aware that you are not the person who was harassed.

✳ *Do not take matters into your own hands but, rather, help the individual to find the appropriate channels either inside or outside of the company.* Unless you are a lawyer or a mental health professional, be aware of your limitations.

Relationships and Their Development

Throughout our lives, we find ourselves in relationships with other people—parents, siblings, and friends. After all, most of us do not suddenly grow up and no longer need caring and nurturing contact with others. This reality makes it extremely important that we understand how relationships develop, how they continue, what constitutes a positive relationship, why we turn to others, and how to communicate effectively within the structure of a relationship.

Development of a Relationship

Relationships vary so greatly that it is almost impossible to formulate any rules about them. Nevertheless, some general principles explain how they develop.[49] Within the first moments of a relationship, internal [intrapersonal] decisions are being formulated that can determine the functions and goals of the relationship. Whether the relationship will be primarily task-oriented, friendship-oriented, or intimate-oriented will more often than not be formulated with the initial interaction.[50]

When two persons meet for the first time, their levels of uncertainty about each other and themselves are fairly high. This uncertainty is generated because people can behave in a number of ways; thus, accurate prediction of behavior and beliefs is difficult. And initial encounters can cause uncertainty in the future as well, because predicting behavior is always difficult and little or no information has been exchanged between the two.

Powerful barriers to establishing intimate connections exist: *fear of exposure* (the decision not to tell certain things as they may be perceived as weaknesses or make you an undesirable partner); *fear of abandonment* (if the relationship begins, what happens if the other person decides to leave it?); *fear of reprisal/attack* (what if something goes wrong and the other person physically or verbally assaults me?); *fear of loss of control* (especially a male issue based on not being able to make decisions for and about oneself); *fear of loss of individuality* (the potential loss of *me* as *I* and *you* become a *we*); and *fear of creating a power imbalance* (the potential for relinquishing power to the partner, thus losing my own power).

Think back to your first meeting with a good friend, your spouse/lover, or a coworker. What went on during that first contact? Why did you decide to pursue the relationship? Did your attitudes change as you got to know the person better? How long did it take you to decide to pursue the relationship? We ask all these questions each time we contact others and decide how far to allow the interaction to go.

It is also recognized that the development of intimacy is difficult. Intimacy depends on acceptance of self, acceptance of others, clear communication, maintaining a balance of power, maintaining a balance of independence and interdependence, and knowledge of the sequential patterns of relational development and maintenance.

Relationships do have a sequential pattern: an *entry phase* (beginning), a *personal phase* (middle), and an *exit phase* (end). But each relationship does not necessarily move through the stages at the same rate. The personalities and needs of the participants determine the rapidity of the movement through the state.

In the **entry relational development phase**, biographical information and general attitudes are exchanged. In the **personal relational phase**, information about central attitudes and values is exchanged. In the **exit relational stage**, questions concerning the future of the relationship are raised and resolved. This stage may include an agreement to continue the affiliation (continuing the personal phase) or terminate it.

Continuing a Relationship

People make judgments about interpersonal contacts by comparing relational rewards and costs—the **economic model of relationships**.[51] As long as rewards are equal to or exceed costs, the relationship becomes more intimate; however, once costs exceed rewards the relationship begins to stagnate and eventually to dissolve.

If one person believes that the investment (**relational costs**) of such factors as money, time, and emotion is met with such factors as security and affection (**relational rewards**), then that person will want to continue the relationship. If he or she is doing all the giving and the partner is only taking, however, then the relationship will probably end.

With this in mind, examine a friendship. Why have you continued to associate with this person? You probably do so because you receive at least as much as you are giving from knowing and being with the person. In contrast, if you have taken the initiative to end an association with someone, your action was probably caused by your belief that you were giving too much and not receiving enough, that the relationship was tilted against you or one-sided.

Positive Relationships

A good relationship allows freedom of expression and reflects acceptance of the idea that the feelings of both people are important. We should remember, however, that any alliance experiences times of uncertainty and anxiety. The persons may change as individuals, what appeared to be fulfilling the economic model may no longer do so, and the reason for the relationship may cease to be.

We must also recognize that we cannot achieve happiness through someone else. If it is to be found, it must be found within ourself. Unfortunately, it is this desire to find happiness in someone else that

Communication is the key
to creating and maintaining
positive relationships.

causes us to try changing people we supposedly love, when in fact our love
should allow them to be themselves and do what they feel is best for themselves. Love is the ability and willingness to allow those that you care for
to be what they choose for themselves without any insistence that they satisfy you. Unfortunately, this idea is easier to present as a concept than to
live as a reality. Most of us spend a great deal of our time trying to alter
and change the people we supposedly love.

Communication is the key to creating and maintaining positive relationships. Research shows that couples who are happily married argue no
less vigorously for their own positions than do those who are not happily
married. But happily married couples come to agreement fairly readily,
through either one partner giving in to the other without resentment, or
compromise. Unhappily married people tend to get caught in a situation

that seems like cross-complaining. Neither partner is willing to come halfway to resolve a dispute; each must continue to have his or her own way.[52]

One theory of successful relational communication centers on five guidelines for making a relationship flourish:

1. *When you are speaking, get into the habit of using "I" messages instead of "you" messages.* Indicate what you are feeling or how you are reacting to the situation rather than accusing the other person. Say "I feel . . ." or "I think . . ." rather than "You did . . ." or "You make me . . . ." Report facts to back up your contentions. Rather than saying, "You are always late" try "I get angry when you tell me you will be here at 2:00 and you arrive at 2:45."

2. *Respond to what the other person has said.* When you go off on a tangent without first having replied to the original statement, you are catching the other person unaware.

3. *Give the other person freedom of speech.* If you want to have the opportunity to state your view you must also be willing to hear out the other person.

4. *Set aside frequent talking time just for the two of you.* We often get so busy that we forget to talk to each other. Don't assume the other person knows what you are thinking.

5. *Do not put labels on either yourself or the other person.* Name calling doesn't solve issues; stating the issue and discussing it can possibly solve it or, at least, get it out into the open.[53]

Also, watch out for some specific communication patterns that cause conflict in intimate relationships. Included among these are blaming, putting someone down, or teasing. In the case of teasing, what can start out as fun usually has an underlying message behind it that is not humor. When people get angry, the labeling can become the source of attack and conflict.

Game playing can also result in relational trouble. Such activities as trying to make a person measure up to preset expectations, making an individual prove how much he or she loves you, and forcing someone with whom you have a relationship to follow your wishes can result in conflicts that are unreconcilable.

Another problem occurs when you attempt to make your partner fuse with you or vice versa. **Relational fusion** takes place when one partner defines, or attempts to define, reality for the other. In other words, the controller dictates what is good, right, and acceptable for the partner. If the partner, at first, allows that to happen, the pattern for the future can be set. Then, when the defined partner wants to break the pattern, abuse may result.

People who are unhappy in their relationships tend to talk at each other, past each other, or through each other, but rarely with or to each other. Just because you're talking doesn't mean you are communicating. Though couples may spend time talking to each other, many lack the skills needed to get their messages across effectively, to express their feelings, or to resolve conflicts without hurting each other or provoking anger.

Communication in Relationships

All relationships have a structure, and each person has a role he or she plays. As long as no one changes the system and each member of the relationship maintains his or her assigned role, the structure is working. But if someone wants alterations, wants to do things that are not normally done, then the system becomes a **dysfunctional system**. A system that is operating to the general satisfaction of the participants is a **functional system**. Assume, for example, that you are dating someone. You and that person look forward to your times together. When conflicts do arise, you are capable of working out the problems without destroying the relationship or building up bad feelings. In contrast, a dysfunctional system is one in which its members are confused about the roles they are to play. For example, if a woman who has been a housewife decides to go to college, there will have to be a redistribution in the family of her former chores, and the family's old system of operation will be thrown out of kilter. Some members in the system may not want to change roles. The husband may not want to do the cooking or child care, or the children may resent not having their mother around. Before the system can become normal again, a new balance will have to be established. This does not mean that the system has to return to the past mode of operation, but a mode of operation in which a pattern of cooperation exists must be instituted.

This does not mean to suggest that dysfunctional systems are not operational. The individuals in the relationship may continue to function quite effectively as they make changes. The usual result of the dysfunction, however, is confusion because each person lacks clarity about what role to play and what rules to follow. For example, questions and protests may arise as to who is responsible for the tasks formerly done by the mother and wife who is now going to college. Common complaints may include "Why should I have to make the meals now?" or "I've never cooked before and it's not fair for that job to be shoved onto me."

The need to reestablish a system is not necessarily disastrous. In fact, most relationships go through adjustments on a regular basis. As a system is being **recalibrated**—restructured—growth can take place. People learn to assume new roles, develop new respect for each other, or make a new team effort. On the other hand, chaos may result as people fight for new role identities, defend their emotional territories, or feel compelled to make changes not to their liking.

In a positive relationship, the participants attempt to adjust to alterations in the normal patterns so that the dysfunctional period is kept to a minimum. This usually takes place because the partners in the dyad (a relationship of two people) have developed effective communication skills and a positive method for solving problems.

Ending Relationships

Whenever we enter any type of relationship, we pay a price for it. A relationship takes time, energy, and commitment. It means giving up freedom, and it means considering another person, adapting to another person, even changing our lives to accommodate another person. When we enter into a relationship, there are possibilities not only for mutual sharing but also mutual or individual hurt.

Whether we are dealing with dating, friendship, or marriage, we must realize that these relationships will not go on forever. Rather, we must accept that the ending of relationships is part of the life cycle. We grow up, relocate, change jobs, have different needs, grow in different directions, and ultimately die. We must realize that just as change is inevitable, so are endings, unless you believe in life everlasting life-after-death, or reincarnation.

The breakup of a relationship can cause hurt. And this hurt usually comes with the realization that there has been heavy emotional and sometimes physical investment. At such times, we feel loss, question who we are, feel alone, search for the reason for the break, and sometimes experience guilt. These emotional difficulties are compounded when one party wants to terminate the relationship and the other does not.

Of course, endings can take many forms. In some cases, the people decide on a mutual split, go their separate ways, and feel little regret. In some cases, as, for instance, when you were a child and your best friend moved, you tried to keep in touch for a while and then your interests and need for each other faltered, and eventually memories faded away. Other times, the breaking is more difficult. It is possible to leave a relationship, if not on a positive note, at least with a feeling of not being rejected or with some gain from the experience. This sort of ending is most likely to occur in a face-to-face meeting in which the participants take time to discuss their own observations and inferences about the relationship and each other in a productive fashion. Though this is seldom done, it can be an insightful experience.

Some relationships end with individuals agreeing to "still be friends." This is very difficult. Being friends is not the same as being in an intimate relationship. Much time and effort often has gone into the relationship, and reverting to a shallow version of the former relationship is almost impossible.

Unfortunately, the endings of most relationships tend to be charged with tension and hostility over feelings of failure and rejection.

IN CONCLUSION →   This chapter dealt with interpersonal communication, with specific emphasis on self-disclosure and relationships. Interpersonal communication is an interactional process in which meaning is stimulated through the sending and receiving of messages between two people. Our interpersonal communication is made up of both logic and emotion. The role of power is important in any relationship. The sequential pattern of a relationship is the entry phase (beginning), the personal phase (middle), and the exit phase (end). People make judgments about interpersonal relationships based on comparisons of rewards and costs. In a functional system, members are clear about the roles they are to play. Males and females do not communicate in the same way.

LEARN BY DOING →   1. Think of an interpersonal problem you have had. Then on a three-by-five-inch card describe your role and the role taken by the other person. The class will be divided into groups of three. Read your card to the other two people in your group, and find out how each of them would have handled the situation. After the discussion, tell them what you did and what the outcome was.

2. Relate to the class a recent personal experience that illustrates the action-reaction principle.

3. Think back to a relationship you have had that has ended. Examine it from the standpoint of the sequential pattern discussed in the chapter.

4. What do you consider the most difficult part of developing a relationship? Give examples to back up your contention.

5. Relate an experience you had in which power was an important element in a relationship. Was the power used to aid or destroy the rela-

tionship? If the power structure had been eliminated, would the relationship have been the same? Why? Why not?

6. Relate a personal experience in which your emotions totally dominated your logic and you said or did something for which you were sorry later.

7. Discuss the statement "Sometimes you have to blow your own horn because no one else knows how to play the tune."

8. Be prepared to take a stand on these topics:

   a. Men are being verbally bashed by women as women attempt to get what they call equal rights.

   b. Stereotyping males and females by their communication patterns is a disservice as it teaches people how others act and sets those patterns for others to follow.

   c. The pop-psychology treatment of male and female communication has trivialized the valid research on the subject.

KEY TERMS →

interpersonal communication
action-reaction principle
self-talk
self-concept
self-love
self-disclosure
self-perceived I
other-perceived Me
self-fulfilled person
power
competitive turn-taking
tag questions
androgyny

genderflex
sexual harassment
entry relational development phase
personal relational phase
exit relational stage
economic model of relationships
relational costs
relational rewards
relational fusion
dysfunctional system
functional system
recalibrated system

chapter 7

Interpersonal Skills

After reading this chapter, you should be able to:

Explain the presentational, listening, and nonverbal concepts of conversation

State the rules for giving details, organizing ideas, and using appropriate terms in giving directions

Discuss the process of ascertaining information, asking for change, and questioning

Define conflict and interpersonal conflict

Explain negotiation, avoidance, accommodation, smoothing over, compromise, competition, integration, and fighting fair as ways to deal with conflict

Differentiate among the win-lose, lose-lose, and win-win styles of negotiation

Demonstrate the simple, empathic, follow-up assertions, and DESC scripting

Explain techniques for handling rejection and criticism

Every day you participate in the act of interpersonal communication. You converse with friends, negotiate with members of your family, become involved in conflicts, and send messages to and receive messages from your instructors. To participate successfully in all these interactions, you need to master certain interpersonal skills, including how to participate in conversations, give directions, request, ask, resolve conflicts, accomplish goals, and handle rejection and criticism.

Participating in Conversations

A **conversation** is an interaction with at least one other person. Almost all of us possess basic conversational skills. Nevertheless, some people try to avoid conversations. Others have difficulty starting and maintaining social interactions even if they are not communicatively apprehensive. Still others need improvement in their conversational skills.

Conversational Presentation Skills

Conversations usually start with small talk and then move to more in-depth sharing. **Small talk** is an exchange of information with someone on a surface level. It takes place at informal gatherings, parties, bars, and meetings. The information exchange centers on biographics (name, occupation or college major, hometown, college attended or attending) or slightly more personal information (hobbies, interests, future plans, acquaintances). Small talk usually goes on for about fifteen minutes, and then in-depth conversation starts. The ground level of communication has been passed when people start talking about personal matters, such as attitudes, beliefs, goals, and specific ways of behaving, or express the desire for social or business interaction, such as a date, a business lunch, or a visit to each other's residence.

You will find that people usually like to talk about themselves and their experiences. For example, you can ask about where a person lives, what it is like to live there, what his or her job is. You can ask whether a person likes the job and how she or he chose it. The key to good conversation is to hit on a common interest between you and the other person.

Other approaches can help you to become a good conversationalist. Keep track of current events; watch nonverbal clues; show interest; if you disagree and want to state your opinion but do not want to offend, try to be tactful. You can say, for instance, "I see your point, but have you considered. . . ." Another approach is to make a comment about an aspect of the situation you are both in or an observation about the person you are

Handling Tough Conversations

If you want to avoid potential stress for you and those you're dealing with, consider these suggestions when you think you're going to be in a stressful conversation:

* **Begin** with agreement. If you know you're going to be disagreeing with someone, start off your discussion with some area on which you both agree. Even if it requires really digging to uncover that common ground, do it.

* **Say** "and"—not "but." "But" acts like an eraser inside people's heads. It erases the value of anything said before it in a sentence.

* **Use lots** of "I" statements. Limit "you" statements. "I" clarifies for the other person what you think and feel, while "you" can make a person feel criticized. "I" also reduces defensiveness and fosters communication.

SOURCE: *Communication Briefings,* as adapted from *Career Success: Personal Stress,* by Christine A. Leatz with Dr. Mark W. Stolar. McGraw-Hill Inc., 11 W. 19th St., New York, NY 10011.

talking with. Say something positive about the person's appearance, ask for advice, or ask a question.

Questions are powerful devices for building conversations. In using questions, remember:

1. *Questions encourage people to open up by drawing them out* (e.g., What university do you go to? What's your major? I've been considering switching my major to communication; do you think that's a good idea?).

2. *Questions aid you in discovering the other's attitudes* (e.g., Why did you decide to be a communication major?)

3. *Questions keep the conversation to the topic at hand.* Whenever a response is irrelevant, ask a follow-up question that probes for more information about the topic (e.g., What do you feel the future job market is for communication majors?).

4. *Questions can be used to direct the conversation.* A question can change the topic, probe for more information, or keep the conversation going.

5. *Questions help you gain information and clarify meanings.* If what the person says is not clear, you can ask for definitions or examples or ask for the source or basis of information.

To use questioning most effectively, start with easy questions, ask short questions, after each question wait for an answer, and let your partner know you are listening by giving nonverbal feedback such as "Uh huh" and "oh," while you are looking at the person.

One of the biggest problems for people who are nervous about conversations is staying calm and not giving themselves negative messages like, "I'm really messing this up." Periods of silence are all right. If the other person does not want to talk to you, that is his or her loss, not yours. You act as your own worst enemy if you convince yourself that you cannot carry on a conversation and that the other person is superior to you.

Remember that some people are difficult to get to know and that there are some people you may not want to get to know any better. The small talk at the start of a conversation often gives you and a new acquaintance an opportunity to determine whether a closer relationship merits exploring.

Also be aware that not all people converse in the same way. In this country we are constantly coming into contact with people who are from other cultures. In general, white male North American conversations are focused—getting right to the point. Behind this is the assumption that a speaker ought to know explicitly the idea or information he or she wishes to convey. North Americans speak in thought patterns emphasizing analysis, which dissects events and concepts into pieces that can be linked into chains and categorized. **Analytical thinking** is not typical for all cultures, however. **Holistic thinking**, which doesn't dissect events or concepts, is more typical in South American and Asian cultures and people descended from those cultures.[1] Storytelling is common in holistic thinking, as a form of interacting. Though the stories may be interesting, they sometimes confuse North Americans, since the stories don't answer questions and often don't come to conclusions.

In addition, Americans, in general, are open to approaching strangers, often start conversations with strangers, and are responsive to strangers who approach them. Other cultures are not as open to invasion of personal space. Asians are generally more standoffish toward strangers, are more reluctant to approach them, and respond less favorably to conversations initiated by people they do not know.[2]

Conversational Listening Skills

Listening is a very important part of conversations. People who can converse with strangers are invariably good listeners. To be a good listener, learn how to paraphrase the speaker's ideas, repeat the person's name as you are introduced, continue to use the name during the conversation as it will help you remember it and make the other person feel that you are centering on him/her, maintain eye contact, and listen to clues for what topics are of interest to the other conversant. But be sure to allow the speaker to finish her or his point before you respond to it, because interruptions can be very annoying, especially to North American women and those from mannerly cultures (e.g., Japan). More specific suggestions about listening in conversations include:

Listen to the concerns of others. Conversations should be two-sided. Both people should get an opportunity to participate. Often people ask questions only so that they can give their own answers. You already know what you think. If you are interested in a conversation, not in giving a personal speech, find out what others think and address their ideas. Nothing is more deadly than an I-I conversation.

Don't assume. Too often we assume one thing and later find we were mistaken. Because physical and oral first impressions are not always accurate, give the other person a chance to prove he or she is worthy of your conversation or repugnant enough to cast aside.

Before speaking, ask yourself what message is needed. Many people do not like to participate in small talk because it appears to offer no opportunity for in-depth discussion or because finding out little tidbits about people whom they are not interested in seems a waste of time. These contentions may be true, but you cannot get to know a person to the degree necessary to have in-depth conversations until you get to know him or her on a basic level and build rapport. People who start right off by stating strong viewpoints and getting too personal are often rebuffed.

Conversational Nonverbal Skills

Nonverbal communication plays an important role in conversation. If you do not think so, pay attention to the facial expressions and postures of the person you are talking to. For example, quick glances away may indicate that the person is anxious to leave, and the same may be implied when that person glances repeatedly at a watch, looks around the room, or shifts from one foot to the other. If, however, the person leans forward, is intently looking at you, or is directly facing you, then the interaction is probably positive. Judge whether to continue or end the interaction based on these cues.

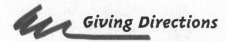

Giving Directions

We often find ourselves giving other people **directions**. These can include instructions for accomplishing a task, achieving an effect, or getting some-

When giving directions, try to be as specific as possible.

where. In giving directions, you are wise to include all the necessary details, organize the ideas in a specific order, and use terms that can be clearly understood.

Giving Details

How many times have you asked someone for directions and been given only a very general description? Others assume that because they know what they are talking about, you do too. "Go down the street to the corner and make a right" may be very clear if you know what street and which corner the person means. Unfortunately, such is not always the case. On the other hand, too many details can be confusing.

Have you ever attempted to assemble an electronic device that was accompanied by vague directions? The frustration can be great because the directions are commonly written by the experts who designed the item. They often assume that you can figure out what to do simply because they can.

When giving directions, try to be as specific as possible. Include such information as names, references (north, south; left, right), descriptions (the size of the item, a sketch of what it looks like), and warnings about where confusion may set in. The procedure should be the same whether you are giving travel directions, assembly information, or a recipe.

Organizing Ideas

Directions are easiest to follow when given in either a chronological or a spatial order. In a chronological order, you indicate the step-by-step procedure by telling what is to be done first, second, third, and so on. This is a good method to use when explaining how something should be assembled.

Spatial orders involve providing descriptions according to geographic directions. A travel plan from the auto club indicating the exact place where you start and the place-by-place order of the cities you will go through is an example of directions that are in spatial order.

Knowing if someone is a linear or global thinker (see Chapter 3 for details and a test to determine your style) can aid you to understand how to package the directions. Linear thinkers prefer maps and written out directions. Global thinkers prefer pictures and oral directions with specific landmarks (the identification of landmarks such as restaurants and gas stations by name).

Using Understandable Terms

If a person cannot understand the directions, then the explanation is of no value. For this reason, make sure that any terms you use are clear or, if you think they might not be, define them. The prospect of operating a computer is often more terrifying than it should be because in many instances the operational procedures are written in computer jargon rather than Standard English. No wonder so many people have computer phobia! Unfortunately, in the case of many computer manuals, the writers appear not to have taken the potential user into consideration, although increased pressure has caused some manufacturers to make manuals more "user friendly" by defining terms and writing from the consumer's standpoint.

Requesting

Requesting is the process of expressing a desire for something. The request, in some instances, takes on the form of a demand. Requests usually fall into one of two categories: requesting information or asking.

Requesting Information

When you request information, specify the exact nature of the information you want and make the request in specific language that includes a suggestion as to how the request is to be carried out. If you ask the research librar-ian, for example, to tell you about Lucerne, Switzerland, she or he can give you volumes of information. But what specifically do you want to know? Maybe you are interested in finding out the most recent population statis-tics. Whatever your interest, try to be as specific as possible.

If you are not presenting the request in person, indicate how you wish to receive the reply—by phone, E-mail, letter, or in person. If the information must be received by a deadline, be sure to specify this as well. This rounds off the entire process so that you and the other person both understand exactly what is wanted and how the request is to be processed.

Asking

People often do not ask questions because they are afraid to do so, do not know how to ask them, or do not know what to ask. Gaining the skills in-volved in **asking**—seeking out information by inquiring—will help you to eliminate misunderstandings, aid you in ensuring receipt of your in-tended message, reassure you that you gained the proper information, and convince the sender that you really do understand.

Asking Questions   Asking questions is important to effective communica-tion. If, for example, a person receives directions to institute a new proce-dure at work, he or she may need to ask questions of the supervisor or trainer who is providing the instructions. A worker who is reluctant to ask for clarification for fear of appearing uninformed is probably just creating more problems for himself or herself. Later, when called on to actually perform the new procedure, the worker may be unable to do so. Re-member, if it is important for a person to know, it is important for her or him to ask.

When you ask questions that probe for information, word the queries in a way so that the listener will know exactly what you need. To do this, determine what it is that you do not understand. Ask a specific question that will clarify your dilemma. If you cannot identify what you do not un-derstand, recognize that confusion usually centers on the need for restate-ment, definition, and/or clarification.

Asking for Restatement   Sometimes in explaining, people state their ideas in such a way that they are unclear. This may be caused by the order in which the ideas were presented. For example, an explanation of an ac-counting procedure that does not tell the first step, second step, and so on will probably lead to confusion. In this case, ask for the ideas to be pre-sented in a step-by-step sequence. This is especially true if you are a linear listener/learner. Linear listeners generally need a clear step-by-step structure to organize the ideas, thus leading to clarity.

Asking for Definitions   Unclear vocabulary is a major problem in the understanding of information. Asking someone to define his or her terms often clears up the misunderstanding. This is usually the problem, for example, with physicians who use medical terms to explain a patient's illness. Many professionals forget that the average person does not have much expertise in the subject and, therefore, does not have access to technical terminology. An explanation appropriate to the layperson's vocabulary is necessary.

Each time you are introduced to a new subject area, you must learn its vocabulary. Chemistry, psychology, and communication, for example, all have a special vocabulary. Students who fail these subjects often do so because they are weak in the subject's vocabulary. In asking for definition, be specific. Ask, "What does [fill in the word] mean?"

Asking for Clarification   Sometimes the basic information in a communication message is simply not enough. In this case, clarification can be achieved through the use of examples, illustrations, and analogies for the clarification. For example, while listening to a lecture, you will find that the first few sentences dealing with each new concept tell the idea, and the rest of the statements clarify. Sometimes, however, senders forget to give examples, illustrations, or analogies. If the illustrations used are not clear, ask for new or additional ones. This is especially true if you are a global listener/learner. Global listeners generally need examples to clarify and make abstract ideas concrete.

As you sit in class, as you participate in a medical examination, as you are being trained to operate a piece of equipment, try to paraphrase what the speaker is saying. If you cannot do so, you probably do not understand the message. In that case, ask questions . . . specific questions!

Dealing with Interpersonal Conflict

When you hear the word *conflict*, what do you think? If you are fairly typical, your list includes such terms as a *fight, dissension, friction, strife,* and *confrontation.* These terms tend to be negative, and many of us have been taught to think of conflict as a totally negative experience, something to be avoided at all costs. In truth, conflict in and of itself is a natural process that can be negative or positive, depending on how it is used. The Chinese word for conflict or crisis is made up of two components (Figure 7.1).

Figure 7.1
In Chinese the words *danger* and *opportunity* are components of the word *crisis*.

The top one stands for "danger" and the bottom part stands for "opportunity." Most people recognize the danger part in a crisis or conflict, but few recognize the opportunity. Conflict can promote relational changes, bring people together, precipitate personal growth, and aid in gaining personal and relational insights.

Conflict Defined

"A **conflict** is any situation in which you perceive that another person, with whom you're interdependent, is frustrating or might frustrate the satisfaction of some concern, need, want, or desire of yours."[3] "The source of conflict or crisis could be your perception of a limited resource (such as money) or an individual difference between you and the other person (such as differences in gender or differences in how you and the other person define your relationship).[4] Conflict is part of everyone's life.

The process of conflict begins when one person perceives that another person has caused him or her to experience some type of frustration; thus they experience interference from each other in accomplishing their goals.[5] This frustration, if put into words, would sound like: "I want _____ (your personal concern, need, want), but _____ (the person perceived as frustrating you) wants _____ (his or her concern, need, want). From these feelings or statements comes a conflict or crisis situation in which incompatible activities occur. These activities prevent, block, or interfere with each other or in some way irritate the participants. "Any situation in which one person perceives that another person, with whom he or she is interdependent, is interfering with his or her goal achievement may be defined as a conflict situation. . . . If it is not expressed in some way, but kept bottled up inside, it is an intrapersonal conflict."[6]

Some people may try to avoid conflict at any cost. In fact, one study indicated that "students try to avoid about 56 percent of their conflicts. They become skilled at turning away from conflict."[7] This sort of behavior is generally not desirable. Conflict can be healthy because it allows for the communication of differing points of view, which can lead to important awareness and changes.

Just as conflict can serve a useful function, so too can it be detrimental. Conflict is detrimental when it stops you from doing your work; threatens the integrity of a relationship; endangers the continuation of a relationship or your ability to function within it; causes physical, mental, or sexual abuse; or leads a person to give up and become inactive in a relationship or life in general.

Not all cultures deal with conflict in the same way. In most of the Middle Eastern and Mediterranean cultures, which are considered **conflict active societies**, conflict is accepted as an important part of life, and men, especially, take great delight and pleasure in haggling and arguing. Haggling is expected when purchasing goods in many Central and South American and Arabic countries. People from **conflict avoidance societies** believe that face-to-face confrontations are to be avoided.[8] Asians find

Resolve Conflict in 4 Steps

Resolve conflict with co-workers, family or friends by following this four-step, interest-based conflict resolution process:

* **Identify** the interests of the disputants. Ask each person, "What do you want?" Then listen to the answer you get.

* **Identify** higher levels of interest by asking, "What does having that do for you?" Too often we dig into a position and refuse to budge or consider alternatives. It is important to understand what people really want.

* **Create an** agreement frame by asking, "If I could show you how to get X, would you do

Y?" X is the person's real interest, and Y is what you want from the person.

* **Brainstorm** for solutions together to find a win-win solution. Do not just hand a solution to the other person and expect him or her to accept it. You get commitment by getting people involved in finding a solution. The solutions must satisfy the interests of all parties.

SOURCE: *Communication Briefings,* as adapted from Terry Bragg, Peacemakers Training, 5485 S. Chaparral Drive, Murray, UT 84123.

haggling distasteful.[9] For example, a Chinese proverb states, "The first person to raise his voice loses the argument."

The conflict avoidance aversion in Japan includes not resolving disputes with lawyers. It is estimated that the Japanese only have one lawyer for every ten thousand people; in the United States, which is a conflict active society, there is one lawyer for every fifty people.[10] Since most of the readers of this book will be dealing with conflict in the North American society, an investigation of that society's conflict patterns will be undertaken; however, even if you are North American, please remember that because the United States and Canada are a nation of immigrants, a great number of the people with whom you come in contact have strong other-culture ties and may follow the patterns of their native culture.

Levels of Conflict

As with all heightening of emotions, conflict develops sequentially and can be understood by examining the levels it travels through. These steps seem present in every type of conflict ranging from neighborly spats to family disagreements, marital problems, labor negotiations, and international incidents.[11] The levels are:

Level 1: No conflict. At this stage, the individuals face no key differences in goals.

Level 2: Latent conflict. One person senses a problem and believes that goal differences exist. Yet the other gives no sign of noticing such differences, or tries to deny that differences exist.

Level 3: Problems to solve. The people express concerns that focus on interests. They choose to confront the problem and take the courage to face the risks associated with that confrontation. The goals do not include personal attacks that move the conflict toward a destructive orientation.

Level 4: Dispute. There is a problem to solve that carries with it a needs-centered conflict. The individuals fight about an issue but insert frequent personal attacks that move the conflict toward a destructive orientation.

Level 5: Help. When the people can no longer manage their dispute because they've gotten out of control, they often seek help. The help can be from friends, relatives, or a professional such as a mental health professional, conciliator, mediator, arbitrator, or adjudicator. It is best if the third party is neutral and invited to participate rather than intrudes. The assistance can be directive or nondirective, but unless required to do so by law the third party should manage the procedure, not solve the conflict. Individuals forced into a solution, such as in court-decreed divorces and child custody cases, and arbitrated labor-management conflicts, almost always hold resentment.

Level 6: Fight or flight. If the help fails, or the parties become so angry that they don't think of asking for help, they either move against and try to defeat or destroy one another, such as in declaring war, or they try to escape from the situation, such as when a teenager runs away from home. It is at the fight stage that physical and verbal aggression, battering, or murder may take place. At the flight level, getting divorced or quitting a job may be the chosen action.

Level 7: Intractability. When people remain at the fight-or-flight level for a long period of time, sustaining the conflict becomes more important than resolving it, that is, the conflict gains a life of its own. People abandon hope for a constructive solution. The conflict may continue until the parties destroy one another or lose the will to continue to fight.

The Role of Personal Anger in Conflict

Explaining their reactions to conflict, many people say something like "He made me mad" or "I was so angry I couldn't control myself." These are statements expressing the emotion of anger.

There are some techniques that can affect your interpersonal expression of the anger so that it can be a constructive rather than a destructive action. Consider, for example, these suggestions:[12]

Do not react immediately when you are angered. The count-to-ten technique is often effective. It stops you from acting on only your emotions and allows you to think through the ramification of your actions.

If possible, don't make important decisions in the heat of an angry moment. A moment of emotional stress is not the time to fire anybody or tell your spouse or lover that your relationship is over.

Use the extra energy generated by anger constructively. When you experience anger (or its first cousin, fear), your body activates its **fight-or-flight** (stay and battle it out, or run away) **mechanism**. This results in an increased flow of adrenaline that makes you temporarily stronger than usual. But instead of beating up someone, go for a fast-paced walk.

In a conflict situation the other person is often attacking you when you are not the cause of the problem.

Apologize if necessary. If you really behave badly during a fit of anger, an apology to those who have been affected is in order. A simple "I'm sorry; I was angry" will probably do.

Dealing with Another Person's Anger in Conflict

To deal with someone's anger, one expert advises, "Don't let them dump on you; it only encourages their craziness."[13] Instead, you must determine what is the best behavior for you and then carry it out. If you give in to another's emotional blackmail (e.g., threats that she or he will leave you or stop being your friend), you have set a pattern by which that person can control you in the future. And the more you give in, the more the person will use the same ploy again.[14] Once the pattern is set the other person will likely assume that you will let him or her aggress against you in the future, and that's how you will be treated.

Remember that in a conflict situation the other person is often attacking you when you may not be the cause of the problem or cannot solve the

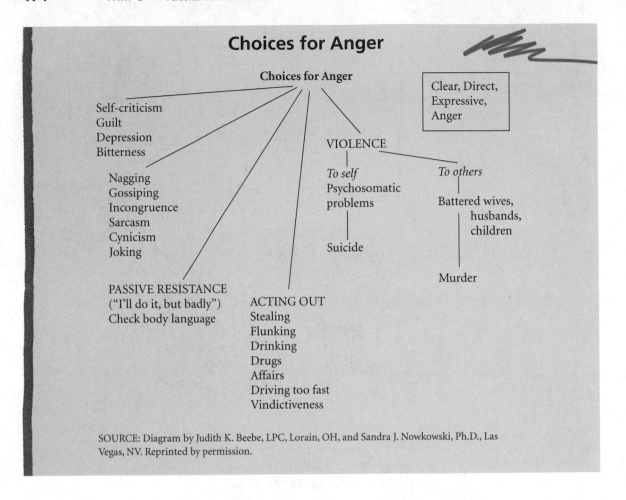

Choices for Anger

Choices for Anger

Self-criticism
Guilt
Depression
Bitterness

Clear, Direct, Expressive, Anger

Nagging
Gossiping
Incongruence
Sarcasm
Cynicism
Joking

VIOLENCE

To self
Psychosomatic problems

Suicide

To others

Battered wives, husbands, children

Murder

PASSIVE RESISTANCE
("I'll do it, but badly")
Check body language

ACTING OUT
Stealing
Flunking
Drinking
Drugs
Affairs
Driving too fast
Vindictiveness

SOURCE: Diagram by Judith K. Beebe, LPC, Lorain, OH, and Sandra J. Nowkowski, Ph.D., Las Vegas, NV. Reprinted by permission.

problem. It may simply be that you are the first person who wandered on the scene after an incident happened. The best approach to follow is to allow the person to vent his or her frustrations, while you remember that the attack is not really against you and try not to react personally. If the person continually uses you as his or her scapegoat, recount factually what the pattern has been and that you will not allow yourself to be a scapegoat. State the facts and how you want to be treated. It's pretty hard to argue with facts! You could say, "Yesterday you yelled at me when Mary didn't get her report in on time, and when John didn't reach his sales quota. I wasn't responsible for either of those things. I know you were angry, but I'd appreciate it in the future if you discussed other people's problem with them, not take it out on me."

Disagreements can actually end up being constructive if you follow the basic principles of "fighting fair."[15]

Dealing with Difficult Behavior

Consider these tactics when you have to cope with people who are difficult to deal with:

* **"Kill" with kindness.** Treat everyone well regardless of how people treat you. Be direct—but likable and polite. It's difficult to treat a thoughtful person thoughtlessly.

* **Listen and respond.** Allow the difficult person to fully express his or her feelings. Then acknowledge your awareness of the situation, describe what you see and hear, reveal what you think and feel, and say what you want. *Tip:* Don't judge ("You shouldn't be that way") or generalize ("You always do that").

* **Don't take** a position—deal with a need. Find out what motivates a person, so you can offer alternative ways of solving the problem. Chances are the difficult person confronting you has simply adopted the most obvious solution. In other words, move from *what* the person wants to *why* the person wants it.

* **Accept blame.** More often than not, you have played some role in bringing about the behaviors others subject you to. Admit what your fault is quickly and emphatically. Whenever you shoulder your share of the blame, others are more likely to own up to theirs.

Tip: Sometimes you can encourage the other person to cooperate by claiming more responsibility than you deserve.

SOURCE: *Communication Briefings,* as adapted from *What to Say to Get What You Want,* by Sam Deep and Lyle Sussman, Addison-Wesley Publishing Co., Inc., Reading, MA 01867.

Fair Fighting

In **fair fighting**, participants work toward an amicable solution to the problem and keep in mind that though the issue is important, the relationship is also important, such as with marital/relational partners, children and parents, and friends. Some fair-fighting strategies include:

Get as much information as you can, and attempt to adjust to the problem based on this information. Fact, rather than hearsay, may show that the supposed cause of the conflict is not the actual cause.

Keep arguments in the present tense. Do not argue about what happened in the past; that can't be changed.

Do not try to make the other person change things that cannot be altered. We cannot trade in our relatives, extensively alter our physical appearance, or become a totally different person.

Do not start a fight when it cannot be finished. It is not appropriate to start a stressful discussion when a person is walking out the door on the way to work, on a tight schedule, or when one or both parties are extremely tired.

The setting can affect a conflict. Disagreeing in public or in front of individuals who are not part of the conflict is not a good strategy.

A fight can take place only if both parties participate. If the conflict is getting out of hand or has gone on too long, then one party should simply stop participating. The length of a constructive argument is normally about twenty minutes; people get tired and their reasonable intentions break down after that. When the participants start repeating the same arguments, they have run out of concepts regarding the issue and it is not uncommon, at that point, for one of the participants to start attacking the other person rather than dealing with the issue.[16]

Listen to your body. If you are aware of your voice getting louder, your body tightening up, your making fighting fists, you should either physically leave or limit your role to that of a passive listener for a while.

Identify realistically what you need to get out of the transaction. Often we enter into a conflict situation without having identified our goals, which means we have no clarity of purpose and don't even know if the conflict is over.[17]

Individual Approaches to Dealing with Conflict

People react differently in dealing with conflict. Some people pull back, some attack, and others take responsibility for themselves and their needs. These actions take on the approaches avoidance, accommodation, smoothing over, compromise, competition, or integration. Most of us use a primary style for confronting conflict. (To determine your usual conflict management style, do Learn by Doing Activity 1 at the end of this chapter.) Knowing your style, and its ramifications, can be helpful in determining whether you are pleased with your interpersonal communication conflict management style. If not, you may need to acquire the skills to make a change in your habitual pattern.

Avoidance   Some people choose to confront conflict by engaging in **conflict avoidance**—not confronting the conflict. They simply put up with the status quo, no matter how unpleasant. While seemingly unproductive, avoidance may actually be a good style if the situation is short term or of minor importance. If, however, the problem is really bothering you or is persistent, then it should be dealt with. Avoiding the issue often uses up a great deal of energy without resolving the aggravating situation. Very seldom do avoiders feel that they have been in a win-win situation. Avoiders usually lose a chunk of their self-respect since they so clearly downplay their own concerns in favor of the other person's. Avoiders frequently were brought up in environments in which they were told to be nice, not to argue, and eventually bad things would go away. Or they have been brought up in home where verbal and/or physical abuse was present and to avoid these types of reactions, they simply hide from conflict.

Accommodation   A person who attempts to manage conflict through **conflict accommodation** puts the other person's needs ahead of his or her own, thereby giving in. In this situation, the accommodator often feels like the "good person" for having given the other person his or her own way. This is perfectly acceptable, if the other person's needs really are more important. But unfortunately, accommodators tend to follow the pattern no matter what the situation. Thus, accommodators are often taken advantage of, and they very seldom get their needs met. Accommodators commonly come from backgrounds where they were exposed to a martyr who gave and gave and got little, but who put on a happy face. They also tend to be people who have little self-respect and try to earn praise by being nice to everyone.

Smoothing Over   The goal of **conflict smoothing over** is to preserve the image that everything is OK above all else. Through smoothing over, people sometimes get what they want, but just as often they do not. Usually they feel they have more to say and have not totally satisfied themselves.

As with avoidance and accommodation, smoothing over can occasionally be useful. If, for example, the relationship between two people is more important than the subject they happen to be conflicting about, then smoothing over may be the best approach. Keep in mind, however, that smoothing over does not solve the conflict; it just pushes it aside. It may very well recur in the future.

Those who use this technique as their normal means of confronting conflict often come from backgrounds in which the idea was stressed that being nice was the best way to be liked and popular. And being liked and popular was more important than satisfying your needs.

Compromise   **Conflict compromise** brings concerns out into the open in an attempt to satisfy the needs of both parties. The definition of the word *compromise*, however, indicates the basic weakness of this approach, for it means that both individuals give in at least to some degree to reach a solution. As a result, neither usually completely achieves what she or he wants. This is not to say that compromise is an inherently poor method of conflict management. It is not, but it can lead to frustration unless both participants are willing to continue to work until both of their needs are being met. Those who are effective compromisers normally have had experience with negotiations and know that you have to give to get, but you don't have to give until it hurts. Those who tend to be weak in working toward a fair and equitable compromise are those who believe that getting something is better than getting nothing at all. Therefore, they are willing to settle for anything, no matter how little.

Competition/Aggression   The main element in **conflict competition** is power! Someone has to win and someone has to lose. This, unfortunately, has been the North American way of operation in many situations—in athletic events, business deals, and interpersonal relations. Indeed, many people do not seem to be happy unless they are clear winners. Realize that if someone wins, someone else must lose. The over-aggressive driver must force the other car off the road.

The value of winning at all costs is debatable. Sometimes, even though we win, we lose in the long run. The hatred of a child for a parent caused by continuous losing, or the negative work environment resulting from a supervisor who must always be on top, may be much worse than the occasional loss of a battle.

Integration/Assertion   Communicators who handle their conflicts through **conflict integration** are concerned about their own needs as well

The main element in conflict competition is power!

as those of the other person. But unlike compromisers, they will not settle for only a partially satisfying solution. Integrators keep in mind that both parties can participate in a win-win resolution. Thus the most important aspect of integration is the realization that the relationship, the value of self-worth, as well as the issue, is important. For this reason, integrative solutions often involve a good deal of time and energy.

People who are competitive by nature, communication apprehensive, or nonassertive, find it nearly impossible to use an integrative style of negotiation. They feel that they must win, or that they cannot stand up for their rights, or that they have no right to negotiate. In contrast, people who tend to have assertiveness skills and value the nature of relationships usually attempt to work toward integration.

Avoidance, accommodation, smoothing over are all nonassertive acts, in that the person does not get his or her needs met. Competition is an aggressive act in that the person gets her or his needs met at the expense of another person. Integration is assertive since the objective is to get your needs met without taking away the rights of someone else. Compromise, depending on how it is acted out, can be either nonassertive or assertive.

 ## Communication Approaches to Resolving Conflict

The communicative approaches to managing conflict include assertive communication, negotiation, arbitration, litigation, and mediation.

Assertive Communication

Have you ever found yourself saying, "I didn't want to come here, but she made me," or "I ordered this steak well done and it's rare. Oh well, I guess I'll eat it anyway"? If so, the communication skill you were probably missing in either of these cases was the ability to be assertive.

Assertive Behavior Defined

Assertive communication takes place when a person stands up for and tries to achieve personal right without damaging others. It begins by acknowledging that you have a right to choose and control your life. A person who is assertive takes action instead of just thinking about it. Rather than saying, "Why didn't I tell her?" or "If the waiter was here now, I'd say . . . ," the assertive person takes action at the appropriate time.

Figure 7.2
A Comparison of Nonassertive, Assertive, and Aggressive Behavior

	Nonassertive	*Assertive*	*Aggressive*
Characteristics of the behavior	Does not express wants, ideas, and feelings, or expresses them in self-deprecating way. Intent: to please.	Expresses wants, ideas, and feelings in direct and appropriate ways. Intent: to communicate.	Expresses wants, ideas and feelings at the expense of others. Intent: to dominate or humiliate.
Your feelings when you act this way	Anxious: Disappointed with yourself. Often angry and resentful later.	Confident. You feel good about yourself at the time and later.	Self-righteous; superior. Sometimes embarrassed later.
Other people's feelings about themselves when you act this way	Guilty or superior.	Respected, valued.	Humiliated, hurt.
Other people's feelings about you when you act this way	Irritation, pity, disgust.	Usually respect.	Anger, vengefulness.
Outcome	Don't get what you want; anger builds up.	Often get what you want.	Often get what you want at the expense of others. Others feel justified in "getting even."
Payoff	Avoids unpleasant situation, conflict, tension, and confrontation.	Feels good; respected by others. Improved self-confidence. Relationships are improved.	Vents anger; feels superior.

SOURCE: Created by Phyllis DeMark. Used with permission.

Many communication problems have the lack of assertion at its roots. You know you are being taken advantage of and are upset because others are getting their needs met and you aren't. You may know how you feel but be afraid to state your needs because you're afraid somebody won't like you, you'll get in trouble, or you don't know exactly how to go about making your needs clear.

Assertion, Nonassertion, and Aggression   As illustrated in Figure 7.2, the goal of assertive behavior is to communicate your needs through honest and direct communication.[18] **Assertiveness** does not mean taking advantage of others; it means taking charge of yourself and your world.

In contrast, the goal of **nonassertive behavior** is to avoid conflict. Nonassertive statements include "Think of others first," "Be modest," and

"Let's keep the peace." The consequences of nonassertive behavior are that you do not get what you want. Because of this, anger may build and you may be alienated from yourself and others.

The goal of **aggressive behavior** is to dominate, to get your own way. If you are aggressive, you are apt to make such statements as "Win at all costs," "Give them what they gave you," and "They only understand being yelled at." Aggressive behavior may well get you what you want, but it can also lead to alienation, thereby putting emotional distance between yourself and others that can lead to loneliness and frustration. **Direct aggression** is the outward expression of dominating or humiliating communication. A statement such as "That's the way it's going to be and if you don't like it, that's tough. I'm bigger, I'm stronger, you lose!" **Passive aggression** attacks or embarrasses but in a manipulative way. This can be done by pretending that there is nothing wrong but derailing any attempt to solve a problem that isn't to your liking in a way that doesn't appear to be aggressive: using sarcasm that sounds like teasing; withholding something from the other person—some service, compliance with a request, or courtesy; or being sweet and polite, but, in fact, controlling what is being done. Passive aggression is a common cultural pattern in such places as England, China, and Japan, where direct aggression is considered bad manners. In the United States, the direct aggressive sign would read, "No Dogs Allowed. This Means You and Your Mutt, Butt-Head!"; in Britain it would say, "We Regret in the Interest of Hygiene, Dogs Are Not Allowed on These Premises."

Principles of Assertiveness   To learn to use assertive communication, you might keep these basic principles in mind:

1. *People are not mind readers.* You must ask for what you want. You must share your feelings if you are hurt, have been taken advantage of, or need assistance.

2. *Habit is no reason for doing anything.* "That's the way it always has been," and "Our family tradition is . . ." are all patterned statements. But the presence of a past pattern does not mean that change cannot occur.

3. *You cannot make others happy.* Others make themselves happy, just as you make yourself happy. Much of the guilt we feel has come from parents and friends making us believe that if we do not act as they want us to, then we are causing them unhappiness.

4. *Remind yourself that parents, spouses, friends, bosses, children, and others will often disapprove of your behavior and that their disapproval has*

nothing to do with who or what you are. In almost any relationship, you will incur some disapproval.

5. *Whenever you find yourself avoiding taking some action, ask yourself, "What's the worst thing that could happen to me?"* Before you let fear act on you, determine what the consequences of the action, the communication, are. If you would prefer to avoid these consequences, then by all means avoid the situation. But in most instances you will probably realize that the potential consequences aren't that bad.

6. *Do not be victimized.* A *victimizer* is a person or establishment that interferes with another person's right to decide how to live his or her own life, and a *victim* is a person who is denied that right. Recent cases of sexual harassment illustrate that women and men have been made victims because they would not stand up to a victimizer. Victimization may be enacted by others, but it can also take the form of *self-victimization*, in which a person prevents herself or himself from deciding how to live. Self-victimizers often go through life thinking of themselves as failures or losers with no capability to achieve.

   When people are functioning as assertive human beings, they use available resources to get out of victimizing situations and victimizing relationships. They report a sexual abuser, or leave situations where they are being victimized. These are communicative actions that say, "I am too valuable a person to be taken advantage of."

7. *Worrying about something will not change it; only action will.* Worrying will not alter the past, the present, or the future. Instead, you must take some action to relieve yourself of anxiety.

8. *Adopt the attitude that you will do the best you can, and if someone else does not like it, that is her or his problem, not yours.* You are responsible to only one person—you. If others cannot and will not accept that idea, that is their problem, not yours. This does not mean that you should not seek out information and advice from those whose opinions you respect; instead, it means that you do not need to seek reassurance for everything you do, think, and feel.

9. *When you decide to be assertive, be aware of the consequences.* Actions have consequences. If you threaten to quit your job if you do not get a raise, you should be ready to start looking for another employer. Don't make a threat unless you are willing to accept the responsibility and take the action.

Assertiveness Skills   If you are not already assertive, you may have decided that you would like to be. Or if you are basically assertive but have not

Figure 7.3
Three types of
responses

1. *Simple assertion:* State the facts.
   If someone shoves ahead of you in the supermarket, you say: "I was here first."

2. *Empathic response:* You recognize the other's position but state your own needs.
   "I know you're probably in a hurry, but I was here first."

3. *Follow-up response:* Repeat a description of the person's behavior, then state your own position.
   "I was here first. I'd like you to go to the end of the line."

SOURCE: Based on a concept of Judith Spencer. Used with permission.

been extremely successful at it, it may be because you lack sufficient techniques to handle a variety of situations. In either case, a number of strategies can be of assistance to you.

Simple, Empathic, Follow-up Assertions   One assertiveness strategy is composed of the simple, empathic, and follow-up assertions. The use of this technique follows several stages. (See Figure 7.3.) When you feel the need to be assertive, start with a **simple assertion** in which you state the facts relating to the existence of a problem. This in itself may be enough to solve the problem because people are often unaware that something is bothering you or that they have done something you consider wrong. A simple assertion alerts them to the problem. If they act, the solution is at hand.

Sometimes, however, you need to recognize the other person's position but state your own needs. This is an **empathic assertion**. It may follow a simple assertion or be the first step in the assertive process. By recognizing the other person's problems or rights, you may find that she or he understands that you are not on the attack. The person may then become quite cooperative.

A **follow-up assertion** is used when the simple or empathic assertion is not successful in getting the desired action. It takes the form of a restatement of the simple or empathic assertion, then a statement of your own position, which may include a direct statement of the action you need or want.

Do not assume that by being assertive you will always get your way. You may not, but you definitely have a better chance than if you are nonassertive. And you probably won't get the negative reactions that you might receive if you were aggressive.

DESC Scripting   **DESC scripting** is a way of dealing with interpersonal conflicts that centers on the process of Describing, Expressing, Specifying, and stating Consequences. This process allows you to "analyze conflicts, determine your needs and rights, propose a resolution to the conflict, and, if necessary, negotiate a contract for change."[19]

This process also allows you to plan ahead, if desirable, to avoid not being able to think of what to say. Most people—especially those who are communicatively anxious—tend to feel more secure if they know exactly what they are going to say. This system allows them to rehearse and eliminate bad scripts or self-defeating statements. The four steps of DESC scripting are:

1. **D**escribe. Describe as specifically and objectively as possible the behavior that is bothersome to you. For example, you may say, "I was told these repairs would cost $35, and I've been given a bill for $100."

2. **E**xpress. Say what you think and feel about this behavior. For example, you may say, "This makes me frustrated because I feel I was not told the truth."

3. **S**pecify. Ask for a different, specific behavior. For example, you may say, "I would like my bill adjusted to the original estimate."

4. **C**onsequences. Spell out concretely and simply what the punishment will be for not changing the behavior. The consequence should be something that you are willing to do and are capable of doing. Threats that go beyond reasonableness will be ignored. For example, you may say, "In the state of Ohio I know you can only charge me $50 over the amount of the estimate. If the change isn't made, I'll contact the state's Consumer Protection Office and lodge an official complaint." (Since this is the law, you can carry through.)

DESC scripting can be used for requesting an adjustment, asking for information or help, clarifying instructions, reconciling with someone, saying no to unreasonable demands, protesting annoying habits, and dealing with unjust criticism.

Negotiation

In contrast to assertion, which is the act of one person attempting to meet her or his needs, **negotiation** is the act of bargaining to reach an agreement with at least two people working on a mutual problem. When negotiating, both parties must be explicit about what they want and why. If you are unable to work out an amicable solution, you must accept that invoking consequences may be necessary. If this is the case, both parties must

Conflict negotiation is the act of bargaining to reach an agreement.

make clear what the consequences will be; they must also make sure that the consequences are relevant to the other person or organization and can be carried out.

A number of considerations must be kept in mind during negotiating:

Look closely at the other party's point of view to understand where you differ. Conflict is often cleared up as soon as one party realizes that he or she did not understand the other person's viewpoint—or his or her own.

Identify your needs. What do you really want? What does the other person want? Are your needs similar, or different?

Decide on a negotiating style. One pattern does not work in all situations. Because of this, one of your basic considerations should be whether you are interested in a win-lose, lose-lose, or win-win resolution.

Win-lose negotiation centers on one person getting what he or she wants while the other comes up short. In a **lose-lose negotiation**, neither person is satisfied with the outcome. In a **win-win negotiation**,

The Five P's of Negotiation

You'll boost your chances of getting what you want in a negotiation if you're:

* **Prepared.** Before you seat yourself at the table, make sure you know as much as possible about the needs of both parties and any external factors that may affect your negotiations.

* **Poised.** Negotiators who become emotional lose points in the negotiation. Those who remain calm win points.

* **Persuasive.** This boils down to two things: You must be able to explain your position and provide support for it.

* **Persistent.** This doesn't mean you should fight for a point until you're "the last one standing." But it does mean that you should not give in at the first sign of resistance to an issue that's important to you.

* **Patient.** Pressing too quickly to conclude the negotiations may cause you to compromise more than you should and leave you with a hollow victory.

SOURCE: *Communication Briefings,* as adapted from Right Associates, Philadelphia, cited in *Industry Week,* 1100 Superior Ave., Cleveland, OH 44114.

the goal is to find a solution that is satisfying to everyone. Although the latter seems to be the ideal for which most people strive, some may aim for a different option. There are times when people feel they must win at all costs, and if they cannot win, the other person is not going to win either.

Set up a conducive climate for negotiating. If the atmosphere is positive, the negotiation will probably go forward. If the atmosphere is negative, however, there may be no way of avoiding a win-lose or lose-lose situation, both of which are fostered by competition. Are you really interested in amicably settling the issue? If so, make an effort to be cooperative. Try and set up a "we" rather than a "you versus me" atmosphere.

Consider the impact of the setting on the process. Trying to negotiate in front of others often places a strain on the participants that can result in a less-than-desirable solution. If the participants feel rushed, tired, or under pressure to meet a deadline, this can influence both their thinking and their emotional attitude.

Keep the discussion focused. Avoid attacking the other person; rather, deal with the issue.

No one has to lose in a negotiation. If both people are satisfied with what is decided, then their needs are met and a win-win situation results.

Arbitration

In **arbitration** a third party is brought in to settle a dispute. The third party hears evidence and makes a decision on how the conflict will be resolved. Both parties have previously agreed that they will abide by the decision. This is a common technique that is used when negotiation has failed. The major communication factors that the disputants should practice is the honest answering of questions and being an active listener so that the questions asked are the questions answered.

Litigation

Litigation is adversarial communication in which a dispute is settled by presenting evidence to a judge or a jury who are given the responsibility of deciding who is right. Litigation is usually conducted by lawyers who call witnesses and question them to reveal information while following a prescribed set of rules that have been established by law and interpreted by the person in charge, usually a judge.

Mediation

Mediation is a process in which a neutral person, who has no vested interest in the outcome, facilitates communication between parties and, without imposing a solution on the parties, enables them to understand and resolve their dispute.[20] Mediators are specially trained in specific communication techniques and are often licensed to perform the act of mediation. Mediation is becoming a communication technique that many courts are mandating instead of litigation in such matters as custody, divorce, and neighbor disputes.

The basic principle in mediation is to get those in conflict to communicate with each other so that they can reach a win-win decision, thus ensuring that the dispute remains settled.[21] It is imperative in mediation that the participants stay in the present tense and discuss how to solve the issue. Therefore, mediation rules usually indicate that the first session may be used by disputants to blame and then they are not to revert to blaming again the rest of the time.

The mediation participants use a joint problem-solving approach, which focuses on their interests. Since most people are not trained to deal with each other in a nonbiased manner of problem resolution, the mediator acts as both guide and teacher in getting the disputants through the process.

The mediator structures the process, encourages information-gathering, assists in defining the issues and generating possible conclusions, guides an exploration of the consequences of various solutions, keeps participants focused, and draws out the parties. The mediator does not advise either disputant or advocate a particular solution.

Though most mediators are professionals, specifically trained to carry out the procedure, the techniques used by mediators can be carried out by anyone. The stages of mediation are: establish the rules, explain the process and the role of the mediator, begin assessment of the problem, begin information-gathering, discuss possible solutions, evaluate the solutions, work toward selection of a mutually agreed-upon solution, and obtain signatures on an agreement that validates the solution.

The hardest part of acting as a mediator is to remain neutral and not step in with advice for either party, even when one appears to be getting the worst of the agreement.

An issue that often leads to conflict is criticism. An understanding of what criticism is and how to handle it can help diffuse its being a cause of conflict.

Handling Criticism

Criticism—the act of judging—is often considered a negative act by the receiver. To handle criticism constructively, without feeling the need to justify yourself or to counterattack, you can try these strategies:

When criticized, seek more information. If someone accuses you of having done something, ask for specifics. For example, if a friend says that you are selfish and do not respect anyone's feelings, ask for some specific examples or the specific instance that inspired the comment.

Paraphrase the ideas of the person making the criticism to clarify them for both of you. Repeat the accusation and ask if that is what he or she really meant. That way you will be dealing with exactly what has been said.

Ask yourself what consequences will result from your not altering the behavior being criticized. Will you personally gain from making the changes or is the criticism based on satisfying the needs of the criticizer?

Listen to the person and, if the criticism is just, accept his or her opinion. Use such techniques as agreeing with the truth, agreeing with the odds (if it is a projection into the future, agree with the odds for its occurrence), agreeing in principle (if the criticism comes in the form of an abstract ideal against which you are being unfavorably compared, you can agree with it in principle without agreeing with the comparison), or agreeing with the critic's perception (agreeing with the right of the critic to perceive things the way he or she does). For example, if you are accused of spending too much time studying and not enough socializing, and you feel this is true, why not simply agree rather than arguing that you have a right to spend your time as you wish?[22]

In dealing with criticism, recognize that much of it is well intentioned. Often, family members, friends, and the boss are telling you how to change for what they perceive is "your own good." This does not mean that they are right or wrong or that you have to take their suggestions. Remember that no one has a crystal ball allowing him or her to see into the future. Your desires, needs, and goals are ultimately your responsibility, and you can do as you wish as long as you are also willing to accept the consequences.

IN CONCLUSION → Every day we participate in the act of interpersonal communication. The basic principle of good conversation is to hit on a common interest between yourself and the other person. Directions include instructions for how to accomplish a task, achieve an effect, or get somewhere. Requesting is the process of seeking out information or change. Conflict is natural, the inevitable result of individual differences, limited resources, and differences in role definitions. The communicative approaches to resolve conflict include assertive communication, negotiation, arbitration, litigation, and mediation. Knowing how to handle criticism is an important communication skill.

LEARN BY DOING → 1. We each have a general pattern by which we deal with conflict. To learn your approach to dealing with conflict, read this story, and rank the six possible conflict confrontation solutions according to the way you would usually handle such a situation.

You and John have been working together for several years. Your offices are near each other on the same floor. While you had always considered each other friends, and helped each other out, lately John has been more and more dependent upon you. He asks you to help him complete work that he doesn't seem able to finish, borrows cash without returning it, and interferes with your normal workflow by talking about his unhappy home life. Until lately, you haven't minded much, but now you are getting tired of John's behavior.

_____ a. Steer clear of John as much as possible. Close your door when you are in the office and don't answer it if you know it is him when there is knocking on the door. Make excuses for why you can't help him with his problems.

_____ b. Do the favors for John, hoping that he'll stop imposing soon. After all, nobody's perfect and it isn't worth making an issue over this.

_____ c. Do the favors for John, but casually hint about the inconvenience involved.

_____ d. Tell John that you are feeling somewhat inconvenienced and ask him if the two of you can sit down and talk about ways that you two might come up with some other way for him to get some of his needs met.

_____ e. Tell John that you've had it with his demands, that he is taking advantage of you, and that if he keeps up the asking and whining, you'll stop talking to him.

_____ f. Tell John how his actions make you feel by factually listing the number of times he has asked for favors, that you still want to be friends, but that he needs to find a way to work out his problem that's less of a strain on you.

Your number one answer is your most usual way of dealing with conflict; your alternative style is your next answer. For an explanation of each style, read the "Individual Approaches to Dealing with Conflict" section of this chapter. Key: a—Avoidance; b—Accommodation; c—Smoothing Over; d—Compromise; e—Competition/Aggression; f—Integration/Assertiveness.

2. Select a place on your campus and write directions from your classroom to that place. Your instructor will divide the class into pairs. One partner is to give the directions orally to the other partner without revealing the chosen destination. See if by following your directions your partner can figure out the place you selected. Then reverse roles.

3. Select an object and write a description of it without revealing its identity. Then read your description to your classmates. At the end of the entire description, they attempt to name the object. When everyone has read his or her description, discuss why the class members could or could not identify certain objects.

4. a. Do something you have wanted to do for yourself but for some reason have not. This is an assertive, selfish act (e.g., call a friend you have wanted to talk to for a while). Record what you did and how you felt.

b. Do something you have wanted to do for someone else but for some reason have not. This is an assertive, selfless act (e.g., visit an ill relative). Record what you did and how you felt.

c. Think of something that someone is doing that bothers you. Using the DESC or simple/empathic/follow-up assertion format, tell that person how you feel, remembering to be assertive, not aggressive. This is an assertive act (e.g., tell your roommate you would appreciate his or her not borrowing your clothes without asking). Record what you did and how you felt.

Do this activity over a period of several days, completing the tasks in the order given. When you are finished, share your experiences with the class. A discussion follows on what you learned about the process of assertiveness. In the discussion, figure out why steps a and b were assertive acts.

5. List a specific situation in which you should have been assertive but were not. Why did you not assert yourself? How could you have asserted yourself? What do you think might have happened if you had asserted yourself? Use your answers as the basis for a discussion on assertiveness.

KEY TERMS →

conversation	assertiveness
small talk	nonassertive behavior
analytical thinking	aggressive behavior
holistic thinking	direct aggression
directions	passive aggression
asking	simple assertion
conflict	empathic assertion
conflict active societies	follow-up assertion
conflict avoidance societies	DESC scripting
fight-or-flight mechanism	negotiation
fair fighting	win-lose negotiation
conflict avoidance	lose-lose negotiation
conflict accommodation	win-win negotiation
conflict smoothing over	arbitration
conflict compromise	litigation
conflict competition	mediation
conflict integration	criticism
assertive communication	

After reading this chapter, you should be able to:

Define what an interview is and identify the types of interviews

List and explain the different purposes for interviews and how those purposes affect what happens in the interview

Demonstrate the organizational structure of an interview

State principles of preparing for and functioning as an interviewee and an interviewer

Identify and illustrate the types of questions used in an interview

An **interview** is a purposeful conversation between two or more persons that follows a basic question-and-answer format. Interviewing is more formal than most conversations, because the participants usually share a preset purpose and use a focused structure.

Although there are many types of interviews, the employment interview is one of the most prevalent. In fact, some people mistakenly believe that it is the only variety of interview. Some other formats are the information-gathering interviews (e.g., medical personnel gathering patient data), counseling interviews (participating in a psychotherapy session), interrogatory interviews (a detective examining someone suspected of a crime), and radio-television interviews (talk shows).

Interviewing Roles

The most effective interviews are conducted at a highly conversational, yet structured level. In the process, the communicators assume fundamental communication roles. In some transactions, the people involved can reverse roles as the interview proceeds. Mainly, however, the roles remain somewhat fixed: one person maintains the position of interviewer; the other, the role of interviewee.

The Role of the Interviewer

The **interviewer** is responsible for the interview's arrangements and takes the lead in conducting the activity. He or she usually establishes the time, location, and purpose of the meeting. Careful preparation is a key to success as an interviewer. Therefore, the interviewer often prepares an **interview format** which outlines the procedures that will be used to achieve the interaction's purpose.

One of the most common mistakes interviewers have been found to make is that they tend to talk too much.[1] "The general rule is that the interviewee should do about 80 percent of the talking."[2]

A good interviewer works at establishing a rapport with the interviewee by providing a climate of trust and support. The successful interviewer must be a sensitive communicator, one who is aware of the nonverbal cues of the interviewee and who can adapt to these responses.

The Role of the Interviewee

The **interviewee**, the person who is being interviewed, should prepare for the session by knowing the purpose of the meeting and what his or her role and responsibilities are. As an interviewee, anticipate what you will be asked and think about how you can best respond.

As an interviewee, don't assume that your only role is to answer questions. Just as a candidate for a position in an employment interview, for instance, responds to the questions asked by the interviewer, so too can the candidate shift roles and ask questions about the position, company, and benefits.

The Interview Format

Once the objectives of the interview are established, the interviewer should prepare the interview format. The basic format, regardless of the interview's purpose, is divided into the opening, the body, and the closing.

The Opening of the Interview

The opening of the interview focuses on establishing rapport between the two communicators. The interviewer should try to make the interviewee feel comfortable. One of the best ways to do this is for the interviewer to do most of the talking at the outset. This technique serves two functions: it establishes the goal of the interview for both communicators, and it gives the interviewee time to become comfortable with the situation and the interviewer.

For example, a journalist conducting an information-gathering interview about black-white relationships as we enter the twenty-first century started with a conversation about the movie *Ghosts of Mississippi*. The discussion of how Whoopi Goldberg portrayed the wife of the slain civil rights leader Medgar Evers offered the interviewee the opportunity to feel comfortable communicating with the journalist before going into the substance of the interview itself.

The Body of the Interview

The body of the interview is the heart of the process. At this stage, the interviewer should ask questions in an attempt to accomplish the purpose of the session.

Types of Interview Questions   An interviewer has a variety of questions to use: direct, open, closed, bipolar, leading, loaded, yes-response, mirror, and the probe.

Direct questions are explicit and require specific replies. For example, "Where did you last work?" **Open questions** are less direct and specify only the topic: "What is your educational background?" **Closed questions** provide alternatives, narrowing the possibilities for response, and probe for opinions on opposite ends of a continuum: "Do you think knowledge of a product or communication skills is the most important asset of a salesperson?" Another form of closed question is the **bipolar question**, which requires a yes or no response: "Would you like to work for this company?"

Leading questions encourage a specific answer: "You wouldn't say you favor gun-control legislation, would you?" This is a leading question because it implies how the interviewee should answer the question. **Loaded questions**, a type of leading question, are designed to elicit a very emotional response. Asking a job applicant who was an officer of the union at a previous job to defend this company's policy of nonunion affiliation would, for example, be a loaded question. Another form of leading question is the **yes-response question**, which is stated in such a way that the respondent is encouraged to agree with the interviewer: "You would agree with me, wouldn't you, that this company's policies are fair?"

Leading, loaded, and yes-response questions are used by interviewers who feel that the only way to get responses showing the true personality and beliefs of the interviewee is to put him or her on the spot. Consequently, interviewees should therefore be aware that questions can carry implications going far beyond what is actually being asked, and they should consider this fact as they answer.

The mirror question and the probe are used to follow up on initial questions. A **mirror question** is intended to get a person to reflect on what he or she has said and expand on it. For example, the interviewee may say, "I've worked for this corporation for years, and I'm getting nowhere." The mirror question might be, "Do you feel you're not moving ahead in the corporation?" Such a response may encourage the interviewee to disclose more about her or his feelings.

The **probe** is used in interviews to elicit a more detailed response. An example of a probe is "Why do you feel that way?" This question encourages the interviewee to discuss his or her point with more direction and depth.

Sequence of the Interview Questions   To accomplish the purpose of an interview, the interviewer should set up a checklist of questions in the categories he or she wants to cover. To do this, the interviewer must first determine the categories needed. For example, in the following job-interview outline, the interviewer selected four categories: educational background, experience, job-related outside activities, and communication skills. These categories and the questions within them are set up from those that are easier to answer to those that are more difficult. The interviewer also sets up the questions so that they move from finding facts to seeking attitudes.

The interviewer also should provide the interviewee with transitions at the end of each category of questions so that he or she knows what direction the interview is taking, can think along with the interviewer, and consequently can provide appropriate responses. Specifically, the interviewer could say, "Now that we've covered your educational background, let's turn to your on-the-job experience."

Interviewer: Personnel director seeking to hire a civilian computer programmer to work on a military base

Interviewee: Computer programmer applying for a programming position

I. Open interview

    A. Specify details of position

        1. Duties

        2. Workdays, hours, benefits, and pay

(Transition to next topic)

II. Education

    A. Why did you choose computer science as your educational major?

    B. Which courses do you feel best prepared you for this position?

    C. Why?

(Transition to next topic)

III. Experience

    A. Describe one problem for which you devised a solution on your last job.

    B. If you were rushing to meet a deadline, how would you go about completing the assignment while keeping quality high? Give an example from your last job.

(Transition to next topic)

IV. Job-related activities

    A. In which computer language or languages are you fluent?

    B. Which language do you like the most? Why?

    C. What specific computer-security measures do you feel should be carried out to protect military information?

V. Communication skills

  A. We cannot read the VTOC on any of a string of disk drives. The CE is stumped and strongly suggests that it is a software problem. You are 100 percent sure that it is a hardware, not a software, problem. If I am the CE, convince me that I am wrong and you are right.

  B. If I were to offer you the following two jobs, which would you choose and why?

    1. One with a $50,000 salary and a job description and responsibility level with which you are not very happy.

    2. One with a $35,000 salary and a job description that fits the type of position you really want.

VI. Conclude interview

  A. Summarize briefly.

  B. Ask for any questions.

  C. Tell interviewee when he or she can expect to hear from you regarding the final hiring decision.

Answering the Interview Questions   Although the interviewer carries the burden of determining the sequence of questions, the interviewee should answer with accuracy, clarity, and specificity. The answers should be backed up with supporting material for clarification and evidence. Some suggestions for answering questions are:

If you don't understand the question ask for clarification. For example, "Would you please restate the question?"

Restate the question in the answer. For example, if asked, "What are your responsibilities in your present job?" The answer might start with, "In my present job, I . . ." In this way, the questioner knows you are listening, and you are clarifying exactly what you are answering.

Answer one question at a time. Often, interviewers group questions together. In general, it is best to answer one question at a time to make sure that the questioner knows specifically which piece of information you are giving. For example, assume that the interviewer asks, "Would you describe your working conditions, and what you like best about your job?" Divide your answer into two parts, such as, "My present working conditions are . . ."; "I like the fact that at my present job I can . . ."

Try to turn negative questions into positive answers. A commonly-asked job interview question is, "What do you think your greatest weakness is?" This negative can be turned into a positive by stating, for example,

"I am aware that I am rather compulsive about my work, so I spend a great deal of time making sure that what I do is done correctly."

The Closing of the Interview

An interview's conclusion should summarize what has been accomplished. If appropriate, discussion of the next step to be taken after the interview has ended should finish the session. When the interview is nearing its end, the interviewer should give the other person an opportunity to make statements or ask questions. A real estate broker, for example, ended a sales interview with a potential buyer with, "I'll write up the contract at the $240,000 price you'd like to offer plus the provision that all the electrical fixtures remain. Do you have any further questions before I leave?"

Types of Interviews

There are numerous types of interviews. The commonly used formats are the employment information-gathering, problem-solving, counseling, persuasive, appraisal, interrogatory, and radio-television. Although not all the varieties may be relevant to you at this point in your academic and/or employment career, you may well be called on to participate in them at some time. Therefore, it is useful to review some considerations of each type.

The Employment Interview

The most crucial interview for many people in their careers is the **employment interview**. It is both a way of entering the job market and a means for changing positions, getting promotions, and achieving salary increases. The job interview format is also sometimes part of the admission processes for colleges and universities, internships or assistantships, and graduate and professional programs.

Since the interview usually follows the prospective employer's examination of prior work experience, grade-point average, and personal recommendations, the interview is often the last hurdle to be jumped before work employment, academic admission, or internship appointment.

The Employment Interviewer   In an employment interview, the interviewer's purpose is to find out about the job applicant. At the same time, the interviewer attempts to sell the organization or the position. Research suggests that interviewers vary widely in their selection decisions and are highly idiosyncratic in their approach to employment interviews. Consequently, selection interviewers are advised to develop selection criteria, determine how the criteria will be assessed, and establish a criteria-based interview guide.[3] Legal ramifications may be forthcoming for failure to have clear criteria and procedures because of federal, state, and municipal employment laws.

The Employment Interviewee   The interviewee also has the responsibility of providing information about her or his background and experiences and, at the same time, convincing the recruiter that she or he is the best applicant for the position. As the job seeker, don't overlook the importance of preparing for an employment interview.

Preparing for the Employment Interview   If you are applying for a job at a new place of employment, you should provide a résumé and a letter of interest so that the recruiter has background information.[4] A résumé is a vital part of your communication image and can often make the difference in whether you are even called for an interview. A résumé and cover letter ought to be tailored to the specific company and particular position for which you are applying. (Information on preparing a résumé and a sample résumé are presented in the appendix to this book.)

Another important aspect of preparation is to be ready to answer the questions posed. The eight most-asked interview questions for entry-level positions are:[5]

1. What are your future career plans?

2. In what school activities have you participated?

3. How do you spend your spare time?

4. In what type of position are you most interested?

5. Why do you think you may like to work for our company?

6. What jobs have you held?

7. What courses did you like best? What courses did you like least?

8. Why did you choose your particular field of work?

Dressing for the Employment Interview   Appearance is an important factor for success in employment interviews. An extreme, but probably

Appearance is an important factor for success in employment interviews.

wise, opinion is, "A lot of people out there have the credentials, the degrees, and the experience. Success comes down to image."[6] A leading consultant who advises businesspersons on what to wear states, "Walk though a door into an office, and instantly people draw a dozen conclusion about you, from how much money you make (or should make) to how trustworthy you are."[7] And though you may not want to believe it, or wish it weren't so, "even the best credentials aren't enough to overcome a poor physical image."[8] Appearance even has an effect on salary. "An initial salary of 8 to 20 percent higher is a result of upgrading a mediocre business appearance to one that is crisp and effective."[9]

Even though some organizations have turned to a more relaxed look, this doesn't normally apply to clothing choices for employment interviews. If you want to succeed, you must package yourself to turn off the fewest number of people and turn on the greatest number of opportunities. This generally translates into the conservative, trustworthy look.

For men that "means dark blue and gray suits in solids or muted patterns. Sport coats are not recommended. Accessories, from ties to shoes to watches, should all be the type that project solidity and never draw attention to themselves."[10] In other words, leave the Nike running shoes, earring, and Mickey Mouse tie at home. A double-breasted suit transmits more authority than a single-breasted suit.[11]

Women should "stick to the classic look—skirt suit or dresses with jackets—in dark colors."[12] Choose natural fabrics over synthetics and avoid polyester. "The number-one lipstick choice is Max Factor #17."[13] Wear neutral-colored stockings. The handbag/attaché case and shoes should be the same color as your suit or dress. Avoid gaudy jewelry, leaning toward conservative earrings such as pearls or small gold loops.

Researchers have identified the following as the five biggest mistakes that men and women make in dressing for interviews:[14]

Men

1. Dirty, wrinkled, ill-fitting clothes

2. Shirt that is too tight at collar or waist

3. Dirty hands, nails, or hair

4. Dirty or improperly colored shoes

5. Improper style clothing for body composition

Women

1. Too much or inappropriate jewelry

2. Too much or too little makeup

3. Inappropriate or scuffed shoes

4. Inappropriate clothing

5. Ill-fitting clothes

Actions during the Employment Interview   What should you do during the interview? In general, it is wise to keep in mind this advice:[15]

Be pleasant and friendly but remain businesslike.

Tell the employer your job preferences as specifically as possible. Avoid a comment like "I'll do anything" because it shows a lack of clarity about your desires and skills and sounds desperate.

Stress your qualifications without exaggeration.

When you discuss your previous jobs, avoid criticizing former employers and fellow workers.

Be prepared to state what salary you want, but do not do so until the employer has introduced the subject.

Few people can fake a role or lie well. Even if you can, employers will hire you for what they see, and if you are not the person you have pretended to be or cannot perform at that level, you'll be terminated.

Ask questions when appropriate. For example, ask about what your initial duties will be, and what kind of training you will receive.

Be enthusiastic; listen for ideas; maintain eye contact.

Take notes during the interview that you can use to remind yourself of questions you want to ask or refer to later.

If the employer does not definitely offer you a job or indicate when you will hear about it, ask when you may call to learn of the decision.

Thank the interviewer for granting you the interview. It is also appropriate to send a letter of appreciation within a day or two after the session.

Answering the Employment Interviewer's Questions   One of the common questions asked by interviewees is, "How should I answer the questions?" A specialist who trains interviewees offered these recommendations:

Listen to the questions asked.

Avoid making assumptions if you do not understand the question.

Answer ambiguous questions to your best advantage.

Make use of pauses and silences to formulate your thoughts.

Establish a rapport with the interviewer.

Treat every question as an important one.[16]

Legal Restrictions on the Employment Interview   An important consideration for both the interviewer and the interviewee is the legal issues that relate to selection process.[17] Both the interviewer and the interviewee should know the federal guidelines as to what questions can and cannot be asked in employment interviews. Unfortunately, the laws are constantly being changed so a review of the current standards must be made. At the time this book was published some of the regulations were:

An interviewer may ask:

How many years' experience do you have?

What are your career goals?

Who were your prior employers? Why did you leave your previous jobs?

Are you a veteran? Did the military provide you with job-related experience?

If you have no phone, where can we reach you?

What languages do you speak?

Do you have any objection if we check with your former employer for a reference?

Interviewers can't ask:

What is your age?

What is your date of birth?

What is your race?

What church do you attend?

Are you married, divorced, separated, widowed, or single?

Have you ever been arrested?

What organizations or clubs do you belong to?

What does your spouse do?

Have your wages ever been attached or garnished?

What was your maiden name?

Unfortunately, in spite of these guidelines, potential job applicants still report that they are subjected to inappropriate questions. If you have experienced this situation and feel you may have lost a position because of it, you have the right to make a formal complaint against the interviewer and the company, and possibly take legal action.

In addition, if you feel that you have been discriminated against because of gender, age, or any of the other classifications approved by your state or legislative district, you have the right to take action. A midwestern utility company, for example, was judged by the courts to have placed too great a reliance on the subjective judgment of its interviewers. As a result, the firm was required to establish a structured means of conducting interviews and a clear rating system for evaluating job applications to make sure that all people were treated fairly. If you plan to take action, be certain that you can document the questions that were asked or the procedure that was followed.

What should you do if an illegal question is asked? You might say, "I'm not trying to be difficult, but I was told in one of the classes I took that asking that question is illegal. I'm afraid if I answer it we could both get into trouble, so, if it's all right with you, I'll not respond." Another approach is to compliment the questioner but refuse to answer the question. For example, "That's an interesting question. Normally I'd love to answer it, but in my business communication class they told us that we aren't legally allowed to answer that." On the other hand, if you think the answer will not be negatively perceived, you might decide to answer the question and hope for the best.

In addition to the employment interview, you might find yourself the interviewee or interviewer in an information-gathering interview.

Journalists use the five-w's-and-an-h approach to develop their reports. This technique can also be used in information-gathering interviews.

The Information-Gathering Interview

In an **information-gathering interview**, the interviewer sets out to obtain information from a respondent. This type of interview is important to journalists, law enforcement authorities, health care workers, students, businesspeople, and mental health professionals. As a student, for example, you may want to conduct an information-gathering interview to collect information to be used in a speech or a term paper. Reporters and newspeople depend on information-gathering interviews to obtain information.

Conducting an Information-Gathering Interview   Information interviews may be done in person, by phone, or through E-mail. Some guidelines for information-gathering interviews include:

1. Make an appointment to interview the potential interviewee if you are appearing in person or conducting a telephone interview.

2. Preplan the questions you want to ask.

3. If possible, send your list of queries to the interviewee in advance of the session.

4. Consider using the *five-w's-and-an-h approach* developed by journalists for getting facts: who, what, when, where, why, and how? *Who* has to do with the person or persons involved in an event. *What* asks for a

description or explanation of the event. *Where* indicates the place the incident happened. *When* provides such information as the date and time of the occurrence. *Why* is an explanation of the reason the event took place. And *how* centers on the exact details of what occurred.

5. Actively listen during the interview. Ask follow-up questions. Make sure that you understand and get all the information you need as you may not be able to do a follow-up session.

6. Take careful notes. If you are going to use quoted material, repeat back what the person has said to be sure you have the information correctly recorded. Or to ensure that you have the exact information, use a tape recorder. Be sure and ask permission when you make your original appointment as to whether recording equipment can be used.

7. Remember that you are taking up valuable time. Ask your questions and leave.

8. Be aware that "certain people can be highly evasive, hard to pin down. You just have to persevere and keep after them. 'I understand what you're saying, but you haven't answered my question.' You've got to try to control the interview without alienating the interviewee so he'll cut off the interview."[18] Sometimes, of course, alienating the interviewee is inevitable. If he or she has something to hide, or if the information could be used in a legal action, then it well may be impossible to find out exactly what you want.

Being the Subject of an Information-Gathering Interview   You may find yourself in the role of the interviewee, giving information. If so, be sure that you understand the questions being asked and that you don't feel pressured into answering against your will.

If you are a witness, say, to a traffic accident, you may be asked to provide information as to what happened. If you are unable to give facts, make sure the interviewer is aware that you are transmitting an opinion. There is a vast difference between saying, "The driver turned left on the red light," and "I couldn't see the light clearly, but I think it was red when the driver turned left."

It is advisable, if you know you could possibly be called as a witness, to write down or tape-record everything you can remember as soon as you can following the incident. Time often alters memory.

A research surveyor or journalistic interviewer may ask for information that you do not want to reveal. You need to make a decision about what and how much you are willing to share. Do not allow yourself to be pressured into an answer you may regret later. Remember, even in a court of law, that you always have the right not to reveal information.

Is what's being shared
faithfully being used?

Another concern is whether what you share is being faithfully used. You may want to stipulate that the information may not be used until you are given a copy of the article or speech in which the ideas are used.

The Problem-Solving Interview

In a **problem-solving interview**, the interviewer and interviewee meet to solve a problem. Problem-solving interviews are very common in business and industry. If a company has a slump in new sales, for instance, it would be strategic for the marketing division to conduct interviews with sales personnel to determine why sales are down, and, further, what can be done to recover the lost business.

In a problem-solving interview, structure the questions in the body of the interview so that the dimensions of the problem—its causes and effects—are discussed before specific solutions are addressed. If the full implications of the problems are not covered first, then a solution may never be derived. Indeed, the greatest drawback to the effective use of the problem-solving format is people's tendency to deliberate about solutions before having a very clear understanding of the problem.

An effective problem-solving format relies on extensive give-and-take in which the interviewer and interviewee shift roles and discuss the matters thoroughly.

Managers in organizations frequently use problem-solving interviews to deal with problems with specific employees. In this context, both parties are encouraged to identify their "stake" in the problem so as to develop a plan that will be acceptable to both. "The problem-solving style is characterized by questions and descriptive language. . . . Questions are used to seek information, probe feelings and discover other points of view. . . . The language is non-judgmental . . . and the amount of time spent talking and listening is equally balanced between the two people."[19]

Knowing a problem-solving technique, such as the one illustrated in Figure 8.1, can aid considerably in keeping the action on track.

The Counseling Interview   We all have problems; some of them require that we have assistance in working through them. The **counseling interview** is designed to provide guidance and support to the interviewee. It is used by mental health professionals, friends, and family members, among others.

In some organizations, managers have been urged to develop basic skills in counseling to improve communication with their employees. In this way, "counseling can provide a service to both the organization and to individuals within it who have particular problems. Counseling can provide a release for the frustrations that are an inevitable part of human interaction in an organization."[20] Any person who is not a trained therapist, however, should keep in mind that harm as well as gain can result from trying to play amateur psychologist.

One approach to the counseling interview centers on the concept that it should not include any evaluation by the interviewer. Using this approach, you would not say to your friend who is not doing well in school, "Have you considered that your study habits may be the cause of your problem?" Instead, you could encourage the person to talk until he or she got to the heart of the difficulties. Such a strategy can be valuable in helping people see their own problems, and giving them a firm foundation for a commitment to solve them. But such **nondirective techniques**—not taking an active role in a solution—can work only if the troubled person accepts that a problem exists, has the skills to identify what is wrong, and deals with it.

An approach used in professional counseling is directive intervention. It is believed by some mental health professionals that allowing unlimited talk by a patient who is not capable of solving his or her own problems in the first place only wastes time and leads to even more problems. Thus, **directive intervention** entails the counselor taking a stand that there should

Figure 8.1
A Problem-
Solving Cycle

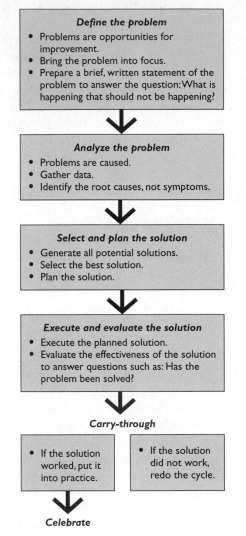

SOURCE: "Tool Kit for Quality," by Joann Horai, *Association Management,* November 1993, p. 65, copyright 1993, American Society of Association Executives, Washington D.C. Reprinted with permission.

be active probing; that specific activities should be carried on outside the counseling session (e.g., writing a letter to or directly confronting a person who has abused the client); that there should be role-playing and activities during counseling (e.g., the letting out of emotions by envisioning that the victimizer is sitting in a chair nearby so the client can tell the imagined person exactly how he or she feels); and that therapeutic hypno-

In the counseling interview, the interviewer serves as a sounding board and listens with empathy.

sis should be used in some cases to deal with certain types of problems.[21] An effective mental health professional fits the nature of the counseling approach to the client and the nature of his or her perceived problem.

Therapeutic interviews go through a definite series of stages: the expectations and objectives of the counseling are spelled out by both interviewer and interviewee; there is an emotional release during which the interviewee elaborates on his or her perceptions of the problem; the problem is explored and, ideally, all its ramifications are probed; the interviewee is reassured or consoled; a confrontation occurs in which the interviewee's contradictions, or "blind spots," are examined; further probing for more information takes place to gain a better perspective about the problem; the interviewee's options are discussed; and finally there comes a time when the interviewee's feeling or behavior may be changed or when the interviewer may wish to refer the person for another type of counseling.[22]

The Persuasive Interview   The purpose of a **persuasive interview** is to change a person's beliefs or behavior. The selection and organization of persuasive points depend on the initial position of the interviewer. If he or she agrees with the beliefs or purpose of the interviewee, then the interviewee's task is to reinforce the agreement. For instance, if a woman comes to a volunteer agency already convinced that she wants to volunteer, then the volunteer coordinator does not have to persuade her to give her time to the cause. Instead, the coordinator can concentrate on explaining the opportunities available.

If, however, the interviewee disagrees with the interviewer's beliefs or purpose, then the interviewer should find some points of agreement and try to build on these before leading the interviewee into areas of controversy. In this way, the interviewer can build an argument to secure the interviewee's acceptance of other points. For example, a management consultant may have to begin with praise and recognition for some aspect of a company's management program before attempting to persuade its executives that their organization needs to develop better internal communication.

The uncertain or neutral interviewee may require more background information before persuasive appeals can be introduced. If, for example, a voter does not know anything about your candidate for mayor, you will have to provide that person with some background information on the candidate before giving any reasons to vote for her or him.

A persuasive interview should maintain a conversational style so that the interviewee is free to raise questions and respond to the interviewer's message. In addition, the interviewee should apply the principles of critical listening and be alert to biased or leading questions.

The Sales Interview   You may not ever have thought of it as such, but the sales process is a persuasive interview. As with all communication, the sales interview process is cultural specific—in different cultures the procedure will vary. In many Middle Eastern cultures, for example, an exchange of personal information and establishment of a friendship are imperative for a successful sale. Negotiation is part of the customs of some cultures, such as in many parts of Mexico and South America.

On the other hand, in North America the procedure is quite different. The **sales interview** usually begins with the salesperson establishing rapport, arousing interest, and getting the customer involved; then the salesperson explores the customer's needs through probing, careful listening, and observing so that the product and the presentation can be linked to these needs. The next step is to present the product or service and illustrate how it will meet the customer's needs. This is followed by an acknowledgment of the potential buyer's objections in which the salesperson probes and answers them. Finally, at the closing of the sale, the salesperson reiterates the reasons to decide favorably, asks for a commitment, and paves the way for future business.[23]

Just as the persuasive interviewer should be well organized and able to adapt to the needs of the interviewee, so too must the interviewee. It is crucial that the interviewee actively participate in the process, critically analyzing the sales approach and appeals, particularly when a great deal of time and money is at stake.

An understanding of just what the interviewer is attempting to do to get the potential purchaser to buy a product or idea can be strong ammunition for dealing with any sales approach. Asking questions, reading any literature that may be available, and going to several different suppliers to compare opposing points of view should prepare you to handle hard-sell techniques.

If the sales pitch is legitimate, and the product or proposal is going to meet your needs, then your acceptance of it may well be in order. But remember that many salespersons are trained to close a sale in order to make a commission or reach a quota; thus they have very strong motivations to do whatever they can to disarm and manipulate you during the negotiation.

As a salesperson, to counter the often negative perception of salespersons, keep in mind that trust can be built by showing knowledge of the product and concern for the needs of the customer, using sales techniques that are not manipulative, being sincere without being condescending, and showing concern for the finances and welfare of the customer. Most significantly, however, the successful sales interviewer must listen. One sales expert has found this to be the case in her own entrepreneurial career: "The more mature I get, the more I recognize the importance of really listening to the customer. . . . I won't find out what he needs if I'm doing all the talking."[24]

The Appraisal Interview   In an **appraisal interview**, sometimes referred to as a *performance review*, the interviewer helps the interviewee to realize the strengths and weaknesses of his or her performance. An appraisal interview takes place when you meet with an instructor to dissect your English theme or in-class speech; however, they are usually associated with employment settings.

Employees are consistently rated on their performance. It is estimated that "over 90 percent of companies and . . . nearly 80 percent of all governmental units have formal systems of personnel assessment."[25] Performance appraisal interviews are useful in improving individual performance by (1) clarifying job requirements and standards; (2) providing feedback on an employee's progress in meeting the requirements; and (3) guiding future performance on the job.[26]

Unfortunately, appraisal interviews may be misunderstood and abused. Too frequently, they are used only for negative criticism instead of positive reinforcement. But when handled well, an appraisal interview can present methods for change while reinforcing the positive aspects of a person's performance.

Twelve points have been identified as characterizing effective performance-appraisal interviews:

1. Identify the positive behavior your employees should strive for.

2. Identify the criteria by which you will evaluate their performance.

3. Maintain a balance between positive and negative in the performance assessment.

4. Do not overemphasize differences between ideal and actual job performance.

5. Bring up performance concerns as needed, not just at the scheduled periodic-review time.

6. Distinguish between an employee who will not work and an employee who cannot work.

7. Separate the performance discussion and the salary discussion of the review for counseling purposes.

8. Avoid becoming defensive.

9. Encourage employees to participate in the development of a good performance-appraisal system.

10. Keep performance appraisals open, honest, and informal.

11. Develop effective communication channels within the organization so that performance-appraisals will be part of an open system of communication.

12. Give employees full, factual, and complete information.[27]

Performance appraisals should be two-way communication. Both supervisor and subordinate should view the process as a careful analysis and, if necessary, problem-solving session. This, of course, is very difficult to carry out in practice, because of the nature of the boss-employee, supervisor-worker, professor-student power relationship. Nevertheless, in organizations in which the boss, supervisor, or instructor has built trust by dealing honestly with the persons with whom she or he works, there is a better chance for true participatory evaluation. This usually takes place when the person in the position of power indicates what is and what is not negotiable, encourages openness regarding questions of authority and does so without repercussions, and does not feel she or he is the only one with the ability to think of solutions to problems. Unfortunately, this type of leader is quite rare.

Just as it requires skill to present constructive criticism in a performance appraisal, so too does it take ability to receive criticism. Unfortunately, criticism can engender a great deal of defensiveness; we all tend to be ego-centered. We feel a need to be right. Even when we recognize we are wrong, we tend to defend our actions. Performance appraisals, from the viewpoint of the receiver, tend to be most productive when the interviewee:

1. Listens carefully to the criticism.

2. Paraphrases the criticism.

3. Asks for specifics.

4. Monitors nonverbal behavior and is aware of the physical signs that indicate possible upset—hand-twisting, teeth-grinding, face-flushing, wiggling in one's seat or shifting from foot to foot if standing, or feeling sudden tightness in the back of the neck or the temples.

5. Responds by agreeing to take the steps necessary to change the situation; or if he or she feels the criticism is not legitimate or beneficial, refusing to take the recommended actions and indicating why.[28]

Remember, if you refuse to accept the recommendations or input, you may well be punished for that action—fired, denied a promotion, put on warning for insubordination, fail a course. Therefore, if you choose to take such an action, be sure you are willing to accept the consequences.

Much of the research on performance-appraisal methods deals with the manager in the workplace. It should be apparent, however, that the same principles apply to a teacher who is trying to improve a student's performance or a parent who wishes to change or improve a child's behavior.

The point of performance appraisal in any field is to improve performance, but improvement can result only if a specific plan is established during the interview. For this reason, the performance-appraisal interview should conclude with a concrete plan in which both parties jointly explore several possible actions; concentrate on one or two specific actions; specify to whom those actions will happen, what will happen, and when; provide for follow-up on the work; and set out in writing the plan to be followed.[29] The Motorola Company, for example, has designed a "Tell the Truth" interview in which a substandard employee's problems are reviewed and then a performance improvement plan is discussed so that the employee knows specifically how to improve to keep the job.[30]

The Reprimanding Interview   In a **reprimanding interview**, the interviewer helps the interviewee to analyze problems caused by the latter so that corrections can be made. Usually a reprimand happens only after an appraisal interview so that an employee has had an opportunity to correct the situation in the meantime. Unlike most of the other types of

How to Respond to Criticism

When a boss or co-worker criticizes you, do you try to win the argument rather than resolve the conflict?

If you do, rethink your approach. Conversations centering on "I'm right, you're wrong," or "I'm being sensible, you're being unreasonable" can lead to heated arguments—not feasible solutions.

The next time you're criticized, consider these tips:

✳ **Ask critics** to explain their criticism. Don't rush to defend your ideas or make a case for your position. *Example:* "What makes you think my approach was arbitrary?"

✳ **Let critics** assert their ideas. Don't reject their opposing position. By making

differences clear, you'll be a step closer to resolution.

✳ **Paraphrase** their ideas. This lets them know you respect the ideas and have taken them seriously.

✳ **Acknowledge** that both of you may be right. But realize that you can't have it both ways. Then ask: "What can we do?" It may take a while to agree on a solution, but you'll be on your way.

SOURCE: *Communication Briefings,* as adapted from *Understanding One Another,* by Thomas F. Mader and Diane C. Mader, Wm. C. Brown Communications Inc., 2460 Kerper Blvd., Dubuque, IA 52001.

interviews that function through the funnel schedule, the **inverted funnel schedule** is most appropriate for the reprimand. In this format, the interview starts out with a clear, specific statement of the performance problem so that there is no question as to what the problem really is. After this discussion, the interview should move to a more general discussion of the person's work, how he or she feels about it, what barriers are interfering with a high level of performance, and so on.

Ideally, the interviewee should suggest a desirable solution to the problem. In fact, some employers like to build counseling techniques into the reprimand, beginning with identification of the problem and then leading to the employee's own explanation of why the problem persists and how she or he can resolve it. Suppose, for example, a lab technician continually fails to replace equipment after using it, a practice causing other technicians to complain to the employer. Through an interview, the employer tries to get the technician to understand the problem, suggests the necessity for correcting the behavior in the future, and encourages the employee to propose an acceptable procedure for correction.

The National Labor Relations Board and the U.S. Supreme Court have ruled that an employee has the right to have third-party representation, in the form of a witness, attorney, or some other person present at any disciplinary interview.[31]

The reprimanding interview is difficult to conduct because the interviewer carries the burden of establishing grounds for the disciplinary action. Using a preset list of questions for which answers are provided may not make the process any less painful, but what is wrong and what is going to be done will be clear:

1. What did I do wrong?

2. Why was it wrong?

3. What is the penalty?

4. Is the penalty fair?

5. What will happen if I do it again?

6. What can I do to improve my performance or behavior?[32]

The reprimanding interview, whether used by managers with workers, parents with children, or teachers with students, ought to be considered the procedure of last resort. The risk involved in the reprimanding interview is great because the procedures can create considerable defensiveness on the part of the interviewee unless handled skillfully.

To be careful communicators in these situations, interviewers should avoid accusatory statements starting with, "you are," and use instead phrases such as "I feel," and stick to factual statements. Interviewers should ask questions that permit the person to express feelings or explain behavior, stay away from verbalizing conclusions during the interview, and try to conclude the interview on a neutral note.[33] Because the interviewer can be held legally liable for any type of punishment that is given, she or he must use factual evidence as a basis for any final decision. The evidence should be available for any legal action that may follow.

The Interrogation Interview   An **interrogation interview** is designed to secure information from an interviewee through extensive use of probing techniques. Lawyers, credit officers, tax specialists, and law enforcement officers use such interviews. Because of the circumstances, the interviewer is sometimes dealing with an interviewee who is reluctant to respond to questions. Consequently, through the phrasing of questions and the manner in which they are verbally and nonverbally presented, the interviewer often uses psychological pressure to elicit responses.

Law Enforcement Interrogation   Law enforcement officers are commonly trained in interrogation interviewing, a format designed to scrutinize an interviewee and, in the case of an arrest, to secure a confession to a crime.

As a result, the interviewer often works to create a climate of stress during the interview to pressure the interviewee into admitting wrongdoing.

Investigators who must use this interview format are advised to attempt to maintain emotional control throughout the interrogation. "Remember, whatever your personal feelings may be toward the person you are questioning, keep them to yourself. Do not shout and do not scream. Keep yourself even-tempered at all times." In spite of this recommendation, there are situations in which strong emotion may be needed to extract the necessary information.

Because the interviewee in a police investigation is likely to be quite hostile, the questioning strategy is very important. A good interrogator works to break through the hostility and get the information she or he needs to complete the case. The interrogator begins this process by informing the suspect of his or her rights. The U.S. Supreme Court's far-reaching *Miranda* decision requires that police officers inform suspects that they have the right to remain silent, that anything they say may be used as evidence against them, and that they have a right to have an attorney present at the interrogation.

An interrogator must establish credibility and take control of the situation. By using different types of questions, the officer constructs a picture of the incident depicted by the suspect. Lies are difficult to maintain. By noticing contradictions or improbable statements, an interrogator can undermine the suspect's story, which weakens resistance and self-confidence, and makes compliance with the investigator's demands easier.[34]

Obviously, the less practiced a person is in resisting an interrogator's techniques, the less will be his or her ability to lie effectively, and the more likely that the interrogator will be successful.

Watching interrogation techniques displayed by television and movie detectives and police officers can be misleading. Remember that the scripted interaction is based on various theatrical techniques and restrictions: the length of the show, the need for dramatic tension, and the general philosophy that the "good guy wins and the bad guy loses." License is often taken with the legalities that is not allowed in real-life situations.

Special Interrogation of a Job Applicant   The interrogation interview is sometimes used to screen job applicants. In the most common technique, a potential employee is put into a stressful situation so that those who are conducting the interview can observe how he or she reacts under pressure. Interviews for prison guards, probation officers, police officers, and hospital emergency-room personnel often take this format. It may be appropriate if the interviewee would have to perform under stressful conditions on the job, but it is a highly controversial strategy for merely "checking out" a potential employee.

Legal Interrogation   Interrogation in court is a firmly established practice. Some trial lawyers attempt to trap a witness by asking questions that elicit information outside his or her factual knowledge. For this reason, witnesses should be on guard so they do not place themselves in the position of answering questions on the basis of opinion rather than proof.

For example, one of your authors once appeared as a character witness for a former student who was on trial for possession of illegal drugs. The prosecutor asked, "Do you think that the defendant has ever used drugs?" and "Would you say that there is a drug problem at the school the defendant attended?" In both questions the prosecutor was asking for information beyond the factual knowledge of the witness. The answers given were, respectively, "I have no way of knowing whether the defendant has used illegal drugs," and "I don't know what you mean by 'drug problem,' and if I did, I would have no way of knowing whether the school has such a problem." The witness was not trying to be evasive or hostile, but the questions were posed for the purpose of leading the witness to conclusions that the prosecutor could then use to influence the jury.

The courtroom interviewee must always be on guard to answer only those questions for which he or she has accurate, factual information.

The Media Interview   The **media interview** takes place when an interviewer asks questions of a guest. The most popular format is the talk show, which can be on radio or television, and be a whole program or a segment. Formats vary greatly: one guest, one host, one host and open lines for listeners to phone in, multiguests with a single or several hosts. Such shows may cover a wide range of topics.

The host's responsibility is to set the format and tone for the program. Some choose the attack-dog approach, others the nice-person role; some are looking for facts, others to incite reaction; some hold strong biases, others try to be more centrists. There is no one best way to format such shows; therefore, the techniques vary great. Some hosts ask questions and politely wait for the guest to answer. Others interrupt, badger, incite. Some hosts insist that all calls be screened, others let any call come through.

If you appear on such a show as a guest, be sure you know and approve of the format. Know if you will be asked to submit questions in advance, whether the host or the listening audience will ask the queries. Agree, in advance, on the topic and set any guidelines of what subjects you are and are not willing to answer. Some guests have been amazed both by the quality of the questions and by the manners of those who ask them.

When you participate as an interviewee in a talk show, consider the implications of what you say. Try to avoid getting trapped with any line of questions, and steer the conversation to the message that you want to present as best as you can. Use transitional bridges such as "Yes, that's an interesting point, and in addition . . ." or "What's really important to consider . . ." to allow you to emphasize your message.

An interesting reversal of roles takes place when a listener calls a talk-show host and asks questions, such as on an open-line segment when a question on any topic can be asked. In that case, the person "in charge" becomes the interviewee. In other cases, callers wish to interrogate the guest expert. If you are a caller and truly want information, here are some suggestions for probing:

1. Ask a short question with only one point. Long, complicated questions confuse the listener and are seldomly answered in whole. If you need to ask more than one thing, and are permitted to do so, break the question down into parts and let the listener know that there are several sections to the inquiry. You can introduce this with such a phrase as, "I have a two-part question I'd like to ask. . . ."

2. Many shows are on what is called a seven-second delay. If you try to listen to the radio or television and ask your question on the phone, you will hear yourself coming out of the speaker in what sounds like an echo. The sound also feeds back into the telephone and is distracting to the host. Turn off your receiver.

3. Ideally, the purpose of your call is to ask a question. Unfortunately, some people want to give speeches. Don't be surprised that you get cut off if you start on a tirade.

4. If you tell the screener what subject you would like to speak about, stick to that topic. The reason the hosts know your name before you come on is that the screener inputs a message to the host via a computer. The host knows all about you before you are on. If you deviate from the topic, you may be cut off.

5. Get right to the point. This is not a social engagement. Asking about the health of the host, or telling that you are a "first-time caller, long-time listener," is of little interest.

6. If you are calling to get advice, listen to the answer, ask clarifying questions, and hang up. Debating the value of the advice is generally not appropriate. You asked, the person gave what she or he thought was right, and that's about as far as this can go.

IN CONCLUSION → The interview is a communication form used extensively to accomplish many goals. Effective participation requires that interviewers and interviewees recognize that an effective interview involves an opening that enables both parties to establish rapport and clarify their objectives; a body of questions and responses that accomplishes the communication objectives; and a close that ties up the conversation and identifies any further steps to be taken.

Interview communicators participate in many different types of interviews, including the employment, the information-gathering, the problem-solving, the counseling, the persuasive, the appraisal, the reprimanding, the interrogation, and the media interview.

LEARN BY DOING →

1. Make an appointment with a person who is or was employed in your present career or career choice. Interview the person to determine what academic courses she or he took to qualify for the job, what specific skills are required for success in the career, what the specific job responsibilities are, and what helpful hints he or she can give you about being successful in the field. Report to the class on not only the results of the interview but also what you learned about the interviewing process.

2. You are paired with another student according to your academic major. Each student is to independently research job descriptions within the field; employment opportunities; communication skills, special talents, and abilities that are needed; types of organizations employing people trained in the field; working conditions; and salary. You are given several weeks to complete your research. You and your partner then conduct a seven- to ten-minute information-gathering interview concerning the selected career during one of your class periods. One of you acts as the interviewee and the other as the interviewer. Before you do so, develop an interview agenda and questions. If your professor prefers, the interviews can be done via audio tape and submitted for evaluation.

3. Two students are assigned to read the same book, short story, or magazine article. In class, one of the students interviews the other concerning what she or he has read. This can be done in small groups or in front of the entire class.

4. Write down the five items you want an interviewer to know about you, then write a sentence about how you plan to convey each of these items. The class is then divided into groups of three, each group having an interviewee, an interviewer, and an observer. After a ten-minute interview, the observer states what he or she believes the applicant has

communicated. The interviewee shares her or his list of five items, and then the entire group discusses how the interviewee might have communicated any items he or she failed to get across. Then change roles and repeat the process until all three members of the group have had a chance to be interviewed.

5. You are paired with another student. You are to select a subject of mutual interest and ask each other a series of questions about the topic. You should first ask each other a direct question, then an open question, then a closed question. Repeat the procedure three times to practice the types of questions. Continue the interview by asking a leading question, a loaded question, and a yes-response question. Follow up with a mirror question and a probe.

6. Prepare a résumé for yourself, following one of the formats given in the appendix.

7. Select an ad from a newspaper for a job you would be interested in applying for at the present time. It should be one for which you are qualified. Use the advice given in this chapter on how to prepare to be interviewed, and write a paper with specific examples describing what you would do to get ready for the interview.

8. Your class will be divided into groups. One person from each group is to call a radio talk show and engage the host in a discussion. Other members of the group should listen and critique the interviewing style of their classmate.

9. Your instructor will assign groups of two people in your class various segments of Richard Bolles's *What Color Is Your Parachute?*[35] to read. Each pair conducts an information-gathering interview about the segment read. These interviews may be done before the entire class, outside of class, or simultaneously while the class is in session. If either of the latter is done, each team is asked to share observations in a class discussion after the interviews are completed.

KEY TERMS →

interview
interviewer
interview format
interviewee
direct questions
open questions

closed questions
bipolar question
leading questions
loaded questions
yes-response question
mirror question

probe
employment interview
information-gathering interview
problem-solving interview
counseling interview
nondirective techniques
directive intervention

persuasive interview
sales interview
appraisal interview
reprimanding interview
inverted funnel schedule
interrogation interview
media interview

chapter **9**

The Theory of Groups

After reading this chapter, you should be able to:

Define what a group is and compare and contrast large and small groups

Explain the advantages and disadvantages of group decision-making

List and define the kinds of groups

Explain and illustrate the norming, storming, conforming, performing, adjourning group phases

Enumerate the Six-Step Standard for Decision-Making and the 1-3-6 Decision-Making Technique

Define voting and explain the four common voting methods: consensus, majority, plurality, and part of the whole

Clarify the role of the setting in group actions

Think back over the last several weeks. How often have you been involved in group activities or heard others speaking about attending a meeting of some type? If you are typical of most people, you probably came up with a considerable list. Businesspeople hold conferences at all levels in an organization, scientists work in teams, educators serve on committees, families meet and discuss mutual joys and problems, students attend classes and hold meetings, citizens serve on juries, and athletes play on a team. All of these are examples of groups in action. In an average person's lifetime, regardless of occupation, each of us will spend more than nine thousand hours—roughly one year—in meetings.[1]

In the North American culture, people join groups for various reasons. You may join because you are forced to do so, such as in a work environment or classroom when there is a required group project. You may affiliate because you are like the members of the group. This is a common reason why individuals join fraternities or sororities. You may join because you believe in the causes that the assemblage espouses, such as their political beliefs. Organizations such as Save the Whales and the Lesbian and Gay Task Force gain membership because of their stances. Some people join because of the meaning or identity a group gives their lives. For example, you might join a church, synagogue, or the Nation of Islam because of your philosophical or religious leanings. Some people affiliate because they think they can gain some contacts or socialization from the members. The American Society for Training and Development, for example, is a way of making business contacts. And social groups allow you to meet new friends.

In the United States, why a person joins a group has a noticeable effect on the productivity and cohesiveness of the group.[2] People who are forced into membership, or do not willingly become members, tend to shun responsibilities and do not actively participate in collective efforts. Think of activities you were forced to join. Did you actively participate? Probably not, or, at best, you did so reluctantly.

Groups Defined

A group is not just any collection or aggregate of persons. Groupness emerges from the relationships among the people involved.[3] A **group** has traditionally been defined as "an assemblage of persons who communicate, face-to-face, in order to fulfill a common purpose and achieve a goal."[4]

Groups are often classified by their size. **Small groups** usually contain three to twelve persons; **large groups** normally have more than a dozen. Research shows that participation rates are affected significantly by differences in group size. For example, six-person juries have greater vocal participation than twelve-person juries.[5]

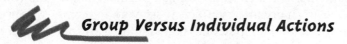

Group Versus Individual Actions

Groups, by the very nature of their collective identity, offer participants both advantages and disadvantages over working alone.

Advantages of Groups

The group process provides an opportunity for input from many people with different points of view. Groups also offer the advantage of challenging ideas before they are put into action. Since a group is composed of people with varying backgrounds and interests, before an idea receives group acceptance it probably will receive the scrutiny of many evaluations. Since any one person's experiences are limited, the aggregate viewpoints should result in a better-thought-out decision.

In addition, taking part in group action can lead to greater commitment among participants to the decisions reached. Workers involved in discussing new procedures, for instance, may approach their tasks with more enthusiasm because they helped to develop those procedures.

Research has revealed what is known as the **risky shift phenomenon**, which holds that decisions reached after discussion by a group display more experimentation, are less conservative, and contain more risk than decisions reached by people working alone before any discussion is held.[6] A group of managers who come together to solve a problem of worker morale, for instance, are more likely to adopt a radical strategy than any of the managers acting alone. A manager by himself or herself is apt to be more careful and assume less risk because he or she is acting alone, rather than together with others.

Disadvantages of Groups

Although the group process does offer these important advantages, it also has some disadvantages. For example, group discussions take much longer than individual decision-making because they involve many people with diverse points of view. The group process also requires participants to give up some individuality for the purpose of compromising with other group members.

Yet another disadvantage of the group process may surface when people blindly commit themselves to group cohesion at the expense of careful analysis. This phenomenon is called **groupthink** and is defined as "the mode of thinking that persons engage in when concurrence-seeking becomes so dominant in a cohesive in-group that it tends to override realistic appraisal of alternative courses of action."[7] The disastrous Bay of Pigs (Cuba) invasion in 1961 is considered a classic example of groupthink. President Kennedy's group of advisers blended so well as a group, and felt that any negative input would be perceived as being disloyal to the group, that even those who disagreed didn't speak up.

To prevent groupthink:[8]

1. Recognize that there is such a problem as groupthink and that it stems from pressure to conform to group norms.

2. Seek information that challenges an emerging concurrence.

3. Develop a norm in the group that legitimizes disagreement.

4. Be aware that though cohesion is normally a positive aspect of group maintenance, the more cohesive a group, the greater is the danger of groupthink.

Since a group has usually made so much effort to reach its conclusion, it is often just assumed that its solution will work. This can lead to the **Pollyanna-Nietzsche effect,** as there is excessive optimism (*pollyannaism*) and an idealized belief (*nietzschism*) that the group is superhuman and can do no wrong. This results in assuming that all is well. To avoid this, groups must evaluate the implementation of any solution and constantly be vigilant to adjusting the recommendations if things do not go as assumed.[9]

Members of any group must be aware that though participation in the decision-making process can lead a person to greater commitment to his or her work or to the decision made, in some cases social loafing may take place. **Social loafing** occurs when group membership leads people to work less than they would individually. When the individual thinks his or her own contribution to the group cannot be measured, his or her output tends to slacken.[10]

Types of Groups

We communicate in various types of groups, including work teams, study groups, committees, media conferences, electronic meetings, public meetings, and town meetings.

The use of work teams leads to improved employee morale and increased quality.

Work Teams

In the professional setting, people may be involved in a number of different kinds of groups. One of the most prevalent groups in American industry is the work team. As organizations work to accomplish their goals, they have found, based on the success of the Japanese and the Swedes, that it is important to set up **work teams**—small groups of workers who function as teams to make and implement decisions about the work to be done. For a work team to achieve its goals, it is necessary for management to "empower" the team. There must be considerable management commitment to training the members to work in a group, and allowing the group the time to carry out its functions and the decisions made.[11] Organizations have found that the use of work teams leads to improved employee morale, greater responsiveness to and flexibility in meeting customer needs, and better quality.[12] .

Study Groups

Study groups are established to enable individuals to work together to study and learn with the assistance of others. Students planning to take the

Graduate Record Examination, for example, often join together, with or without a tutor, to work toward learning the materials on the test.

To be productive, a study group should follow some basic principles:

1. Limit the group to participants who will help in the learning process.

2. Meet on a regular basis in a location that lends itself to studying, not to socializing or allowing interruptions, and insist that beepers and cell phones be turned off.

3. Insist that all members of the group attend and participate.

4. Require that each member be prepared for sessions.

5. Allow each member to take a turn in leading and providing explanations.[13]

Support Groups

A **support group** is a system that allows people to interact with others who share similar goals or problems. "The purpose of a support group is to increase people's knowledge of themselves and others, assist people to clarify the changes they most want to make in their life, and give people some of the tools necessary to make these changes."[14]

"People are coming together in record numbers both to cope with affliction and to deal with normal processes in life."[15] It is estimated that nearly 1 million special types of support groups have been established in the past few years. Growth groups have a vast number of purposes. Examples are those which deal with gaining preventive and remedial aims (e.g., Alcoholics Anonymous); treatment of eating disorders (e.g., Weight Watchers); learning coping skills (Adult Children of Alcoholics); managing relationships (Marriage Encounter); offering support for grieving (Mended Hearts); making family adjustments (Parents Without Partners); and being the parent or friend of a gay or lesbian (P-Flag).

In the counseling setting, some therapists believe that support groups may be more effective than individual counseling because they can provide the empathy and knowledge of people who have gone through similar experiences and can share their thoughts and feelings.[16] Support groups are considered an effective means for those working through trauma caused by rape, incest, physical abuse, battering, physical illness, and phobias. One study indicated that women with advanced breast cancer who had group therapy, in addition to medical treatment, lived twice as long as women who were given medical treatment alone.[17]

A newspaper advice columnist encouraged the use of support groups when she told a troubled correspondent: "I can't say enough about the groups that operate on the theory that people who share the same problem can get strength from one another. If you are having a problem with children, parents, family, friends, or with yourself, there is probably a self-help group for you."[18]

Committees

Most organizations rely heavily on committees. Because it is often difficult for a large group of people to accomplish much more than voting on policy matters, it may become necessary to send certain tasks to a **committee**—a small group responsible for study, research, and recommendations about the issue at hand. The committee's actions are usually then brought back to a larger group for final action.

To ensure that committees work effectively, a series of guidelines have been proposed. The ten recommendations are to (1) have clear objectives, (2) include a diversity of members from throughout the organization, (3) be flexible in allowing members to move in and out of the committee, (4) be sure that everyone is allowed a voice in the deliberations, (5) balance the needs of the committee with the needs of the rest of the organization, (6) cooperate, (7) work as a team, (8) enjoy the experience, (9) share the results throughout the organization, and (10) assume the responsibility for study, review, guidance, direction, and evaluation but allow the implementation to be handled by management.[19]

Media Conferences

It is estimated that 20 million face-to-face meetings are held every day in the United States.[20] But, as technology becomes increasingly sophisticated, organizations do not have to always rely on in-person meetings to conduct their business. Technological advances have led to the popularization of the **media conference**, which allows a group to conduct meetings via telephones, computers, or television.

Media conferences bring with them special communication demands, because electronic channels cut out visual messages if the telephone is the channel, or intensify attention to visual cues if the videophone is used.

Corporations such as Marriott, Bank of America, and Aetna Insurance Corporation make regular use of media conferences, as do nonprofit and collegiate associations. Many universities and hotels have built media-conferencing centers in their facilities for their own as well as public use. Recognized as the fastest-growing segment of the telecommunications industry, **teleconferencing**—the use of interactive television broadcast to various settings—has become a $150-million-a-year business.[21]

Some techniques that should be used for audio and video meetings include:[22]

* Speakers should be close enough to the microphones to be easily heard.

* Participants should control the noise of papers, tapping on the table, and other distracting habits that the microphones will pick up.

* High-quality graphics must be prepared to fit the television format.

* Materials that are needed must be mailed or faxed in time for reference during the session, if it is audio or the materials are too complex to be seen on video.

* Participants should be identified continuously during the process.

* Departures and entrances should be announced.

* Wait until the camera is on you if you are participating in a video conference.

* Limit the agenda to no more than an hour. If longer, a break should be scheduled.

Focus Groups

Motivational research has led many organizations to the use of focus groups. **Focus groups** are designed to test reactions to a particular product, process, or service offered by an organization. A randomly selected group of participants who are representative of the user or consumer group are brought together with a professional facilitator to discuss, for example, a new product. The reactions are carefully recorded and quantified in a report to the organization as input for decision-making.

The Family as a Group

Although you may not have ever thought of it as such, the family is a group. In fact, it is one of the primary groups in which most of us participate. Families are groups operating as a system by the very nature of their purposes and functions—decision-making, interpersonal relationships, and mutual dependency.

A **family** is an assemblage of people who have legally been declared a group, or who have defined themselves as such. Typical kinds of families include natural families (a married couple with or without children), blended families (families created by divorce and remarriage or death and remarriage), single-parent families (one parent with a child or children), extended families (a cluster of relatives that may also include friends), and self-declared families (heterosexuals living together, homosexuals living together, communal groups, religious cults).[23]

There is no one best way for a family to operate. Some families learn to operate under stress and chaos. Some families have open channels of communication and operate in cooperative harmony.

Most family communication follows a structure that resembles a mobile. The parts (family members) are segments of the same unit, and any reverberation of a problem goes through the system and throws off the mobile's balance. How well the family functions depends on the members' abilities to communicate with one another and balance the various parts of the system.

Family discussions center on answers to some basic communication questions. What are members allowed to talk about (e.g., death, alcohol use, sex, money)? What words can be used to talk about certain subjects (e.g., death is "passed on"; alcoholism is "Daddy is sick")? Where can members talk (e.g., in the kitchen, at the table while eating, in the bedroom, in the car, "only in our own house—this is nobody else's business")? Who can talk about it (e.g., mother and father only; father talks, others listen)?

Most families typically enforce rules randomly and lack consistency in their methods of operation. In some families, however, rules of communication are established and upheld at all costs, resulting in praise, cooperation, abuse, punishment, and/or banning.

Public Meetings

In addition to the use of internal group interactions, some organizations find it necessary to conduct **public meetings**, in which members of interested individuals may attend the sessions. Corporations must hold stockholders meetings. Government organizations, such as school boards and city councils, may need to hold their meetings in public to ensure that the decisions they reach are in the best interests of the public they serve, and to fulfill the legal requirements of many states to hold open meetings.

Public meetings can follow a number of formats. The members may discuss among themselves and then let the audience ask questions. Or there may be a series expert(s) or witness(es) in a **symposium** format, in which participants give prepared speeches with no interaction between each other or the audience. These presentations are often then followed by a **forum**—an interaction during which questions are fielded by the participants from each other as well as from any audience present.

Town Meetings

In a **town meeting**, the presenter opens with some short, prepared statement that establishes the framework for the meeting. Individuals in the audience then engage in a forum with the speaker. The ensuing dialogue can be useful for both speaker and audience, to explain their positions and to share viewpoints on issues. The town meeting has a long history in some areas of the United States, such as New England, where it is still used in some communities for town decision-making. It came into contemporary prominence when it was used by President Clinton in his 1992 campaign, and it was the format selected for a 1996 presidential debate between candidates Bill Clinton and Bob Dole.

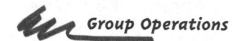 ## Group Operations

Groups are continually evolving. Normally, the evolution comes forth in five phases: norming, storming, conforming, performing, and adjourning.[24]

Group Norming

Group norming is the orienting aspect of people coming together and starting a group, or welcoming new people into an existing group. Depending on the nature of the assemblage, an exchange of names and other demographic information usually takes place. In new organizations, discussion is often cautious and doesn't deal immediately with the purpose or goals of the group. The norming process usually proceeds more rapidly when new people enter an existing group.

During this stage, **group norms**—the rules by which the group will operate—are developed. The obligations of the members, what they can and can't do, and the mode of operation are normally decided upon. These norms can be explicit (written and agreed upon, as in a constitution) or implicit (understood but not formalized).[25]

The source of the group's norms may be influences outside the group. They may be rules preset by others, such as when a judge charges a jury; handed down, such as when a local chapter of an organization is given rules by the national organization; developed by the group based on their past experiences or through trial and error; or influenced by a member or leader who either has experience in the group process or strong enough persuasive skills to influence others. Whatever the means, setting boundaries is a critical group function.

Group procedures that generally need to be determined include:[26]

1. *Planning an agenda.* Group meetings normally follow an **agenda**—the list of the topics to be discussed or the problems that must be dealt with in the order in which they will be acted upon.

2. *Handling routine "housekeeping" details.* Such details include the taking of attendance and agreeing on the rules of how decisions will be made.

3. *Preparing for the next meeting.* If this is an ongoing group, it is necessary to decide when it will reconvene. It is sometimes necessary to designate who will be responsible for certain details for the next session.

Group Storming

Although it might be ideal, and make group decision-making much easier, groups seldom norm and work toward their goal without some disagreements. Most groups, during either the process of setting rules or working toward their goal, enter into a period called **group storming**, when conflicts erupt. The disagreements may be caused by a power struggle among those interested in being the leader, conflict over the rules of operation, or personality conflicts among group members. Storming can be a positive aspect of group operation since it often alerts the group to underlying problems. Storming brings the conflicts into the open, allows the members to deal with them, and allows open sessions to follow. Though storming is common, don't assume that something is wrong if a group you are in doesn't go through storming. Just be sure that the lack of storming is not the cause of groupthink.

Primary Group Tension   Two types of social tensions are at the base of storming. **Primary group tension** refers to the normal jitters and feelings of uneasiness experienced when groups first congregate. Think of an experience you've had when entering a group for the first time, for example, entering a class on the first day or going to work on a new job. Group interaction at this point is usually of very low intensity. Often there are long periods of silence, discussion of frivolous topics, tentative statements, overpoliteness. Interruptions evoke profuse apologies. This phenomenon can be compared to boxers feeling each other out.[27] There is tendency, especially among North Americans, to want to get through this "meaningless stuff" quickly and get down to business. Your strategy as a competent communicator is not to avoid primary tension but to let it take its natural course. Primary tension tends to be short-lived and cause for little concern unless it escalates to an unmanageable level. With time it normally disappears.

Differences of opinion can be a cause of secondary group tension.

Secondary Group Tension   **Secondary group tension** is the stress and strain that occurs within a group later in its development. Having to make a decision is often the cause of the problem. Shortage of time to accomplish the task is another frequent cause. Differences of opinion are still another, as is a difficult member.

Signs of secondary tension include abrupt departure from the group's routine, a sharp outburst by a member, a sarcastic barb, or hostile and antagonistic exchanges between members. Extreme secondary tension can be unpleasant. If left uncontrolled, the group's existence may be threatened. The goal is not to eliminate the tension, but to use it in a positive way. Tension can be energizing, a source of creative thinking, and can bring a group together.

Some general storming strategies you should consider are the following:

1. Include a get-acquainted period before the first meeting so that group members get to meet each other informally.

2. Schedule an informal chat period before each meeting so that there is unpressured interaction between participants.

3. Remind the group both that disagreement can help achieve a superior outcome and that the purpose of the assemblage is to achieve the group goal, not individual goals.

4. Tolerate, even encourage, disagreement and deviance. The trick is to keep disagreement within tolerable limits. Be aware, however, that some people can't tolerate any disagreement. They may have a history of physical or verbal abuse and panic when bickering starts, fearing it will escalate into a full-fledged war. Others have been brought up to believe that fighting is to be avoided at all costs because it is rude. Whatever the situation, even though allowing some disagreement can be a positive force in a group, be aware of the possible deep-seated sensitivity of some members.

5. If appropriate, use humor, joking, and shared laughter to lighten the mood.

6. Stick to attacking the issues, not the person who disagrees with your stand. Don't keep repeating the same argument over and over.

7. Be an active listener. Even though you have a clearly defined viewpoint, be aware that the other person believes his or her viewpoint is as valid as yours. If you really listen, you might find that the other's view has some validity.

8. Look for possible places to compromise. Be careful, however, in reaching a compromise that you don't water down the solution so much that it will not achieve its goal of relieving the problem.

The Role of Power   One of the major causes of storming is the role of power. Competition appears to be unavoidable in human transactions, and one of the major centers of competition is who holds the power. **Power role** is the ability to influence another's attainment of goals. Power can center on controlling another person or persons, influencing the efforts of others, and accomplishing a goal.

All groups have a power structure. One person may exert power because he or she has information or expertise that will allow the group to reach its goal. For example, a group dealing with a financial crisis may turn to the person most knowledgeable in economics or accounting for advice. In some cases, power centers on some type of legitimate authority. The person who is appointed chairperson of the committee by the company president holds the position legitimately and therefore can act as the leader no matter the feelings of the group. Sometimes the power figure has the ability to give rewards or punishments. A parent, for example, often has the ability to decide on allowances and curfew times, thus putting her or him in a control position over children. A supervisor often has the power to fire an employee who disagrees.

Another type of power centers on personal qualities. That is, some people have the charisma or likability to become a power source. It is often believed that our most effective leaders, whether presidents or athletic coaches, are those who get people to follow them willingly, and do so because of their charisma.

Unresolved Storming   Do not assume that all groups make it through the storming stage. Some find that because of the personalities of the members, the inability to decide on norms, or the lack of clarity of purpose, they simply cannot work their way through storming. In this case, they either cease to exist, continue to operate in a storming fashion, or members gradually fade away and the group folds when members stop coming to meetings because they see no reason to attend since nothing is being accomplished.

Group Conforming

Groups that work their way through the storming stage are those that can go on to work together. This coming together is called **group conforming**. The group will know that it is in the conforming stage when such issues as norms, the group's purpose, and how to handle the role of power have been settled. At this point, the group is ready to work toward the agreed-upon mission, recognizing that it may revert back to storming and will then have to work again toward conforming.

Group Performing

Group performing is the action stage of group process. During this phase, the membership clearly starts to work toward goals. They have developed a history and know each other, have worked out their mode of operation, and have agreed to move forward to accomplish their task and maintenance roles.

All decision-making in a group contains both task and maintenance dimensions. These are not independent entities that stand in opposition to each other; they are interrelated.

The **task dimension of groups** includes decision-making, informing, appraising/examining, problem-solving, and creating interest in staying on track. Some consider accomplishing the goal the entire purpose of the group and concentrate solely on making sure that the group stays "on task." However, most groups also need to attend to the **maintenance dimension of groups**—meeting the interpersonal needs of the members. The main purpose of maintenance is developing **group cohesion**—the interconnectedness of the members.

As social beings, many of us like to be with others, interact with them, express opinions and feelings. Ignoring these aspects of group process, by concentrating only on task functions, can lead to an empty experience for some of the participants.

Group Adjourning

Some groups find it necessary to go through **adjourning**—going out of existence. In business settings, certain groups are constituted to accomplish a particular task. At the completion of the task, the group disperses. Study groups are formed to get the participants ready for a test. Once the test is over the group's purpose is completed. Such adjourning requires no specific action, other than awareness that the task is done.

On the other hand, some groups have no specific end goal but are ongoing. Even these groups may come to an end. Members may lose interest, people may leave the organization therefore depleting the membership, or group members determine that the group no longer has a purpose. In these cases, the members vote the group out of existence or simply stop holding meetings. It is advisable that group members take an action to formally bring the group to an end. If not, they may feel that they have not reached a true ending and feel incomplete, similar to not completing the process of saying good-bye to someone who suddenly dies.

Making Group Decisions

One of the most prominent functions of the group communication process is that of decision-making. Traditionally in the North American society, effective decision-making tends to follow a step-by-step procedure that allows group members to explore the dimensions of a problem, seek out solutions, and select a solution the members think is most appropriate.

Developing a process leads a group to consider the rules of operation to be followed to reach decisions. Formal organizations, such as city councils and fraternities usually develop a constitution and bylaws clearly spelling out procedures. A set of parliamentary guidelines, such as *Robert's Rules of Order*, is usually adopted as a framework for handling procedural agreements and disagreements.[28] Individuals who chair formal meetings should learn these rules of order. Less formal organizations may allow the leader of a group to determine the operational procedures. Whatever method is used, however, it should be agreed on before any formal work is undertaken by a group in order to have a clarity for how action will occur.

Formulating an Agenda

For the members of a group to be aware of the order in which things will be handled, an *agenda*—the order of business for a meeting or discussion—is formatted. It allows the group to cover topics systematically and accomplish the task in the most efficient way possible. An agenda should be used like a road map. It should contain just enough detail to allow the group to travel the path to the task but should not be so rigid that it does not allow for any detours.

In a typical meeting, the agenda format is:

I. Calling the meeting to order

II. Reading the minutes of the previous meeting

III. Committee reports

IV. Discussion of unfinished business

V. Proposal of new business

VI. Adjourning the meeting

Sometimes the agenda is not for how the meeting should be run, but, instead, how to go about solving a specific problem. The participants start their work by wording a **discussion question**—the issue or problem that will be dealt with. For example, if the group's purpose is to decide what type of grading system should be used on campus, the question could be: "What should be done to solve the problem of inconsistent grading policies on campus?"

Some general principles for wording a discussion question are:

1. *Propose the issue in a question form.* Since the major issue of a problem-solving discussion is "What should we do to solve the problem?" the discussion should center on answering the question.

2. *Keep the question short and simple.* Clarity is important.

3. *Word the question so that it does not show bias.* You cannot honestly discuss a question that states the expected conclusion.

Set an Agenda With Questions

When writing an agenda for a meeting, ask these four questions for each topic on the list:

✳ **What specific** issues will we discuss?

✳ **What outcome** do we want from the discussion?

✳ **What system** will we use to move the discussion along?

✳ **How much** time will we devote to the issue?

SOURCE: *Communication Briefings,* as adapted from Robert Levasseur, author of *Breakthrough Business Meetings,* cited in *Successful Meetings,* 355 Park Ave. S., New York, NY 10010.

4. *Word the question so that it cannot be answered with a yes or no*. You need to allow for other alternatives.

In some instances, the group is formed because the dilemma is clear and the group's task is to solve the preworded problem. On the other hand, some groups may be given a general idea of what is wrong and need to formulate a discussion question. One way to plan a discussion question is for each member to prepare his or her own in advance. Then the group can meet for a short time to share individual questions and blend them into a question the group can agree upon. No discussion of the issues should take place while the question is being put together.

Once the question is agreed upon, a format for a discussion may be in order. This step of the process involves developing a discussion agenda. Let us assume that you are in a group that is going to discuss the question, "What can be done to solve the problem of computer hardware and software incompatibility?" Your problem-solving agenda might look like this:

I. What is the problem?

    A. What terms do we need to know to deal with the problem?

        1. What is computer hardware and software?

        2. What is meant by "computer hardware and software incompatibility"?

    B. How does this problem concern us

        1. As professionals?

        2. As consumers?

II. What are the causes of the problem?

    A. Is the desire for profits the cause of computer hardware and software incompatibility?

        1. Is competition among leading companies a cause of incompatibility?

        2. Is the purposeful creation of more profitable products a cause of incompatibility?

    B. Does the swiftly growing and changing nature of computer design cause incompatibility?

    C. Does a lack of standards contribute to incompatibility?

III. What are possible solutions?

    A. Would government guidelines bring about greater compatibility?

    B. Would public encouragement of hardware and software compatibility solve the problem?

    C. Would forming a group of manufacturers bring about greater compatibility?

D. Could groups dedicated to enforcing standards solve the problem?

IV. What is (are) the best solution(s)?

    A. Which of the solutions proposed is workable?

    B. Which of the solutions proposed is desirable?

    C. Which of the solutions proposed is practical?

V. How can the best solution(s) be put into effect?

Following such an agenda allows for complete discussion and, hopefully, a well-thought-out solution.

In addition to developing a system for conducting business and arriving at results, a group has responsibilities for determining how decisions will be made and accepted by all its members.

Voting

Voting takes place when members are given an opportunity to indicate agreement, disagreement, or no opinion on an idea or candidate. The purpose of voting is to ensure that members know of the outcome of the discussion and the decision made.

There are four common voting methods: consensus, majority, plurality, and part of the whole. It is imperative that the method of voting be agreed on before the group starts working toward the final solution, for any alteration of the method can affect the outcome of the group's action.

Consensus means "all."[29] Thus in a consensus decision, every member of the group must agree on a proposal before it can be put into action. This is often the method used for decisions in which dire consequences can result from the outcome of the action. For example, most juries operate by consensus.

In a **majority vote**, the winner must receive more than half of the votes, excluding those who do not vote or who abstain (i.e., do not want to vote).[30] For example, if there are ten people in a group and all vote, it will take six votes for a majority to rule. If, however, one of the people does not vote, then it will take five votes for passage according to the majority method.

Plurality means "most."[31] Often when more than two options are available, a group may turn to plurality voting. If, for example, three candidates are running for an office, in plurality voting the one getting the most votes is declared the winner. In the same way, if five ideas have been proposed as solutions to a problem, the solution selected will be the one receiving the greatest number of votes.

Part-of-the-whole voting occurs when a specific number or percentage of those who are eligible to vote is required to bring about some action. For

Voting allows each member to indicate agreement, disagreement, or having no opinion on an idea or candidate.

example, some of the rules of operation of an organization can be changed only if 75 percent of those eligible to vote agree to the change. A group has the right to set any number or percentage it wishes to allow action to take place. These numbers need to be set before starting the decision-making process.

The method selected for the voting can have a profound effect on the outcome of a proposed action. In a historic case, the proposed federal Equal Rights Amendment was not enacted as a U.S. constitutional change, even though more than a majority of the states approved its inclusion. This happened because the part-of-the-whole method was used and a two-thirds vote was needed but was not obtained. If a majority voting system had been used, the amendment would have passed. Juries, which use consensus, require all twelve jurors to vote in favor of conviction. If the vote is 11 to 1, which is a clear majority, the person is not convicted.

Decision-Making Techniques

In the North American culture, there are a number of approaches to structuring a decision-making discussion. These approaches seem to center on two concepts. First, "effective group decision-making requires an analysis and understanding of a problem before members search for solutions"[32] and second, "effective decision-making groups normally engage in creative exploration of unusual, even deviant, ideas during initial discussions."[33] These two steps ensure that the group works toward solving an agreed-upon problem and that all the resources and creativity of the members are utilized. Two methods of decision-making are the Six-Step Standard Agenda and 1-3-6.

The Six-Step Standard Agenda   The **Six-Step Standard Agenda for Decision-Making**[34] is a direct outgrowth of the traditional reflective-thinking process, which stresses that a problem be identified and analyzed, solutions sought, and a solution selected and implemented.[35] The procedure for this method is as follows:

Step 1   *Problem identification.* A question is worded that states the problem. The query may be a **question of fact** (whether something is true and to what extent); a **question of value** (whether some thing is good or bad, right or wrong, and to what extent); or a **question of policy** (whether a specific course of action should be undertaken in order to solve a problem).

Step 2   *Problem analysis.* Collect the necessary information needed to identify the problem. This includes gathering facts, determining how serious the problem is, determining what harm is associated with the problem, deciding whether the harm is serious and widespread, and determining what causes the problem.

Step 3   *Solution criteria.* Before the solutions are addressed, determine what criteria will be used to evaluate the possible solutions. One of the most common sets of criteria centers on workability, practicality, and desirability. *Workability* is whether the solution will solve the problem. *Practicality* is whether the solution can be put into effect. *Desirability* is whether harm will be caused by implementing the solution.

Step 4   *Solution suggestions.* Brainstorm for possible solutions to the problem. **Brainstorming** consists of generating possible solutions without evaluation of them at the time of their proposal. Guidelines for brainstorming include:[36]

   a. Don't evaluate ideas while brainstorming.

   b. Don't clarify or seek clarification of an idea during the collection.

   c. Encourage zany ideas. Some of the best solutions are those that haven't been tried before or are out of the normal stream of action.

   d. Record all ideas without reference to who contributed the idea.

e. Encourage participation from all group members.

Step 5 *Select a solution.* Explore the merits and demerits of all the ideas collected during brainstorming, and apply the already-agreed-upon criteria. Another method of selecting the solution is to apply an evaluation technique entitled RISK.[37] The basic steps of RISK are:

a. Think of any risks, fears, or problems associated with the solution.

b. Brainstorm potential negative consequences either individually or as a group.

c. Post all potential problems on a chart or blackboard for all members to see.

d. Give time for additions to the list.

e. Discuss each negative again.

f. Weigh the risks and consequences against the perceived benefits as a group.

g. Make a decision to implement, delay for further study, modify, or kill the proposal and search for (a) better alternative(s).

Step 6 *Solution implementation.* Put the solution into effect and monitor it by follow-up testing and observation to make sure it is working. If it is not working, repeat steps 4 through 6.

The 1-3-6 Decision-Making Technique The **Nominal Group Technique of Decision-Making** centers on the concept of brainstorming without direct group interaction. This technique encourages idea generation from all individuals but avoids criticism, destructive conflict, and long-winded speeches.[38]

The **1-3-6 Decision-Making Technique**[39] is a format for using the nominal group technique. It takes place after the specific decision to be made or problem to be solved is agreed upon by the group, and members are ready to work toward solution. The technique gets its name from how the participants work—alone (1), then in a group of 3, and then in group of 6. The steps, illustrated in Figure 9.1, are:

Step A Each individual in the group lists what he or she thinks should be done to solve the problem, or the best possible decisions regarding the issue. This process is a brainstorming session. All ideas generated should be listed, with no evaluation made of the suggestions.

Step B Participants are divided into groups of three. Each group combines its members' lists. No items are deleted, but possibilities are

Create, Don't Evaluate

Keep the creativity spigot running by starting all brainstorming sessions with this statement: "We won't decide everything today," and ending with this statement: "We won't finalize anything until we sleep on it."

SOURCE: *Communication Briefings,* as adapted from *Creativity for Leaders,* by Gary Fellers, Pelican Publishing Co., 1101 Monroe St., Gretna, LA 70054.

Figure 9.1
The 1-3-6 Decision-
Making Technique

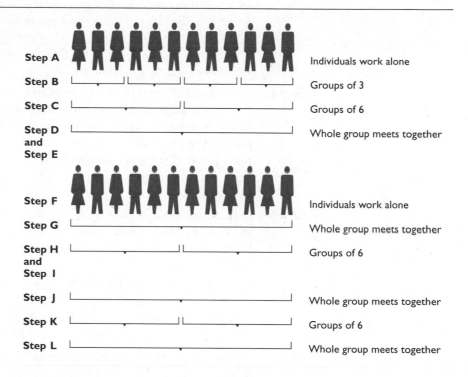

Step A	Individuals work alone
Step B	Groups of 3
Step C	Groups of 6
Step D and Step E	Whole group meets together
Step F	Individuals work alone
Step G	Whole group meets together
Step H and Step I	Groups of 6
Step J	Whole group meets together
Step K	Groups of 6
Step L	Whole group meets together

    combined and solutions or decisions reworded. There should be no discussion of the value of the ideas during this step.

Step C   Each two subgroups of three people meet and combine their lists. Again, duplicate ideas are eliminated and solutions or decisions reworded. No evaluations are made.

Step D   The whole group reassembles. A spokesperson for each subgroup reads its list aloud. All items are written on a long sheet of paper or on a blackboard. (It is important that everyone in the room be able to read the lists, so large writing is imperative.)

Step E   The items are numbered.

Step F   Each person prioritizes the entire list, ranking in order all items with no ties. The most important or best solution or decision should be numbered 1, the next 2, and so forth. Each person's rankings are recorded on a sheet of paper.

Step G   The rankings are collected and tallied. The top items are identified, the final number of which should be a proportion of the number of items generated in Step D. If thirty or more items were generated, the top ten would be a reasonable final list. For fewer items, about one-half to one-third of the total is appropriate. (Determine this in advance to alleviate conflict over how many should be included in the final list.)

Step H   Individuals select their top choices and then are randomly divided into subgroups of no more than six persons. If possible, a representative of each of the subgroups in Step C should be in each of the newly formed units. (This is not imperative, but in cases where there is lack of clarity in a statement, the individual from the subgroup that generated the idea may be able to clarify its meaning.)

Step I   Each subgroup selects what it considers the best solution using the individual selections from Step H. At this step, evaluations are made. Statements may be reworded, but no new solutions may be introduced.

Step J   Spokespersons for each subgroup report on the decision of the subgroup. If all subgroups have selected the same solution, the process is completed. If not, solutions that received the support of at least one subgroup are retained and the others eliminated.

Step K   Subgroups reassemble and select what they consider the best solution from those remaining on the list.

Step L   A spokesperson for each subgroup reports on the selection of his or her subgroup.

Steps K and L are repeated until a single solution is chosen.

Some smaller groups adopt an alternative approach, using only Steps A through F, and then have all members meet together to reach a final solution. Smaller groups also can adapt the procedure to be a 1-2-4 process.

The Group Setting

Although you might not have given it much consideration, where a group meets—the size, shape, color, temperature, and decorations of the room—and where participants sit can all affect the success of a group. Group meeting spaces represent a particularly important type of microenvironment that can affect the quality and quantity of communicative interaction, the participants' perceptions of each other, and the task performance of a given group.[40]

Two specific variables of importance in group settings that can affect group action are seating choices and the configuration of the tables.

Seating Choice

Where you sit at a meeting may determine whether you are selected as the leader, how much you will participate, and how others perceive you. This is an important concept for you to consider if you aspire to leadership, or wish to just quietly sit and watch the proceedings. For example, the person who sits at the head of a rectangular table significantly increases his/her chances of being perceived as the leader.[41]

Studies about seating have demonstrated that:

✳ "It seems to be a norm, in the United States at least, that leaders are expected to be found at the head or end of the table."[42] At family dinners, for example, the head of the household is usually seated at the head of the table. Elected group leaders generally put themselves in the head positions at rectangular tables, and the members place themselves so they can see the leader.

✳ At a round conference table, whoever sits at the twelve o'clock position is the most powerful, with power diminishing as it moves around past positions at three o'clock, six o'clock, nine o'clock. The least powerful person sits at the eleven o'clock position.[43]

✳ Individuals who choose a seat along the sides of a table not only decrease their chances of being perceived as leaders but also are apt to be perceived as individuals with lower status and less self-confidence.[44]

✳ People seated in a circle will feel more comfortable and interact more than they would if they were in straight rows or seated around a rectangular table.

✳ In a group consisting of all women, the one at the head of the table is perceived as the leader. However, in a mixed-gender group, a woman at the head position is much less likely to be perceived in a leadership role than a man who occupies the end position.[45]

✳ At round tables, if several people sit at one arc of the table and the others spread themselves around the rest, the two seated together tend to be perceived as the leaders. This is considered the visual center of the table as the others tend to turn to face the two seated together.[46]

Table Configuration

Table configuration or shape is also an important variable in group interaction. The quality and amount of communicative interaction is less with T-shaped or L-shaped seating arrangements than with rectangular arrangements, and less at a rectangular table than in a round configuration.

The round configuration is the most neutral.[47] At rectangular tables, communication usually flows across the table rather than around it.[48]

People seem to be aware of the different perceptions related to different seating positions. When people were asked to select seats to convey different impressions, they chose end positions to convey leadership/dominance, the closest seats to convey interpersonal attraction, and seats that afforded the greatest interpersonal distance to indicate they did not wish to participate.[49]

In classrooms arranged in rows, students who participate the most tend to form a triangle from the center of the room. For example, in a room with six rows of chairs, most class participation tends to come from those seated in the first four seats of the row closest to the front, the three seats behind them, the two seats behind them, and the one seat behind them. The least participation tends to come from the very back corners and those seated in the end rows.[50]

The Effect of the Physical Environment

The physical environment should be comfortable. A meeting can unravel if the room is too large or small, if it is too warm or cold, and if the lighting or the acoustics are not conducive to hearing and seeing one another. Groups seem to function more effectively if snacks are provided. Attention to these kinds of details will pay off in member satisfaction with the group and, hopefully, greater contribution to the group process and product.

On the other hand, the **meet while standing theory** requires a meeting place without any furniture. The concept is that people forced to stand will make decisions more rapidly and meetings are shorter because the participants get tired and want to finish their business and find someplace to sit.

IN CONCLUSION → Groups are an assemblage of persons who communicate, face to face, in order to fulfill a common purpose and achieve a goal. Group members influence one another, derive some satisfaction from maintaining membership in the group, interact for some purpose, assume specialized roles, and depend on one another. Groups are often classified by size, with small groups containing three to twelve persons and large groups more than a dozen. One of the most prominent functions of the group communication process is that of decision-making. There are advantages and disadvantages to both participating in a group and having groups make decisions, versus working alone. Groups normally go through five phases: norming, storming, conforming, performing, and adjourning. Where a group meets and where participants sit can affect the success of a group.

LEARN BY DOING ➔
1. Be prepared to defend or counter this statement: "The advantages of working in a group outweigh the disadvantages." Go beyond the arguments given in the chapter and use personal examples to develop your answer.

2. Consider a group in which you have worked that was not successful in reaching its goal or that had difficulty in reaching its goal. What specifically was the problem? How could the problem have been solved?

3. For your next examination in this class students will be divided into study groups to prepare for the test. After the exam, a class discussion will be held on the value or lack of value of this approach.

4. Mentally revisit a group in which you have participated. Write a short paper (which may be given as an oral presentation) analyzing its norming, storming, conforming, and performing stages.

KEY TERMS ➔

group	secondary group tension
small groups	power role
large groups	group conforming
risky shift phenomenon	group performing
groupthink	task dimension of groups
Pollyanna-Nietzsche effect	maintenance dimension of groups
social loafing	group cohesion
work teams	adjourning
study groups	discussion question
support group	voting
committee	consensus
media conference	majority vote
teleconferencing	plurality
focus groups	part-of-the-whole voting
family	Six-Step Standard Agenda for
public meetings	Decision-Making
symposium	question of fact
forum	question of value
town meeting	question of policy
group norming	brainstorming
group norms	Nominal Group Technique of
agenda	Decision-Making
group storming	1-3-6 Decision-Making Technique
primary group tension	meet while standing theory

chapter **10**

Participating in Groups

LEARNING OUTCOMES →

After reading this chapter, you should be able to:

Explain that people from different cultures possess varying attitudes about being a group participant and about procedures for working in groups, making decisions, procedural structure, and using information

Discuss the role of gender as a factor in group activities

Define and explain the role of the participants, the leaders, and leadership in groups

Compare and contrast the role of disagreement in the group process

Acknowledge the role of the hidden agenda in the group process

List the types and explain the communicative role of group networks

Define the authoritarian, democratic, and laissez-faire leader types

Explain why a person would want to be a group leader and demonstrate how the person would proceed to acquire the leader or leadership role

Groups are made up of people. Those who comprise a group play the roles of leaders, leadership, and participants. **Participants** are those members of a group who interact to bring about the actions of the group. **Leaders** are those who guide the group. **Leadership** refers to those who influence the group to accomplish its goal.

Members of groups, whether they are playing the participant or leader role, come to that group with cultural influences. These influences affect the way in which group members function.

Cultural Differences in Groups

We each are a product of the culture in which we were brought up. We learn the customs and patterns of our culture and they carry over into all phases of our lives. Research shows that people from different cultures possess varying attitudes about making independent decisions and being a group participant, about procedures for working in groups, making decisions, procedural structure, and using information.

Cultures and Groups

"The United States has the highest individualism index. We [Americans] are, without doubt, the most individualistic culture on earth."[1] This individualism—putting oneself before group loyalty—has a strong historical base; the United States was founded by adventurers and dissidents. In the North American culture, membership in groups (except those that are mandatory because of a person's work or academic environment) tend to be voluntary. While recognizing that there may be traditions, such as membership in a particular religion, Americans tend to decide on their own whether they want to belong to a group. You, for example, choose whether to participate in a social group or a fraternal organization. Once a part of the group, if you don't like being a member, you can resign.

Because of this ability to join and leave, allegiance tends not to be a lifelong commitment. This, however, is not the case in other parts of the world. For example, in many East Asian countries, Confucianism is the basic philosophy of much of the population. The **Confucian principle of i** requires that a person be affiliated and identify with a small and tightly knit group of people over long periods of time. These long-term relationships work because each group member expects group members to aid and assist each other when there is a need; sooner or later those who assisted will have to depend on those they aided. This mutually implied assistance pact makes for group interdependence.[2]

Cultural differences surface in the way a person works in a group.

Native Americans use "discussion as a means to maintain or restore harmony."[3] It is important for group members to work toward consensus. "In the absence of consensus, talk goes on interminably, with great respect for the conventions of oratory."[4] Discussion continues "until those in opposition feel it is useless or impolite to express further disagreement."[5]

Not only does the attitude toward being in groups vary by culture, but there is a difference in the training needed in certain cultures for group participation. Many North Americans, because they seldom participate in groups, need to learn about group operational methods when they enter into organizations. The same is true of people from other countries who have a high degree of individualism, such as Australia, Great Britain, Canada, New Zealand, and Denmark.[6] In contrast, people from societies where group adherence is stressed have clearer understandings of how groups operate since they are encased in groups all their lives. Those areas and countries that are the least individualistic tend to be in Asia and South America.[7]

Cultural differences also are reflected in the way a person works in a group. In many East Asian countries, for example, the Confucian principle of i leads to a strong distaste for purely business transactions. This is carried over into meetings, where the tendency is to mix personal with public relationships. Business meetings, for example, may take place over a long period of time in order for people to establish personal relationships; include activities like sports and drinking; foster an understanding of the personalities of the participants; and develop a certain level of trust and a favorable attitude.[8]

A good example of where the business is mixed with the personal is Japan, which is known as a nation stressing group culture, where individualism is submerged, and expression occurs in hidden ways. This, of course, is almost the opposite of how Americans operate. In the United States, individuals work in groups to get *tasks* accomplished. In Japan, the individual's sense of identity *is* the group. This is based on a long history of ruling families who created a social structure that bound families, villagers, and strong leaders together. In the United States, the stress has been on rugged individualism, with the group coming second to the individual. In Japan, the word for describing a group is "we." In the United States, groups often are divided between "us" and "them." For example, administrators and faculty members are part of the same group—the university—but often find themselves on opposite sides in decisions.

Contrasts in Cultural Group Decision-Making

If the assumption is made that one of the important tasks of a group is decision-making, another cultural variation comes into play. It is important to realize, when working in decision-making groups, that there are vast cultural differences in how people think, apply forms of reasoning, and make decisions.

In the Western view, it is generally believed that people can discover truth if they apply the scientific method of decision-making process. The usual procedure is: identify the problem, search for solutions, test those solutions, and put a solution into practice. The final decision is often based on a majority vote of the membership, with those who will have to implement or live with the decision often not part of the decision-making team. For example, few students are ever included in university discussions on curriculum requirements. The Japanese, on the other hand, depend heavily on everyone affected by the decision to be included in the process.[9]

Other societies use different decision-making approaches. For example, for the Chinese, "decision-making is more authoritative than consensual; decisions are made by higher authorities without the inclusion of subordinates."[10]

"Middle-Easterners can be described as using an **intuitive-affective decision-making approach**. Broad issues that do not appear to be directly related to the issue at hand are brought up; issues are linked together on the basis of whether or not the speaker likes the issues."[11] Although subordinates are consulted informally, the leader always makes the final decision.[12]

Meanwhile work groups in Mexico tend to use a **centralized decision-making process**. Mexicans often view authority as being inherent within the individual, not his or her position. Making tradeoffs is common for Mexican negotiators, including adding issues that are not part of the original business at hand.[13]

Cultural Contrast of the Role of Information for Groups

Even what information or ideas are used for making decisions may differ among cultures. American negotiators tend to compartmentalize issues, focusing on one issue at a time, instead of negotiating many issues together. "They tend to rely on rational thinking and concrete data in their negotiations."[14] In the United States, negotiating toward the final decision usually takes on a form of **proposal-counterproposal negotiating**, in which a plan or solution is presented and then a counteroffer made. For example, in a group meeting concerning salary negotiations, the employees will propose a particular salary and explain why they think this is the appropriate amount. Management would then make an offer of a lesser amount and offer counterarguments. This process continues until an amount is agreed upon and may be accompanied by a threat of the workers going out on strike, an action unheard of in other cultures.

The French, on the other hand, seem to "have no problem with open disagreement. They debate more than they bargain and are less apt than Americans to be flexible for the sake of agreement."[15] "They start with a long-range view of their purpose, as opposed to Americans, who work with more short-range objectives."[16]

"Japanese negotiators make decisions on the basis of detailed information rather than persuasive arguments."[17]

Because this book is directed primarily at individuals who will find themselves most often participating in groups in the North American culture, the material in this chapter deals mainly with North American participant and leader conventions and patterns. However, because of the multiculturalism of this country, you will often find that you are working with people from a variety of cultural backgrounds. Also, with the internationalization of business, it is becoming more and more common for North American businesspeople to be working in international settings, so knowledge of other cultures' group procedures can be helpful.

Male and Female Roles in Groups

Besides cultural differences based on nationality, the cultural roles of males and females play an important role in leader and participant operational modes.

Is gender a factor in group tasks or maintenance? Generally, the studies on leadership and group process indicate that differences do occur in the way the genders operate in a group. For example, "women tend to be more process-oriented than men. Men are more goal-oriented. For women, the process is as important, or more important, than the product."[18] Other studies indicate that "individuals prefer managers who possess masculine characteristics."[19] This carries over into courtrooms, where men are more likely than women to be selected as foreperson of a jury.[20] Research in educational groups indicates that students believe classes led by women to be more discussion-oriented, and classes taught by men to be more structured and emphasizing content mastery more.[71] In addition, male college professors are perceived to be less supportive and less innovative than are female instructors.[22]

Do you believe that men are more assertive in a group than women, or that women are too emotional to make rational decisions? If you answered yes, research proves you wrong. Several supposed truisms about men's and women's participation in groups have proven to be untrue, including the belief that women are too emotional to make rational decisions; that women have a low commitment to work compared with men; and that men are inherently more assertive than women.[23] However, being a member of one gender or the other does seem to affect group participation and perception. For example, "being the only member of one's sex in a mixed-gender group affects the perceptions of other group members and often skews the opportunities to communicate and the feedback one receives."[24] In addition, men are perceived to be more dominant and women more submissive during group communication involving both men and women, whether the communication is verbal or nonverbal.[25] And research on juries shows that male jurors typically offer 40 percent more comments during deliberation than do female jurors.[26] It also has been shown that "male students initiate more interactions with teachers than female students initiate,"[27] and that males tend to dominate classroom talk.[28]

Thus, it appears that there are differences, or at least perceived differences, between the genders as they participate in groups in the North American culture.

The Group Participant

Participants in groups have various responsibilities to themselves and to the group. They normally perform communicative maintenance and task roles, form networks by which they relay messages, and must deal with other members.

Responsibilities of Group Members

All participants should remember that an entire group is responsible and accountable for final decisions. Thus, being a member of the **silent majority** (those who say nothing during the decision-making process) does not release you from accountability for that decision. For example, if the group decides that each member should pay $15 more in dues, you must pay the extra fee, even though you may not have said anything during the discussion and may not have even voted on the issue. Despite your lack of participation, if you expect to remain a member of the group, you cannot announce after the decision is made, "I didn't say anything and I didn't vote, so I don't have to pay!"

All group members should be knowledgeable. In the Western logic system, although personal beliefs are important, expert opinions and facts reveal what authorities believe and what testing has proven, and this is the basis for sound decision-making. In other words, the use of supporting evidence can help ensure that your conclusions have substance and will probably be perceived as having some credibility. Consider how you can apply evidence such as statistics, testimony, and illustrations to your discussions. Your participation is enhanced if you use this research to support your comments clearly and concisely.

Some groups are plagued by people who insist on dominating the discussion and the decision-making process. These people may, at worst, destroy the group and, at best, irritate members and make decision-making difficult. Though it is sometimes very difficult when you have strong opinions and believe you are right and others wrong, each participant should try to respect as much as possible the rights of the others. This does not mean you should not participate if your views differ from others. It does mean that a point can be reached where continued bickering can be destructive to the group's mission. Let us say that after presenting your point of view, it appears that your ideas are not going to be accepted. Your task, then, is either to try and work toward reaching a compromise into which you can enfold your ideas or to accept the fact that you have done everything you could to get your viewpoint presented and accepted but have failed to achieve your goal.

It is important not to assume that rejection of your idea is a rejection of you personally. Unfortunately, many people have difficulty making this distinction. They assume that if one of their ideas is rejected, they too have been deemed unworthy. Not understanding this concept causes people to "fight to the death" for acceptance of their beliefs. In reality, what they are fighting for is to establish or retain their own legitimacy. This often causes the rejected person to start attacking others rather than sticking to the issues. Personal attacks often do little to get your stand accepted; rather, they cause alienation within the group. They often cause other people to take stands, not on what solution is right or wrong, but on who is right or wrong. This choosing up of sides often divides the group, causing internal rifts and destroying the chances for group cohesion and goal accomplishment.

Normally, group members should assume an active role in communicating with each other so that the entire group can benefit. Of course, there are times when, for whatever reason, you may feel that you do not want to participate. You may think that you do not have the necessary information; or you might not have strong enough feelings to interject; or that your beliefs have already been presented by someone else. Whatever the reason, if you knowingly and willingly don't participate, this is your privilege. However, remember that choosing not to participate is an act of abdicating responsibility as a group member.

Participants in a group discussion, much like therapeutic listeners, also must try to set aside their own prejudices and beliefs so as to listen and respond to what others have to say. This ability to suspend judgment is difficult. Try to resolve conflicts by adopting an openness to compromise and conciliation; that is, if you feel this is in the best interests of the group process and you can live with the compromise. Remember that compromises can result in giving up beliefs and moving to "watered-down" solutions, unsatisfying to all concerned. Do not allow a verbal bully to force you into a compromise or to adopt a solution you feel is not in the best interests of the group. Note that the last sentence says the best interest of the *group*, which may not necessarily be in *your* best interest!

Communicating as a Group Member

As a group member, you perform varied communication activities. Foremost of these are speaking and listening. In the process of participation, you probably evaluate information, propose concepts, and agree and disagree with the ideas of others. Group interactions seem most effective when participants are aware of their maintenance and task roles.

Performing Group Maintenance Tasks   In general, group participants should treat other members with respect. For most people this is not a great problem. Hopefully, you and others realize that you will not always agree. There should be an understanding that disagreement can be helpful as it opens the decision-making process to a variety of viewpoints and allows differences of opinion to be aired.

It is generally understood that having positive attitudes about what you are doing makes for a more committed and active group member. Think back to times when you have been proud of your group, the way it

Having positive attitudes about what is being done makes for a more committed and active group member.

acted, its achievements—having been on a winning athletic team or planned an event and been pleased with the results. Accomplishments help build group pride.

It is hoped that group members have pride in the group and show commitment to it. If this is not the case, maybe one of the tasks of the group should be to investigate why there are negative attitudes. Dealing with this issue may make working in the group more pleasurable and increase the productivity of the membership.

Taking an active role in a group through volunteering ideas, showing willingness to work on subgroups and committees, and making supportive comments are important components of a communicator helping a group to work cohesively.

Research shows that individuals who are communicatively supportive of maintenance functions reinforce others' ideas, participate in a constructive way, separate people from ideas, try to remain flexible, express their feelings, and describe their reactions.[29]

Performing Task Roles   Besides maintenance roles, participants need to perform task roles, which include initiating ideas, encouraging diverse ideas, using reasoned thought, staying open-minded, and being aware of hidden agendas; in other words, making sure the group accomplishes its goal.

Initiating Ideas   Group actions are based on someone first proposing actions, putting forth ideas, proposing solutions to problems. Initially, in most groups, people tend to be a little shy about presenting ideas. But as the group moves from norming to participating, this reluctance to put forth ideas is overcome. As a group member, if the others aren't proposing ideas, make a suggestion. This may encourage others to participate. If you know that suggestions will be sought, and you know the topic of the discussion or the nature of the problem, come in to the meeting prepared to propose ideas.

Encouraging Diverse Ideas   Another important aspect of task roles is to encourage diverse ideas. Conservative thinkers stick to the "tried and true." They tend to exclusively re-create past solutions to problems, sticking mainly to the status quo. Creative idea-generators go beyond the norm and search for different solutions. Their ideas may seem crazy at first, but many daft ideas have satisfied major needs. Historically, space travel, the invention of the computer, and even the light bulb, were all "far out" ideas. Don't be stifled by the tried and true; think creatively, even if you risk being called a dreamer or an idealist. Joining Alexander Graham Bell, Michelangelo, George Washington Carver, Madame Marie Curie, and other inventors, scientists, and explorers who have made a difference isn't a negative act.

Using Reasoned Thought   One of the important roles of task communication is to operate on the basis of reasoned thought. Being able to support sound ideas, develop well-thought-out concepts, being able to separate fact from opinion, criticizing weak or unsubstantiated ideas, using good critical thinking, offering evidence, and integrating ideas are important obligations of a constructive task communicator.

Staying Open-Minded   In general, most of us come to a conclusion, believe it is correct, and defend it no matter what. But ideally, we are open to the possibility that someone else's ideas may be as valid, if not more valid, than ours. There are often ideas we haven't thought of, approaches we haven't been exposed to, ideas that challenge our beliefs. Don't overlook the possibility of joining ideas together to make for a blended solution.

Being Aware of Hidden Agendas   Be aware that not all members of a group will be as open, caring, and responsible as you. Some individuals will attempt to accomplish their goals at the expense of others. Some members of a group enter the task process with a **hidden agenda**—an objective or purpose that goes beyond the constructive interests of the group as a whole. When individuals work for their own unstated ends rather than for the group's objectives, the result is usually counterproductive. A hidden agenda is apparent, for example, when a department manager, discussing budget allocations, promises to support any plan that divides the resources equitably among departments but then opposes every plan presented. In this case, the manager has a hidden agenda—he or she may want most of the funds for his or her department and thinks a delay will tire the participants and lead to a decision that favors that department. Thus the manager is trying to manipulate the group toward a personal goal.

In your role as an effective task communicator, listen carefully to the proposals and arguments of other members and be alert to the possibility of hidden agendas.

Being Cognizant of Time Constraints   A group participant should be sensitive to time factors, both to ensure that time is used wisely and that the group is not manipulated by a clever user of time.

If you use a great deal of time, and dominate a discussion with too many statements or lengthy comments, you run the risk that you will be tuned out, or that your contributions will be so overpowering that the group process will be lost in your dominance. Use time effectively, and make sure that you allow others the time they need.

Be wary of the participant who knows the meeting is coming to a close and that time is short, yet suggests a new, untested, or undiscussed solution. This is a device commonly used by individuals who know that when time pressures become a dominant factor, group members may act impulsively. If someone suggests a solution late in the discussion, make sure it is not acted upon immediately, before the group has time to really think about the advisability of taking the proposed action.

Encouraging Participants   Being encouraging rather than discouraging also can aid in task accomplishment. Negative messages during a group discussion can easily shut down communication. **Communication stoppers**—phrases that put down the ideas of others in a way so that they stop participating and that may cut off valuable input. Statements such as "That will never work," "We've tried that before," or "That's ridiculous" can shut down a group's communication.

Attending to Nonverbal Messages   The effective group communicator also attends to nonverbal messages. It is important to maintain eye contact with those speaking, and to actively engage, physically, in the discussion. The person who faces the speaker is usually showing attentiveness. The person who looks away or turns her or his body from the speaker could be communicating that he or she really does not care about the discussion, or disagrees with the comments being made.

Research shows that a rapid speech rate, fluid gestures, relaxed posture, verbal fluency (e.g., avoiding "uh," "things like that," or "you know") are positive nonverbal communicators.[30] "To keep a meeting moving along and under control," suggests one meeting management specialist, "let your own body language be one of your strongest allies."[31]

Roles of Group Members

Participants in small groups function in a variety of roles. It is helpful to recognize these roles and monitor not only your own behavior but that of others. Monitoring often allows you to understand why you and others are doing what you are doing. And this awareness opens the possibility of altering behavior, or alerting others to the role they are playing if actions being taken are detrimental to the group's progress. It also allows for self-praise and praising others if you discover that the roles being played are productive. Remember that titles and role descriptions are only classifications to explain the roles that group members may assume in their task and maintenance functions within groups. These designations are by no means all-encompassing, nor are they mutually exclusive. Like any model, they are simply ways to easily identify certain patterns of role behavior in task and maintenance.[32]

As a participant in a group, you or others may assume roles that are considered positive for group action. These roles include:

Initiator-contributor—presenting new ideas or perspectives

Information seeker—asking for facts and clarifications

Opinion seeker—asking for opinions to get at group values

Information giver—presenting facts and opinions

Opinion giver—presenting values and opinions

Elaborator—providing examples and solutions, and building on the contributions of others

Coordinator—identifying relationships among the ideas presented

Orienter—clarifying ideas for the group through summaries and identification of the group's direction

Evaluator—analyzing the group's decisions

Energizer—stimulating the group to greater productivity

Procedural technician—handling mechanical tasks such as paper distribution and seating arrangements

Recorder—recording the transactions of the group

Encourager—supplying positive reinforcement to group members

Harmonizer—mediating various differences among group members

Compromiser—attempting to resolve conflicts within the group

Gatekeeper—keeping channels of communication open by encouraging the members

Standard setter—establishing group norms and patterns of behavior

Communication Networks

Groups operate by different formal and informal patterns that link members together. As participants speak, they develop patterns that result in their talking to, through, or at others. These patterns can be analyzed and help the group to understand why and if their communication patterns encourage or discourage communication. These patterns are called **group communication networks**.

Early research on communication networks indicated five basic network patterns. These are illustrated in Figure 10.1. Each of the dots repre-

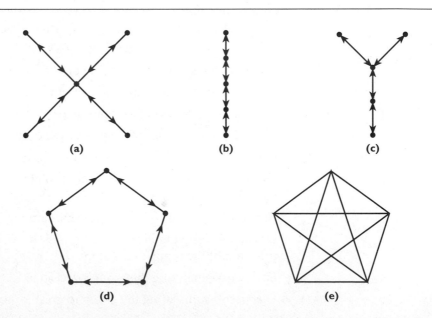

Figure 10.1
Communication
Networks:
(a) wheel
(b) chain
(c) Y
(d) circle
(e) all-channel

(a)   (b)   (c)

(d)   (e)

sents an individual communicator; the arrows, the way the information flows. The leader, or the person of influence, is at the center of each flow of information. For example, in the wheel, the chain, and the Y, there is a clear leader or power figure. All information flows toward and through them. Therefore, these patterns are referred to as **centralized group communication networks**. In general, centralized networks are most effective for groups dealing with simple problems. They are systems that often depend on a strong leadership figure to guide the proceedings. They can work more rapidly than other patterns because the leadership normally has a great deal of influence and can direct participation toward accomplishing the task.

In the circle and the all-channel patterns, there is no central focal person; information does flow from or through a single person. **Decentralized group communication networks** describe these patterns. In decentralized networks ideas flow freely, and they are more effective for solving complex problems. Decentralized networks can often result in greater member interaction and satisfaction because there is more interplay between participants and less influence by a power figure. The leader in a decentralized network plays less the role of director and more that of a participant.

Research concerning communication networks indicates that group members have higher morale in a decentralized than centralized communication network; that decentralized communication networks are more efficient when groups must solve complex problems but centralized networks are more efficient when groups must solve simple problems; and that centralized networks are more likely to result in work overload for the leader than are decentralized communication networks.[33]

Dealing with Difficult Group Members

Many people in groups are a joy to work with. They are cooperative, participate, assume leader/leadership roles in noncontrolling ways, and are willing to be open-minded in dealing with others. Then there are those who cause dissent, are self-centered, attack others rather than dealing with the issues, and won't stick to the agenda.

A theory told about problems that groups encounter centers on the idea that 90 percent of the people who are members of groups are reasonable most of the time. There are conflicts and differences of opinion, but people work for the good of the group and work things out. About another 9 percent of the members are somewhat difficult to work with; they have hidden agendas, disagreeable personalities, and seem to be marching to the tune of a different drummer much of the time. Then there is the remaining 1 percent. These people were created, but no one is exactly sure why! Their obstructive nature gets in the way of any attempt to cooperatively deal with them.

Using this theory as a basis, you can understand an aspect of conflict in a group and how to deal with different group members. To deal with the 90 percent, applying the concepts presented in this chapter on effective group communication should be sufficient to work things out and work toward task.

As for the 1 percent—the impossible people—there is very little you can do to work constructively with them. Reasoning with them, or giving in to their demands, accomplishes little. These individuals simply are out to make life miserable for themselves and everyone around them. They often are incapable of listening, processing, and working toward group cohesiveness. They tend to be so self-absorbed that there is no way to work things out short of giving in. But giving in seems only to encourage their behavior, which only escalates their negative actions because they know that eventually the group will give in to their tantrums and negativism again.

One coping method is to expel the impossible ones from the group. Another is to ignore them. A third is recognizing that they must have their say but it is no one's obligation to listen. Unfortunately, if one of these is the group leader—the boss, the professor, the parent—the problem is compounded. Even group experts and psychologists have no recommendations for what participants should do if this is the case. Quitting a job or leaving a group may be your only salvation if things get too bad.

That leaves the 9 percent who are considered difficult group members. Difficult people are those who cause problems regarding the task and/or maintenance functions of a group, actions such as frequent disruptions, long speeches, irrational requests, insulting behavior toward others, and interruption of participants.

Actions of counterproductive group members have been identified and titles given to them based on the destructive acts they perform. These include:

Aggressor—attacks the group and its members

Blocker—provides negative feedback and opposition, with no constructive suggestions

Recognition seeker—attempts to focus attention on himself or herself and ignores group issues

Playboy/girl—purpose of the group is for them to have a place to play around, with little or no regard for the group or its task

Dominator—attempts to take over the group and, if he/she can't do that, does everything possible to stop group progress

Help seeker—turns group sessions into self-help sessions with her or his problems at the center of the process

Special-interest pleader/evangelist—disregards what is best for the group and presents only the case for some special group or cause

Before taking any action, though, be sure that the actions are actually taking place and that the person is in fact difficult. Sometimes we perceive a person to be difficult because his or her ideas are different from ours. Is the person really difficult, or is the problem yours?

Experts seem to agree that to deal with difficult people, six general axioms should be followed:[34]

1. *Don't placate the troublemaker.* Allowing the disrupter to manipulate the group in order to keep the peace rewards the troublemaker for objectionable behavior and only encourages similar future actions.

2. *Refuse to be goaded into a reciprocal pattern.* Resist the temptation to meet fire with fire.

3. *Don't provide a soapbox for the troublemaker.* You cannot ignore disruptive behavior, especially when it becomes chronic.

4. *Try to convert disruption into a constructive contribution.* There is a difference between being disruptive and being constructive. Use the person's ideas to ask for other ideas. This takes the discussion away from the person and allows others to speak.

5. *Confront the difficult person directly.* If tirades or other actions are disruptive, tell the person so. Continual disruptions and other negative actions that stop task and maintenance progress are not in the best interest of the group and need to be dealt with. Ideally, the confrontation should be assertive, factual, and focused on the issue— state exactly what the person has done. For example, instead of saying, "You are always making stupid and irrelevant remarks," state, "The last two times we have discussed the issue of selecting a new advertising campaign, you changed the subject to why you believe the club should have more social events and why you believe you should be serving on the finance committee. Neither of these statements had to do with the topic being discussed and didn't help us to solve the issue at hand."

6. *Separate yourself from the difficult person if all else fails.* Some individuals leave no other option but ostracism by the group. As already

stated in the discussion of dealing with impossible people, quitting the job or leaving the group may be your only recourse.

We operate in groups not only as participants but also as those who perform the roles of leader or leadership. Understanding this aspect of group communication can get you ready to assume such a role.

The Group Leader and Group Leadership

The strength of a group is found not only in effective participation but also in meaningful leadership. The **leader** of a group is the person who is recognized as being responsible for guiding the group through its tasks (see Figure 10.2). The leader may be *elected* (e.g., president of the speech honor society), may be *appointed* by an outside source (e.g., the board of trustees appoints the university president), may *volunteer* (e.g., a person volunteers to chair the social committee), or may *emerge* by taking control (e.g., a father in a family). A group may also have more than one leader; for instance, a group may have several chairpersons. Furthermore, in some groups the recognized leader may not be the only one guiding the group; other members may share this function by either being appointed or assuming such responsibility.

**Figure 10.2
Berko-Wolvin-Wolvin Model of the Leader/Leadership Relationship.**

The leader is the group's guide. Leadership is the ability to influence, which can be used either positively or coercively. Both leader and leadership functions can be carried out by (a) the same person(s) or (b) separate persons.

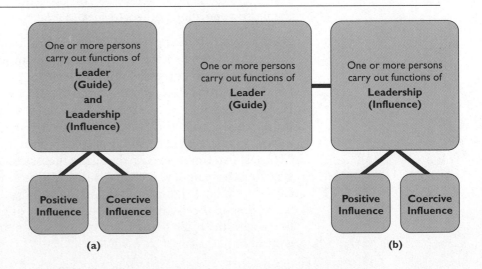

The strength of a group is found not only in effective participation, but also in meaningful leadership.

The ability to influence others' opinions and actions is known as **leadership** (see Figure 10.2). It can be demonstrated by one or more people in a group, and the use of the power that derives from leadership can be viewed as enforcing obedience and the ability to influence others to perform.

Leadership power can be defined, first, as enforcing obedience through the ability to withhold benefits or to inflict punishment. In this sense, power is coercive. **Coercion** centers on offering a selection of choices, all of which are undesirable. For example, in a meeting of nurses to discuss whether shifts should be rotated, many of the participants may not want this action to be taken. But if the head nurse is in favor of rotating shifts, then the power of the position may come into play. He may say that it's his responsibility to determine staff assignments, and that anyone who cannot accept this idea can request a transfer to another department. Thus the decision has been made through coercive power because the options offered may not be desirable to the nursing staff. Similarly, in a family, a mother can control the members by stating, "As long as you are living in my house, you will do as you are told or get out."

But leadership power also can be defined as the ability to influence others to perform or produce results. This kind of power does not use force or coercion. With this type of power, the influence of the person, rather than the authority of the position, is paramount. For example, in the meeting of nurses, the head nurse may suggest a solution whereby those nurses who want to be on a rotating shift may do so, and those who do not may select a permanent shift. The head nurse presents reasons for this solution and asks the others for suggestions. Eventually, the group accepts the head nurse's suggestion, with or without changes, because it was explained well and because he was willing to accept alterations and perhaps has a record of being flexible in such situations. This influence through positive leadership is a productive way to use power for the benefit of the entire group.

The tendency of certain people in leadership positions to act coercively has given rise to an examination of alternative leadership styles. One of these styles is **transformational leadership** in which the person takes on the role of transforming agent. A transforming agent is one who can change both the behavior and the outlook of his or her followers. This person keeps the interest of the group and its goals in mind rather than forcing her or his will on the group. Therefore, she or he gives up the command-and-control model of leadership.[35]

Another style is **superleadership**, in which people are led to lead themselves and thereby release the self-leadership energy within each person.[36] Such an approach is especially appropriate in today's scaled-down organizations, where not all qualified employees have the opportunity to move up the corporate ladder into management and/or executive positions. Consequently, each person can and should be encouraged to develop his or her leadership skills to stay productive in changing organizations.

Types of Leaders

Regardless of leadership style, leaders use their power to influence the outcome of any group effort. As such, leaders exhibit characteristics by which their style of leadership can be categorized. Three basic types of leaders have been identified:[37]

An **authoritarian leader** dominates and directs a group according to personal goals and objectives, regardless of how consistent these goals are with group members' goals.

A **democratic leader** directs a group according to the goals of its members and allows them to form their own conclusions.

A **laissez-faire leader** is nondirective and lets group members "do their own thing."

Evidence suggests that neither the directive nor nondirective approach is consistently more effective. Each approach works better under certain conditions. "The key to leadership effectiveness is matching the appropriate style to the group environment."[38] Thus, if group members are very task-oriented, they may be productive working with a laissez-faire leader. The laissez-faire style may be disastrous, however, if group members are unable to function productively on their own. Similarly, a democratic leader works well with a group that requires minimal supervision. If group members cannot accomplish their tasks because they lack self-discipline, an authoritarian leader may be needed to direct activities and assign specific responsibilities. Research on leadership style suggests that the power position of the leader, the task at hand, and the needs of the group should determine how and when a leader must adapt his or her style to any given group.[39]

Patterns of Leader/Leadership Emergence

If a leader is not appointed for a group, one of the questions that arises is how a person interested in becoming a leader proceeds. Research shows that emergent leaders exhibit a significantly higher rate of participation than do nonleaders.[40] In addition, "leaders become leaders when they exert influence over others on behalf of the group."[41] Leaders also tend to conform to the group's norms, values, and goals, while displaying the

Ways to Become a Leader

To make the leap from being a manager to being a leader as well:

✳ **Be seen** not only as the one who runs the operation but also as someone who's involved in it. Get out among your employees regularly and be open to ideas from both staff and peers. Make sure your people are working *with* you, not just *for* you.

✳ **Expand** your boundaries. Don't let a job description restrict you. Instead of defining what people do, job descriptions often define what they *don't* do. Read the description once, for understanding, and then decide what you should be doing.

✳ **Become** known as someone who's willing to consult by being willing to give up some control. Ultimately, you'll be more effective.

✳ **Cultivate** your intuition. Your decisions must be based on good data, of course, but an intuitive manager relies on both hunches and specific information.

✳ **Respect** established practices. This is a good way to win higher management's respect and—if necessary—to alter those practices. But win the respect of your peers and staff first. Respect from higher-ups will follow.

✳ **Be willing** to take risks. It's better to be a contributor than a perfectionist. Taking appropriate risks yourself is one of the surest ways to be an effective leader.

SOURCE: *Communication Briefings*, as adapted from *Management Letter*, 24 Rope Ferry Road, Waterford, CT 06386.

motivation to lead—knowing the rules of order, having charisma, being positive about themselves, encouraging others to communicate, and being a supportive listener.

Why People Desire to Be Leaders

Knowing that a great deal of responsibility is laid at the foot of leaders, that leaders often find themselves the target of attacks, and that they are blamed if things don't go right, why would anyone want to be a leader?

People want to be leaders for five basic reasons:

1. *Information.* The leader is privy to special information. Many leaders like to be "in the know."

2. *Rewards.* Leaders receive praise, attention, payment, power, and special privileges for being in their positions. Being a corporate executive making several million dollars a year seems to be more satisfying to some than working for a five-figure dollar amount, in spite of the responsibilities and time constraints. Some people also like to be in the public eye. Note that a number of corporate and business leaders do advertisements for their companies.

3. *Expectations.* Certain people have enough faith in themselves to believe that they can accomplish a task, or that they have better solutions than someone else. Listen to politicians running for office. They have platforms that attempt to explain why they are more capable of making things better than are their opponents.

4. *Acceptance.* Some people equate the title of president, chairperson, or boss with being accepted, liked, and admired.

5. *Status.* Acquiring status in one group can bring status in other groups. That is, record of past leadership often is the basis for selecting someone for another leadership position. Members of boards of directors of hospitals and banks are often the same people who hold leadership in other organizations. The president of the United States is almost always someone who has been a senator, member of the House of Representatives, or a state governor.

Leadership: Communicative Perspective

There is a fundamental link between human communication and leadership. Influential leaders such as Winston Churchill, Golda Meir, Martin Luther King, Sitting Bull, Gandhi, Mao Tse Tung, Barbara Jordan, and

César Chavez were compelling communicators. A communicative perspective on leadership emphasizes the group as a product of communication and the leader as a catalyst for the communication.[42] Leaders not only use words well but also "exhibit significantly more nonverbal cues than do nonleaders in task-oriented and informal small groups."[43]

Effective Leadership Questioning

One of the most important responsibilities of a leader is to monitor the proceedings and interject appropriate questions to stimulate discussion, clarify ideas, and resolve conflict. Some problems and model questions to ask include:[44]

> Issue: Drawing out a silent member
>
> Question to ask: "Does anyone who hasn't spoken care to comment?" Or, "Amad, what is your opinion of . . . ?"
>
> Issue: Calling attention to points that have not been considered
>
> Question to ask: "Does anyone have any information about this matter?" Or, "Lamont, would you care to explore this angle of the topic in more detail?"

When Participants Disagree

If you're in charge of a meeting or just a participant, you might want to use some of these suggestions to help deal with disagreements:

* **Find a** way to agree. *Example:* "I agree that this is an unfortunate situation, and I would remedy it differently from the way you suggested."

* **Use humor** to defuse tension. A spontaneous laugh can sometimes offer the fresh perspective the group needs.

* **Use peer** pressure to keep off-the-topic comments to a minimum. Ask the group early in the discussion to remind one another to stay on the topic. Agree on a signal that members can use to suggest the speaker get back to the point.

* **Avoid** "triangling," complaining about a person who is not part of the conversation.

Speak directly to a person if you want a conflict resolved.

* **Restate** a person's critical comment and ask if you understand it correctly. It shows that you're taking the disagreement seriously.

* **Seat a person** who is hostile toward you to your side rather than across from you. Confrontations will be less likely to occur.

* **Describe** observations in non-threatening, non-judgmental language. Don't say: "You claim that . . ." This suggests that the person might be lying. A better response: "Is my understanding correct? Are you saying that. . . ?"

SOURCE: *Communication Briefings*, as adapted from *Busy Manager's Guide to Successful Meetings*, by Karen Anderson, Career Press, 180 5th Ave., Hawthorne, NJ 07507.

A leader is responsible for guiding the group toward accomplishing its task.

Issue: Keeping the discussion focused on the subject

Question to ask: "That's interesting, but just how does this point fit in with the issue being considered?"

Issue: Using conflict constructively

Question to ask: "Since we do not seem to be able to resolve this difference now, could we move on to the next point?"

Issue: Suggesting the need for more information

Question to ask: "Is it agreeable to the group if we ask a subcommittee to investigate and bring back the needed information to our next session?"

Issue: Calling attention to the source of information

Question to ask: "Where did this information come from?"

Issue: Preventing a few from monopolizing the discussion

Question to ask: "May we hear from someone who hasn't expressed an opinion?"

Issue: Suggesting the need for closing the discussion

Advice for Meeting Leaders

To encourage creative thinking and idea generation when you're in charge of a meeting:

* **Ask open-ended** questions. *Reason:* Participants will have to answer with more than just a "yes" or "no."

* **Encourage people** to continue—even if they start to back off because they're repeating points made earlier.

* **Paraphrase ideas** when someone makes an unclear point.

* **Don't force** your views on others. Always remain neutral. *Reason:* A dominant tone will repress discussion.

* **Make sure** everyone contributes to the discussion. *How:* Direct questions to people who have not spoken. *And:* Ask for examples and elaboration.

* **Have opposing** sides state one another's opinions when conflict occurs.

* **Direct questions** to other people—or ask to hear another view—when one person tries to dominate the discussion.

* **Say to** the last person who spoke, "Tell me more."

SOURCE: *Communication Briefings,* as adapted from *How to Facilitate a Productive Group Session,* by Floyd Hurt, 1004 East Jefferson St., Charlottesville, VA 22902.

Question to ask: "We're scheduled to finish discussion in about five minutes. Is there a final comment?"

Responsibilities of Leaders

Regardless of style, a leader has the responsibility for guiding the group toward accomplishing its task and maintaining the group as a functioning unit. An effective leader needs to know when to sit back and let the group work on its own, when to step in and make suggestions, when to warn about such potential problems as groupthink, how to motivate the building of cohesion, and how to instruct on the need to critically evaluate ideas and express doubts. In other words, an effective group leader needs to know her or his responsibilities and how to carry them out.

A leader has responsibilities before, during, and following a meeting. These responsibilities might include the following:[45]

In Preparation for a Meeting:

* Define the purpose of the meeting.

* List specific outcomes that should or must be produced from this meeting.

How to Plan A Meeting

If you're in charge of a meeting, here are some planning steps to consider

✳ **Write down** the reason for the meeting—and your goals.

✳ **Specify the** type of meeting you're going to have. *Examples:* Will it be a sales, brainstorming, training or other kind of meeting?

✳ **Find out** how many people will attend.

✳ **Determine who** will be in charge of what. *Examples:* taking notes, providing food, setting up equipment, etc.

SOURCE: *Communication Briefings,* as adapted from *The New Robert's Rules of Order,* by Mary A. De Vries, Penguin Books USA Inc., 375 Hudson St., New York, NY 10014.

✳ Establish the starting and ending times of the meeting.

✳ Notify members of purpose and/or the agenda, their necessary preparations, and the time and place of the meeting.

✳ If specific resource persons are needed, advise them and prepare them for the meeting.

✳ Make necessary physical arrangements.

✳ Get necessary work items (e.g., pencils, paper, charts, data sheets, reports).

During the Meeting:

✳ Describe the importance and purpose of the meeting.

✳ Make an effort to establish a climate of trust and informality (if appropriate).

✳ Stimulate creative thinking (if appropriate).

✳ Stimulate critical thinking.

✳ Promote teamwork and cooperation.

✳ Equalize opportunities to participate and influence.

Follow-up to the Meeting:

✳ Remind members who agreed to do "after-meeting work."

✳ If minutes are kept, see that they are written and distributed.

✳ If the group decision should be forwarded to another person, see that this is done immediately.

✳ If work is necessary before a future meeting, be sure it is done.

IN CONCLUSION → Groups are made up of people. People from different cultures possess varying attitudes about making decisions or being group participants. Participants are those members of a group who interact to bring about the actions of the group. Leaders are those who guide the group. Leadership refers to those who influence the group to accomplish its goal. Group members, their leaders, and their leadership perform task and maintenance roles.

LEARN BY DOING → 1. Your class will be divided into groups. Each group is to take twenty minutes in which to agree on what a time traveler should take into the future, using this information for the decision:[46]

A time machine travels to the year 5847. By then, the world has been destroyed in a nuclear holocaust, and all that remains are a few men and women living a primitive existence and having no record or memory of the past. The traveler in the time machine decides to rebuild the world but can make only one trip back and forth in time. On the trip, which can encompass any years between the dawn of humanity and this year, the traveler may collect such useful items as living things, printed materials, food, toilet paper, and so forth. The only limitation is one of weight: excluding the weight of the time traveler, no more than 200 pounds of material may be carried through time. What should the time traveler take into the future?

After the small-group discussion, the class meets to discuss the following questions:

   a. What effect did differences in members' backgrounds have on the group's decision?

   b. What was the role of the leader in the group?

   c. What was the greatest problem the group encountered in reaching its decision? Could this have been resolved? How?

   d. What inferences about how groups operate can be drawn from this experience?

2. a. The following are statements on which you are required to take a stand. You may thoroughly agree (TA), agree (A), disagree (D), or thoroughly disagree (TD). Mark each statement with the relevant code.

   (1) Prayer should be allowed in public schools.

   (2) Corporations have an obligation to their stockholders to make profits; this obligation supersedes all others.

   (3) We have little control over what we communicate about ourselves to others.

   (4) Every member of an organization should be permitted to present views at a meeting, regardless of how long this may take.

   (5) The changing moral structure of current society has led to confusion and a breakdown of traditional morality.

   (6) Television is a major factor in desensitization to violence.

   (7) Advertising is necessary for continuation of the free-enterprise system.

   (8) War is an inevitable result of international conflict.

   (9) Same-sex persons should be allowed to get married.

    b. You are assigned to a group when you come to class. Each group is to elect a leader who will be responsible for leading the discussion. Keep in mind the responsibilities of a good leader and participant as discussed in the chapter. The group must reach consensus—total agreement—on one of the four responses (thoroughly agree through thoroughly disagree). Group members may rewrite a statement if it will help them come to agreement on one of the responses.

    c. At the end of the discussion each person answers these:

      (1) What two things did the leader do that helped the group in reaching its goals?

      (2) What one thing could the leader have done that would have helped the group in reaching its goals?

      (3) One thing I did as a participant that pleased me was . . .

      (4) One thing I did as a participant that I should not have done was . . .

      (5) This group did/did not work well because . . .

3. Using the discussions that were done in dealing with either #1 or #2, each person in your group is to analyze all of the group members, including himself or herself by identifying the roles each played using the identifiers in the "Roles of Group Members" section of this chapter. Share your lists with the members of the group and discuss the observations.

4. Identify a specific culture (e.g., ethnic, racial, or gender group), and prepare a short paper (which may be given as an oral presentation in class) indicating what research shows about characteristic patterns of this culture as group members.

KEY TERMS →

participants
leaders
leadership
Confucian principle of i
intuitive-affective decision-making approach
centralized decision-making process
proposal-counterproposal negotiating
silent majority
hidden agenda
communication stoppers

group communication networks
centralized group communication networks
decentralized group communication networks
leadership power
coercion
transformational leadership
superleadership
authoritarian leader
democratic leader
laissez-faire leader

PART three

Communicating in Public

chapter 11

Public Speaking: Planning and Presenting the Message

LEARNING OUTCOMES →

After reading this chapter, you should be able to:

Define public communication/public speaking

Explain the role of the participants, setting, and purpose/topic in public communication

Define and explain the roles of prior, process, and postspeech analyses

Clarify the role of the statement of central idea of a public speech

Discuss how to develop an impromptu (or ad lib), extemporaneous, manuscript, and memorized presentation

List pointers on preparing an oral style manuscript

Explain the advantages and disadvantages of the impromptu, extemporaneous, manuscript and memorized modes of presentation

Identify the oral and physical factors that lead to an effective presentation

Clarify how to use visuals in a presentation

Explain public speaking anxiety and some ways of dealing with it

276

F or many, the thought of giving a speech is exciting. For others, standing before an audience conjures up feelings of terror. No matter your attitude, you can learn to be a competent public speaker! Really!

The act of **public communication** involves a transaction between a speaker and an audience. You may think that public speaking is something you do not need to be concerned about, but this is not the case. In fact, "a surprising number of persons . . . do speak to audiences of ten or more people fairly frequently."[1] No matter what your college major or present position, odds are that you will be doing some type of public speaking.

Preparing a Speech: An Overview

Research shows that preparation is an important key to effective public speaking. The quality of a speech performance normally correlates positively with the total preparation time, the amount of research done, the time and effort spent in preparation of speaking notes, the time spent preparing visual aids, the number of rehearsals, and the time spent rehearsing out loud.[2]

Even though there is no universally agreed-upon one best way to prepare a speech, there is a process that seems to work well for many people.

The act of public communication involves a transaction between a speaker and an audience.

The first step is to decide on a topic or accept the topic assigned to you. Next is the formulation of a statement of central idea. Then, any necessary research is done to collect material that develops the statement of central idea. The next step is to construct an introduction that will get the attention of the listeners and provide them with the necessary background so that they will be ready to hear the particulars of the topic. The body of the presentation is then formulated so that the goal can be achieved. Then, necessary aids, such as visuals and computer generated graphics, are prepared. Last, the ending is developed, which summarizes the points and wraps up the presentation.

Parameters of Public Speaking

Any act of communication is based on three parameters: the participants, the setting, and the purpose of the communication. In a speech, these three parameters may affect the topic selected, the language used, the types of examples and illustrations chosen, and the aids needed to support and/or clarify ideas.

The **speech participants** are the speaker and the members of the audience. The **speaking setting** includes where the speech is given, what the time limit is, when the presentation is made, and the emotional attitude of the audience. The **purpose of the speech** centers on the speaker's expected outcomes for the presentation.

To give effective speeches, analyze the three parameters. Such an investigation should be conducted in three stages: prior analysis, process analysis, and postspeech analysis. The majority of the work takes place during the **prior to the speech analysis**, before the speech is given. But observing the audience for feedback (the **process of the speech analysis**) and paying attention to reactions following a speech (the **postspeech analysis**) are also important.

Prior to the Speech Analysis

In considering what you are going to say, you need to consider several factors. This information will aid in dealing with such actions as selecting or refining a topic, developing the speech, selecting appropriate language, and determining what information to include in the presentation. This information, the **audience analysis**, consists of assessing the demographic, psychographic, and rhetorographic characteristics of your prospective listeners.

Demographics

Demographics—factors that make the listeners unique based on their descriptions and backgrounds—include such factors as the prospective listeners' ages, gender, religions, ethnicity, educations, occupations, and race.[3]

Age   The general age level of your audience should be considered. Make sure that the examples and language you use are appropriate for the age level of group being addressed.

Gender   Knowing whether the audience will be primarily made up of males or females may help you in deciding how to approach the topic or what types of examples should be used. It is important not to stereotype all men or women as being universally the same; however, using examples that are appropriate to the gender makeup of the group can enhance the listeners' interest level. Further, be aware that sexist statements may turn listeners against the speaker.

Religion   A speaker can establish or destroy a common bond with specific religious groups through his or her language and examples. If the group is all of the same religious persuasion, using examples of people or principles of that group could lead to the acceptance of your views, just as an inappropriate reference might turn listeners against you.

Ethnic Background   The ethnic background of an audience often is as important as its religious affiliation. Appropriate ethnic references, if they fit the topic, can enhance a speaker's credibility. Try and select references that put the ethnic group in a positive light unless you are intentionally trying to incite negative feelings.

Educational Background   Understanding the educational background and training of your listeners is important. A speaker must choose material that can be understood at the appropriate level. For example, a highly expert audience at an informative briefing will expect a more detailed analysis of Internet capabilities than would a group of listeners who have just purchased home computers.

Occupation   Occupational interests and experiences often serve as the communication bond for speakers and listeners. Using examples that are specifically aimed at members of a particular work group can result in clarity, pride, and a feeling of togetherness.

Racial Background   Like ethnic background, the racial composition of your audience may be a critical consideration. Just as it is important not to make stereotyped statements when addressing all men or all women, so, too, it is important not to make assumptions about any particular racial group, especially if you, the speaker, are not of the same race as your listeners, or if you are intending to instigate strong reactions.

Psychographics

In addition to the demographics, the **psychographics**—attitudes and beliefs of the audience members—are an important consideration. This profile can be determined by analyzing the listeners.

Conservative/Liberal Dispositions   In dealing with issues such as abortion, the death penalty, genetic engineering, homosexuality, and school prayer, you are taking on topics about which the listeners may well have an emotional investment that comes out of their conservative or liberal dispositions. It is helpful to know the predispositions of your listeners as you select arguments and appeals to get them to respond.

Political Affiliation   The listeners' political affiliations usually correspond to their conservative/liberal dispositions. And they may have religious roots as well. You may want to know if your listeners were primarily independent voters, or registered as a member of a particular political party, before putting together your message in order to trigger the responses you desire by appealing to their loyalties.

Rhetorographics

Just as you analyze your audience, so must you analyze the **rhetorographics**—the place, time limit, time of day, and emotional climate for the speech.

Place   The place can affect the tone and topic of a speech. Such factors as size of the room, temperature, lighting, arrangement of the furniture, and physical comfort or discomfort of the audience all affect your communication. Do the acoustics of the room enable the listeners to hear you clearly? Is there a microphone? When using slides, can you dim the lights or do you have to turn them off completely? How is the seating arranged?

Time   Both the time limit and the time of day affect a speaker's performance. Whatever the reason for the time limit, a speaker has an obligation to stay within the prescribed boundaries, so it is important to prepare carefully so that you don't run over the time limit.

Speakers also should be aware that time of day can affect an audience. Early morning and late night hours, for instance, often are difficult times to hold the attention of an audience. You might want to plan a shorter speech if you know you are speaking near the end of the day or the finish of a conference.

Emotional Climate   The setting for public communication also may be affected by its emotional climate—the overriding psychological state of the participants. A community recently devastated by a tornado, for example, certainly would have a special emotional climate. Thus, a speaker called on to present a speech in such a setting would have to adapt his or her message to the tragedy and deal with the fears, bitterness, and trauma experienced by the audience.

From the information obtained in the prior analysis, you should be able to reach a reasonable conclusion about a topic that will fit you and the audience concerning the language and the supporting materials needed to develop the speech.

Applying the Prior Analysis

Assuming you have completed your prior analysis, how do you use the information?

Topic Selection   Typically, speakers are asked to make presentations because of their knowledge, experiences, or expertise; for example, a businessperson is told to present a new plan for reorganizing her department. Or a speaker decides that she or he has something to say and finds an audience who will listen.

On the other hand, sometimes a speaker is given limited or total leeway in selecting a topic. For example, in the academic setting, to help students learn how to plan and prepare speeches, instructors may let the students figure out what topic should be used for a class assignment.

If you are given latitude in selecting your topic, be aware that you are your own best resource. An examination of your life experiences and interests can be useful for selecting topics. For example, consider your hobbies and special interests, places you have lived or traveled, or the things you know how to do. Some people like to develop a speaking inventory to help them in the topic identification process. To develop such a list, do the first acivity in the Learning by Doing section at the end of this chapter.

Using the information presented so far, let's examine the process leading up to the presentation of the speech:

Picking a General Topic: An Example

Chan is a twenty-year-old college sophomore. In filling out his speaker inventory, he discovered that his interests and knowledge all center around his having worked at McDonald's restaurants for the past four years. He is now in their management training program and is in college to fulfill requirements for becoming a district manager. He would like to talk about McDonald's! He now has a general topic. The next question is, what specifically will he speak about? The answer to that question takes further analysis.

Using Demographic Information: An Example

Chan remembers that during the first day everyone was introduced. Almost all of the students are health care, premedicine, social work, preschool, education, and psychology majors. He is one of two business majors. A number of the older students have young children. The topics he considers include how a McDonald's restaurant is managed, what his job consists of, his possible future employment with the restaurant chain, the Ronald McDonald House program. He would feel comfortable talking about all of these, but which would be best for this audience? Based on the major academic fields of the audience, he eliminates managing the restaurant and possible employment—these would be more appropriate for business majors. He eliminates speaking about what his job consists of because it is of interest to him but probably not to anyone else. He selects the Ronald McDonald House program, since it deals with health care and social service issues and is aimed at working with children and parents, which fits the audience demographics.

Using Psychographic Information: An Example

Chan reconsiders his choice based on the psychographics. It doesn't appear, from what he can tell of the class, that any political or conservative/liberal disposition would be negatively stirred by his topic selection, so he decides to stick with his choice.

Using Rhetorographic Information: An Example

Chan now needs to test his topic regarding place, time limit, time of day, and emotional climate. The classroom, during a regular class session, doesn't seem to have any negative effect on the topic selection, though he is aware that his idea of showing snapshots isn't going to work in the large room, with a class of 30 students, so he decides to use slides and large posters instead. There doesn't seem to be any existing emotional climate he has to deal with. The time limit of the speech, however, is going to be a factor. He has a maximum of five minutes to speak. There is no way he can inform the class about all the activities of McDonald House in that time, so he is going to have to limit the breadth of the

The language selected for use during a speech must be adapted to the audience.

topic. He decides to tell the purpose of Ronald McDonald House and give two personal examples of children he has assisted as an active volunteer with the local project and university hospital.

Language Selection   Like the topic, the language selected for use during a speech also must be adapted to the audience. The average thirteen-year-old's vocabulary is not the same as an adult's. By the same token, certain terms that are common to a specific occupational or cultural group may be unknown to individuals who are not members of that group. And a person who is well versed in a specific subject can easily forget that the audience may not have the same knowledge or know the same terms.

It is crucial to adapt the vocabulary to the level of the audience. Be careful not to talk down to your listeners or use language that is so technical or abstract that they cannot understand.

Selecting Appropriate Language: An Example

Chan, in thinking about the subject, the audience, and any language that they might be unfamiliar with realizes that he has to make sure not to use terms that are not generally understood by those not working or familiar with the facility. For example, he must avoid calling the site "Willard's Place, the volunteers' nickname for it." (The first person to portray Ronald McDonald was the now nationally known TV weatherman Willard Scott who has been strongly identified with the place.) He must also be sure that he clarifies the services offered by Ronald McDonald with names the public will understand.

Statement of Central Idea   In developing a message, a speaker should know specifically what she or he wants to communicate. Thus, before even starting to develop the actual presentation, public speakers find it useful to compose a **statement of central idea,** which defines the subject and develops the criteria by which to evaluate the material to be included in the speech. A statement of central idea centers on what you want the audience to know, to be able to do, to believe. The statement of central idea typically consists of three parts: the goal of the speech; the statement of the topic; and the method or process to be used to develop the speech.

Goal   The **goal of the speech** is expressed in terms of its expected outcome. To *inform* (impart new information and secure understanding or reinforce information and understandings acquired in the past), or to *persuade* (attempt to get the listener to take some action, to accept a belief, or to change a point of view) are the goals of speeches.

Topic   The **topic of the speech**—the subject—should be stated as specifically as possible.

Method of Development   As you determine your statement of central idea, you also want to consider how to approach the presentation through the **method of speech development**. If the topic requires an in-depth study of one fact, then a detailed development of a single issue is done. For example, a theater director might discuss only how cast members are chosen. If, however, the topic requires a complete survey of ideas, a multiple number of topics may need to be covered; for example, how a play is cast, rehearsed, and performed. Just as in language selection, the method of development depends a great deal on your determination of how much your listeners know about or, indeed, need to know about the topic you have selected.

Key words can assist the informative speaker in developing a statement of central idea. Samples of such phrases include: *by explaining*; *by summarizing*; *by contrasting*; *by describing*; *by demonstrating*; *by analyzing*.

In a persuasive speech, key phrases for the method of development section of the statement of central idea can include the following: *to accept that*; *to attend*; *to support*; *to agree with*; *to contribute to*; *to serve*; *to share*; *to vote for*.

Wording the Statement of Central Idea   With the knowledge that the statement of central idea consists of the goal of the speech, the statement of the topic, and the method or process to be used to develop the speech, a statement can be prepared.

An informative speaker might word statements of central idea such as:

1. To inform the audience why competency testing is being used as a determination for high school graduation by discussing the three major reasons for its use.
2. I want the audience to know of the important effect that the Beatles had on modern music. To do this, I will demonstrate the changes in modern music before and after the Beatles' era.

Examples of persuasive statements of central ideas are:

1. I want the audience to fill out and sign living wills. To do this, I will list five reasons for them to take the action.
2. To persuade the audience to accept the concept that getting help from a mental health professional can be a positive act by examining the five most common reasons people seek mental health help and the statistics showing the success rate of treatment for those problems.

By keeping these factors in mind, you can avoid some of the major pitfalls of neophyte speakers. These pitfalls include not finishing the speech in the time limit, not accomplishing the speech's purpose, and not allowing the audience to gain the information.

Writing the Statement of Central Idea: An Example

Chan feels he is now ready to prepare his statement of central idea: "To inform the audience about the Ronald McDonald House project, by explaining the purpose of the project and presenting two examples of children who have been aided by Ronald McDonald House." He checks to make sure his statement contains a goal (to inform), a topic (the Ronald McDonald House project), and a method of development (explaining and presenting). Chan is now ready to develop his speech.

The speaker's preparation thus extends to doing a careful prior analysis of the audience and the setting and drawing up of a statement of central idea that will be appropriate to his or her level of expertise and knowledge and to the intended listeners.

Process of the Speech Analysis

As the speech is being presented, you actively analyze the feedback you receive during the speech itself. This process of the speech analysis is important to the accomplishment of your speaking goal. Speakers frequently need to adjust the materials as they present. For example, President Clinton diffused a hostile situation by adapting through good process analysis. During his first term, he was presenting a speech about his proposed health care plan when a man in the audience jumped up and started to verbally attack the president's efforts regarding AIDS research. Clinton paused, dissuaded the Secret Service from removing the heckler, and invited the man to present his point. The president then responded to the arguments, went back to his prepared remarks, and built references to this unplanned interaction into the remainder of the presentation.

Verbal interruptions are not typical. More typical are nonverbal cues of attentiveness and agreement, or of boredom or hostility, conveyed through posture and facial expression. Some speakers are sensitive to the *cough meter*. If you have lost your audience's attention, you will often hear people clear their throats, cough, and become physically restless.

Effective process analysis requires that you interpret cues accurately and then adapt to them. Be careful not to assume, for instance, that one person nodding off represents boredom on the part of all of your listeners. However, if most of the audience looks bored, you should be concerned.

You can adapt to the feedback you receive in various ways. For example, if you feel the audience does not understand a point, add an illustration, clarify your terms, or restate the idea. If you sense that the audience is not attentive, change the volume of your voice, use a pause, move forward, or insert an interesting or humorous story. Another technique used in the classroom is to ask questions of the audience members to get them involved in the presentation.

Most people don't feel totally comfortable in departing from their preplanned notes during a speech. The more confidence you have in your speaking abilities, the more comfortable you are with the topic, the more willing you will be to adjust to the feedback. Some people make mental notes about what is happening and then try and figure out afterward what went wrong so they can adjust their material or presentational style for the next speech. Besides noting what is going on during the speech, postspeech analysis can be of help in perfecting your speaking skills.

Postspeech Analysis

Postspeech analysis enables you to determine how a speech affected the audience. This information can be useful in preparing and presenting future speeches. A direct way to conduct a postspeech analysis is to have a question-and-answer session. The questions your audience asks may reveal just how clear your presentation was. The verbal and language tone of the questions may reflect the general mood of the listeners, telling you how positively or negatively they received you and your message. Informal conversations with members of the audience after the speech also can reveal a great deal.

Other postspeech techniques include opinion polls, tests, questionnaires, and follow-up interviews. These techniques are often used by professional speakers, such as politicians, to evaluate their presentations.

In addition to planning your speech, you need to attend to the presentation of your message.

Presenting the Message

To prepare for a speech, you should be aware that there are several basic means of channeling a message. These include the oral and physical elements of the presentation. You also should be aware that these elements are sometimes affected by the mode of presentation that is selected and used.

Modes of Presentation

Four basic **modes of speech presentation**—the preparation method and reference aids to be used during the speech—are the impromptu or ad lib, extemporaneous, manuscript, and memorized.

The Impromptu or Ad Lib Mode

Sometimes a speaker uses information acquired from past experiences, speaks with little or no preparation, and organizes ideas while he or she is communicating. This approach is referred to as **impromptu speaking**. Some speech theorists distinguish this from **ad lib speaking**, in which a speaker has no time to organize ideas and responds immediately when answering a question, volunteering an opinion, or interacting during an interpersonal experience. The impromptu mode gives a speaker a short period of time to decide what to say; therefore, the speaker does not communicate quite as spontaneously as he or she does when ad libbing. For example, when a teacher asks a question in class and gives students a minute or so to think of the answer, students use the impromptu mode

Facing a Last-Minute Speech

If you have to present with little notice, follow these tips:

✳ **Write down** a single phrase describing what you need to communicate to your audience. Then, write three actions, reasons or qualities supporting that phrase. *Example:* If you want to communicate how to increase sales, three actions to do so could be: make more cold calls, ask for referrals and survey customers. Mention the points during your speech. *Tip:* Write them on the back of a business card for easy reference.

✳ **Answer the** questions *who, what, when, where, why* and *how. Example:* If you're talking about change that will occur in your organization, tell the audience *who* will be in charge of the change effort, *what* the change is, *why* it's necessary, *when* it will occur, *where* it will take place and *how* it will be achieved.

✳ **Refer to** a current event or personal story and link either to your main point. Audiences will remember these more easily than facts or figures.

✳ **Use an** analogy to help get your message across. *Example:* If speaking about a new product, say, "Our new widget is like a stealth fighter because it gets the job done and you don't even know it's there."

✳ **Memorize four** or five quotes about motivation, communication, teamwork, etc., and mention them in your talk.

SOURCE: *Communication Briefings,* as adapted from *Smart Moves for People in Charge,* by Sam Deep and Lyle Sussman, Addison-Wesley Publishing Co., 1 Jacob Way, Reading, MA 01867.

---

when responding. Getting called on and being required to give an immediate answer is an ad lib.

These forms of speaking offer the advantage of being natural and spontaneous and tend to represent a speaker's real feelings because so little time is available to develop defenses.

Both of these modes are weakened, however, by the lack of time a speaker has to develop organized and well-analyzed statements. Another drawback, which derives from the impossibility of doing research, is the speaker's lack of opportunity to use statistics, examples, or illustrations to explain his or her ideas clearly, unless he or she is an expert on the topic. Still another liability is the speaker's tendency to ramble or use unnecessary phrases such as "you know" and "stuff like that" to gain thinking time or gloss over nonspecific information. Finally, lack of preparation can also result in oral uncertainty.

Putting together an impromptu speech requires quick work and immediate decisions. The process is the same as preparing for any other type of speech, except that there is less time to get ready. As you try to organize your thoughts, keep these ideas in mind:

1. Ask yourself what topic you wish to present.

2. Word a statement of central idea that represents the topic.

3. List the major headings that develop the statement of central idea. If paper is available, jot the ideas down. Write these in the vertical middle of the sheet of paper so you have time to add the introduction above them later, if time is available. Leave space between the major headings so that if you have time for developing subpoints you will be able to write them in.

4. Arrange the major headings according to one of the methods of organization (spatial, chronological, topical, causal, comparison-contrast, or problem-solution). Use the list you developed in step 3 and number the order of each heading.

5. Decide on an introduction. Most ad lib speakers tend to use a question or a reference to the topic, but often you can think of a story that relates to the topic. Because you probably will not have time to write out the whole introduction, jot down several key words so you will remember what you want to say.

6. Restate the major points you made as the speech's conclusion.

7. If you have time, go back to see if you can think of any illustrations, examples, or statistics that develop the major ideas you want to present. Write them in at the appropriate place in the outline. If not, try to think of some as you speak. Make sure that you clarify or define any words that may be unfamiliar to your listeners.

The Extemporaneous Mode

People who have more time to prepare for their presentations most often use the **extemporaneous speaking mode**, developing a set of "talking points," such as notes or an outline to assist them in presenting their ideas. The speaker knows in advance that she or he will be giving a speech and can prepare by doing research and planning the speech.

The extemporaneous mode offers these significant advantages: time to find the information needed to help accomplish the statement of central idea; the security of having notes or an outline to refer to throughout the speech; use of quotations, illustrations, and statistics in written form for backing up ideas; and a more spontaneous and natural oral presentation and physical presentation than are likely in the manuscript or memorized mode.

As with any presentational mode, the extemporaneous mode of delivery has some disadvantages as well. For example, if a speaker does not allow sufficient time for preparation and rehearsal, he or she may get mentally lost during the presentation. Furthermore, if a speaker refers to the notes or outline too frequently during the speech, or has too many notes, she or he may fail to interact with the audience. And, because extemporaneous material is never written out word for word, a speaker will not have a permanent record of the speech.

Preparing the Extemporaneous Speech   Most speakers use either notes or an outline when they present an extemporaneous speech. Notes can consist of a list of words that guide the speaker through the presentation or a series of phrases or sentences to act as clues. Most commonly, extemporaneous speakers use an outline.

Many speakers start out with a **speech planning outline**, a brief framework used to think through the process of the speech. It contains the major ideas of the speech, without elaboration. It is your means of thinking through the things you wish to say and putting them in a structured order. Some speakers use this for practice and then go on to use it while speaking. However, others prepare a **speech presentation outline** in which they flesh out the outline with details such as examples and illustrations, and write in internal summaries and forecasts.

The basic concept in outlining is that the speaker has a clear step-by-step structure of what will be said and in what order. Some speakers simply list the headings and subordinate points in a sequential order. Others use a formal outlining method. In formal outlining, the letters and numbers allow for easy visual remembrances of what stage of the outline the speaker is using. The traditional format is:

I. Major heading

  A. Major point (level 1)

    1. Subordinate point (level 2)

      a. Subordinate point (level 3)

        (1) Subordinate point (level 4)

          (a) Subordinate point (level 5)

Many rules have been developed for how to structure an outline.[4] Some instructors will be very specific as to what the outline is to look like, indicating that the discipline of developing the outline aids the speaker in making sure that all parts of the speech are well developed and ordered. Others will simply state, "The outline is for your benefit. Prepare it so that you are comfortable with the material and the outline helps you remember what you need to say."

Formal outlining rules often include:

1 *Block information for clarity of ideas.* Use consistent indenting so that each major head is flush with the left margin, each major point is indented five spaces, each level 2 subordinate point indented ten spaces. This allows you to visually find your place as you proceed through the speech.

2 *Be consistent in format.* Decide whether you wish to use sentences, phrases, or words or a combination of sentence/phrases/words. The consistency will allow you to anticipate exactly how you will be using the material as you speak.

3 *Use subordinate points to support the preceding major point.* The purpose of subordinate points is to flesh out the major ideas by adding clarifiers, examples, and illustrations. Some outlining purists contend that "for every A there should be a B and for every 1 there must be a 2." In general, this makes sense. If you are subdividing an idea, breaking it into parts, then by definition you must have at least two subideas. This does not mean, however, that if you are supporting an idea with an example, you must have two examples. Again, the important thing is that the outline help you develop and present a clear and organized speech.

4 *Include internal summaries and forecasts.* Internal summaries restate each major point before proceeding to the next major point. Forecasts tell the listener what is coming next. To ensure that they remember to include these in the oral presentation, many speakers write the statements into the outline.

5 *Write notes in the margins to remind yourself of necessary information.* If you need a reminder to slow down in certain sections, or to use a visual aid to emphasize a point, write yourself a note in the margin of the outline. Use a color ink that stands out. Though the marginal notes are not an official part of the outline, they are yet another device to help make the speech effective and to help you feel comfortable and gain confidence.

6 *Avoid overoutlining.* To avoid having an excessive number of notes, you should limit the quantity to those you absolutely need to trigger your thoughts. In determining just what is essential, you are wise to consider this analogy. The first time you drive to a particular site, you may need a detailed set of directions complete with route numbers, road markers, and indications of exact mileage. On your second trip, you need less information; and by the third trip, you need almost none. So it is with your use of notes and outlines. You should have

enough information to feel comfortable and free to navigate through the presentation with no fear of getting lost. The only way to discover the extent of your readiness is to take several test drives through your speech to ascertain how much prepared information you really need to have with you in the form of written prompts.

The Manuscript Mode

In the **manuscript speech mode**, the material is written out and delivered word for word. This method offers the advantages of providing accurate language and solid organization. In addition, it gives the speaker a permanent written record of the speech.

But the manuscript mode also has some disadvantages. Because the manuscript provides a word-for-word record of the speech, the speaker cannot easily adapt it to suit the audience during the presentation. The speaker is stuck with the message as written. As a result, the speaker must depend only on prior audience analysis to ensure that the message is tailored to the listeners.

Members of an audience will feel involved in the presentation if the speaker looks at them.

The manuscript mode of delivery requires the ability to read effectively from the written page. An effective speaker should use extensive eye contact, vocal inflections, and physical actions to maintain rapport with the listeners. Unfortunately, most people are not very good oral readers. They tend to read monotonously, make reading errors, get lost in the script, and fail to establish good eye contact. Many novice speakers turn to the manuscript mode because they feel more secure with it. However, manuscripted speeches, in the hands of many people, are dull and boring presentations.

Usually speakers adopt the extemporaneous mode rather than the manuscript mode because it allows them to interact more freely with the audience and to adapt better to feedback. At times, however, preparing an exact word-for-word presentation is necessary. For example, the manuscript mode must be used when speakers are going to be quoted, when they must meet specific time requirements, or when they need precise word selection.

Preparing the Manuscript   Unlike a reader, who has the opportunity to reread a passage, the listener has only one opportunity to receive, understand, and interpret the oral message (unless he or she uses an audio or videotape recorder and can replay passages).

When composing something that will be heard rather than read, you must write as though you are speaking, not reading. To do this, write as you would talk, say the material aloud as you are writing, and practice reading the material aloud. These pointers may help you prepare a manuscript:[5]

1. Use the active, not passive, voice.

2. Keep sentences short.

3. Use short, simple words.

4. Use repetition to reinforce major ideas.

5. Express ideas that create emotional or sensory allusions for the listener.

6. Avoid using technical terms that the audience may not understand.

7. If you use one person's name and then another person's name, avoid "he" to refer to one or the other afterward; the audience will not know to which one you are referring.

8. If a member of the audience is expected to apply the material to himself or herself, then the word *you* is appropriate. If the reference is to an experience that you, the speaker, had, or something you are going to do, then use *I*.

9. The word *we* is more involving than the word *you*.

10. Unless it is absolutely necessary not to do so, round off any numbers you use.

11. Use language with which you are comfortable. The purpose of language is to convey a message, not impress the audience.

12. Remember the rule of the bumper sticker . . . express specific ideas by employing clear ideas in a few well-chosen words.

Reading from the Manuscript   Using a manuscript can be difficult, because you must look at the audience at the same time that you are trying to read your material with animation and naturalness. You will have to work out some system for following the script in an unobtrusive way so that you also can look at the audience without losing your place. Be careful not to move or flip manuscript pages unnecessarily; this draws attention away from you and toward the manuscript. Also, try to avoid falling into a flat-sounding reading style. Instead, read according to the meaning by stressing important words and ideas, and vary your tone of voice so that you are speaking naturally. Some speakers run the index finger of their left hand down the side of the manuscript so that they are continuously pointing to the start of the next printed line they will be reading. This way, when they look up, they can find their place when they return to the manuscript.

One method for establishing eye contact with an audience while following a manuscript in an unobtrusive way is *eye span*. This involves training your eyes to glance down quickly, pick out a meaningful phrase, and deliver it to the audience. As you reach the end of the phrase, but before you have finished saying it, glance down and grasp the next phrase to be spoken. It is helpful to underline key words and mark off phrases.

It also helps to arrange the script in a manner that keeps you from getting lost. Double- or triple-space the information; number the pages; do not divide sentences by starting them on one page and finishing them on another; do not write or type on the backs of the pages; and use a large font. If you are going to use note cards, write on only one side so you don't get lost, and number each card.

The Memorized Mode

In the **memorized speech mode**, a speech is written out word for word and is then committed to memory. Public speakers seldom use this mode of communication, because it is potentially disastrous. Whereas speakers who use the extemporaneous or manuscript mode can refer to written information, those who use the memorized mode have nothing available for reference as they speak. Forgetting one idea can lead to forgetting everything. Also, the memorizer may be so concerned about getting the exact word in exactly the right place that the meaning of the words becomes secondary.

The few advantages of the memorized mode include the ability to select exact wording and examples, look at the audience during the entire speaking process, and time the presentation precisely. The disadvantages of memorized speaking usually so overshadow its advantages that few people choose to use this mode.

Oral and Physical Presentation

People who capture their listeners' attention are apt to share certain qualities. These include confidence and ease, authority, conviction, credibility, sincerity, warmth, animation, enthusiasm, vitality, intensity, concern, and empathy. They also make effective use of eye contact, conversational tone, and variety of pitch, pacing, projection, and phrasing.[6]

Vocal Delivery

A well-prepared speech can be enhanced by effective vocal and physical delivery. Audience members tend to listen with attention when a speaker is dynamic and enthusiastic.

Vocal Variety   Someone who speaks in a monotone—a flat, boring sound resulting from constant pitch, volume, and rate—eventually will cause the audience to tune out. Most people speak about 125 to 150 words per minute, the equivalent of one-half to two-thirds of a double-spaced typewritten page, which is a comfortable pace. Speaking slower than that can lead to listener boredom. On the other hand, speaking so rapidly that the listener can't understand will result in confusion.

Pronunciation   "There are many different and acceptable ways of pronouncing American English, because our language is spoken differently in various parts of the United States and Canada."[7] Standard American English—that spoken by well-educated Canadians and Americans of the midwest, mideast, and far west—tends to be the most acceptable of the regional dialects. Speech becomes substandard if pronunciations cause misunderstandings and sets a negative tone for the presentation.[8]

Because you will be evaluated on the basis not only of what you say but on how you say it, you should be aware of some common pronunciation problems and their causes.[9]

1. *Sloppy or incorrect articulation.* If you say "air" for *error* and "dint" for *didn't,* you are mispronouncing because of laziness in the use of articulators. Be conscious of dropping the *g* sound at the end of words ending in *ing,* such as *going, doing,* and *watching.* Also be aware of slurring words together. "Alls-ya-godado" is not an understandable substitute for *all you have to do.*

2. *Ignorance of correct pronunciation.* Most of us have reading vocabularies that are far greater than our speaking vocabularies. In preparing a speech, look up in a dictionary or a pronunciation guide any word whose pronunciation is unfamiliar.

3. *Vowel distortion.* Some of us have grown up in environments in which words are mispronounced because of vowel substitutions. *Milk* may have been pronounced as "melk"; *secretary* may have been "sekatury"; and *many* may have been "miny." Being aware of the distortions allows some people to begin monitoring their own pronunciations and correcting themselves.

4. *Pronunciation outside the normal pattern.* If we assume that Standard American English is the norm, certain pronunciations usually are not considered acceptable in the marketplace of business, education, and the professions. *Asked* is not "axt," *many* is not "miny," and *picture* and *pitcher* are not the same word.

Physical Elements

The physical elements of public communication include gestures, movement, posture, and eye contact. The way you use visual aids is another physical element.

Gestures   Gestures involve the use of hands, body movements, and facial expressions. Researchers have determined that people who use hand movements when they talk appear freer, more open, and more honest to an audience.[10]

Knowing the importance of movement, students in speech classes sometimes ask their instructors to teach them how to gesture. Unfortunately, it is impossible to do so because gesturing is the result of the speaker's degree of involvement, excitement, dynamism, and their personality. Each person uses his or her own characteristic gesture pattern while communicating. Some people use a great number of gestures, whereas others use only a few.

Gestures should be natural. That is why you should not worry about what to do with your hands; forget them and they will take care of them-

Rest Your Hands When Speaking

Unsure of what to do with your hands while giving a speech? Rest them lightly on the corners of the lectern.

Don't drop them at your sides or touch your notes except when "absolutely necessary."

This will permit you to begin your speech without appearing unsure and use gestures naturally as you "get into" the substance of the speech.

SOURCE: *Communication Briefings,* as adapted from Dr. Jim Vickrey, professor of speech communication, Troy State University, Troy, AL 36082.

selves. Your hands will be active when your body calls for movement—unless you are gripping the lectern so tightly that you cannot let go or have your hands jammed inside your pockets and cannot get them out. If you are orally dynamic, so will be your body. If you are orally boring, so will be your body.

Eye Contact   Establishing **eye contact**—looking into the eyes of your audience as you speak—is another key to effective speaking. Members of an audience will tend to feel involved in the presentation if you look at them. Maintaining eye contact also helps you receive feedback so you can adjust your presentation accordingly. To use eye contact effectively, look directly

The Magic V

Let's say there are 500 people in your audience. It's very difficult to make actual eye contact with 500 people. However, there's a trick to help called the Magic V (see the figure). When you look at someone, everyone in a *V* behind that person thinks you are looking at them.

Divide the room up into a tic-tac-toe board. Look at one of the "squares" and use the *V* and the mind touch to lift that section. Once you have them, move to another square.

When the crowd is large, use the Magic V. Draw a "tic-tac-toe" in your mind over the crowd. As you look at each square, you are actually looking at all the people, in a "V" behind the person you are really looking at.

After you have made contact with that group emotionally, switch to another square. Make sure you work the squares at random.

SOURCE: From *Secrets of Successful Speakers* by Lilly Walters, pp. 138–139. Copyright © 1993. Reproduced with permission of McGraw-Hill, Inc.

When Speaking

If you need notes to refer to during a presentation, retain eye contact with your audience by using "hidden notes."

Place your brief notes in the frame of a transparency or below your main headings on the flip chart. A quick glance will prompt you to get to the next key point.

SOURCE: *Communication Briefings,* as adapted from Norman B. Sigband, 3109 Dona Susana Drive, Studio City, CA 91604.

at listeners, not over their heads. Also shift your focus so that you are not maintaining contact with just one section of the audience, and be especially careful not to overlook those in the front or back rows.

Use of Visual Aids Keep these basic suggestions in mind when you use visual aids in a presentation:

* Do not stand between the visual aid and the audience; you will block their view.

* Speak toward the audience, not toward the visual aid.

* Know the visual aid well enough so that you do not have to study it while you talk.

* Point to the particular place on the aid that you are discussing.

* Use the aid at the point in your presentation where it will have the greatest impact.

* If you do not need the aid for part of the speech, put it down, cover it up, or turn it over. If it is electrical, turn it off.

In addition to preparation for speaking, understanding and dealing with speaker anxiety can help you be a more effective speaker.

Public Speaking Anxiety

Very few speakers escape the "butterflies." "Speech anxiety is a serious problem for a large number of people and has been found to affect career development as well as academic performance."[11] (If you would like to ascertain your public speaking anxiety level, complete Activity 2 in the Learn by Doing section of this chapter.)

Public speaking anxiety is a phobia known as **speechophobia.** It is characterized by by these characteristics: (1) there is persistent fear of a specific situation out of proportion to the reality of the danger, (2) there is a compelling desire to avoid and escape the situation, (3) it is recognized that the fear is unreasonable and excessive, and (4) it is not due to any other disorder.[12] As with most phobias, it is curable. A lack of knowledge of how to prepare and present a speech leads to anxiety.[13] Hopefully, as you read this book and practice developing speeches, you will gain the knowledge to overcome this major roadblock to overcoming public speaking fear. Here are some suggestions for dealing with speaking anxiety:

Does Your Heart Flutter Before a Big Speech?

Psychologists have identified and recorded three stages of heart rate increase that occur before and during a speech. Keep in mind that the average resting heart rate is between 60-80 beats per minute.

Anticipation Stage:
This is the time just before a speaker stands up to begin a presentation. The average heart rate is 90–140 beats per minute.

Confrontation Stage:
This stage occurs during the first 30 seconds of a speech. The average heart rate is 110–190 beats per minute.

Drop-off Stage:
The average heart rate goes back down to 90–140 beats per minute after the first 30 seconds.

SOURCE: "Speak with Impact," Communication Development Associates, Inc., 21550 Oxnard St., #880, Woodland Hills, CA 91367.

Do not avoid the experience of giving a presentation. The more you speak, the more comfortable you will get. Although your nervousness may not go away completely, it should let up as you get more practice.

Do not fail to prepare, assuming that the longer you avoid confronting the situation, the less time there will be to build up anxiety. If you are not prepared, the panic will probably be greater than it would be if you had the material to get you by.

Accept that you will experience some anxiety. All speakers encounter at least a moment of anxiousness as they begin, because they are, essentially, facing the unknown. Indeed, a study of what Americans fear the most reveals that public speaking is our greatest fear![14]

Do not take drugs or alcohol because you think they will relax you. All they will do is dull your reflexes and increase your chances of forgetting and making a fool of yourself.

Use relaxation techniques.[15] Before beginning a presentation, some speakers find it helpful to take several deep breaths and expel all the air from their lungs. Others like to shake their hands at the wrists to "get out the nervousness." Some people favor grabbing the seat of their chair with both hands, pushing down, holding the position for about five seconds, and repeating this movement about five times. This tightens and then loosens the muscles, which causes a decrease in physical tension.

Recognize the anxiety. Another approach is to think of the experience of getting up before the audience, and feel the anxiety. Let it stay in your mind, imagining that you are going through the experience. Let yourself be as nervous as you can; psychologically push it as far as you can. Some people report that by imagining the upcoming experience in its worst way, the actual experience becomes much easier.[16]

Practice visualization. We all tend to perform the way we expect to perform, so expectancy restructuring is based on the idea that if you expect to do well, then you will do well. To overcome the fear, prepare a well-structured and documented speech so that you have confidence that the material will be well received. Then go through the process of visualization—seeing yourself in the actual setting in which you are going to give the speech and making a successful presentation. Picture yourself getting out of your chair, walking to the front of the room, arranging your materials on the podium, looking at the audience, and giving the speech. As you see yourself presenting the material, look at various people. They are nodding their heads in agreement; they are interested and are listening attentively. Then imagine yourself ending the speech and returning to your chair, feeling good about yourself. The more you visualize this positive experience, the more your expectation level of success should increase. Soon you will be expecting success, not failure.

Rehearsing the Speech

Common sense can also dictate the forms your rehearsal might take. The following are some of the possibilities:

1. Read the speech over several times, silently.

2. Read the speech several times aloud.

3. Practice your delivery, including the entire address, standing in front of a mirror. This gives you the opportunity to observe not only your general attitude but also your gestures, posture, and facial expression.

4. Read the speech into a tape recorder and listen to the results. Then listen to them again. At this stage you will make an astounding discovery. Things begin to become apparent to you at a second listening (or, for that matter, a tenth) that had escaped your attention earlier.

5. If you have access to videotaping equipment, make a record of your performance in that way.

6. If you have cooperative family members, deliver the speech to them and ask for their honest comments. Don't make the mistake of welcoming only compliments and tuning out messages that are analytical or critical. If your spouse says something like "I think it's quite good but you were talking too fast," don't argue the point, whether or not your ego will permit you to agree at that moment. Just absorb the message and let it bounce around in your internal computer.

SOURCE: From *How to Make a Speech* (McGraw-Hill) © 1986, material reproduced with permission of Steve Allen.

Rehearsing the Speech

If possible, start to prepare far enough in advance so that you have enough material, the speech is well structured and well organized, and you have a chance to practice it. Some speakers try to convince themselves that they will do better if they just get up and talk, with little or no thought about what they will say. This is a fool's contention; it is usually the excuse of a procrastinator or a person who is not properly aware of his or her responsibility to audience and self. Yes, some speakers can get up and "wing it," but the normal mortal usually cannot. So prepare and practice!

There is no one best way to rehearse. For some people, sitting at a desk and going over the material by mumbling through the outline or notes is the starting point. This will alert you to ideas that do not seem to make sense, words you cannot pronounce, places where you go blank because you need more notes, and/or areas that need more or fewer examples. Make the changes, and continue to review your notes orally until you are satisfied with the material.

Once you are satisfied with the material, try to construct the setting in which you are going to speak. Duplicate as closely as possible what you are going to do. If you are going to use visual aids, use them. The more familiar you become with exactly what you are going to do, the more likely it is you will be comfortable doing it.

Stop practicing when you are comfortable with your material and have worked out the problems related to using notes and supplementary aids. You can never become perfect. You are striving to become as comfortable as you can in what is a stressful situation for almost all of us.

Dealing with Difficulties During a Speech

As you proceed through the speech, you can do several things to assist in making this a positive experience for both you and the audience. Some suggestions include:

Try to be relaxed as you speak. Some interesting research has shown that how you stand affects your ability to avoid your body tightening. The tightening often results in shallow breathing, dry mouth, and shaking hands and legs. Using the *triangle stance* can help you stop your body from stiffening. In the triangle stance (Figure 11.1), you

Figure 11.1
Foot Placement to
Aid in the Relief of
Speaker Anxiety

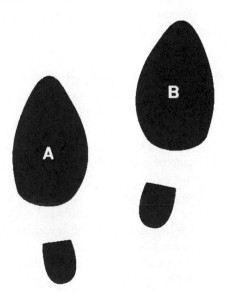

place one foot—foot A—at a slight angle and foot B at about a forty-five-degree angle, as if it were coming out of the arch of foot A. Keep your feet about six inches apart. Shuffle your feet slightly until you feel comfortable and balanced. Place your weight on foot A. You will feel leg and foot B relax. You may also find that it helps if you slightly extend the hip on the foot-A side of your body. As you proceed through a speech, you can alter your stance by changing the positions of feet A and B, but always remember to put your body weight on the foot that is farthest back.

Look at the people in the audience who are alert during the presentation. You can find these people by watching for those whose heads nod in agreement or those who smile at you as you speak. It normally makes a person feel good if they get positive reactions.

Remember that we all make mistakes. If you fumble words, remember that professional speakers and media announcers fumble words fairly often. If it is a minor fumble, just ignore it and keep going. If it is a major error, fix it. Simply repeat the correct word or words and continue your speech recognizing that you can't erase the mishap.

Take time to get yourself organized at the lectern. Arrange your papers on the lectern so that page 1 is on the left and the rest are on the right. Halfway through page 2, slide (don't flip) the page over to cover page 1. Continue to do this so that you are not pausing at the end of each page to turn it over. Sliding allows you to move pages without calling attention to the act; flipping pages can be distracting as it draws attention to the pages for no reason.

IN CONCLUSION → The act of public communication involves a transaction between a speaker and an audience. As in any act of communication, the participants, the setting, and the purpose of the communication affect a public speech. These three parameters may affect the topic selected, the language used, the types of examples and illustrations chosen, and the aids needed to support and/or clarify ideas. To investigate the parameters, an audience analysis is done through prior speech analysis, process of speech analysis, and post-speech analysis.

The public speaker can use one of four basic modes of presentation: impromptu or ad lib, extemporaneous, manuscript, and memorized. In presenting the speech, the vocal elements and the physical elements are important. Some people have a fear associated with giving a speech. Techniques are available for lessening the fear.

LEARN BY DOING →

1. One of the keys to giving an effective oral presentation is to choose a subject you are interested in and about which you have some knowledge. To learn your interest and knowledge base, fill out this speaker inventory.

   a. Hobbies and special interests

   b. Places I have traveled

   c. Things I know how to do (sports I can play, skills I have)

   d. Jobs I have had

   e. Experiences (accidents, special events)

   f. Funny things that have happened to me

   g. Books I have read and liked

   h. Movies and plays I have seen and liked

   i. Interesting people I have known

   j. People I admire

   k. Religious and nationality customs of my family

   l. Talents I have (musical instruments played, athletic abilities)

2. This instrument is composed of six statements concerning feelings about speaking in public.[17] Please indicate the degree to which each statement applies to you by marking whether you (1) strongly agree, (2) agree, (3) are undecided, (4) disagree, or (5) strongly disagree. Work quickly. Record your first impression.

   _____ a. I have no fear of giving a speech.

   _____ b. Certain parts of my body feel very tense and rigid while I am giving a speech.

   _____ c. I feel relaxed while giving a speech.

   _____ d. My thoughts become confused and jumbled when I am giving a speech.

   _____ e. I face the prospect of giving a speech with confidence.

   _____ f. While giving a speech, I get so nervous I forget facts that I really know.

   To obtain your score: Add 18 to your scores from items a, c, and e, and then subtract your score from items b, d, and f. This is your final score.

Interpretation: Scores can range from a low of 6 to a high of 30. If your score is 18 or above, you are like the overwhelming majority of Americans in that you display public speaking apprehension.

3. What questions would you ask a person who has invited you to give a speech on the topic of your choice to a club or organization? Why did you pick these questions?

4. Use a topic related to your academic major to develop a statement of central idea for an informative speech to be presented to a group of classmates. Then prepare another informative statement of central idea for the same topic but for a different, nonclassroom audience. Based on the different statements of central idea, how will the speeches vary?

5. Prepare a statement of central idea informing a group of high school students about your college for a speech of fifteen minutes. Now write a statement of central idea for the same speech in which you will only have five minutes to speak. Why did your statement of central idea change according to the time frame?

6. The class sits in a circle. The instructor throws a ball to someone in the circle and passes an envelope to that person. The person selects a statement from the envelope, takes a minute to prepare, and gives a one- to two-minute presentation on the topic. Before speaking, the first person tosses the ball to someone else, who will be the second speaker. While the first person is speaking the second person selects a topic and prepares a speech. Each speaker tosses the ball to another speaker until all members of the class have spoken.

7. On a three-by-five-inch card, list three topics you think you could speak about for a minimum of two minutes. Your instructor selects one of these for you to give an impromptu speech about. You have two minutes to get ready. You may use any notes you can prepare within that time.

8. Some of the most commonly mispronounced words in general American speech are listed here. Look up each word in a dictionary or pronunciation guide. During a class session, you will be asked to pronounce these words and use them in sentences: *across, acts, actually, all, ambulance, any, asked, because, catch, doing, familiar, fifth, genuine, going, horror, hundred, introduce, just, library, next, nuclear, particular, picture, prescription, probably, pumpkin, recognized, sandwich, secretary, Washington, with.*

KEY TERMS

public communication
speech participants
speaking setting
purpose of the speech
prior to the speech analysis
process of the speech analysis
postspeech analysis
audience analysis
demographics
psychographics
rhetorographics
statement of central idea
goal of the speech

topic of the speech
method of speech development
modes of speech presentation
ad lib speaking
impromptu speaking
extemporaneous speaking mode
speech planning outline
speech presentation outline
manuscript speech mode
memorized speech mode
eye contact
speechophobia

chapter 12

Public Speaking: Developing the Speech

L istening to a speech can be an exciting, interesting, or uplifting experience. It can also be a frustrating, boring, or confusing one. The differences between positive and negative listening experiences are often based on whether the speaker has done such things as defined terms, offered clarifying examples, explained abstract concepts, presented proving statistics, restated ideas, and illustrated thoughts with supplementary aids.

Sources of Information

Most of the information we use to develop messages is based on personal experiences, personal observations, or learning acquired through sources such as school, the media, and reading. As we are exposed to information, we retain a certain amount of it, and this knowledge forms the core of our communication. We select words and examples from this storehouse, and we use it to organize messages.

Sometimes, however, to develop a message, we need information that is not in this core. In such cases, we must find outside sources to aid us.

As you search for sources of information to support your points, you should make every effort to locate **primary sources of information**— sources of information that represent the original reports of the observations or research. When the original work is not available to you, you may find it necessary, then, to go to **secondary sources of information**— sources of information that report, but did not generate, the observations or research.

Research from major sources has been made easier with our access to computerized databases. "The past decade has seen a remarkable expansion in digital networks in the U.S. research and educational community, from a state where networking was the purview of the privileged few to one where it is considered an essential tool by millions of researchers and educators."[1] Because of the wide use of computers, research data may be accessed from places outside libraries. Many libraries have made their card catalogs available through the Internet or similar access systems. The National Science Foundation is heading an effort to develop ways to digitize all the world's library holdings. This system, known as the **information highway**, is an assemblage of networks hooking primary and secondary schools, public and private institutions, commercial enterprises, individuals in their homes, and foreign institutions together for collaboration. They include the traditional reference sources, plus

The information highway is an assemblage of networks hooking together people, schools, and institutions for collaboration.

national phone directories, sound and voice recordings, images, video clips, scientific data, and private information services such as stock market reports and private newsletters.

In addition to locating information, a speaker must assess its validity. All sources of information reflect certain perceptions and biases. Consequently, it is wise to attempt to determine the bias of a source and to interpret its information accordingly.[2] Thus, when doing research for a presentation, it is a good idea to find several agreeing authoritative sources so that your supporting details will be credible to your listeners.

Sources of information that speakers seek out include books, magazines, newspapers, special journals, indexes, government publications, and the publications of special-interest groups. Additional sources include nonprint materials such as tape recordings, records, films, videotapes, charts, and models, as well as interviews or correspondence with knowledgeable people in a particular field.

Books

Personal, academic, and public libraries can be the sources of much information; nevertheless, you must know how to find the materials you need. In academic and public libraries, books are shelved according to a numerical system and can be located by looking in the electronic card catalog under the title, the author's name, or the general subject.

Unfortunately, not all subjects are easy to locate. For example, an average library's electronic card catalog would reveal no information if you looked under the word *Arapesh*. Thus, to learn which books contain material about this subject, you would need some additional information. By looking in an encyclopedia, you would discover that the Arapesh are a primitive, mountain-dwelling people of New Guinea, whose society was investigated by anthropologist Margaret Mead and discussed in her book *Sex and Temperament in Three Primitive Societies*. Based on this information, you could look in the electronic card catalog under such subjects as *anthropology, Margaret Mead, New Guinea,* and *Sex and Temperament in Three Primitive Societies*.

Books are of great value in supplying information, but they can quickly become out of date. It generally takes at least a year for an average book to move from the author's final draft through the printing process and onto the shelves of a library. Some subjects change little, and in these areas books are a good research source. But for quickly changing subjects, more up-to-date sources are needed for a thorough investigation.

Magazines

Most magazines are designed to print recent information quickly. Many magazines are published weekly, so their information is current.

At one point the only way to access a magazine was to locate a copy of the publication. Now, however, magazines are piling up on the information highway.[3] The publications have bought into the electronic distribution and can be electronically accessed.

Researchers must be aware, however, that because these sources gather their data so quickly, some inaccuracies may occur. In addition, the editorial staffs of magazines—like the authors of books—sometimes have political and ideological biases that may temper what they write or influence what subjects they include.

To find information in magazines, you can search electronically, if your library is so equipped, or start with the *Readers' Guide to Periodical Literature*, a publication that indexes magazine articles by subject, title, and author, or the *International Index*. By using the World Wide Web and other accessing sources, key word or topic searches will often reveal sources.

Newspapers

Newspapers, like magazines, contain current information that is published daily, weekly, or monthly. As is the case with magazines, because of the speed with which newspapers are written and printed, you must be aware of the possibility of error. Many libraries do not keep past issues of newspapers, but some store the information on microfilm, or make them available through electronic sources. Many newspapers can be directly accessed on the information highway.

Journals

Professional organizations often publish journals reporting research and theories in their specific fields. The National Communication Association, for example, publishes such journals as *Communication Education*, *The Quarterly Journal of Speech*, *Communication Monographs*, *The Journal of Applied Communication Research*, and *Critical Studies in Mass Communication*. Thus, students interested in finding out about some area of speech communication can refer to these journals. The organization also has a CD/ROM available for doing word, topic, and article searches.

Indexes

Encyclopedias, atlases, and bibliographical guides are all indexes that provide descriptive information in certain categories. An index gives a minimal amount of information. Thus, if you want in-depth material, indexes may not be the best sources.

When using encyclopedias, recognize that many of them are expensive to produce and, therefore, are not totally updated each year. This has been somewhat rectified by CD/ROMs, which update the indexes on a regular basis.

Government Pamphlets

The U.S. government publishes pamphlets, available at minimal cost, on a variety of subjects. These can be found at bookstores in federal buildings in many major cities of the country and also can be accessed through the U.S. Government Printing Office's home page.

Special-Interest-Group Publications

Special-interest groups such as the American Cancer Society and the American Society for Training and Development publish information regarding their research and programs. A telephone call or letter to such an organization often brings a prompt response, or materials can be accessed through an organization's home page. To find the name of an organization and their E-mail address, look in *Gale's Encyclopedia of Associations*.

Nonprint Media

Much information also is available from nonprint media. Libraries and audio-visual departments of colleges and universities often have tape recordings, records, films, filmstrips, and videotapes from commercially and locally prepared sources covering a variety of topics. These sources usually are cataloged in a manner similar to that used for books and periodicals. Some nonprint materials are available for general circulation, but

A researcher can get information by going to a library and searching in the electronic card catalogue.

others must be used on the premises. Local radio and television stations often sell audio or visual copies of their programs.

Interviews

Interviews can be used to find information that is not available from written or audio-visual sources. After all, what better way is there to find out, for example, how the budget of your college is developed than by talking to the treasurer or the budget director? Such interviews can be conducted in a variety of ways. If someone is not available for a face-to-face or telephone session, you can submit a series of questions to be answered through either writing or tape-recording. In addition, contacting a person on the Internet often brings an immediate response.

Computer Searches

Historically, a researcher got information by going to a library and looking in the card catalog or *Readers' Guide,* or asking the reference librarian what sources are available. At present, a great deal of research can be done in a library's electronic card catalog or from the comfort of a person's home or office. Through various electronic hookups it is possible to access local, national, and international resources. Almost daily, through the electronic highway, even more of this type of service is becoming available. One of the new challenges of researchers is not only to find information but also to keep up-to-date on how to access the resources.

A major advantage to this method is the time saved, as a computer retrieves in minutes information what otherwise would take much longer to compile. Another feature is the timeliness of the material; these databases are frequently updated.

Recording Your Research

When you do research, keep a record of where your information came from so you can refer to the source to find additional information, answer questions about a source, or give oral footnotes during a speech. When you write a term paper, you must footnote **quotations**—material written or spoken by a person in the exact words in which it was originally presented—and **paraphrases**—someone else's ideas put into your own words. You do the same in public speaking, except orally. For example, in a speech concerning male-female communication, this **oral footnote** is appropriate: "Deborah Tannen, in her book *You Just Don't Understand*, observed, 'Habitual ways of talking are hard to change. Learning to respect others' ways of talking may be a bit easier. Men should accept that many women regard exchanging details about personal lives as a basic ingredient of intimacy, and women should accept that many men do not share this view.'"[4]

In some instances, you also may feel that it is necessary to establish a quoted author as an authority. In this case, your oral footnote might be, "Deborah Tannen, the author of *You Just Don't Understand*, has received grants from the National Endowment for the Humanities and the National Science Foundation and is a professor of linguistics at Georgetown University."

There are many ways to record both bibliographical information and notes that result from your research. One method is to use a running bibliography listing the names of authors; sources used; and places, publishers, and dates of the materials' publication. The list is numbered so that it can be used while taking notes. An example is:

Bibliography

1. Deborah Tannen. *You Just Don't Understand* (New York: William Morrow, 1990).

2. Julia T. Wood. *Gendered Lives: Communication, Gender, and Culture* (Belmont, CA: Wadsworth Publishing Company, 1994).

3. Lea Stewart, Pamela Cooper, Alan Stewart, and Sheryl Friedley. *Communication and Gender*, 3rd ed. (Scottsdale, AZ: Gorsuch Scarisbrick Publishers, 1996).

As you do your research and record your information, you can refer to the source by number, thus eliminating the necessity of continually writing out the same bibliographical material. You can refer to the male-female quotation above, for example, as 1-122 (source 1 in the bibliography, page 122). Because the material is directly quoted, put quotation marks around it. If it is paraphrased, the use of quotation marks is not necessary, but be aware that the material is not original to you but from another source.

Notes can be taken on three-by-five-inch or four-by-six-inch cards or on sheets of paper. If cards are used, a footnote reference would look like:

**A Tip for You
When Speaking**

For every major point
you make, try to do the
following:

✳ Tell a story.

✳ Use a quote.

✳ Give an example.

✳ Use appropriate
humor.

   Not everyone is capa-
ble of doing all four of
these. Pick those that work
for you and try to support
each major point with one
of them.

SOURCE: *Communication
Briefings,* as adapted from
Presentations Plus, by David A.
Peoples, John Wiley & Sons
Inc., 605 3rd Ave., New York,
NY 10158.

Topic: Gender Communication
Reference: 1-122

Information: "Habitual ways of talking are hard to change. Learning to respect others' ways of talking may be a bit easier. Men should accept that many women regard exchanging details about personal lives as a basic ingredient of intimacy, and women should accept that many men do not share this view."

After assembling all your research, if you used a computer, you can print out the material. If you used paper, you can just proceed with step two—cutting the material into strips, separating them by topic, and writing or outlining directly from these. Some people go so far as to arrange the slips on sheets of paper and then attach the slips to the pages with transparent tape, and use these as their outline for the speech. An alternative to this is to connect the strips and then duplicate them on a copying machine, thus creating a final outline. The advantages of using or copying the actual slips of paper center not only on saving time but also on allowing you to have all your footnote sources available if you are asked about them during the question-and-answer session.

Supporting Material

Supporting speech material should clarify a point you are making in the speech or offer proof to the validity of the argument presented. The forms of support you select depend on your purposes, but the most common are illustrations, specific instances, expositions, statistics, analogies, and testimony.

Illustrations

Examples that explain a subject through the use of detailed stories are called **illustrations.** They are intended to clarify a point, not offer proof. They may be hypothetical or factual.

   If the illustrations are hypothetical, the speaker should make this clear by saying, for example, "Suppose you were . . ." or "Let us all imagine that. . . ." Hypothetical illustrations can be used, for instance, by a medical technician taking a listener on a theoretical trip through the circulatory system.

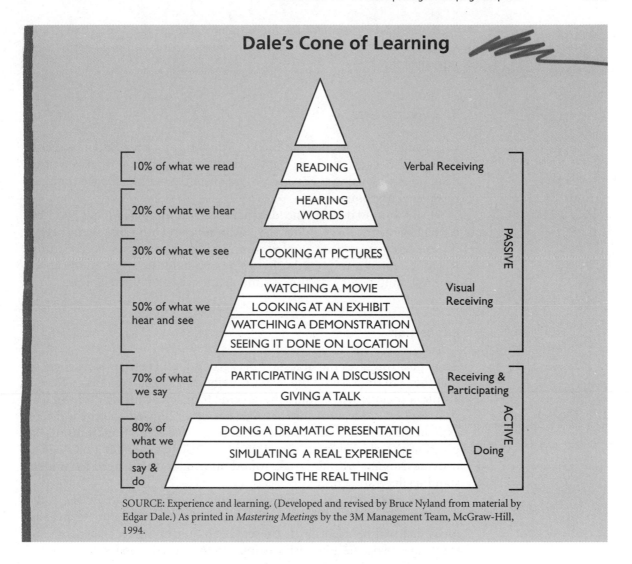

Dale's Cone of Learning

10% of what we read — READING — Verbal Receiving

20% of what we hear — HEARING WORDS

30% of what we see — LOOKING AT PICTURES

50% of what we hear and see — WATCHING A MOVIE / LOOKING AT AN EXHIBIT / WATCHING A DEMONSTRATION / SEEING IT DONE ON LOCATION — Visual Receiving

70% of what we say — PARTICIPATING IN A DISCUSSION / GIVING A TALK — Receiving & Participating

80% of what we both say & do — DOING A DRAMATIC PRESENTATION / SIMULATING A REAL EXPERIENCE / DOING THE REAL THING — Doing

PASSIVE

ACTIVE

SOURCE: Experience and learning. (Developed and revised by Bruce Nyland from material by Edgar Dale.) As printed in *Mastering Meetings* by the 3M Management Team, McGraw-Hill, 1994.

In contrast, a factual illustration is a real or actual story. It can be introduced by statements such as "When I came to school this morning . . ." A speaker developed a speech on safety codes with this illustration:

Where Memorial School stands today, Jefferson School once stood. One day a devastating fire struck Jefferson School. Eighty students and four teachers lost their lives in that tragic fire, and hundreds of others were seriously injured. The new Memorial School can never eradicate the memories of those who died during the tragic fire.

Think back to some of the more memorable speakers you have heard. Undoubtedly, they used a number of relevant, interesting stories to support their points.

Specific Instances

Condensed examples that are used to clarify or prove a point are **specific instances**. Because they are not developed in depth, you can say a great deal quickly by using them and provide listeners with evidence they can relate to your point.

If you want to develop the idea that speech communication is an interesting major for college students, you can support your point with specific instances of careers that employ communication majors: speech writing, teaching, research and training in business and industrial communication, political campaigning, health communication, and public relations.

Exposition

An **exposition** gives the necessary background information to listeners so that they can understand the material being presented. Sometimes, for example, a speaker needs to define specific terms, give historical information, explain the relationship between herself or himself and the topic, or explain the process that will be used during the presentation. In using exposition, the speaker must also attempt to anticipate or alter a message to provide listeners with the background information they need for understanding the transaction.

More specifically, the speaker, realizing an obligation to aid the audience in understanding the message, may feel a need to define terms and ideas that will be used in the presentation. For example, a speaker who wants to explain the advertising campaign to be used in marketing a product may find it necessary to clarify such terms and phrases as *bandwagoning* and *plus-and-minus factor of surveying*.

An audience may need historical information as well. For listeners to understand the outcome of the Whitewater investigation, for instance, they may need to know the specific events that led to the decision to launch the investigation.

Listeners also may need a bridge between the speaker and the topic, to understand why the speaker is discussing the subject or to establish the speaker's expertise. For example, a student nurse who is explaining the nursing program he recently completed should share his educational background with the audience.

In addition, indicating the process to be followed during a presentation or the results the speaker wants to achieve also may be helpful to listeners. An outline of the major points to be made can be distributed or displayed, or the speaker can explain what she or he will do and will want the audience to do as the speech proceeds.

Statistics

Any collection of numerical information arranged to indicate representations, trends, or theories is an example of **statistics**. Statistics are used by communicators to provide a measurement (e.g., The upper limit of hearing by the human ear is 20,000 Hz per second); to compare (The normal intelligible outdoor range of the male human voice in still air is 200 yards; female screams register higher readings on decibel meters than male bellows[5]); and to demonstrate amounts (The census indicates that the population of Ecuador is 8,053,280 people[6]).

Nevertheless, before accepting statistics as proof, the wise speaker asks these questions:

1. Who says so?

2. How does he or she know?

3. What is missing?

4. Did somebody change the subject?

5. Does it make sense?[7]

When statistics have been accurately collected, properly interpreted, and are not out of date, their use is a valid aid in reaching conclusions. Unfortunately, not all statistical studies are accurately done, properly interpreted, or current.

Statistical Surveying Statisticians have developed methods for collecting data—statistical surveying—that can be used with some degree of assurance that resulting information will be correct.[8] Ideally, to find out everyone's opinion on a particular issue, everyone should be asked, but of course this is usually impossible for large groups of people. Thus, to make educated guesses, statisticians have devised methods of random sampling that allow less than the entire population to be surveyed. These methods recognize the probability of error, and a speaker should indicate this fact when giving the statistical results of a survey.

For clarity, a speaker can display an outline of the major points being made in the speech.

Proper Interpretation of Data   If a particular group or person is trying to get a specific result, that tester may keep testing until she or he gets the desired conclusion, or ignore results that do not agree with the goal. For this reason, be wary of statistics that are taken out of context, are incomplete, or do not specify the method used to collect the data.

Currency of Data   Studies and surveys conducted in the past may have been perfectly accurate at the time they were done. This does not mean, however, that they are accurate now. It is important that you use or receive the latest data and not allow yourself to be influenced by information that is out of date.

Reporting the Data   Remember that a person can retain only a limited amount of information. Thus, extensive lists, complicated numerical combinations, and long numbers may well be lost if you do not help listeners by simplification or visualization. For example, a long list—such as the figures representing the cost of each material used to produce a piece of machinery—can be written on a chalkboard or poster or projected on a screen. In this way, listeners view as well as hear, and they can refer to the numbers as needed.

Simplify numbers. A statistic such as $1,243,724,863 is difficult to comprehend, but the phrase "approximately $1.25 billion" is within the grasp of an audience. If a statistic is important enough to include in a speech, you must be sure that the listener can grasp the information.

Analogies

A speaker may use an **analogy** to clarify a concept for listeners; that is, the speaker compares an unfamiliar concept to a familiar one. For example, in the section of this text dealing with the processing capacity of the human cortex, an analogy was drawn between a cybernetic process and a computer process. This comparison was not intended to indicate that the cortex and the computer are one and the same, but to demonstrate that if a reader understands the functioning of a computer, he or she may also understand the basic operation of the cortex.

Remember that an analogy is effective only if the listeners are familiar with the object, idea, or theory being used as its basis. Contrasting a patient on an operating table to stars in the sky may confuse listeners who are unfamiliar with either astronomy or surgical techniques.

A speaker also should be careful not to overextend the comparison or contrast. A college president once developed an inaugural speech by comparing the school to a football team. The analogy compared faculty members to team players, students to spectators, the president to the coach, and on and on and on! After a while, the listeners became confused and stopped paying attention; the intended effect was lost.

Testimony

Testimony may be a direct quotation (actual statement) or a paraphrase (reworded idea) from an authority. Speakers provide testimony to clarify ideas, back up contentions, and reinforce concepts. Thus, a speaker may turn to this type of supporting material when it is believed that an authority is more knowledgeable than the speaker about the topic being discussed or that the opinion of an authority will make listeners more receptive to a particular idea.

An **expert** is a person who, through knowledge or skill in a specific field, gains respect for his or her opinions or expertise. We trust experts' opinions because their knowledge has been acquired through personal experience, education, training, research, and observation. We also respect people who have academic degrees, who are licensed or accredited, or who are recognized by peers as leaders in their fields.

Selected quotations should be true to the intention of the source. Before you accept testimony as support, assess its validity by asking some basic questions:

1. *Is the material quoted accurately?*

2. *Is the source biased because of position, employment, or affiliation?* A quotation by the chairperson of the board of directors of a major

tobacco company that cigarette smoking may not lead to cancer should be suspect because of the speaker's biased position.

3. *Is the information relevant to the issue being discussed?*

4. *Is the source competent in the field being discussed?* For example, what qualifies an actor to recommend changes in U.S. foreign policy?

5. *Is the information current, if currency is important?*

Vehicles for Presenting Supporting Material

Three means of presenting and focusing supporting material are internal summaries, forecasting, and use of supplementary aids.

Internal Summaries

As a listener, have you ever been on the receiving end of a message and found yourself totally confused because of the amount of material involved? To avoid listener confusion, summarize each segment of a presentation by presenting an **internal summary**, a short restatement of what just has been said in the section that you are about to leave, before proceeding to the next segment. For example, after spending several minutes proposing that the United States should adopt a more aggressive foreign policy, the speaker could bridge out of that unit with the internal summary, "Our nation, then, needs to pursue a more vigorous, definitive approach to its international relations."

Forecasting

A **forecast** is a statement that alerts the audience to ideas that are coming. A sample of a forecast is, "Let's now examine the three examples of how bulimics purge food." This alerts the audience to get ready to listen to the three points.

Supplementary Aids

Many speakers find **supplementary speech aids**—visual, audio, audio-visual, and computer-aided graphics—valuable in augmenting the oral

When Preparing Audio-Visuals

When preparing slides or overheads, you should limit punctuation. Specifically, avoid using:

✳ **Slashes.** *Example:* "yes/no." *Why:* When seen from a distance, slashes can resemble letters. They'll confuse your audience, which may think you're using longer words that don't make sense.

✳ **Em-dashes,** short dashes that serve to separate expressions. *Example:* ". . . is of course—hypothetically speaking—. . ." *The problem:* When these expressions are knocked to the next line as a single word, you'll get awkward line breaks.

✳ **Exclamation** points. *The problem:* When projected, an "!" may resemble a "1."

SOURCE: *Communication Briefings,* as adapted from Roger C. Parker, writing in *Technique,* 10 Post Office Square, Ste. 600 s, Boston, MA 02109.

segments of their presentations. Aids are intended to facilitate listener understanding, not function as decorative touches; therefore, a speaker should ask two questions before using aids: Is the aid relevant to the presentation? And, will listeners better understand the material through the use of an aid?

In a speech, statistical differences can be greatly enhanced by the use of charts. In a classroom, supplementary aids can be used to teach particular techniques. For example, nurses sometimes insert needles into grapefruits so they can learn how to give shots and a videotape of an interrogation can supplement a discussion for law enforcement students. These aids are intended to supplement the speaker's voice.

Visual Aids   **Visual aids** appeal to our sense of sight. As in using any other supplementary aid, speakers must be careful that the visual aids truly *aid* the presentation. These guidelines can serve as an aid to developing effective visuals:

1. Don't tell the whole story.

2. Keep it simple.

3. Make the message the heading.

4. Make it readable.

5. Make sure all letters and numerals read horizontally.

6. Fancy typefaces or multiple typefaces can make your visual hard to read.

7. Avoid using all capital letters, because they are difficult to read.

8. Be consistent.

9. Vary the type of visuals you present.

10. Avoid distortions.[9]

Visual aids can be real objects; models, photographs, pictures; diagrams; charts; cutaways; mockups; and presentation graphics.

Real Objects   To demonstrate the process of swinging a hammer, why not use a real hammer? Or, use an actual form to show how a traffic ticket is filled out. These are examples of using real objects as visual aids.

Models   At times, it is impossible to use real objects. In such cases, a scale model (in exact proportion to the dimensions of the real object) or a synthetic model (not in proportion but nevertheless representative) may be used. For example, although a Boeing 757 jet cannot be brought into an aviation classroom, a scale model certainly can be.

Photographs, Pictures, and Diagrams   A photograph of a death scene and the victim can be shown to a jury in a murder trial in order to reconstruct the scene or the violence.

Charts   A chart is a visual representation of statistical data that gives information in tabular or diagrammatic form. For example, a series of columns representing the number of doctors available to a hospital compared with the number needed presents a striking visual image of the problem.

Cutaways   It often is difficult to look inside certain objects. A cutaway allows us to see what we normally would have to imagine, thus enabling us to better visualize and understand. To show the layers of materials used to construct a house, a wall is cut in half so that we see the aluminum siding, the insulation, the studding, the wallboard, and the wallpaper.

Mockups   A mockup shows the building up or tearing down of an article. For example, a biology textbook may include an outline drawing of the human body on a page with a series of clear plastic sheets attached. Each of these plastic overlays shows a specific drawing that, as it is flipped onto the original sketch, adds an aspect of the human anatomy.

Presentation Graphics   **Presentation graphics** are a series of visuals that are projected via an overhead projector while the speaker is discussing each point. The slides enable the speaker to visually illustrate with statistics, cartoons, short quotes, maps, or other materials.

Many computer programs are available for developing presentation graphics. Microsoft's® PowerPoint, for example, provides templates for creating slides, outlines, speaker notes, handouts, and presentations. Slides, with various fonts, colors, and even clip art can be formatted and printed out to make transparencies for projection on an overhead projector. Or an LCD projector system allows for direct projection from a computer. You can display one line of a slide at a time, or fade from one image to another with a click of your computer mouse.[10]

Audio Aids   **Audio aids** appeal to our sense of hearing. Such devices as records, tape recordings, or duplications of sounds may be the only way to accurately demonstrate particular sensations for listeners. For example, playing a recording of Martin Luther King's "I Have a Dream" speech is an excellent way to demonstrate his dynamic oral style.

Audio-visual Aids   **Audio-visual aids** such as films, videotapes, and tape-slide presentations combine the dimensions of sight and sound. A video clip of a seeing-eye dog assisting his or her person can illustrate the support that such animals can provide. In the same way, a videotape of an executive's speech is an excellent way to illustrate his or her vocal and physical mannerisms.

IN CONCLUSION →   The sources of information available to a speaker include personal experiences, personal observations, and accumulated learning, plus information derived from research and interviews. Research information may be found in books, magazines, newspapers, journals, indexes, government publications, and publications from special-interest groups. Additional information can be found in nonprint media and interviews. When doing research, you should keep a record of where the information came from. Supporting material is used in a speech to clarify the speaker's point or to demonstrate that the point has some probability of being true. Supporting material can include illustrations, specific instances, expositions, statistics, analogies, and testimony. Three means for presenting and focusing supporting material are internal summaries, forecasting, and the use of supplementary aids.

LEARN BY DOING →   1. Select a controversial subject area (e.g., abortion, euthanasia, legalization of drugs, confiscation of handguns) and identify a person who is an authority on the subject. Interview that person and give an oral presentation to the class about your interview. You should clearly state the interviewee's stand concerning the issue and the reasons for the stand. After all of the presentations have been made, participate in a class discussion on the value of the interview as a means for collecting data for a speech.

2. Use the information collected from the interview in Activity 1 to research the same topic. Look for the views of other authorities on the subject. Prepare a presentation in which you compare the results of your interview with the results of your research.

3. Make a presentation to the class in which a supplementary aid is absolutely necessary for the listeners' comprehension of the message

(e.g., a description of Van Gogh's style of brush stroke, the music of the Grateful Dead in comparison with that of the group Chicago; the architectural styles of the Mayas of the Yucatan).

4. Research each of these and compile a set of note cards and a running bibliography as explained in this chapter (pages 313-314).

   a. The name of one book about the teachings of Aristotle

   b. A magazine article about nuclear-waste disposal

   c. The longitude and latitude of Omaha, Nebraska

   d. Three encyclopedia entries about the White House

   e. The name of a journal exclusively about nonverbal communication

   f. The definition of the word *cacophony*

   g. The 1950 population of the United States

   h. The birthplace of John Grisham

   i. The title of a government pamphlet dealing with AIDS

   j. The gross national product of the United States in 1996

   k. The name of the lyricist for the musical *Miss Saigon*

5. Use the format explained in the chapter to make three notecards for a speech with the purpose statement "to inform the class of the effects of the Salk polio vaccine." Two are to be quotations; one, a paraphrase. Use a different source for each card.

6. Find a factual illustration, or create a hypothetical one, that could be used for the speech described in Activity 5.

7. What expository materials do you think would be needed by members of your class if you were to present the speech in Activity 5?

8. Locate and footnote three sources of testimony concerning the effects of secondary smoke on nonsmokers.

9. Find a humorous story that you could use as an introduction for a speech about the American educational system, gender differences, or sports.

KEY TERMS →

primary sources of information
secondary sources of information
information highway
quotations
paraphrases
oral footnote
supporting speech material
illustrations
specific instances
exposition
statistics

analogy
testimony
expert
internal summary
forecast
supplementary speech aids
visual aids
presentation graphics
audio aids
audio-visual aids

chapter 13

Public Speaking: Structuring the Message

Have you ever sat through a class lecture and found yourself thoroughly confused because the instructor kept jumping from idea to idea, and then back to a former one while discussing still another thought? If so, you were experiencing organizational confusion.

If a speech is well ordered, the chance of its success increases. One of the most effective approaches to enhancing listener comprehension of a message is the development of well-supported points.[1] "Experienced speakers know (1) that if a presentation is to be effective, it must be understood and (2) that if a presentation is to be understood, it must be organized logically."[2]

Speakers who can plan and then build in repetition of their points foster listening comprehension. Television commercials use redundancy by repeating extensively, to reinforce the message in the viewer's mind. This is not done by accident, nor is the repetition random. Ideas are presented, clarified, and then represented.

Listeners often have limited attention spans, constantly tuning in to and out of speakers' messages. Consequently, it is important to present a carefully structured message that enables the listener to get back on track when he or she tunes back in to the speech.

A careful plan for putting together a speech is a major part of the process of preparing and developing effective presentations.[3] The plan should aid in eliminating the confusion, produce a well-supported presentation, foster listening comprehension, and maintain attention.

When Preparing Your Speech

The next time you're preparing a presentation, remember this tip:

The first 30 seconds and the last 30 seconds have the most impact. Don't waste these precious seconds with "Ladies and gentlemen" or a weather report. Launch right in with a startling statement, quote or story. End with a bang, not a whimper.

SOURCE: *Communication Briefings,* as adapted from Patricia Fripp, 527 Hugo St., San Francisco, CA 94122.

The Basic Elements of a Speech

A public communication message should be arranged into four parts: introduction, central idea, body, and conclusion. This structure may be outlined as:

I. Introduction—attention-gaining and orienting material

II. Central idea—the purpose of the presentation and a specific statement of its main idea

III. Body—the major points to be expressed in the presentation. The body of the speech may be expanded into as many divisions as necessary to develop the intent of the message.

IV. Conclusion—a summarizing and possibly a motivating statement

An audience can get thoroughly confused if the speaker jumps from one idea to another, with no organization framework for the speech.

The Introduction

Speech Starter

If you're looking for a way to get an audience's attention when you start a speech, try this:

"I'm going to make this talk short because I read the other day that the No. 1 fear of many people is having to make a speech. The No. 2 fear might be having to listen to one."

SOURCE: *Communication Briefings,* as adapted from IdeaBank® online database, 11 Joan Drive, Chappaqua, NY 10514, cited in *The Executive Speaker,* P.O. Box 292437, Dayton, OH 45429.

The purpose of the **introduction to a speech** is to (a) gain the listeners' attention and (b) orient them to the material that will be presented.

Attention Material

It is imperative to gain the listener's attention at the start of the speech. If the speaker fails to convince the audience to listen immediately, getting them to turn on later is almost impossible. Attention-getting techniques include presenting personal references, humorous stories, illustrations, rhetorical questions, action questions, unusual or dramatic devices, quotations related to the theme, or a statement of the theme.

Personal References   Introductions containing personal references give a speaker's reasons for undertaking a presentation on a specific topic. For example, to introduce a presentation that appeals for funds, a patient may relate the personal experience of receiving aid from the Muscular Dystrophy Association.

Humorous stories are often an effective way to start a presentation.

Humorous Stories   People like to laugh and enjoy themselves; therefore, humorous stories often are an effective way to start a presentation. The humor should fit the audience and the occasion, be relevant to the material that follows, and set the desired tone.

The humor should parallel the intent of the speech. A speaker, for example, could begin a presentation with a humorous anecdote: "A railroad agent in Africa had been bawled out for doing things without orders from headquarters. One day headquarters received a telegram from the agent which read, 'Tiger on platform eating conductor. Wire instructions.'"[4] From this story, listeners would expect a speech about worker empowerment or creative decision-making.

It is important to consider, too, whether humor is appropriate to your communication style. Some people are not very comfortable telling funny stories or jokes, and that discomfort will be revealed to the audience. Other speakers have a good ear (and memory) for relaying humorous anecdotes and find the form to be successful for them.

Putting Humor in Its Place

Humor has a place in your presentations and your work with others. Even if you feel you can't tell a joke, you can still make humor work for you.

Humor should be relevant to the message you are giving. Link it to a point you are making, and make it the type of humor that is in good taste.

* **Analogies** are one way to use humor. Linking your present situation or problem to something else often provides an opportunity for humor. The link can be either logical or illogical and could even be a personal anecdote.

* **Another way** to use humor—and an easy one for the person who falls into the "cannot-tell-jokes" category—is to use funny quotes. Get a book of humorous quotations.

Also: Have you seen an amusing cartoon in the paper or in a magazine? Describe it. Show it on a screen.

Some specifics on using humor:

* **When you** are telling jokes or quips, don't pre-announce them. Just insert them here and there.

* **Avoid** anything offensive or sarcastic. If in doubt, leave it out.

* **Remember** that sometimes things occur—such as power failures, dead mikes, etc.—during presentations. Have a joke or comment ready for emergencies.

SOURCE: *Communication Briefings,* as adapted from Dr. Stephanie Slahor, P.O. Box 2615, Palm Springs, CA 92263.

Illustrations Illustrations such as stories, pictures, and slides help to make ideas more vivid for listeners because they create a visualization or image of the topic to be discussed. For example, showing pictures of the results of a new skin-grafting process for burn victims clearly illustrates the topic to be discussed. Similarly, a speaker who is going to talk about the need for well-equipped police cars can begin a speech by saying, "Picture yourself on a dark road some night with car trouble or maybe even an injury that prevents you from driving. Suddenly you see the headlights of a car. It could belong to almost anyone. But wouldn't you feel better if it turned out to be a police officer with all the equipment you needed?"

Rhetorical Questions Questions for which no outward response is expected are called rhetorical questions. For example, a speaker may say to an audience, "Have you ever asked yourself what you would do if someone tried to rob you?" In this case, the speaker does not intend to count how many have or have not asked themselves the question. Instead, his or her purpose is to have audience members ask themselves the question so as to build their curiosity or interest.

Although sometimes overused, rhetorical questions can still be an effective method of getting the audience to ponder a topic.

Action Questions   Action questions are presented as a means of getting the audience involved in a speech and making listeners think and respond. For example, a speaker started a presentation by asking, "How many of you have been involved in an auto accident?" After the hands went up, the speaker said, "For those of you with your hands up, do you remember that instant when you knew the accident was going to happen and you couldn't do anything about it? What flashed through your mind?" After getting some answers from the audience, the speaker said, "Yes, a common response is helplessness and fear." Thus, the speaker involved the audience and was able to move their attention into the next segment of the speech, which centered on how to overcome the feelings of helplessness caused by fear and despair.

Unusual or Dramatic Devices   Unusual or dramatic devices get the attention because of their curiosity or shock value. In one dramatic opening, a medical lab technician set up equipment and drew blood from a student volunteer to show how blood is analyzed.

Quotations Related to the Theme   Speakers sometimes begin quoting a famous person or expert, reading an account of a specific event, reciting a section of a poem or play, or read a newspaper editorial. The quotes should be relevant to the topic and read meaningfully. The greatest mistake many speakers make in presenting a quote is to select an appropriate piece and then speed through the reading or fail to stress the meaning.

Stating the Theme   Theme statements are used to indicate to the audience exactly what the speaker is going to talk about. Unfortunately, many untrained speakers start out their presentations by saying, "Today I am going to tell you about. . . ." This is not a creative or attention getting opener.

A more creative theme statement is likely to hold the audience's attention. For example, a mechanic started her presentation by saying, "There is a right and wrong way to change a tire. Doing it the wrong way can result in death or permanent injury. I'm going to share with you a simple technique to ensure you do it the right way."

Orienting Material

Orienting material is presented to give the audience the background necessary to understand the basic material of the speech. It is designed to tie the material to the central idea, provide necessary information, establish personal credibility for the speaker, and/or make the subject important to the listener. Orienting material can include such clarifiers as providing a historical background, defining terms that will be used in the presentation, tying the speaker's personal history to the subject, and illuminating the importance of the ideas to the listener.

Historical Background Often a speaker has to explain what led up to present occurrences so an audience can gain the necessary historical background. For example, a speech intended to persuade the audience to vote for a renewal of a school levy ought to include the facts that illustrate the history of the levy.

Definition of Terms   Though terms are usually defined at the place they are used in a speech, sometimes the very nature of a speech depends on an understanding near the start of the presentation. For example, in a speech about agoraphobia, the definition of it as an emotional illness that manifests itself in the victim not wanting to appear in public should appear near the beginning of the presentation. Only those terms that are universal to the speech should be included in the orientation.

Personal History and/or Tie to the Topic   A speaker often can gain credibility if she or he has some personal tie or experience related to the topic. A speaker intending to demonstrate the steps in mouth-to-mouth resuscitation should include his Red Cross training and background as a lifeguard. This documentation establishes the speaker's authority to speak about the subject.

Importance to the Listeners   One of the most critical parts of the orienting material is relating the subject to the listeners in some way. Listeners pay attention to ideas and issues that are relevant to them, so it is helpful if the speaker makes that link at the outset. One good strategy is to show the importance of the topic based on the interests of the audience. For example, "The Internal Revenue Service reports that an average of 107,000,000 income tax forms are filed yearly. Your tax form was probably one of these."

The Central Idea

The **statement of the speech's central idea** is intended to keep the speaker on course for developing a purposeful and well-organized speech. It also indicates the response the speaker wants from listeners. If, for example, the central idea of a speech is "I will present to you two reasons why we should all vote for the school-bond issue on November 2," both the speaker and the audience are clear about the topic, the method of developing that topic, and what is desired from the audience.

The importance of actually stating the central idea in a speech cannot be overemphasized. Speakers who skip this important part of the speech deprive the listeners of the clue they may need to be sure of what the exact point of the speech really is. The central idea should be presented as a statement, because a speaker who uses a question (e.g., "Should the federal government provide financial aid to private educational institutions?") is not indicating to listeners what the main point really is. But a speaker who presents the point as a statement ("There are three reasons why I believe the federal government should provide financial aid to private educational institutions") is clarifying the stand that will be advocated.

The Body

The **body of a speech** develops the major points as well as any subpoints pertaining to a speaker's central idea. In this way, the listeners should have little trouble in understanding the message.

When a speech lacks this sort of organization, listeners may become so confused they simply give up trying to understand it. For example, a military analyst who starts a lecture by talking about the causes of World War I, then wanders into a discussion of the marriage customs of Greece, goes back to the cause of World War I, and then comments on the Equal Rights Amendment will probably have confused listeners! To avoid such problems, the points of the body of a speech should be sequenced through one of the methods of issue arrangement.

Not all cultures regard the Western world's Aristotelian mode of structuring a speech to be the best or the only way to develop a presentation. Historically, speakers of Western cultures make use of a process that calls for stating a contention, supporting that contention, and drawing a conclusion for the listeners. This is accomplished in a step-by-step manner. On the other hand, in some cultures a **spiral form of explanation** is used. In this mode, a statement is made and then a story or analogy that deals with the statement is presented. It is often left to the listener to apply the parallels and draw outcomes related to the original statement. Because this book is being written primarily for public speakers in the United States where the Western mode of reasoning is the general format, the discussion of how to develop a speech will follow the Aristotelian guidelines. This is

Mind Maps

"If I'm concerned about having too much to say or what to cover in a speech, I organize it by mind mapping the material. I put the topic or theme in the middle of the page. Then brainstorm everything I can think of about that topic. I write just a word or so that represents each of those thoughts. I put little squiggles around each word, just for fun. I then look at the thoughts and number each one in the way I might use them. I don't draw pictures or get elaborate in terms of colors—my wife, Marge, does like to organize her talk that way."

Dr. Ken Blanchard

Yellow elephant.

As you read that phrase, did you think of letters Y-e-l-l-o-w-e-l-e-p-h-a-n-t. Or did you see an image? Of course, you saw the image. The mind thinks in images and pictures. Mind mapping was developed by Tony Buzan, author and brain researcher, as an alternative to outlining. He suggests you organize your material by drawing pic-tures. For example, you might draw a simple picture of a yellow elephant (assuming you were doing a talk that involved a yellow elephant), then a line with an arrow to the next thought you want to talk about.

When you try to force your mind to think in a traditional outline form—with words and sentences—you may wait around forever, staring at a blank paper, waiting for Roman numeral *I* to bounce into your head. But in mind mapping you draw each idea as it pops up, then connect the pictures later into a speech.

As you draw your mind map, you can more easily see when you've got too much stuff in one place and not enough in another. If you can't easily connect one line to another, then you can see it may not belong in the presentation at all.

SOURCE: From *Secrets of Successful Speakers* by Lilly Walters, pp. 86–87. Copyright © 1993. Reproduced with permission of McGraw-Hill, Inc. and Lilly Walters.

not to say that other formats or approaches are inferior or that they should not be learned or used when appropriate.

Methods of Issue Arrangement

The **method of issue arrangement for the body of a speech** normally takes one of six forms: spatial arrangement, chronological/time arrangement, topical arrangement, causal arrangement, comparison-contrast arrangement, or problem-solution arrangement. The method selected acts as a guide for sequencing information for listener clarity.

Spatial Arrangement Many people organize information automatically even though they are not aware of it. Suppose some friends of yours are visiting you at your college. They have never been on campus before, so they ask you to tell them about the institution. You start by describing the building located on the south end of the campus and then proceed to talk about all the other buildings, noting their locations from south to north. You have organized your presentation according to the **spatial method of issue arrangement**. You have set a point of reference at a specific location and followed a geographic pattern. The pattern can be left to right, north to south, or from the center to the outside. This is a common method for giving directions or describing something by its location.

We can see how spatial arrangement can be used for the body of a speech with the central idea "to inform the audience of the financial tax base of the state of Maryland by examining the state from west to east" with the following outline of the body of the speech:

III. Financial tax base of the state of Maryland

    A. Western Maryland

        1. Cumberland

        2. Hagerstown

    B. Central Maryland

        1. Baltimore

        2. Rockville

    C. Eastern Maryland

        1. Annapolis

        2. Ocean City

The major headings in the body of this speech, thus, are spatially arranged according to geographical location.

Time Arrangement   Another method of organization is the **time method of issue arrangement**, which orders information from a beginning point to an ending one, with all the steps developed in numerical or time sequence.

For example, chronological arrangement can be used to develop the body of the speech with the central idea "to inform the audience of the accomplishments of the last four Chinese dynasties." The body outline for the speech would read:

III. The last four Chinese dynasties

    A. A.D. 960–1280—Song (Sung)

        1. Paper money invented

        2. Primitive printing press developed

        3. Scholars active

           a. Books printed

           b. Painting reached zenith

B. A.D. 1280–1368—Yuan

1. Became part of an empire that stretched to Europe

2. Silk Road reopened

3. New religions introduced

C. A.D. 1368–1644—Ming

1. Agricultural methods of production developed

2. Great sea expeditions undertaken

D. A.D. 1644–1911—Qing (Ching)

1. Tobacco and corn industries developed

2. Lost Korea, Taiwan, and the Pescadores Islands

Topical Arrangement   Ideas also can be organized on the basis of their similarities. Thus, in using a **topical method of issue arrangement**, a speaker explains an idea in terms of its component parts. For example, in speaking about dogs, a speaker may discuss cocker spaniels, poodles, and then collies, developing ideas about each breed (the component part) completely before going on to the next one. The speaker can also organize the presentation of ideas by talking about the temperament of each breed, then about the size of each breed, and finally about the coloring of each breed. In this way, the speaker is organizing the ideas by classifying the animals according to specific identifiable characteristics (the component parts) and then developing each subsection into identifiable patterns of information.

To illustrate this process, we can construct an outline of the main headings of the body of a speech whose central idea statement is "to inform the audience about three operations of WordPerfect 3.0 for the Macintosh: editing, page formatting, and merging operations":

III. Three operations of WordPerfect 3.0 for Macintosh

A. Editing

1. Inserting and deleting text

2. Starting a new line

3. Wrap-around typing

4. Inserting text in paragraphs

B. Formatting

1. Setting margins

2. Changing point size

3. Adding a heading

C. Merging operations

    1. List processing

    2. Fill-in forms

    3. Automatic printing

Causal Arrangement   The **causal method of issue arrangement** shows how two or more events are connected in such a way that if one occurs, the other will necessarily follow. In other words, if one incident happened, it caused the second incident to happen. This is a good method to use when a specific observable result can be understood by determining what happened.

For example, this outline was developed for the body of a speech whose central idea was "to list and discuss the theory that a series of identifiable events can result in the development of agoraphobia":

III. Series of events resulting in agoraphobia

    A. Sequence of events

        1. First event

            a. Physical symptoms such as heart palpitations, trembling, sweating, breathlessness, dizziness

            b. No apparent cause for the physical symptoms

        2. Second event

            a. Duplication of physical symptoms in a place similar to the site of the first event

            b. Increasing awareness of fear of going to certain places

        3. Third event

            a. Symptoms occurring when there is a thought of going to a place similar to the site of the first event

            b. Feeling of being out of control when thinking of leaving the safety site (usually the home)

    B. Result—agoraphobia

        1. Personality changes

            a. Frequent anxiety

            b. Depression

            c. Loss of individual character

        2. Emotional changes

            a. Impassiveness

            b. High degree of dependence on others

            c. Constant alertness

Note that the events leading up to the final result are listed, with the final result discussed last. An alternative form would have been to give the final result first and then list the events leading up to it. The former method is called cause(s) to effect; the latter, effect from cause(s).

Comparison-Contrast Arrangement Suppose you are asked to explain the similarities between a community college and a four-year institution. Your explanation will probably follow the **comparison method of issue organization**, in which you would tell how two or more examples are alike. In the case of the colleges, you could talk about the similarities in curriculum, staff, facilities, activity programs, and costs. If, however, you are asked to tell the differences between the two, you would use the **contrast method of issue arrangement**, developing the ideas by giving specific examples of differences between the two types of institutions. A speech based on the **comparison-contrast method of issue arrangement** tells about both similarities and differences.

The body of a speech with a central idea of "informing the audience of some similarities and differences between state-sponsored two- and four-year colleges in Ohio" would be:

III. Similarities and differences between two- and four-year state-supported Ohio colleges

A. Similarities

1. Are governed by the Board of Regents
2. Receive state funding
3. Offer general studies courses
4. Must receive permission to add new curricula
5. Are governed by a board of trustees appointed in part by the governor

B. Differences

1. Two-year colleges: funded in part by their local communities; four-year colleges: not funded by communities
2. Two-year colleges: offer associate degrees; four-year colleges: bachelor's and advanced degrees
3. Two-year colleges: have certificate and two-year terminal programs; four-year schools: no certificates or terminal programs
4. Two-year colleges: less expensive

Problem-Solution Arrangement The **problem-solution method of issue arrangement** is used when a speaker attempts to identify what is wrong and to determine how to cure it or make a recommendation for its cure.

A well-developed speech allows listeners to share a complete picture of the speaker's reasoning process.

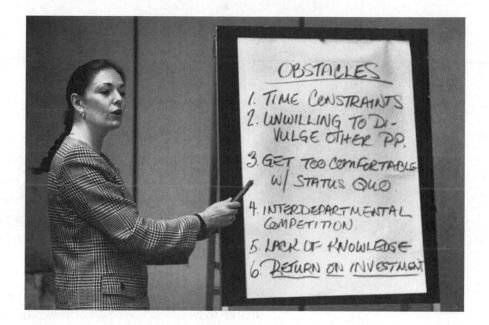

This method can be used to think through a problem and then structure a speech. A person dealing with the problem of child abuse, for instance, may wish to begin by analyzing the problem: the influence of family history, lack of parental control and/or knowledge, and the different types of child abuse. Such an analysis may then lead to a consideration of various solutions, such as stricter legislation mandating penalties for child abuse, stronger enforcement of child-abuse laws, improved reporting procedures, and greater availability of social services to parents and children alike.

An alternative form of the problem-solution method is the see-blame-cure-cost method. In this approach, the evil or problem that exists is examined (see); what has caused the problem is determined (blame); solutions are investigated, and the most practical solution is selected (cure); and what finances, time, or emotions will have to be expended (cost) are examined.

When you develop a problem-solution message, state the problem, its cause, the possible solutions, and the selected solution. This allows your listeners to share a complete picture of your reasoning process.

Here is an example of a speech outline using problem solution for the body of a speech with the central idea "to inform the audience why I believe that one of the solutions for the acid-rain problem is to require coal-burning companies and smelting plants to build taller smokestacks, use scrubbers, and wash their coal before using it":

III. Solution to acid-rain problem

A. Problem

1. Acid rain is caused by substances such as sulfur oxides and nitrogen oxides.

2. Acid rain falls anywhere that is downwind of urban or industrial pollution.

3. Acid rain has significant negative effects.

a. It decreases the fertility and productivity of soils.

b. It causes freshwater lakes and streams to become barren of fish, amphibians, invertebrates, and plankton.

c. It damages such materials as stone, marble, and copper.

d. It affects human health through contamination of the water we drink and fish and wildlife we eat.

B. Solution

1. Coal-burning companies and smelting plants should be required to build taller smokestacks to disperse the pollution.

2. Scrubbers—traps in smokestacks that can catch up to 90 percent or more of the sulfur oxides emitted—should be required for all industrial users of smokestacks.

3. All coal burned by industrial users should be washed before it is used.

A more detailed presentation of the speech can include discussions of the testing of each element of the solution. This can be accomplished by including subdivisions under each of the statements of the solution to explore whether it is workable (developing why the suggestion will solve or help solve the problem), desirable (explaining why the suggestion will not cause greater problems), and practical (indicating if and how the suggestion can be put into practice).

Major and Internal Methods of Arrangement For each speech, the speaker usually selects one major method of development, always keeping in mind that other methods may be used as necessary to present subdivisions of the complete idea. For instance, in developing a presentation on the causes of World War II, a speaker may decide to use a chronological arrangement as the major method of development and a spatial method for some of the subtopical segments of the presentation. Thus, the speaker may talk about the political and social changes in the 1920s in England, France, Germany, Russia, and Japan; then proceed to tell about events in the early 1930s in these countries; then discuss happenings in these countries in the mid–

1930s. In this way, the audience can develop a listening pattern that allows for clarity of comprehension . . . the year span and then place.

No matter which pattern you utilize to develop a message, maintain that pattern consistently throughout your presentation. Otherwise your audience will be confused by sudden shifts or failure to follow a sequence to its logical conclusion.

The Conclusion

Depending on the purpose of a speech, the **conclusion of a speech** can be used to summarize, to pull thoughts together, or to motivate listeners to take a prescribed action.

Summary

Whatever the purpose, a presentation should end with a **summary of a speech** that restates the major points so that the listener can recap what has been covered. The guide for developing the summary is to refer to the major headings in the body of the speech and indicate how they develop the statement of central idea.

The Clincher

Summarize

Don't end your presentation with "Here's one final thought." *Reason:* You'll only confuse your audience by introducing a new idea in your conclusion.

SOURCE: *Communication Briefings,* as adapted from *Communicate to Win,* by Heinz Goldman, cited in *The Competitive Advantage,* P.O. Box 10828, Portland, OR 97210.

Some communication theorists believe that all speeches should end with a summary of the major points, followed by a clincher. The outline of the conclusion section of a speech that includes a clincher would be:

IV. Conclusion
    A. Summary
    B. Clincher

The advantage of including a **clincher to a speech** is that it gives the speaker one more chance to reinforce the major ideas she or he has presented and then wraps up the presentation with a final message to clinch the selling of the central idea. Clincher techniques are similar to attention-getting introduction methods and include personal references, humorous stories, illustrations, rhetorical questions, unusual or dramatic devices, or quotations:

By using a *personal reference*, a heart specialist who established expertise at the start of a speech can reestablish his or her authority in the conclusion.

A speaker may find it appropriate to end a presentation with a *humorous story* that summarizes his or her ideas, such as summarizing a presentation about public speaking anxiety with the statement, "The mind is an amazing thing; it starts working the moment you are born and never stops until you get up to give a speech."

A person who became dependent on drugs can end a speech with an *illustration* of how difficult it is to turn away from the drug scene.

A speaker who posed a *rhetorical question* at the beginning of a presentation can conclude by answering it.

A speaker concluded a speech about the necessity of proper dental hygiene by passing out a small cup of disclosing solution and small mirror to each member of the audience. She then asked them to rinse out their mouths with the solution, which turned plaque and other substances on or between the teeth bright red. The results of this activity effectively illustrated the importance of proper brushing—and the value of *unusual or dramatic devices*.

Quotations that restate the major theme of a presentation can be used in ending it. A speaker could summarize a speech against the death penalty, for example, by reading the vivid description of an execution presented in Truman Capote's book *In Cold Blood*.

Methods for Formatting a Speech

In organizing a speech, you make decisions about the type of introduction, statement of central idea, methods of arranging the material in the body of your speech, and various techniques you can use to conclude. Some theorists believe that a speaker should go beyond this basic four-step structure and use an overall organizational structure.

The overall organizational structure can utilize the partitioning, unfolding, and case methods.

The Partitioning Method

The **partitioning organizational speech structure** depends on a great deal of repetition and is the easiest of the three overall methods for listeners to follow.

**Getting Around
18-Minute Wall**

Listeners lose concentration
after 18 minutes of a
speech, according to a Navy
study reported in *The
Articulate Executive*, by
Granville N. Toogood. To get
around the 18-minute wall:

✳ **Give them** the basics
in 15 minutes. Then, devote
half an hour to Q&A to expand your main points.

✳ **Alternate** 18-minute
segments with an associate
speaking for two minutes to
amplify a point in your
speech.

✳ **Speak for** 18 min-
utes, show a 10-minute
video and then restart your
18-minute clock.

SOURCE: *Communication
Briefings,* as adapted from
Across the Board, 845 3rd Ave.,
New York, NY 10022.

When using this type of organization, you start with the introduction and lead into your central idea. Then you state the central idea, restate it, and divide it by listing the main issues you will cover in the order in which you will cover them. This restatement and division constitute what is called the **partitioning step**. For example, a speaker whose central idea is that "there are several problems with the use of radiation therapy" could state: "To understand these radiological difficulties, we will look at the harmful effects of radiation therapy and the poor quality of radiation facilities in hospitals."

From the partitioning step, you move into the first issue of the body of the speech by using a transition that forecasts the first issue. For example, the speaker could say, "Turning, then, to our first point, let us consider the harmful effect that radiation therapy has had." Restatement is also important, for as new material is added, the speaker should hold the audience's attention and clarify his or her points by repeating those points in different words.

In moving from one issue to the next in the body of the speech, a speaker should use **transitions**, which provide a connection between the points. A good transition consists of two parts: a restatement of the previous issue and a forecast of the next one. For example, a speaker presenting a talk on marine biology provided a transition between two issues by stating, "From the evidence presented, it appears that the problems of water pollution are massive. How, then, can we tackle these problems?"

Once the last issue in a partitioned speech has been discussed, the presentation concludes with a summary that restates the central idea and the main issues. This summary gives listeners a chance to review in their own minds the points that have been discussed.

Successful partitioning organization follows the format "Tell the audience what you're going to tell them, then tell them, and then tell them what you've told them."

A general outline for the partitioning sequence would look like this:

I. Introduction

    A. Attention material

    B. Orienting material

II. Central idea

    A. Statement of central idea

    B. Restatement of central idea

    C. Division (listing of issues by some method of issue arrangement)

        1. First main issue

        2. Second main issue

        3. Third main issue (and so on)

III. Body (Transition: forecast of the first issue)

    A. First main issue

        1. Discussion of first main issue through examples, illustrations, and explanations

        2. Discussion of first main issue through examples, illustrations, and explanations (and so on)

    (Transition: restatement of first main issue and forecast of second issue)

    B. Second main issue

        1. Discussion of second main issue

        2. Discussion of second main issue (and so on)

    (Transition: restatement of second main issue and forecast of third issue)

    C. Third main issue

        1. Discussion of third main issue

        2. Discussion of third main issue (and so on)

IV. Conclusion

    A. Summary (restatement of issues and central idea)

    B. Clincher

The following outline develops a speech according to the partitioning method of organization:

Central Idea: To inform the audience of the alternatives an intake counselor has by listing and discussing the options.

I. Introduction

    A. Attention material: Each of us probably makes hundreds of decisions every day. We decide what to eat, what to wear, what television program to watch, what time to go to bed.

    B. Orienting material: In my work as an intake counselor with the Department of Juvenile Services, I must make decisions that can seriously affect a child's life. An intake counselor gets the police report when a juvenile commits a crime, calls in the parents and the child to decide what actions should be taken, and counsels them. An investigation of such work can help you to understand some of the procedures that local governments use to combat the problems of juvenile delinquency.

II. Statement of central idea

    A. Let us consider the alternatives an intake counselor has.

    B. The counselor can select from three major decisions.

    C. These decisions are to

        1. Send the case to court.

        2. Close the case at intake.

        3. Place the child on informal supervision for forty-five days.

III. Body

    (One decision a counselor may make is to send the case to court.)

    A. The law states that you must send the case to court if

        1. The charge is denied.

        2. The juvenile has a prior record.

        3. You notice signs of trouble in the family.

        4. The case is like Felicia's. Felicia . . .

    (Thus a case may be sent to court. A counselor may also decide to close a case at intake.)

    B. There are several reasons for closing the case at intake.

        1. The child admits guilt.

        2. The incident was a first offense.

        3. The parents are supportive and the home life is stable.

        4. An example of a case closed at intake was Henrietta's. . . .

    (As a result, a case may be closed at intake. A counselor may also decide to put a juvenile under informal supervision.)

    C. Supervision for forty-five days is warranted if

        1. The child or the family is in need of short-term counseling.

        2. The procedure is not used often.

        3. The court has never ordered this in the past.

        4. The case is like Lamont's. Lamont. . . .

    (Through informal supervision, some children can be helped.)

IV. Conclusion

    A. Summary: The basic decision is whether to arrange court appearances, stop the action at the beginning, or supervise the client.

    B. Clincher: The goal of the whole intake process is to provide whatever is best for the child so that he or she will have proper care, treatment, and supervision.

Though partitioning organization can be used for a speech of any purpose, it especially is well suited to informative speaking and informative briefing. Because the aim of such a speech is to increase the listener's comprehension of a particular body of information, a clear structure and repetition of the major points are warranted.

The Unfolding Method

The **unfolding organizational speech structure** can be used for a speech of any purpose, but if you want to persuade your listeners, you will find this format the most useful. Unfolding organization differs from partitioning organization in two important ways: it does not restate the central idea or include the division step.

The unfolding format may be appropriate for an audience that initially agrees with the central idea and issue the speaker plans to develop.

Here is one possible sequence for an unfolding format:

I. Introduction
 A. Attention material
 B. Orienting material

II. Statement of central idea

III. Body (organized by some method of issue arrangement)
 (Transition)
 A. First issue
  1. Discussion of first issue through examples, illustrations, and explanations
  2. Discussion of first issue through examples, illustrations, and explanations (and so on)
 (Transition)
 B. Second issue
  1. Discussion of second issue through examples, illustrations, and explanations
  2. Discussion of second issue through examples, illustrations, and explanations (and so on)
 (Transition)

IV. Conclusion
 A. Restatement
 B. Clincher

If members of the audience oppose your stand, it does not make sense to alienate them by stating your central idea early in the presentation. Instead, lead them through the main points, moving from areas of shared agreement into areas of controversy. If you arrange the main issues subtly and word them carefully, you may be able to establish acceptance of your purpose statement just before you reach the conclusion. In proceeding, follow this variation of the unfolding format:

I. Introduction

    A. Attention material

    B. Orienting material

    (Transition)

II. Body (organized by some method of issue arrangement)

    A. Discussion of first issue

        1. Examples and illustrations

        2. Examples and illustrations (and so on)

    B. Statement of first issue

    (Transition)

    C. Discussion of second issue

        1. Examples and illustrations

        2. Examples and illustrations (and so on)

    (Transition)

III. Statement of central idea

    (Transition)

IV. Conclusion

    A. Restatement

    B. Clincher

For instance, if you are trying to persuade a group of people to vote for a candidate and you know the audience is not committed to the person, you are wise to develop your position by stating the issues, stands, and actions of the candidate; stressing the positive aspects of your candidate; and building strong support for him or her. After establishing this argument, you then reveal the voting action you want from the audience. Some members may be swayed.

The unfolding method is more flexible than the partitioning method because it lends itself to a variety of formats. For example, in the unfolding method of organization, you can move the statement of the central idea anywhere in the speech as long as it comes before the conclusion. And your transitions do not have to restate and forecast issues; they simply have to establish clear connections. Furthermore, in this method, you do not have to restate all the issues and the central idea in the conclusion. Remember, however, that a good conclusion should summarize and conclude your presentation.

As a speaker, you want to maintain a clear framework so that the speech moves forward sequentially. Remember that a speech is of no value if the audience does not clearly understand your central idea at the conclusion.

This outline develops a speech according to the unfolding method of organization:

Central Idea: To persuade each member of the audience, by listing and discussing the reasons, that he or she should donate his or her body to science.

  I. Introduction
     A. Attention material: Picture a three-year-old girl attached to a kidney dialysis machine once a week for the rest of her life—or for as long as the machine is available. Picture a little boy whose world is blackness, or a father who is confined to his bed because he has a weak heart.
     B. Orienting material: Such pictures are not very pleasant. But you can do something about them.

 II. Statement of central idea: You should donate your body to science.

III. Body
     A. Scientists need organs so that others may function normally.
        1. List of organs that can be donated
        2. The need for speed in transplanting organs (Thus specific organs can be used)
     B. Your body can be used as an instrument for medical education.
        1. Who can donate and how
        2. The need to eliminate shortages
     (As a result, your entire body can continue to serve a useful purpose.)

IV. Conclusion
     A. Summary
        1. Organs are needed so that others can function normally.
        2. Your body can be used for medical education.

B. Clincher

1. I am a benevolent person who believes that everyone is born with a benevolent nature. I know that you and I will help those less fortunate than we are. I am a potential organ and cadaver donor through my will. A donor's card can be obtained through any medical foundation. I cannot overemphasize the need for body and organ donations.

2. Don't, as the proverb states, wait for George to do it. You do it! Take immediate action to become an organ and cadaver donor.

The Case Method

In some respects, the **case method of organizational speech structure** of organization is less complex than the partitioning and unfolding methods, because the speaker discusses the central idea without breaking it into subpoints. As a result, this format is especially suitable for speeches designed to entertain, commemorate or present a single issue. If, for example, your central idea is that "kids say the funniest things," then the body of a speech you organize using this method includes a series of examples of children's clever sayings connected by clear transitions.

When you use the case method, be careful not to develop subpoints in the body of the speech so that they become main points in themselves. The danger of subdividing is that you may not develop each subdivided point fully, and your listeners may become confused. If, for instance, in the "kids say the funniest things" example you say in one of the transitions, "Kids say funny things at school and at camp," you have subdivided your central idea into two issues.

Here is the general format for a speech developed by case organization:

I. Introduction

A. Attention material

B. Orienting material

(Transition)

II. Central idea

(Transition)

III. Body (organized in a sequence)

A. Example (a case)

(Transition)

B. Example (a case)

(Transition)

C. Example (a case; and so on)

(Transition)

IV. Conclusion

    A. Summary

    B. Clincher

The following outline develops a speech according to the case method of organization:

Central Idea: To inform the audience of some ways in which left-handers are discriminated against by listing some examples.

I. Introduction

    A. Attention material: Have you ever pondered the design of a butter knife or the structure of a gravy ladle?

    B. Orienting material: These structural problems are important to all of us who are afflicted with a key social problem—left-handedness.

    (Those of us who are left-handed believe that . . .)

II. Statement of central idea

    A. Left-handers are discriminated against.

    B. Let's look at some examples.

III. Body

    A. Example: Tell a story of the difficulties encountered when using scissors.

    (Transition: Another experience I've had . . .)

    B. Example: Tell a story of the problems with school desks designed for right-handed people.

    (Transition: This experience points out another one . . .)

    C. Example: Tell a story of the problems with words such as *gauche* and *southpaw*.

    (Transition: So you see . . .)

IV. Conclusion

    A. Summary: Left-handers are discriminated against all the way from the design of scissors to the names they are called.

    B. Clincher: If you are left-handed, however, no matter the descrimination, you are in good company: eleven presidents of the United States have been left-handed!

IN CONCLUSION  A public communication message is usually divided into four parts: introduction, central idea, body, and conclusion.

Attention material can be comprised of personal references, humorous illustrations, references to the occasion or setting, rhetorical questions, action questions, unusual or dramatic devices, quotations related to the theme, or statements of the theme.

Orienting material, which includes historical background, definition of terms, personal history and/or the speaker's tie to the topic, and the topic's importance to the listeners, gives an audience the background necessary to understand the basic material of the speech.

Issue arrangement takes one of six forms: spatial arrangement, chronological or time arrangement, topical arrangement, causal arrangement, comparison-contrast arrangement, or problem-solution arrangement.

A summary restates the major points of the speech. Clinchers can include personal references, humorous stories, illustrations, rhetorical questions, unusual or dramatic devices, and quotations.

The basic approaches to overall speech organization are the partitioning, unfolding, and case methods.

LEARN BY DOING ⟶ 1. Your instructor asks for a volunteer and gives him or her a card that has a drawing on it. Each member of the class has a sheet of paper and a pencil. The volunteer tells the class how to draw the diagram exactly as it appears on the card. No one is allowed to ask any questions. When the volunteer has finished giving directions, the members of the class compare their drawings with the original. After the activity, the class discusses these questions:

   a. If the volunteer did not do so, would it have helped if he or she had given a general overview of what to draw before beginning to give directions? Discuss this question in relation to your reading about the purpose of an introduction.

   b. Did the instructions have a conclusion? How could a conclusion restating the major points have helped you?

   c. Were any words used in the directions that caused noise to enter into the communication? What were they? How did they cause problems?

   d. Was the structure of the directions clear?

   e. Do you think a question-and-answer session following the instructions would have been valuable? Why or why not?

2. Do Activity 1 again. This time, the next volunteer builds on the positive things the first volunteer did and makes improvements based on the discussion. This time the activity is followed by a question-and-answer session. Note how many people altered their drawings during the question-and-answer session. Draw some conclusions about the value of question-and-answer sessions.

3. A speaker informs the class about an unusual topic—something which the audience has no knowledge about. Sample topics are the language of bees, the Christmas customs of Puerto Rico, rafting on the Colorado River, or organic architecture. Be sure the speech has a clear structure and lasts no more than five minutes.

4. Select a subject about which you are expert and present a speech to your classmates in such a way that when you finish they too have an understanding of the topic. Clearly structure the speech, and take no more than six minutes to deliver it.

5. Prepare a speech of no more than five minutes informing the class about a controversial theory. Sample topics: The Loch Ness monster exists; Rational emotive therapy can alter behavior; Alcoholism is an inherited disease. Explain the theory and the various arguments concerning the theory. Do not include your views in the presentation. Be sure the speech is clearly structured.

6. You are going to give a speech about your education (elementary, high school, college). Prepare an introduction for the presentation representing each of these introductory devices:

    a. Personal reference

    b. Humorous story

    c. Rhetorical question

    d. Unusual or dramatic device

KEY TERMS →

introduction to a speech
orienting material
statement of the speech's
    central idea
body of a speech
spiral form of explanation

method of issue arrangement for
    the body of a speech
spatial method of issue arrangement
time method of issue arrangement
topical method of issue
    arrangement

causal method of issue
  arrangement
comparison method of issue
  organization
contrast method of issue
  arrangement
comparison-contrast method of
  issue arrangement
problem-solution method of issue
  arrangement
conclusion of a speech

summary of a speech
clincher to a speech
partitioning organizational speech
  structure
partitioning step
transitions
unfolding organizational speech
  structure
case method of organizational
  speech structure

chapter 14

Informative Public Speaking

LEARNING OUTCOMES →

After reading this chapter, you should be able to:

Define informative speaking

Discuss the need for informative speaking in the information age

List and explain the classifications of informative speeches

Explain how to develop an informative speech

List and explain the steps a successful informative speaker takes in developing a speech

W̲e live in an era that has been dubbed "the information age." "Knowledge is doubling at the rate of 100 percent every twenty months."[1] One social commentator suggests that the need for people who can retrieve and explain information is going to greatly increase in the future.[2]

The Role of Informative Speaking

With the ever-expanding development of information, we need to have a source for obtaining the information. The traditional sources, such as television, radio, and the newspapers, have been supplemented by the Internet and CD/ROMs. In addition to the usual sources, institutions depend on information resource people, professors, and guest speakers to provide information that employees and students need.

Businesses are representative of the recognition of the need for information. According to one corporate communication expert: "A factor vital to the health of any corporation is the constant exchange of accurate information. Although traditional, written forms of business communication remain important, the oral exchange of information occupies an increasingly important role in the functioning of today's companies."[3] Organizations hire consultants and engage information specialists to disseminate new material and to train their employees to instruct others on how to use new equipment and adjust their job skills in an ever-changing new information environment.

The Concept of Informative Speaking

Traditionally, **informative speaking** has been defined as discourse that imparts new information, secures understanding, or reinforces accumulated information. At present, however, controversies persist among communication theorists about this definition. For instance, some scholars argue that all speaking is persuasive in nature, that the traditional distinction between informative speaking and persuasive speaking is simply a matter of theoretical degree.

This text assumes that all communication contains elements of persuasion. After all, the audience in the traditional informative-speaking format must be persuaded to accept information presented by the speaker. Indeed, even the act of using materials to gain attention is persuasive because the speaker is asking listeners to pay attention to the speaker rather than to any other competing stimuli. If there are distinguishing elements between an informative and a persuasive speech, they center on the structure of the message and the appeals used in the persuasive format. The importance of understanding this argument, for you, the student, is to be alert that developing an informative and a persuasive speech is not exactly the same task. As you study this and the next chapter, you will be notified of the differences and your responsibilities as a preparer and presenter of speeches.

Characteristics of Informative Speaking

As in any type of speaking, the development of an informative presentation depends on analysis of the audience. Consideration must be given to the listeners' present knowledge about the subject, concepts known by the audience that can function as a foundation to their gaining the information, and the extent to which definitions, understandable analogies, examples, and clarifiers need to be used. A speaker also must determine appropriate language level, attention devices to be used, and the structure of the message that will best fit the group. Research suggests that the speaker, as the information source, may think his or her listeners lack necessary information, whereas the listeners themselves may not feel the same way.[4] An astute speaker determines the real needs of the audience members through thorough audience analysis and uses that information to develop the speech.

In an informative presentation, a speaker must always keep the purpose of the presentation in mind. Thus a clear statement of central idea is essential. Consider these examples: "To inform the audience of what the Heimlich maneuver is, how it was developed, and how this technique can prevent people from choking to death"; "At the conclusion of this speech I want the members of the audience to know what the Heimlich maneuver is, and what steps are necessary to do the maneuver." Note that in the examples, although the subject is the same, the goal is different. The former explains the maneuver and its value. The latter explains the maneuver and then teaches the steps for performing it.

These statements of central idea may sound rather formal, but they are stated in a manner that narrows the subject and indicates specifically what will be included in the speech. Thus the statement of central idea serves as a fence around the territory to be covered in a presentation and indicates how to "corral" the information. If you do not set up these sorts of boundaries, you may find yourself discussing many things but not achieving your desired outcome.

I Didn't Get a Standing Ovation Today

I didn't get a standing ovation today
But I learned afterwards a woman in the front row with cancer
Nodded in agreement as I spoke of overcoming circumstance.

I didn't get a standing ovation a week ago
But a small group stayed late after the program.
They bought the beer and we shared great stories.

I didn't get a standing ovation a month ago,
But a manager from that program sent me a note.
He said my presentation encouraged him to keep trying.

I did get a standing ovation recently,
I gave a pretty good speech, but after the applause,
I don't remember much else that was remarkable that day.

I didn't get a standing ovation today
Instead, somehow I connected with the human spirit
And I got much, much more.

SOURCE: From Mark Sanborn in *Secrets of Successful Speakers* by Lilly Walters, p. 148, 1993, McGraw-Hill, Inc. Reproduced by permission of Mark Sanborn.

 Classifications of Informative Speaking

There is no universally-accepted classification of informative speeches. One classification system examines presentations about objects, processes, events, and concepts. At the same time, this system accepts other specific types of informative speeches that can be identified by the setting in which they are used or by their uniqueness. Examples include informative briefings, technical reports, lectures, question-and-answer sessions, and speeches of introduction.

Speeches About Objects

Speeches about objects describe a particular thing in detail. The object may be a person, place, animal, structure, machine—anything that can be touched or seen. First the object is identified, and then details concerning some specific attribute of the object are discussed.

Examples of statements of central idea for informative speeches about an object are: "To inform the audience about the role of the Presidential Volunteer Office during the Clinton presidency" (topical arrangement); "To inform the audience of the experiments being done to identify the language capabilities of dolphins by discussing two of the experiments."

Speeches About Processes

Speeches about processes instruct the audience about how something works, is made, or is done so that listeners can apply the skills learned. The end purpose may be either to gain understanding of the process or to be able to do something. This technique is used in training workers to operate a piece of equipment or in explaining a manufacturing process. Statements of central idea for informative speeches about processes include "To inform listeners of the step-by-step process of using the move feature of the Word word-processing program" (time sequence arrangement); "To demonstrate the process used to fill out the income tax short form."

Speeches about processes often lend themselves to development according to a chronological method of organization. In this method, the speaker describes the first step of the process, then the second, and so on.

Speeches About Events

Speeches about events inform the audience about something that has already happened, is happening, or is expected to happen. This type of presentation tends to work well in a chronological, comparison-contrast, or spatial arrangement. Here are several statements of central idea for informative speeches about events: "To inform the audience of the spread of the AIDS virus through a statistical examination of the years 1980 to 1996 in the United States" (time sequence arrangement); and "To inform the audience of the similarities and differences in the American and Russian revolutions based on their economic causes" (comparison-contrast arrangement).

Speeches About Concepts

Speeches about concepts examine theories, beliefs, ideas, philosophies, or schools of thought. Much of the formal educational process deals with speeches about concepts.[5] Concept topics include explanations and

Speeches about processes instruct the audience about how something works, is made, or is done, so that the listeners can apply the skills.

investigations of business theories, philosophical movements, psychological concepts, and political theories.

Because many of the ideas relating to concepts are abstract, a speaker must be sure to use precise language, define terms, give historical background, avoid undefined slang and jargon, and use clarifying support materials such as audio, visual, and audio-visual aids. Examples of statements of central idea for informative speeches about concepts are: "To inform the audience about the theory that abused children grow up to be child abusers through an examination of three classic research studies" (cause-to-affect arrangement); "To inform the audience that musical theater composers Alan Jay Lerner and Frederick Loewe used the theme of the search for a perfect time, perfect place, and perfect love story as the basis for their musicals."

Informative Briefings

Business, organizational, and technical communicators often gain current knowledge in their fields as a result of informative briefings. The fundamental objective of an **informative briefing** is to present information to a specialized audience, followed by the exchange of data, ideas, and questions among participants.[6] This technique is used by organizations, for example, to explain new or existing organizational policies, procedures, and issues. Examples of informative briefings are a sales manager of an automobile agency informing her staff about the new models or the Dean of Students explaining a college's academic policies to a group of entering freshmen.

As with any speech, preparation for an informative briefing requires careful analysis of the audience to determine what background and definitions will be needed to ensure audience comprehension. If the audience has extensive knowledge, the speaker does not have to cover background material in as much depth as he or she would for uninformed listeners. For example, the automobile agency sales manager does not have to go into detail with her experienced staff about the auto manufacturer and the history of the agency; on the other hand, for a meeting of new salespersons, she should give this background.

Technical Reports

The **technical report** is a concise, clear statement describing a process, explaining a technique, or discussing new elements, either to people within a business or industry or to people outside it. In spite of the fact that the technical report is a major communicative activity in corporate America, recent college and university graduates do not seem prepared to give such presentations. A survey of business executives revealed that fewer than 20 percent of the people they worked with were capable of giving a concise, clear oral report and that they had far greater difficulty training people to do this than to write a clear letter.

In presenting a technical report, the speaker must know who will be in the audience. If the report is to be given to nontechnical people, all technical words must be defined, and analogies familiar to the audience should be included to clarify the ideas presented. This does not mean a speaker has to water down the material so that it is invalidated. Instead, the speaker should be sure to define words, give examples, and present ideas in a variety of ways to make sure that the audience understands the concepts being set forth.

If your presentation includes technical drawings or a number of statistics, use handouts so that everyone can examine the materials. If the group is small, consider allowing audience members to ask questions as you develop your ideas so that they have the opportunity for immediate clarification where necessary.

One of the major factors in the development of a technical report is determining the structure. When you structure a technical report that involves a recommendation, start with a statement of the proposal unless there is a compelling reason not to do so. (You may want to hold the recommendation until the end if you know the audience will be hostile to the

Inviting inquiries during a presentation can facilitate listeners' understanding and keep them interested.

proposal, or if you want to lead up to the recommendation by giving total background before revealing your solution or recommendation.) After you have proposed the idea, explain how you arrived at the conclusions or recommendations. Make sure you know exactly how much time is allotted for your presentation. Plan the presentation so that you can stay in that time limit.[7]

Lectures

Probably the most familiar type of informative speaking to all of us is the **lecture**, the formal presentation of material to facilitate learning. Lectures are an integral part of academic life, serving as the main vehicle for presenting information in many subject fields. In addition, lectures are used in other settings: invited lecturers for lunch or dinnertime seminars in corporate headquarters and public lectures by distinguished authorities in museum, arts, religious, or public settings.

A good lecture should be carefully adapted to the intended audience so that the speaker does not make inaccurate assumptions about the level of knowledge and vocabulary of the listeners. An effective lecture should be clearly organized, with transitions that allow listeners to stay "on track" and anticipate what is coming next. The speaker should use supporting details to elaborate each of the points made. Like all informative speaking, lectures often tend to be top-heavy with explanations and consequently are considered dry. A variety of supporting materials (stories, statistics, analogies) enhance explanatory details and involve listeners more readily. The insertion of humor is also a way of getting and holding attention, as is the use of interaction that involves listeners by asking them questions, probing for information, and inviting inquiries during the presentation instead of waiting until the question-and-answer session. Supplemental aids can facilitate listeners' understanding and keep them interested in the presentation.

The timing of a lecture is another key to success. Lecturers should be aware of the time frame available. The audience expects a lecturer to stay within the framework of the assigned time (such as a class period).

We have all sat through good and bad class lectures, lectures that held your attention and from which you learned, and those that put you to sleep. If you are ever asked to present a lecture, ask yourself what the good lecturers did . . . then duplicate that style.

Question-and-Answer Sessions

The **question-and-answer session** that follows many speeches is a type of informative speech in itself. It is an on-the-spot set of unrehearsed answers that measures a speaker's knowledge, alerts a speaker to areas in a speech that were unclear or needed more development, and gives listeners a chance to probe for ideas.

In some instances, a question-and-answer session allows receivers to point out weaknesses in a speaker's arguments or present alternative views. These occur more frequently after persuasive speeches than after informative presentations. If confronted by a hostile questioner, the speaker has to determine whether she or he wants to deal with the issue or remind the prober that the purpose of this part of the speech is to ask questions, not give a counterspeech or engage in debate.

When you enter into a question-and-answer session, set the ground rules. Ask the program chairperson about the process to be used and the time limit. Tell him or her of any restrictions you wish to place on this segment of the speech. Some speakers like to call on participants; others prefer that the chairperson entertain the questions. Some presenters want all questions written out beforehand so they can select the questions they will

When You Answer Questions

If you've made a presentation and are fielding questions from the audience, here are some ways to build credibility:

* **If you don't** know the answer to a question, don't pretend to. Admit you don't know and offer to get the information to the person.

* **Refer to** your professional and personal experience when addressing questions. Just be careful not to sound as if you're bragging.

* **Quote experts** on the topic being discussed.

* **Offer as** many facts as possible.

* **Establish** a bond. *Example:* "I can certainly appreciate your concern."

* **Recognize** the importance of the question being asked. But be careful not to sound patronizing.

* **When possible,** dissociate yourself from a problem caused by a previous administration. *Example:* "That was the policy during the last administration. Our policy is . . ."

* **Prepare** one-liners that you'll be able to weave into the answers—key points you want the audience to remember.

SOURCE: *Communication Briefings,* as adapted from *Power Communications,* by Valerie Wiener, New York University Press, Washington Square, New York, NY 10003.

answer. If you have any restrictions, let the chairperson know of them before you give the speech, and inform the audience of the rules.

The most difficult part of many question-and-answer sessions is to get the first question asked. Once this hurdle is overcome, however, questions may flow spontaneously. To overcome the first-question trauma, you may want to have someone in the audience prepared in advance to ask a question. Another technique is to ask a question yourself. This can be accomplished by stating, "I've often been asked my views concerning . . ." and then answering by indicating your views.

Here are some additional suggestions for conducting a question-and-answer session:

Before you answer a question, restate it so that everyone hears the inquiry. If the question is complicated, simplify it in the restatement.

Do not speak only to the questioner; speak to the whole audience.

Be patient. If you have to repeat material you have already covered, do so briefly.

If a question goes on and on, prompt the questioner to summarize the question.

Keep your answers short. Restate the question, give your response, clarify any vocabulary necessary, give an example if appropriate, and then

The question-and-answer session that follows many speeches.

stop. Following the response, some speakers ask the questioner whether the answer was satisfactory.

Back up your responses with examples, statistics, and quotations.

If a question is overly complicated or of interest only to the asker, suggest a discussion with the questioner after the speech or via correspondence.

If a question is irrelevant, indicate that it is interesting or thought-provoking but does not seem appropriate to the presentation. Do not get sidetracked from the purpose of the speech or pulled into a private debate with a questioner.

If you do not know an answer, say so. You can offer to find out the answer and report back later.

Limit the discussion to one question per person, and avoid getting caught in a dialogue with one person. Others who have questions will become frustrated, and those who do not will get bored.

Be willing to be corrected or at least to recognize another's viewpoint. Thank a person for his or her clarification or acknowledge that more than one point of view is possible (e.g., "That's an interesting idea," or "The idea can be viewed that way"). You may win a battle of words

When you enter into a question-and-answer session, set the ground rules. Let the audience know the format, including any restrictions.

by putting down or insulting a questioner, but you will lose the respect of the listeners in the process. Indeed, it is futile to get involved in a battle of words with a heckler or a person with a preconceived attitude or bias.

Know when to end a session. Do not wait until interest has waned or people begin leaving. You can lose the positive effect of a speech by having an overlong question-and-answer session.

Speeches of Introduction

The purpose of a **speech of introduction** is to identify the person who will be speaking to the audience and give any other information that may spark listeners' interest in the speaker or the topic. Too often, speeches of introduction are ineffective because the presenter has not carefully prepared remarks appropriate to listeners' needs. When you introduce a speaker, clearly identify who the speaker is by whatever name, title, and identification he or she wants used. You can also talk about where the speaker is from, as well as his or her accomplishments and when they were achieved. Establish the credibility of a speaker by highlighting aspects of his or her credentials and background that indicate knowledge or expertise in the subject being discussed.

A speech of introduction should be short and to the point. Remember, listeners have come to hear the speaker, not the person making the introduction.

Some suggestions concerning a speech of introduction include:

Do not overpraise a speaker. Indicating that he or she is the best speaker the audience will ever hear gives the presenter an almost impossible goal.

Avoid using phrases such as "It is an honor and a privilege" or "This speaker needs no introduction." These are overused and often insincere.

Set the proper tone for the speech. If, for example, you know that the speech is going to be humorous, try to fit humor into the introduction.

Be sure you can pronounce a speaker's name as he or she wants it pronounced.

Get the information you need from a speaker as far in advance as possible so that you have time to work on the presentation.

If possible, ask what a speaker wishes to have highlighted.

Developing the Informative Speech

Every informative speaker has a challenge: to get the audience to understand and retain the information presented. When you consider that the typical listener remembers only about 10 percent of an oral presentation three days after hearing it, you recognize how great the challenge is.[8]

Learning-theory specialists stress that the basis for retention and understanding is the establishment of relationships (associations and connections) with physical or mental activities. We can learn through repetition—hearing ideas over and over again. We can learn through experiencing—doing a task to see what it is.[9] We are more likely to remember things that have relevance to us. We remember information we are exposed to that will somehow make life easier, teaches us something we did not know before, or we will be rewarded for knowing. In other words, we remember when we see a reason to do so. We also remember when

Focus on Why

When preparing a presentation, conduct a "so why?" test. Pretend you're a member of the audience and ask, "So why do I need to know this?" If you don't have a clear answer, your audience won't either.

SOURCE: *Communication Briefings,* as adapted from *Simple Steps to a Powerful Presentation,* Quill, 100 Schelter Road, Lincolnshire, IL 60069.

something makes sense to us—when the order in which the material is presented makes the idea(s) easy to understand, or the examples and other developing materials make the idea clear.

When you plan an informative speech, consider using supplementary aids to help your listeners remember your message. Understanding how we learn can be of assistance in determining the approach to take. It is estimated that we learn 1 percent through taste, 1.5 percent through touch, 3.5 percent through smell, 11 percent through hearing, and an astonishing 83 percent through sight.[10] Thus, you must realize that your best chance of getting people to remember is to have them hear and see the content of your presentation. Such devices as slides, charts, illustrations, pictures, and models help to reinforce and/or clarify what you say. Keep in mind these pointers when developing an informative speech:[11]

Order your ideas clearly. Select a method of organization that helps your audience follow the step-by-step development of the speech.

Use a time sequence method of delivery if a speech lends itself to a first-second-third progression or is date-oriented (years or ages). Sample subject: explaining an experiment that requires a specific progression.

Use a spatial method of delivery if a speech has some geographical basis that lends itself to an east-west, top-bottom, or inside-out organization. Sample subject: tracing the voyage of Christopher Columbus from Spain to the New World.

Use a topical method of delivery if a broad subject area can be divided into specific parts. Sample subject: describing the life cycle, characteristics, and dangers of the killer bee.

Use comparison-contrast when a topic centers on illustrating similarities and differences. Sample subject: comparing Nebraska's unicameral (one-house) legislature with the two-house legislative system of all other states.

Use the familiar to explain the new. An excellent clarifying technique is to use an analogy that compares something unfamiliar to the familiar. For example, you can explain how an AM radio signal travels by comparing it to the way a bow and arrow work. The arrow goes as far as the bow projects it. If something gets in its way, the arrow stops moving. Similarly, an AM signal goes as far as its thrusting signal power allows it to move unless something gets in its way and stops it.

Use vivid illustrations. Descriptions, stories, comparisons, contrasts, and verbal pictures add to the possibility of gaining and holding the audience's attention. An audience member who can visualize something is likely to remember it.

Avoid being too technical. If you have ever tried to follow directions for using a computer program when you knew nothing about computer language, you know the difficulty of understanding materials geared for an expert, not a layperson. If your subject is technical, evaluate the vocabulary level of audience members. Choose terms that are unlikely to confuse or clarify the technical terms you do use. The purpose of a speech is not to impress an audience with your vast vocabulary; it is to accomplish an informative objective. Select words that will help, rather than hinder, your task.

Personalize your message. Audiences are more attracted to real, human-element examples than fictional or hypothetical examples. If at all possible, use illustrations that allow your audience to identify with the plight of a victim, understand the joy of what happened to someone who mastered the process you are teaching, or learn how someone's life was altered by the historical event you are sharing.

Do not speak down to your audience, but do not overestimate audience knowledge. There is no clear guideline for evaluating an audience's knowledge level other than to learn as much as you can about what the audience knows, specifically and generally. It is senseless to draw an analogy to the familiar if it is not familiar. For example, professors brought up during the John F. Kennedy era often forget that most present-day college students were not even born during JFK's presidency. Drawing comparisons between today and that time may be beyond the conceptual level of today's students in a freshman level class.

Use as much clarification and detail as you think necessary to ensure listener understanding. If anything, err on the side of overexplanation. Most audience members appreciate a speaker who makes an effort to communicate clearly.

The Informative Process in Action

It is helpful to study the process of speech preparation by investigating the steps a professional speaker once took in developing a speech. Figure 14.1 outlines what is involved in effective lobbying techniques as keys to influencing decisions in legislative bodies. The speaker is well known to her listeners as a successful lobbyist.

Figure 14.1
Sample Speech
Outline

Central Idea: to inform the audience about the value of investing money by examining the various asset classes, the perceived risks, and the need for portfolio diversity.

Attention material using reference from an authority with statistics.	**I. Introduction:** A. Attention Material: According to Mercer Global Advisors, only 3% of the people in the U.S. can retire at age 65 with the same level of comfort they had before retirement. Because we are a nation with the highest standard of living in the world, this is unacceptable.
Orienting material demonstrating how topic affects listeners	B. Orienting Material: Because of inflation, in order to live comfortably when you retire at age 65, you will need to have over $2M set aside. This is possible. The most successful investors start early because compound interest works in one's favor. For instance, if you save $4000 a year for 8 years (for a total of $32,000 saved) after graduation, then never save again but let it grow at 9% interest, you will have $757,966 in 40 years.
Topic of speech	**II. Central Idea:** A. Along with starting at an early age, researching various aspects of investing is crucial to success.
Partitioning step (preview of issues)	B. In evaluating investment needs, we will look at different classes of investments, perceived risks, and the importance of portfolio diversity.

Statement of the first issue
 	
Discussion of asset classes with examples
	III. Body
	A. Research various asset classes
	  1. Debt Investments
	    a. This includes Treasury Bills (T Bills) and Certificates of Deposits (CDs).
	    b. The investor lends the bank money for the income.
	    c. The investor is a creditor or debt holder.
	  2. Equity Investments
	    a. This includes investments such as stocks and mutual funds.
	    b. The investor is entitled to all free cash flows that exceed the debt payment obligations.

Transition

Statement of the second issue
Discussion of perceived risks of
assets with definitions

Explanation and elaboration

Discussion of personal risk level

Explanation and elaboration

Transition

Statement of the third issue

Definition of diversity

    c. Potential for profit is greater
       and is paid through dividend
       payments, or the investor may
       elect to reinvest the profits back
       into the business.
(These different types of investments do
carry with them perceived risks.)
B. Perceived risks
  1. The risk of the asset (debt versus
    equity) is determined by the volatil-
    ity of the asset (potential of a secu-
    rity to go up or down in value).
    a. If a stock has high volatility,
       there is a great risk; however,
       the opportunity for a profit also
       increases.
    b. Because of the agreed-upon fu-
       ture interest and payment in
       debt investments, they are
       nearly risk free.
    c. There is a greater risk in equity
       investments because the in-
       vestor is risking the entire
       amount of the investment and
       is also running a risk that if the
       business goes bankrupt, the in-
       vestor loses all.
  2. Additionally, each individual has a
    risk level that they are willing to
    tolerate which adds to the decision
    of which asset class to invest in.
    a. This risk level takes into consid-
       eration how quickly money may
       be needed.
    b. Another determining factor on
       the risk level is the age of the
       investor.

(Because there are perceived risks to the
various categories of investments, portfolio diversity is essential.)
C. Portfolio Diversity is essential for
   success.
  1. In diversifying, one allocates in-
    vestments among different classes
    of assets in a certain proportion
    because, when investing, portfolio
    design is what matters most.

Elaboration of importance in diversifying

2. Risky funds aren't so risky if they're part of a fund portfolio. This way, if you're a conservative investor, you can invest in one risky fund, benefit from the long-term gains, and still be secure.

3. Stock fund performance is not an accurate guide to future results. Even the best funds have their bad years, so it is necessary to have a well-balanced portfolio.

IV. Conclusion
    A. Summary

Reiteration of main points

1. It's imperative to start investing early in order to have enough money set aside to live comfortably when you retire.

2. When researching investments, one must keep in mind the differences between debt and equity investments and understand the risk of each.

3. One must also be sure to maintain a diversified portfolio.

Closing phrase to emphasize importance of investing money

    B. Keep in mind that it's better to have your money work for you rather than you having to work for your money!

IN CONCLUSION → Informative speaking imparts new information, secures understanding, or reinforces accumulated information. Types of informative speaking include presentations about objects, processes, events, and concepts. Informative speeches, when classified by setting or uniqueness, include informative briefings, technical reports, lectures, question-and-answer sessions, and speeches of introduction. The challenge for an informative speaker is to get the audience to understand and retain the information presented. To develop an informative speech, order ideas clearly, use the familiar to explain the new, use vivid illustrations, avoid being too technical, personalize the message, and do not speak down to the audience.

LEARN BY DOING → 1. In class, your instructor will match you with a partner. With the assistance of your partner, select a topic for a speech based on audience analysis (your class), setting (your classroom), and purpose (an informative speech of three to five minutes). After you have both selected your topics, meet with another group. Present a short informative speech indicating what topic you have selected and why this subject suits you, the audience, the setting, and the purpose. The speech should use a structure that includes an introduction, statement of central idea, body, and conclusion.

2. Bring to class an object or piece of machinery (e.g., a camera, food processor, or microscope) that you feel members of your class cannot operate or that you have a different approach to operating. Be prepared to teach someone else how to use the equipment. In class you are placed in a group with four of your classmates. Decide the order in which you will present the material. After this is done, the first speaker gives a two- to four-minute presentation on how the object works. Then the second speaker demonstrates how the object operates. Your success as a speaker is based on whether the person following you can operate the object.

3. Before a series of speeches to be given by class members, your instructor assigns you the name of a person in your class whom you will later be introducing. Interview that person, and collect all the information you will need to prepare a speech of introduction (topic of the speech, some background information on the speaker, why the subject was chosen, the qualifications of the speaker to present a speech on this topic, and so on). On the day of your partner's speech, introduce her or him.

4. You are going to give a "what-if" speech. On each of three 3-by-5-inch notecards, indicate something that could go wrong immediately before, during, or after a speech (e.g., you drop your speech outline in a puddle of water just outside your classroom building; an audience member challenges your statistics during the question-and-answer period). The instructor collects the cards, shuffles them, and hands them out one by one. When you get your card, immediately give a presentation that includes a restatement of the occurrence and a contingency plan for dealing with the situation. (This assignment may take place when a short amount of time remains at the end of any class period.)

5. All students present one-minute speeches in which they state something that bothers them in everyday life. They should tell what the peeve is, why it is a peeve, and what they would like to see done about it, if anything.

6. Use your vocational preference, or an occupation you may be interested in, to investigate some phase of the career and present an informative speech about it. The presentation must include use of a supplementary aid. Sample speech topics: a future audiologist explains the differences among several brands of hearing aids; an accounting major illustrates how a balance sheet is prepared; an aspiring musician demonstrates how music is scored.

KEY TERMS →

informative speaking
speeches about objects
speeches about processes
speeches about events
speeches about concepts

informative briefing
technical report
lecture
question-and-answer session
speech of introduction

chapter 15

Persuasive Public Speaking

Every day you, as a listener, are bombarded with messages intended to convince you to take some action, accept some belief, or change some point of view. And almost every day you, knowingly or unknowingly, attempt to bring about these changes as a speaker. You have been participating in the act of persuasion.

Persuasion is the process of influencing attitudes and behaviors. The bottom line in being a successful persuader is to find the means to answer the question, "What's in it for you?" The bottom line for the person who is the recipient of a persuasive message is, "Is what the speaker proposing in my best interests?" Most people will take actions and/or adopt beliefs if they can figure out how they can benefit from them—monetarily, socially, physically, philosophically, spiritually.

Persuasive Speaking

A **persuasive speech** is intended to influence the opinion or behavior of an audience. Its materials are derived from problems about which people hold differing beliefs and opinions, such as controversial matters that call for decisions or action. The persuasive speaker tells listeners what they ought to believe or do.

A persuasive speech or presentation may have as its end goal either conviction or actuation.

In a **speech of conviction,** the speaker is attempting to convince the listener to believe as the speaker does. Topics that fall into this category could include: "There is no real danger of nuclear fallout from atomic plants," or "XYZ Corporation has developed a clear set of equal opportunity guidelines."

A **speech of actuation** should move the members of the audience to take the desired action that the speaker has proposed: buy the product, sign the petition, go on strike, or adopt the plan presented.

The Process of Persuasion

Much is known about what motivates people to act. Unfortunately, in spite of our knowledge, there are flaws in the system or no candidate for office would ever lose, no charity would fail to reach its goal, and no product would ever go unsold. This chapter presents the theories that appear to explain the process of persuasion and how—if you are developing a persuasive speech to individuals from the North American culture—you might use those theories to accomplish your end goal.

The basic process of persuasion centers on making a claim, then backing up the claim with reasons and emotional appeals that will make listeners accept the claim. To do this, you must analyze the audience and develop arguments that will appeal to that particular group.

Several concepts, including the theories of field-related, group, and individual standards, help explain what to do.

The **theory of field-related standards** establishes that not all people reach conclusions in the same way and thus may react differently to the same evidence or psychological material. Therefore, in establishing your arguments, you may want to include as many appeals as you can to cover the various thought processes of members of your audience. For example, in establishing arguments for why your listeners should vote for a particular candidate, you can list several of the candidate's positions rather than just one.

Group norm standards—the thinking of a particular group—may be used as a guide for developing your arguments. For example, if you are speaking to a group of union members, you can assume that on labor-related issues they will have views that favor the union rather than management. Thus, if you are going to propose a change in the present style of plant operation, show how it will be good for the union and its members.

Individual norm standards—the thinking of those people within a group who have influence over the group's members—also might be included in the criteria for persuasion. If these influential members can be persuaded to go along with a proposal, then the entire group will probably go along. But who are the leaders? If your presentation deals with your need to use this appeal, find out. For example, if the elected president of the city council agrees, the rest of the group who elected her may follow her lead.

To be persuasive, you also should develop your materials so that listeners feel the solution, plan of action, or cure that you are presenting is reasonable. Two methods you might consider using are critical thinking and comparative-advantage reasoning.

To apply **critical thinking**, you establish criteria and then match the solutions with the criteria. For example, if you are proposing a plan of action for solving a club's financial problems, you can set criteria that include not having to raise members' dues and planning an activity that can raise money quickly, without extensive planning. You may then propose that the club stage a lottery and sell raffle tickets, establishing how the lottery fulfills the established criteria.

In contrast, when you use **comparative-advantage reasoning**, you begin by stating possible solutions. Then demonstrate how the proposal is the most *workable* (can solve the problem), *desirable* (does not cause any greater problems), and *practical* (that it can be put into operation). Establish why this particular proposal has fewer disadvantages than any other. To achieve the goal of raising funds, for example, use the comparative-advantage reasoning process. Propose that a lottery be set up, explain why this is a workable plan by indicating that other organizations have used the process, and present statistics on the amount of money raised by these groups. Then indicate that a lottery is desirable because it will not cost members a great deal of money and the risk of losing money is not great. Next, show that the proposal is practical as the tickets can be ready by the next week and the finance committee has worked out a plan for distributing the tickets and handling the money. Finally, you explain why this system is better than raising dues.

The Role of Influence in Persuasion

The purpose of the persuasive process is to influence. The persuasive process, for instance, occurs when salespersons from different data-processing corporations present speeches in an attempt to secure the sale of their system to the purchasing agents of a company. Based on the presentations, the purchasing agents were influenced to buy products from salesperson A, say, because of her arguments stressing her product's lower cost and ease of operation.

Normally, the intended audience has choice of what actions to take. However, a particular form of influencing takes place when listeners are not given a voluntary choice. For example, a speaker at a union meeting says, "Either we accept the proposal as presented or we go on strike." You might not want to choose either of those options, yet if the vote is set up with only those two, you must choose. This attempt to change behavior relies on force and is known as **coercion**.

Another form of influence includes various psychological appeals aimed at emotionally stirring audience members to action. Such factors as fear, hatred, social pressure, and shock can be used to dull listeners' senses to the point where they perform acts they may not consider if they were to step outside the emotion of the situation and objectively evaluate potential consequences. German dictator Adolf Hitler before and during World War II used emotional appeals focused on building a "master race" that included destruction of all those he deemed inferior—Jews, Gypsies, homosexuals, and his political enemies. Many people responded to these appeals, participated in the destruction of other human beings as a result, and later came to regret their actions.

Persuasion also may be accomplished by repeated exposure to messages. Seldom does one persuasive message result in any major change of

Psychological appeals are aimed at emotionally stirring audience members to action.

belief on the part of the receiver. As a result, massive amounts of time and money are spent waging persuasive campaigns by systematically and repeatedly exposing listeners to a message with the objective of enhancing retention of its basic persuasive thesis. This is the reason that you are inundated with speeches and other publicity about candidates during political campaigns.

Do not assume that all persuasion is negative or immoral. Persuasive communication strategies are essentially amoral—neither good nor bad. It is only how the strategies are used, and to what ends, that give communication a dimension of morality. By knowing this and being equipped to recognize manipulative and coercive methods, you may be able to protect yourself from being taken advantage of.

Components of Persuasive Message

The classical Greek philosopher/rhetorician Aristotle first described Western culture's system of persuasion as based on the use of three components.[1] These three components can be identified as speaker credibility

The classical Greek philosopher/rhetorician Aristotle first described Western culture's sytem of persuasion.

(**ethos**), logical arguments (**logos**), and psychological appeals (**pathos**). Although Aristotle wrote more than two thousand years ago, his theory still characterizes what are considered to be the components of the development of an effective persuasive message. Be aware, however, that this is a theory, not a proven concept, and not infallible.

Speaker Credibility

The reputation, prestige, and authority of a speaker as perceived by the listeners all contribute to **speaker credibility**. In most public speaking persuasive situations, listeners' acceptance of the speaker as a credible person will make it easier for the speaker to get acceptance of the message. If you, as a listener, dislike, mistrust, or question the honesty of a person, she or he will have a difficult time persuading you to accept her or his beliefs.

As a speaker, you must realize that credibility, or lack of it, may exist even before you speak. A person's prior reputation with an audience can help or hinder his or her persuasive ability. For example, if Dr. David Ho, the AIDS researcher who was *Time Magazine*'s 1996 Man of the Year, addressed an audience about the need for increased funding for research on communicable diseases, he would have initial credibility and his views

Two Words That Persuade

Two key words will make you more persuasive. *The words:* "if" and "then."

Whether you're trying to sell a car or an idea, the message that works is "If you will take this action, then you'll get this reward."

The next time you're planning to try to persuade someone, think about using these two words to get what you want.

SOURCE: *Communication Briefings,* as adapted from *Overcoming Resistance*, by Jerald M. Jellison, Simon & Schuster, 1230 Avenue of the Americas, New York, NY 10020.

would have an excellent chance of being accepted. But an unknown or negatively perceived speaker would have a much more difficult persuasive task.

Establishing Credibility   How does a speaker establish credibility? A speaker who has a reputation for being knowledgeable about the topic, is a celebrity, or has a positive personal reputation with the audience comes with credibility. One of your authors has been invited for the past eight years to speak on a communication topic to a group of cosmetologists at their conference. Each time, audience members flock around him before the presentation and tell them how much they are looking forward to the presentation. He has little problem in persuading them to take the actions he proposes during the speech.

If you have no reputation with the audience, you are going to have to establish it.

Credibility is sometimes characterized as being composed of the three Cs: competence, charisma, and character.

Competence   Competence refers to the wisdom, authority, and knowledge a speaker demonstrates. For an audience to feel that you are competent in the subject area being discussed, you must demonstrate that you know what you are talking about. This ordinarily means including up-to-date information and/or familiarity with the material. A salesperson who has just made a presentation to a group of executives can ruin a potential sale, for example, if he displays a lack of knowledge about the product during the question-and-answer session.

Another way to establish credibility is to build on someone else's knowledge. For example, if you aren't an expert on a topic, you can strengthen your position by quoting recognized experts in the field. In this way, listeners draw the conclusion that if experts agree with your stand, then your contention may have merit.

If possible, associate yourself with the topic. For example, suppose you are proposing a plan of action concerning safety regulations. If you have had experience on a construction crew and refer to this experience, your listeners will more readily accept your point that the construction industry needs more stringent safety regulations than if you did not have the personal experience. Use phrases such as, "It has been my experience that . . ."; "I have observed that . . ." to establish the tie.

Charisma   Another characteristic of credibility is **charisma**. Words synonymous with charisma are *vigorous, concerned, enthusiastic,* and *sincere.* People with charisma are compelling and have the ability to entice others. A charismatic speaker grabs and holds attention. John F. Kennedy and Martin Luther King Jr. were capable of getting masses of people to follow them because of their ability to mesmerize audiences. Some religious

The reputation, prestige, and authority of a speaker as perceived by the listeners all contribute to speaker credibility.

speakers are capable of getting their followers to give vast amounts of money and even be cured because of the power of the listener's unwavering belief in the messenger. Few of us, unfortunately, are capable of that kind of charisma.

Character   Your reputation, honesty, and sensitivity all aid in developing your character. Some people are assumed to be of high character. They engender trust. Sometimes this is based on the experiences they have had, the positions they hold, or the comments others have made about them.

Positively perceived speakers often find audiences receptive to their messages. Speakers who are negatively perceived need to try to alter their listeners' beliefs by emphasizing qualities about themselves the audience may respond to positively. For example, a former convict, speaking to an audience about the need for altering prison procedures, started his presentation with these comments:

I am a paroled convict. Knowing this, some of you may immediately say to yourself, "Why should I listen to anything that an ex-jailbird has to say?" It is because I was in prison, and because I know what prison can do to a person, and because I know what negative influences jail can have on a person, that I want to speak to you tonight.[2]

Sometimes speakers can change the feelings of audience members who disagree with their views by directly taking on the issues of disagreement and asking listeners to give them a fair chance to be heard. For example, a Democratic candidate speaking before a predominantly Republican audience stated:

I realize that I am a Democrat and you are Republicans. I also realize that we are both after the same thing—a city in which we can live without fear for our lives, a city in which the services such as trash and snow removal are efficient, and a city in which taxes are held in check. You, the Republicans, and I, the Democrat, do have common goals. I'd appreciate your considering how I propose to help all of us achieve our joint objectives.

Not only are competence, charisma, and character important, but developing a logically constructed speech is critical to persuading listeners.

Logical Arguments

If it doesn't make sense, the audience is less likely to be swayed. To a North American audience, "making sense" generally means that the statements you make and the evidence you give add up to a reasonable match. Listeners, especially when they are dealing with information about which they know little or are skeptical, probably look for logical connections in the messages they are receiving.

Be aware that the use of logic, though important in the Western world, is not a universal. If you are speaking to an audience primarily composed of Arabic or Hispanic members, for example, be aware that the basic method of conveying information is through the use of stories that illustrate the point being made but do not necessarily state the conclusion to be reached. Therefore, in planning a presentation, be sure to recognize that cultural adjustments may have to be made. If you are to speak outside of your norm culture, you may need to consult an expert in the persuasive cultural patterns of the listeners.

The Structure of Logical Arguments   Even in the North American culture, there is no one best way to get everyone to agree with you. However, in the North American society, many individuals have been taught to look for:

1. A clear statement of the purpose of the speech so the audience knows what the speaker is proposing.

Logical Reasoning
by Jeanine Walters Miranda

Deductive Process

Spinach makes me sick.

Spinach souffle is tonight's main dish.

Conclusion: by deductive process I will get sick if I eat tonight's main dish.

Inductive Process

If we are to draw our conclusion about spinach, the evidence might be . . .

When I was five, I ate spinach and became sick.

When I was seven, I was forced to eat spinach and became ill.

When I was nine, creamed spinach made me ill.

When I was thirteen spinach salad also made me ill.

At twenty I tried spinach again and became ill.

Conclusion by inductive process: spinach makes me ill.

SOURCE: Lilly Walters, *Secrets of Successful Speakers: How You Can Motivate, Captivate, and Persuade* (New York: McGraw-Hill, 1993), pp. 82–83.

2. Reasons why the speaker believes or wants you to believe in the proposal.

3. The use of and mention of credible sources, if the person is not an expert himself/herself.

4. Arguments that follow some structure for ease of understanding and that develop the main point(s).

5. A statement of desired outcome/stand/action desired.

6. Absence of false facts, partial information, and biased stands.

To lead your listeners to your conclusion, it often is wise to choose an argumentive structure that fits your analysis of what approach is most likely to sway the listeners. The most commonly used Western logical structures are the inductive or deductive formats.

An **inductive argument** is based on probability—what conclusion is expected or believed from the available evidence. The more specific instances you can draw on in an inductive argument, the more probable your conclusion will be. Inductive argument can take one of two forms: the generalization conclusion or the hypothesis conclusion.

In a **generalization conclusion**, a number of specific instances are examined. From these, you attempt to predict some future occurrence or explain a whole category of instances. Underlying this is the assumption that what holds true for specific instances will hold true for all instances in a given category.

Speaking at the National Conference on Corporate Community Involvement, a representative of the American Association of Retired

Persons described the "graying" of America by developing this inductive argument:

> Because of better medical care, nutrition, and activity, more people are gliding into their 60s and beyond in good physical shape. . . . Mental ability does not diminish merely because of age, according to researchers. In fact, it may improve. . . . The economic health of today's older generation has improved to the point where advertisers are already targeting the "maturity" market.

Using evidence to support each of the claims, he drew an inductive conclusion:

> The upshot of all this change in better physical, psychological, and economic well-being is that we are looking at a new breed of older person vastly different from former negative stereotypes.[3]

In the **hypothesis conclusion**, a hypothesis is used to explain all the available evidence. For the argument to have substance, however, the hypothesis must provide the best explanation for that evidence. Reviewing a number of cases in which terrorists had been tried and convicted throughout the world, the U.S. Department of State ambassador-at-large for counterterrorism argued that "the rule of law is working against terrorists, and fewer terrorists are being released without trial" in an effort to convince his audience that "we, the people of the world's democracies, will ultimately prevail over those who would through terror take from us the fruits of two centuries of political progress."[4]

The **deductive argument** is based on logical necessity. If you accept the premise of the deductive argument—the proposition that is the basis of the argument—then you must also accept its conclusion.

One type of deductive argument is the **categorical syllogism**, an argument that contains premises and a conclusion. For instance, in a speech with the central idea of persuading the listeners of what the symptoms are that lead doctors to diagnose chronic fatigue syndrome, a speaker might state:

> (*Premise*) A proven sign of chronic fatigue syndrome is an off-balance immune system.
>
> (*Premise*) A proven sign of chronic fatigue syndrome is a positive diagnosis for human herpes virus 6.
>
> (*Premise*) A proven sign of chronic fatigue syndrome is a positive diagnosis for human B-cell lymphotropic virus.
>
> (*Conclusion*) Therefore, a person diagnosed with an off-balance immune system, human herpes virus 6, and human B-cell lymphotropic virus can be diagnosed as having chronic fatigue syndrome.

Another form of syllogism is the **enthymeme**—in which one premise is not directly stated. The omitted premise is shared by the communicators and therefore does not need to be verbalized. For example, while speaking to those attending a conference on writing assessment, a speaker concluded, "If we can teach our children, from all backgrounds, to write with joy, originality, clarity and control, then I don't think we have much else to worry about," a conclusion based on the premise shared by his listeners that children today should be taught effective writing skills.[5]

Another type of deductive argument is the **disjunctive argument**—an either/or argument in which true alternatives must be established. Talking about the United States and the collapse of the Soviet Empire, a speaker pointed out that the United States faced an either/or choice: "To follow our fears and turn inward, ignoring the opportunities presented by the collapse of the Soviet Empire, or to answer the summons of history and lead toward a better future for all."[6]

Still another form of deductive argument is the **conditional argument**, which sets up an if/then proposition. In this form, there are two conditions, one of which necessarily follows from the other. The chief executive officer of a major accounting firm proposed that the federal government adopt a new accrual accounting system so that the public and Congress could monitor the federal budget. He argued that "if citizens were to demand the financial information to which they are clearly entitled, incentives would be created for sound fiscal management—and, perhaps, for more enlightened political leadership. We could then expect to see better-informed decision making—less fiscal recklessness—and a reduction in the risks caused by the misallocation of capital."[7]

Persuasive Evidence   The persuasive speaker, in Western cultures, not only must structure the persuasive argument but also must support these contentions. What is perceived to be the most persuasive form of supporting material—**evidence**—includes testimony from experts, statistics, and specific instances. If you can offer solid data to support your contentions, it will lend substance to your argument. For example, a speaker who attempts to persuade listeners that the U.S. Food and Drug Administration (FDA) needs more funds to hire inspectors can cite specific instances from the agency's files. Real cases are on record of potatoes contaminated with insecticide, and ginger ale containing mold, which were sold to consumers. The speaker can also cite statistics indicating that only five hundred FDA inspectors are available to monitor sixty thousand food-processing plants in the United States.

Reasoning Fallacies   Speakers sometimes, intentionally or not, present material that contains flaws in reasoning. As a speaker you should be aware that you might fall prey to using these fallacies. Wise listeners are aware that they must protect themselves from accepting fallacious reasoning. Types of

When Analyzing That Data

How you analyze marketing data that you've collected is just as important as deciding to collect the data. Here are some suggestions:

✳ **Use the** data correctly. Don't try to adjust the information to produce the results you were hoping for. Don't give prominence to favorable evidence and lose negative data in the shuffle.

✳ **Make solid** and reliable deductions. Don't try to read big news into commonplace results.

✳ **Keep the** results as simple as possible. Don't let any analysis develop into a mass of statistics that few can understand. Remember, the goal is to produce summary information out of raw bulk details.

✳ **Be sure** the sample size is big enough to project comfortably. If you want to use the results based on a small sample, flag them with a warning that they are based on an insufficient sample.

✳ **Don't equate** opinions with facts. Point out the difference in the data presented. When looking for cause-and-effect relationships, be thorough. Misreading the relationships can severely damage the validity of an analysis.

SOURCE: *Communication Briefings,* as adapted from *Marketing for Nonmarketers,* by Houston G. Elan and Norton Paley, AMACOM, 135 W. 50 St., New York, NY 10020.

---

reasoning fallacies include: hasty generalizations, faulty analogical reasoning, faulty causal reasoning, ignoring the issue, ad hominem argument, ad populum argument, and ad ignorantium argument.

A speaker who makes a **hasty generalization** reaches an unwarranted, general conclusion from an insufficient number of instances. For example, a speaker may argue that gun-control legislation is necessary and demonstrate this argument with some instances of freeway shootings in Los Angeles, thus limiting the scope and numbers of possible cases in support of the need for gun control.

Another reasoning fallacy is **faulty analogical reasoning**. No analogy is ever totally "pure" because no two cases are ever identical. Speakers use faulty analogies when they assume that the shared elements will continue indefinitely and/or that all the aspects relevant to the case under consideration are similar. The speaker who, for example, argues that the current AIDS crisis is analogous to the bubonic plague that ravaged Europe in earlier eras overlooks the medical advances that make the AIDS crisis very different (although no less serious).

A further reasoning fallacy is **faulty causal reasoning**. Faulty causal reasoning occurs when a speaker claims, without qualification, that something caused something else. If the claim overstates the case, faulty reasoning has been used. Rather than saying "a common cause" or "a probable cause," the speaker would argue, for example, that the increase in the number of illegal immigrants into the United States is the direct result of the liberal welfare laws.

An entire set of reasoning fallacies can result from **ignoring the issue**. In ignoring the issue, the speaker uses irrelevant arguments to obscure the real issue. The **ad hominem argument**—attacks on the personal character of a source—is one example. For instance, some attacks on the mid-1990s proposal for health system reform centered on the fact that Hillary Rodham Clinton was one of its codevelopers. Since she wasn't elected by the people, it was argued, she shouldn't have been on the proposal commission; and, therefore, the bill should not be passed.

The **ad populum argument**—an appeal to people's prejudices and passions rather than a focus on the issue at hand—is another characteristic of ignoring the issue. For example, in 1994 when O. J. Simpson was initially arrested in connection with his ex-wife's murder, many sports fans insisted he was innocent. Their devotion to him as a football hero overshadowed any evidence that was presented that implicated him.

Yet another example of the fallacy of ignoring the issue is the **ad ignorantium argument**—an attempt to prove that a statement is true because it cannot be disproved. For example, supporters of pit bull terriers argue that they are not dangerous pets because dog-bite statistics show pit bulls to rank ninth in number of bites, after poodles and cocker spaniels. Of course, the number of pit bulls in this country is minuscule in comparison to the number of more popular breeds such as poodles and cocker spaniels.

Psychological Appeals

The third component of the persuasive message, **psychological appeals**, enlists listeners' emotions as motivation for accepting your arguments. Just as you must select your arguments and enhance your credibility on the basis of what you know about your listeners, so must you select psychological appeals on the basis of what you think will stir their emotions. The purpose of incorporating some emotional appeals in your speech is to keep your listeners involved with you as you spell out your persuasive plan, even though they probably do not distinguish the emotional from the rational in your presentation.

People tend to react according to whether their needs are being met. Several theories attempt to illustrate what needs people have, and persuasive speakers can use these to organize their emotional appeals by triggering need satisfaction.

One theory of need satisfaction is the **Hierarchy of Human Needs** (Figure 15.1), a theory devised by Abraham Maslow. Based on this view, a speaker must determine the level of need of a particular group of listeners and then select appeals aimed at that level.[8] Although Maslow's theory is

Figure 15.1
Maslow's Hierarchy
of Needs

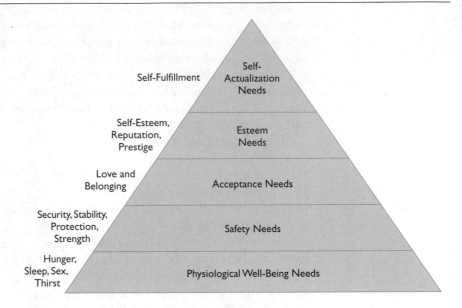

hierarchical, these need levels can function at the same time. Therefore, a speaker need not deal with only one level at a time.

Maslow suggested that all human beings have five levels of needs. The first, most basic level is comprised of *physiological needs*—hunger, sleep, sex, and thirst. Normally, these needs must all be satisfied before a person can be motivated by appeals to higher levels of need. For example, the U.S. Agency for International Development offers aid to developing nations in order to persuade them, through appeals to physiological needs, that the democratic form of government offers self-government, free elections, and food and medical care.

The second level of human need, *safety needs*, encompasses security, stability, protection, and strength. Organizations that have had to reduce their work forces and lay off employees have found it persuasive to offer seminars on job searches, résumé preparation, and other career skills. Employees concerned about the security of their positions are quick to sign up for such offerings.

The third level consists of *acceptance needs*—the needs for love and belonging. College and university alumni representatives use this need in speeches intended to motivate alumni to contribute to endowment funds for the sake of being part of their alma mater.

Esteem needs form the fourth level identified by Maslow. Human needs at this level involve both self-esteem (desire for achievement and mastery) and esteem by others (desire for reputation and prestige). Athletic coaches use appeals to esteem in their pep talks before games to persuade team members to do their best.

Finally, Maslow identified *self-actualization needs*—desire for self-fulfillment or achieving one's greatest potential as the ultimate level for which people reach—as the fifth level in the hierarchy. Recruiters attempt to influence potential military personnel with slogans such as, "Be the best that you can be."

The **Ethnographic Theory of Human Drives** theory, another attempt to explain human needs, indicates that survival of the species, pleasure-seeking, security, and territoriality must be satisfied.

Persuasive speakers using the *survival-of-the-species* aspect of this theory try to appeal to such factors as the physical and psychological safety of the person and his or her family. Public speakers talking to teen groups, for example, regarding the need for safe sex often discuss the fatal effect of AIDS.

Pleasure-seeking centers on the idea that people spend a great deal of their lives seeking out happiness. For example, in discussing why a city income tax is needed, a municipal spokesperson might indicate that the funds would be going toward refurbishing all of the city's recreation facilities.

Security, here, means keeping things on an even keel, in balance, under control. In analyzing an audience, look for instances of fears about things being changed. For example, people might have to be dissuaded that new legislation will change the way things were in the "good old days."

We all mark off and defend territory. This is *territoriality*. To activate this appeal, you must ascertain that audience members are concerned over what is already theirs; or you can instill the belief that something will belong to listeners. An army recruiter, for example, might appeal to the need to "defend your country" as her way of getting potential recruits to join.

Appeals to Motivate Listeners

Once you have determined your listeners' need level(s), you can then build into your speech the appropriate psychological appeals. A variety of motivational appeals are available. This alphabetical discussion of the most typical appeals can assist you in determining which ones will best match the need level of your listeners.[9]

Adventure   Here the speaker stresses listeners' desire to explore new worlds, see exciting places, take part in unusual experiences, or participate in different events. A speaker in the travel industry might motivate potential travelers by describing what it would be like to go on a tour to an unusual place.

Companionship   This taps our desire to be with other people. A speaker might make this appeal in an attempt to recruit membership for a senior citizen's group.

Deference   Showing respect for the wiser, more experienced, higher authority can also be a successful strategy. Robert Dole, in his 1996 presidential campaign, continually referred to his years of public service.

Fear   This appeal is used to raise apprehension in a listener. A representative of the food industry speaking to individuals who have had heart attacks or bypass surgery could use this approach to discuss no-salt and low-cholesterol products.

Although the fear appeal can be powerful, there can be a danger in using this appeal. Listeners can become frightened because the situation is perceived as hopeless.[10] Long-time smokers, for example, may assume that because of their long history of smoking, there is no sense in quitting because it's too late.

Gender   Appealing to women's rights, stressing the need for understanding the male point of view, or criticizing sexual harassment can all be useful tools in persuasion.

Guilt   People may feel guilty for both doing and not doing something. Many sermons are based on this appeal.

Humor   People enjoy laughing and are often taken off guard when they are enjoying themselves. "Humor can engage, entice, coax and persuade."[11]

Loyalty   Appeals to reverence—to respect the nation, friends and family, organizations—motivate. The "Buy American" campaign is an example of an appeal to national pride.

Reverence   Audiences are often motivated by hero worship. Referring to a famous person who feels like you do about a subject may be the motivating factor to convince an audience to take a desired action. AIDS fundraisers often refer to the work of Elizabeth Taylor and Magic Johnson on behalf of the cause.

Revulsion   An appeal to disgust can be effective. A speaker, for instance, can illustrate the effects of water pollution on Chesapeake Bay by showing

A variety of motivational appeals may be used to aid in persuading the audience.

listeners some water samples in an attempt to motivate them to support legislation to clean up the Bay. As with fear, revulsion can arouse such strong feelings that listeners may tune out the message. Antivivisectionists might overwhelm their listeners with photographs of maimed laboratory animals.

Shame   Related to guilt is the response of shame. "Properly calibrated, shame falls somewhere between mild embarrassment and cruel humiliation."[12] Some welfare reformers, for example, argue that stigmatizing those who abuse the welfare system is the only way to recover the system itself.

Sympathy   By showing photographs or films of starving children or impoverished elderly people, a speaker can compel listeners to give time, money, or other resources. A sympathetic bond, often coupled with guilt, is created with those less fortunate.

A speaker has a wide variety of options from which to choose in developing persuasive appeals. The speaker should analyze the audience to determine need levels, and select appeals that will meet these needs.

The Structure of the Persuasive Message

The structure of a persuasive speech should allow the listener to reach the behavioral or mental change the speaker desires. The most common method of developing a persuasive message is to use the problem-solution arrangement. The speaker identifies what is wrong and then presents the cure or recommendation for its cure.

The structure of the body of a speech that develops inductively would be:

III. Body

    A. Identify the situation (what is wrong).

    B. Identify the problem (what has to be changed).

    C. List the possible solutions to the problem.

    D. Evaluate the solutions for workability, desirability, practicality.

        1. Workability—Can the proposed solutions solve the problem?

        2. Desirability—Will the proposed solutions cause bigger problems?

        3. Practicality—Can the proposed solutions be put into effect?

    E. Recommendation of the solution that is most workable, desirable, and practical.

When listing the possible solutions (division C), two strategies are available: placing the strongest argument first, so that it will have the greatest impact on listeners at the outset; or placing the strongest argument last, to ensure that listeners retain it.

Another consideration is whether to develop part D by simply listing the reasons why the solution to be proposed is workable, desirable, and practical or to investigate both sides of each solution, including the one to be recommended. One potential problem in developing both sides of an argument is that you may raise issues and ideas your listeners have not previously considered.

An alternative to the illustrated pattern would be to place what is division E at the start of the body, thus revealing the solution, then explain why this solution was selected. In general, if you feel that the audience is or may be on your side, state your arguments first, and allow your listeners to believe along with you for the rest of your presentation (a deductive mode of reasoning). But if you perceive your audience to be hostile to your position, build the background and then present the arguments when you feel that your listeners are ready for them (a more inductive line of reasoning).

8 Great Speech Blunders

1. **Dullness itself: Relying on only one or two illustrations to make your points.**
   Use salient statistics . . . timely quotes . . . appropriate industry examples . . . and personal stories to help your listeners visualize your message—and remember it.

2. **NOT repeating your message enough.**
   Repetition is crucial to retention. Half an hour after a presentation, the average listener has already forgotten 40 percent of what was said. By the end of the week, 90 percent is usually forgotten. The more you repeat and illustrate your message, the more retention you'll get.

3. **NOT answering the audience's most major question, "What's in it for me?"**
   You must understand the payoff: why your audience is willing to come and listen to you. If you can answer this question, you can tailor-make your speech for them—and reach them in a very personal way.

4. **Burying your point.**
   You can lose your audience, even if you have something that they want to hear, unless you point out the most vital sections for them, in advance. Use signal phrases (like "What's important here," or "This can't be overemphasized") to focus people's attention on the most important parts of your message.

5. **Forgetting to practice (and time) your speech out loud.**
   This little item can cause major embarrassment. A short spoken rehearsal will eliminate tongue twisters . . . make sure the speech's spoken length is appropriate . . . ensure that your opener is no more than the recomended three minutes long . . . and that you close snappily, in 30 seconds or less.

6. **Forgetting to check visual aids for readability.**
   You can only have yourself to blame if you lose your audience over this! Look at all your visual aids in advance. If anything you present cannot be read from the back of the room, get rid of it. Now.

7. **Answering hypothetical questions after the speech.**
   You can get into real hot water on this one, because these questions have no boundaries, no budget or time constraints, and can pin you down to a future you'd rather not have. Turn the question, instead, back to reality by saying, "Based on these facts and the existing situation, this is how I would handle the situation."

8. **Getting distracted before you speak.**
   Very few speakers can answer a phone call or deal with some minor emergency before they speak, and NOT have it distract from their presentation. Always take five minutes (or more) to collect your thoughts, focus on your message, and breathe before stepping up to the podium. Don't allow distractions to ruin what you've taken days to prepare.

 The Persuasive Process in Action

Psychological appeals, coupled with a speaker's credibility and well-reasoned and well-supported arguments, provide a sound, honest approach to influencing others to change their beliefs or actions. The sample speech outlined in Figure 15.2 illustrates the interaction of these persuasive elements.

Figure 15.2
Sample Speech
Outline

Statement of Central Idea: To persuade the audience that voting is not only a privilege and a responsibility as an American citizen, but also a necessity.

Attention material to involve
listeners

Orienting material to relate topic
to listeners and to establish
speaker credibility

Topic of the speech

Statement of the first issue: the
problem
Ways in which the problem is
defined

Statistics to demonstrate the extent of the problem

I. Introduction
   A. Attention Material:
      Did you know that one vote gave Adolf
      Hitler leadership of the Nazi party?
   B. Orienting Material:
      A one vote difference has also occurred in our American history. For
      example, according to the American
      Archives, had Hubert Humphrey received one additional vote in every
      precinct, he would have won the presidential election over Richard Nixon.
      Imagine how history may have
      changed if that had been the case.

II. Central Idea: Voting is not only a privilege and a responsibility as an American
    citizen, but also a necessity.

III. Body
   A. The lack of voting interest in our
      democracy
      1. There are many justifications for
         nonparticipation that define the
         lack of interest.
         a. My vote doesn't make a
            difference.
         b. I don't have time to register/
            vote.
         c. I'm not familiar with the
            candidates.
         d. I'll vote for a candidate when
            he/she cares about issues that
            affect/concern me.
      2. Apathy in young citizens
         a. According to the Voting and
            Registration Supplement of the
            Current Population Survey, citizens age 18–24 have the lowest
            voter turnout.
         b. According to statistics from the
            1992 elections, only 52 percent
            of citizens, age 18–24 even
            bothered to register.
         c. Only 42 percent of those in that
            age bracket voted.

	d. Compare this with 78 percent of those age 65 and older who registered and 70 percent who voted.
Definition of democracy	3. Definition of democracy a. Government exercised directly by the people or through elected representatives b. A political or social unit based on democratic rule c. Rule by the majority d. The principles of social equality and respect for the individual within a community
Elaboration demonstrating inconsistency between democracy and the problem	4. Do young adults *want* democratic rule? a. If so, how can we have democratic rule when our leaders are not elected by the majority but by a fragment of citizens? b. If so, how can the principles of social equality be exercised when fifty percent of young adults don't bother to vote?
Transition	(As you can see, there is a disturbing trend developing within our society where many young citizens have decided to act passively regarding decisions affecting their futures. This trend must not continue; more young citizens must become involved.)
Statement of second issue: What has been done to refute justification of the problem? Refutations of justifications	B. What has been done that discredits justifications for the nonparticipation problem? 1. One vote has made a difference in our historical past. a. 1845: one vote brought Texas into the Union. b. 1941: one vote saved the Selective Service system just weeks before the attack on Pearl Harbor. 2. There are many opportunities which make registering/voting more convenient. a. Because of Motor Voter legislation passed in 1995, we can now register to vote at the same time we register our cars.

   b. Many states have election day
      registration.
   c. All states allow for absentee
      ballots.
3. There is no excuse not to be familiar with the candidates.
   a. As American citizens, we have a
      responsibility to learn about is-
      sues that affect our future and
      our children's futures.
   b. There are many resources such
      as the League of Women Voters
      that put the candidates and
      their issues in language that
      is easily understood.
4. Voting for a candidate when
   he or she starts caring about
   issues that concern/affect us is
   irrational.
   a. This is putting the cart before
      the horse.
   b. Elected officials are just as self-
      interested as the individual citi-
      zens who elect them and will
      look after the interests of those
      demographic groups who vote
      for them.

Transition

(There are no reasonable justifications
for *not* voting yet there are many reasons
why we should.)

Statement of third issue: What
should be done
Elaboration on solutions to the
problem

C. What should be done to solve the
   problem?
   1. We must participate to reaffirm the
      belief that those who fought to earn
      this privilege did not die in vain.
      a. Because our American govern-
         ment has made the process of
         voting so easy, it can be easily
         taken for granted until it's taken
         away.
      b. Recall 1971: because of strong
         insistence, those 18–20 were
         given the privilege to vote by
         virtue of the 26th Amendment.
   2. We must become informed to be-
      come responsible citizens.
      a. It is our single-more important
         duty.

        b. It shows we like being an American citizen.

        c. We cannot have free will and liberty without responsibility.

        d. We must not let others make critical decisions for us.

   3. We must show concern for our future because it is necessary.

        a. We cannot sit back and complain about government actions if we do not vote.

        b. Young adults have many economic, educational, crime, and health concerns.

        c. Voting provides a way to gain more control over our lives and futures.

        d. Voting makes politicians aware that young Americans are a vital source of election support.

IV. Conclusion

   A. Restate the issues

Reiteration of main issues

     1. There is a great deal of nonparticipation in voting, particularly those age 18–24.

     2. There are no reasonable justifications *not* to vote.

     3. Only *we* can change the trend of nonparticipation and there are many reasons why we must.

Final appeal

   B. Clincher: Don't throw away your responsibility to vote, your ability to change and influence our government and to determine our future. Remember, if it wasn't for one vote cast in 1776, we'd be speaking German today instead of English.

IN CONCLUSION → Persuasion is the process by which one party purposefully secures a change of behavior on the part of another party. The basic process of persuasion centers on a speaker making a claim and backing it up in such a way that listeners accept the claim. Successful persuasive strategies appear to center on use of speaker credibility, logical arguments, and psychological appeals.

LEARN BY DOING →

1. Prepare a speech on a topic about which you have strong feelings. Propose a change in a current procedure, take a stand on a view concerning the subject, or propose a plan of action. The topic should be one to which your listeners can relate and react so that you can persuade them. An example of a central idea for this speech might be "This school should not raise tuition."

2. Select a controversial topic and prepare a speech in which you advocate a particular solution to the problem. Your task is to persuade your listeners to accept your solution. A central idea for this speech might be "Euthanasia should be a legal option for terminally ill patients."

3. Prepare a speech analyzing the persuasive strategies used by some group in advocating a particular cause (e.g., gay rights or Native American rights). Select a number of persuasive messages by spokespersons for the group you choose, and use examples from these messages to illustrate your analysis of the persuasive strategies.

4. Find a speech or letter to the editor that illustrates one or more of the psychological appeals described in this chapter.

5. Make a list of what you perceive to be the difference in preparing persuasive speeches and informative speeches.

6. Attend a persuasive speech by someone in a public forum, or analyze a persuasive manuscript in *Vital Speeches of the Day*. Prepare a descriptive analysis of the use of persuasive strategies by this speaker similar to that demonstrated in Figure 15.2.

KEY TERMS →

persuasion
persuasive speech
speech of conviction
speech of actuation
theory of field-related standards
group norm standards
Individual norm standards
critical thinking
comparative-advantage reasoning
coercion
ethos
logos
pathos
speaker credibility
charisma
inductive argument
generalization conclusion
hypothesis conclusion

deductive argument
categorical syllogism
enthymeme
disjunctive argument
conditional argument
evidence
hasty generalization
faulty analogical reasoning
faulty causal reasoning
ignoring the issue
ad hominem argument
ad populum argument
ad ignorantium argument
psychological appeals
Hierarchy of Human Needs
Ethnographic Theory of Human
    Drives

APPENDIX: the resumé

 **Resumé Guide**

20 Seconds is All You Get!

This is the average time a manager takes to scan a resumé and determine if the applicant should be granted an interview. It's true—you may have spent thousands of dollars on education and training, and all you now have is just 20 seconds to sell yourself to a prospective employer.

For this reason, the materials you use to market yourself MUST project a professional image. Your resumé should present your abilities and what you have accomplished in your jobs. It must make the reader want to meet you by asking, "How did they accomplish that?"

The Importance of Premium Paper

Because your resumé serves as one of your first introductions to a prospective employer, it needs to present a quality, professional image. This is why the color and quality of the resumé paper you choose are so important:

❋ high-quality, acid-free 100% cotton 24 lb. paper

❋ sophisticated color selections

❋ watermark placed one inch above center

❋ matching envelopes

Accomplishment Statements—Selling the Sizzle!

When preparing a resumé, most people make the critical mistake of detailing their *duties* and *responsibilities* instead of highlighting accomplish-

Source: From Kinko's, a registered trademark of Kinko's Graphics Corporation. Permission granted by David Bowman, President of TTG Consultants, Los Angeles, CA—A Career Management and Human Resource Consulting Firm.

ments. In advertising jargon, this would be selling the *steak,* instead of the *sizzle*—a marketing error that could cost you an important interview.

A potential employer has only a secondary interest in the duties and responsibilities you performed in a previous job. So what if you sold widgets to the aerospace industry, or were the senior accountant in a candy factory, or even Vice President of Marketing for a furniture company? Titles and duties say nothing about *performance* (the sizzle), or what you can bring to this new employer that is unique and worthy of consideration. On the other hand, if your resumé indicates that you increased widget sales by 20%, receiving "Salesperson of the Year" honors, or discovered accounting errors that saved $50,000, or designed a new production system that reduced material costs, saving $200,000 annually, you can bet an interview will follow.

Your accomplishment statements need not be dramatic, but they should always *enlarge* upon your basic duties and responsibilities. The best way to do that is to *quantify*, by adding *numbers* or *percentages,* when possible. Here are some examples of the type of questions you must ask yourself:

✳ How *many* payroll checks, involving how much money, did you issue each week?

✳ How *much* time and/or money did your new procedure save the company?

✳ How *large* a budget did you manage?

✳ By *what* percentage and/or number of dollars did you increase sales?

It is this kind of self-questioning that will help you develop accomplishment statements that will generate employer interest. Remember, you're the product—your accomplishments are the sizzle.

The Dos and Don'ts of Resumé Preparation

Dos

✳ Make sure your resumé is easy to read. Use concise, unambiguous sentences and avoid over-writing or flowery prose.

✳ Know your audience—use the vocabulary and speak the language of your targeted field.

✳ Keep the overall length of your resumé short. Depending upon your experience, one or two pages is ideal.

✳ Stress your past accomplishments and the skills you used to get the desired results.

✷ Focus on information that's relevant to your own career goals. If you're making a career change, stress what skills are transferrable to support your new career objectives.

✷ Begin accomplishment statements with action verbs (see below) instead of pronouns like *I, we,* or even *the company.*

✷ Neatness counts. A poorly structured, badly typed resumé is a reflection of the applicant.

Don'ts

✷ Your salary history or reasons for leaving a previous job should never be included on a resumé.

✷ If you're considering enclosing a photograph of yourself, don't! You may bear a striking resemblance to someone the reader doesn't like.

✷ Don't include personal references on your resumé. A potential employer is interested in references only after they are seriously considering hiring you. At that time, you may be asked to provide reference information.

✷ Don't stretch the truth! Misinformation or untruthful statements will inevitably come back to haunt you.

✷ Avoid references to hobbies, activities and memberships that are not business-related or haven't any application to your current career goals or job objectives.

✷ Last, but certainly not least, don't have any unreasonable expectations of what a resumé can do. Employers do not hire resumés, they hire people.

Action Verbs Make a Difference

When describing your accomplishments, the use of action verbs can make the difference between a statement that attracts attention and one that seems commonplace and uninteresting.

achieved	developed
added	designed
broadened	eliminated
consolidated	established
coordinated	expanded
created	evaluated

generated	reduced
identified	saved
increased	simplified
initiated	streamlined
invented	strengthened
maintained	supervised
managed	trained
negotiated	transformed
organized	utilized
performed	verified
planned	worked
purchased	wrote

Skills Based/Functional Resumé Format

This format is best suited for multi-industry or function careers (different industries and function/skills) and/or when there are gaps in employment history.

ALAN WINTER
2432 Bayard Drive
Edgeware, NJ 10216
(515) 221-6453

An experienced sales executive in the electronic, scientific and real estate fields. A well-organized individual, who utilizes excellent communication and leadership skills to gain the respect and confidence of clients and co-workers.

SIGNIFICANT ACCOMPLISHMENTS

Sales
- Named "Salesperson of the Year" for a real estate firm with 70 full-time associates.
- Developed a new new sales territory, achieving a 10% market share among six established electronics competitors in a one-year period.
- Maintained 22 major existing accounts and added seven new customers, exceeding annual sales budget by 72%.

Marketing
- Restructured ten sales territories, resulting in a 40% increase in cost effectiveness.
- Initiated new, more competitive pricing policies, incorporating term and volume discounts, increasing sales by 20% annually.

Training
- Demonstrated technical products at 15 trade shows, resulting in 23% sales increase.
- Trained seven-member technical service staff in effective customer communications, receiving "Staff of the Year" award from CEO.

EXPERIENCE

HALL-MARK ELECTRONICS	1990–Present
Fairfield, New Jersey	

- Sales Engineer

HAMILTON INSTRUMENTATION	1983–1990
Newark, New Jersey	

- Sales Representative

MAX E. WYNN, INC.	
Chester Pennsylvania	1981–1983

- Director of Development and Finance
- Real Estate Sales Associate

EDUCATION

B.S. in Chemistry, Park College, Kansas City, Missouri
Graduate Coursework, Northwestern University, Evanston, Illinois

Chronological Resumé Format

This format is best suited for single industry or function careers, and when there are no gaps in employment history.

SHARON SUMMER
23 Old Colony Road
Los Angeles, CA 90031
(216) 556-7878

A payroll professional with increasingly responsible positions, including five years with a multi-million dollar cosmetics company.

PROFESSIONAL EXPERIENCE

RICHARDSON-BARRON, INC.   1986–Present
Los Angeles, California

Payroll Administrator
- Resolved several hundred discrepancies in employee pay and benefits, maintaining excellent employer/employee relationships and morale.
- Developed and formatted a new PC compensation tracking system which contained a breakout of salaries and benefits for employees, consultants and temporary personnel, reducing processing time by 70%.
- Assisted corporate accountants in filing federal and multi-state tax returns, with no requests for government audit.
- Administered the 2000-employee corporate payroll function during a conversion from an outside supplier to an in-house fully automated system, maintaining full continuity.
- Analyzed corporate financial reports, successfully balancing inter-related accounts for the closing of office.

BARCLAY ELECTRIC   1980–1989
Milwaukee, Wisconsin

Senior Payroll Clerk
- Managed payroll for 250 union employees, including posting hours and auditing payroll with no discrepancies or requests for audit.

EDUCATION
Milwaukee Area Technical College: Major, Data Processing
West Los Angeles College: Major, Travel and Transportation

NOTES

Preface

1. Marilyn Hanf Buckley, "Focus on Research: We Listen a Book a Day; We Speak a Book a Week: Learning from Walter Loban," *Language Arts* 69 (December 1992): 623.
2. Dan B. Curtis, Jerry L. Winsor, and Ronald D. Stephens, "National Preferences in Business and Communication Education," *Communication Education* 38 (January 1989): 6–14.
3. "What Work Requires of Schools: A SCANS Report on America 2000," The Secretary's Commission on Achieving Necessary Skills, U.S. Department of Labor, Washington, D.C., June 1991, p. vii.
4. Anita Vangelisti and John Daly, "Correlates of Speaking Skills in the United States: A National Assessment," *Communication Education* 38 (April 1989): 132–143.
5. Ibid.
6. James McCroskey and Virginia Richmond, *Quiet Children and the Classroom Teacher* (Bloomington, IN: ERIC Clearinghouse on Reading and Communication Skills in cooperation with the Speech Communication Association, Annandale, VA, 1991), p. 20.
7. For an extended discussion on public speaking and communication apprehension, see Virginia R. Richmond and James C. McCroskey, *Communication: Apprehension, Avoidance and Effectiveness,* 4th ed. (Scottsdale, AZ: Gorsuch Scarisbrick, 1995).
8. Roy Berko and Carolyn Perry, ed., *Speaking, Listening, and Media Literacy Standards for K through 12 Education* (Annandale, VA: Speech Communication Association, 1996), p. 2.
9. Ibid.
10. Ibid.
11. Michael Cronin, ed., "The Need for Required Oral Communication Education in the Undergraduate General Education Curriculum," an unpublished paper, 1993, available from the National Communication Association, Annandale, VA.
12. Wendy S. Zabava Ford and Andrew D. Wolvin, "The Differential Impact of a Basic Communication Course on Perceived Communication Competencies in Class, Work, and Social Contexts," *Communication Education* 42 (July 1993): 215–223. Also see David R. Seibold, Sami Kudsi, and Michael Rude, "Does Communication Training Make a Difference?: Evidence for the Effectiveness of a Presentation Skills Program," *Journal of Applied Communication Research* (May 1993): 111–131.

Chapter 1

1. Rebecca B. Rubin and Elizabeth E. Graham, "Communication Correlates of College Success: An Exploratory Investigation," *Communication Education* 37 (January 1988): 14.
2. Ibid.
3. Dan B. Curtis, Jerry L. Winsor, and Ronald D. Stephens, "National Preferences in Business and Communication Education," *Communication Education* 38 (1989): 6.
4. Isa Engleberg and Dianna Wynn, "DACUM: A National Database Justifying the Study of Speech Communication, *Journal of Communication Administration* 1 (1995): 28–38.
5. Anita Vangelisti and John Daly, "Correlates of Speaking Skills in the United States: A National Assessment," *Communication Education* 38 (April 1989): 132–143.
6. Ibid.
7. James C. McCroskey and Virginia P. Richmond, *Quiet Children and The Classroom Teacher* (Bloomington, IN: ERIC Clearinghouse on Reading and Communication Skills; and Annandale, VA: Speech Communication Association, 1991), p. 20.
8. For an extended discussion of public-speaking apprehension, see Virginia P. Richmond and James C. McCroskey, *Communication: Apprehension, Avoidance, and Effectiveness,* 4th ed. (Scottsdale, AZ: Gorsuch Scarisbrick, 1995), Ch. 3.
9. Unisys Corporation, "How Can We Expect Him [Her] to Learn When We Haven't Taught Him [Her] How to Listen," advertisement reproduced in Roy Berko, Andrew Wolvin, and Darlyn Wolvin, *Communicating: A Social and Career Focus,* 6 ed. (Boston: Houghton Mifflin, 1995), p. 81.
10. Michael Cronin, ed., "The Need for Required Oral Communication Education in the Undergraduate General Education Curriculum" (unpublished paper, 1993, available from the National Communication Association, Annandale, VA).
11. Based on David K. Berlo, *The Process of Communication* (New York: Holt, Rinehart and Winston, 1960).
12. Advertisement, "WordPerfect-Macintosh," WordPerfect Corporation, Ogden, UT.

13. Milt Thomas, "Cultural Self-Identification in the Basic Course" (unpublished paper presented at the Central States Speech Association convention, Oklahoma City, 1994), p. 8.

14. Ibid.

15. Kim Walters, "Coalescence in the Basic Course" (unpublished paper presented at the Western Speech Association Convention, Albuquerque, NM, February 15, 1993).

16. *Oxford English Dictionary,* 2nd ed. (Oxford, England: Clarendon Press, 1989).

17. William A. Henry III, "The Politics of Separation," *Time* (Fall 1993, special edition), p. 75.

18. Deborah Atwater, "Issues Facing Minorities in Speech Communication Education: Moving from the Melting Pot to a Tossed Salad," *Proceedings of the 1988 Speech Communication Association Flagstaff Conference Report* (Annandale, VA: Speech Communication Association, 1989), p. 40.

19. *Report on the Population* (Washington D.C.; Reference Bureau, n.d.)

20. Atwater, p. 41.

21. Factors that cause communication difficulties are sometimes called interference. In this text, these factors are referred to as noise.

22. Helen Dewar, "Free Speech Free-for-All," *Washington Post,* October 21, 1993, p. A–1.

23. Franklyn S. Haiman, *Speech Arts and the First Amendment* (Carbondale, IL: Southern Illinois University Press, 1993), p. 1.

24. "Sex Policy Raises Questions of Academic Freedom," *Cleveland Plain Dealer,* November 27, 1993, p. A-16.

25. Matt Helms, "License to Hate," *National College Magazine,* September 22, 1992, p. 14.

26. Haiman, p. 3.

27. Rich Hodges, "Speech Codes on Campus!," *Washington Post,* November 27, 1993, p. A–25.

28. Ibid.

29. Alan Deshowitz, "Imprisonment of Ideas: What Is the First Amendment?" (speech presented at the Eisenhower Symposium, Johns Hopkins University, Baltimore, MD, October 20, 1991).

30. Scott Jaschite, "Nominee Reflects on 'Hate Speech' Sees Supreme Court Taking Up the Issue," *Chronicle of Higher Education,* August 4, 1993, p. A-23.

31. Richard L. Johannesen, *Ethics in Human Communication,* 4th ed. (Prospect Heights, IL: Waveland Press, 1996), p. 2.

32. Ibid.

33. Thomas Nilsen, *Ethics in Speech Communication* (Indianapolis: Bobbs-Merrill, 1966), p. 139.

34. For an extensive discussion about being an ethical speaker, see Nilsen.

35. Nilsen, p. 14.

36. Michael Purdy, "Listening Ethics: Little Things Mean a Lot" (unpublished paper presented to the International Listening Association, December 1995).

Chapter 2

1. Pamela Butler, as noted in Robert McGarvey, "Talk Yourself Up," *USAir Magazine* (March 1990): 90.

2. Ibid.

3. Gail Dusa, as noted in McGarvey, p. 90.

4. Dave Grant, as noted in McGarvey, p. 93.

5. Bernie Zilbergeld, as noted in McGarvey, p. 94.

6. Leon Festinger, *A Theory of Cognitive Dissonance* (Evanston, IL: Row, Peterson, 1957).

7. Sveri Wahlross, *Family Communication* (New York: Macmillan, 1974), p. xi.

8. Long Beach City College of Theatre Arts and Speech, *Communicate,* 3rd ed. (Dubuque, IA: Kendall/Hunt, 1976).

9. William James, *The Principles of Psychology* (New York: Holt, Rinehart and Winston, 1890).

10. Ruth C. Wyle, *The Self-Concept* (Lincoln: University of Nebraska Press, 1979), p. 9.

11. The verb *to be* provides us with our basic label of our selves. Native Americans and those from some other cultures, such as West Africans, may have difficulty understanding and applying this concept because of linguistic and other cultural differences. Most North Americans, however, should find it an easy concept to grasp.

12. Joseph A. Luft, *Group Process: An Introduction to Group Dynamics* (Palo Alto, CA: National Press, 1963), Ch. 3.

13. Based on Lawrence Rosenfeld, "Relational Disclosure and Feedback" (unpublished paper available from Lawrence Rosenfeld, Department of Communication, University of North Carolina, Chapel Hill, NC).

14. Based on an untitled curriculum proposal prepared by the Communication Department, Loyola University of Chicago, W. Barnett Pearce, Chair, 1994.

15. For a discussion of communication and ethnography, see Stuart Sigman, "A Matter of Time: The Case for Ethnographies of Communication" (unpublished paper presented at the SCA Convention, November 23, 1996); and H. L. Goodall, "Transforming Communication Studies Through Ethnographic Practices" (unpublished paper presented at the SCA Convention, November 23, 1996).

16. The description presented is based on a synthesis of theories about ethnography.

17. See, for example, Joe Ayres, A. Kathleen Wilcox, and Debbie M. Ayres, "Receiver Apprehension: An Explanatory Model and Accompanying Research," *Communication Education* 44 (July 1995): 223–235; and Joan E. Aitken and Michael R. Neer, "College Student Question-Asking: The Relationship of Classroom Communication Apprehension and Motivation," *The Southern Communication Journal* 59 (Fall 1993): 73–81.

18. Beth Azar, "Shy People Have Inaccurate Self-Concepts," *American*

Psychological Association Monitor, November 1995, p. 24.

19. Ibid.

20. Joe Ayres and Tim Hopf, *Coping with Speech Anxiety* (Norwood, NJ: Ablex Publishing, 1993), p. 4.

21. James McCroskey and Virginia Richmond, *The Quiet Ones: Communication Apprehension and Shyness* (Dubuque, IA: CommComp, Gorsuch Scarisbrick, 1980), p. 21.

22. "Americas #1 Fear: Public Speaking," *Bruskin/Goldin Research Report* (February 1993), p. 4.

23. "Is Shyness Inherited?" *Healthy Decisions* (Georgetown University Medical Center), Winter 1997, p. 2.

24. Azar, "Shy People."

25. For an extended discussion of the causes of communication apprehension, see Virginia Richmond and James McCroskey, *Communication: Apprehension, Avoidance, and Effectiveness*, 4th ed. (Scottsdale, AZ: Gorsuch Scarisbrick, 1995).

26. Azur, "Shy People.

27. Ibid.

28. Richmond and McCroskey , pp. 97–101

29. Ibid., p. 36.

30. Ibid., p. 49.

31. Printed by permission of James C. McCroskey. For an in-depth discussion of this and other communication apprehension evaluation tools, see Richmond and McCroskey.

Chapter 3

1. Based on materials developed by Robert Montgomery as they appear in Roy Berko, Lawrence Rosenfeld, and Larry Samovar, *Connecting: A Culture-Sensitive Approach to Interpersonal Communication Competency*, 2nd ed. (Fort Worth, TX: Harcourt Brace College Publishers, 1997), p. 100.

2. Ibid.

3. Marilyn F. Buckley, "Focus on Research: We Listen a Book a Day; We Speak a Book a Week: Learning from Walter Loban," *Language Arts* 69 (1992): 622–626.

4. For a comprehensive review of information on listening, see the 1990 issue of the *Journal of the International Listening Association*; and Andrew D. Wolvin and Carolyn Gwynn Coakley, eds., *Perspectives on Listening* (Norwood, NJ: Ablex, 1993).

5. National Institute on Deafness and Other Communication Disorders, *Biennial Report of the Director, National Institutes of Health, 1991–1992* (Washington, DC: The Institute, 1993), p. 84.

6. Ibid.

7. Marcia Warren, CCC-A, licensed audiologist, interviewed, December 26, 1996.

8. Berko, Rosenfeld, and Samovar, p. 100

9. Dorothy Singer and Jerome Singer, "Is Human Imagination Going Down the Tube?" *Chronicle of Higher Education*, April 29, 1979, p. 56.

10. Ralph G. Nichols and Leonard A. Stevens, *Are You Listening?* (New York: McGraw-Hill, 1957), p. 107.

11. Norbert Wiener, *Cybernetics* (Cambridge, MA: MIT Press, 1961); and Norbert Wiener, *The Human Use of Human Beings* (Garden City, NY: Doubleday, 1964).

12. Jack C. Richard, "Listening Comprehension: Approach, Design, Procedure," *Tesol Quarterly* 17 (June 1983): 219–240.

13. For a discussion of the left/right brain theory, see Betty Edwards, *Drawing on the Right Side of the Brain* (Los Angeles: Jeremy Tracher, 1989); Constance Pechura and Joseph Martin, eds., *Mapping the Brain and Its Function* (Washington, DC: Institute of Medicine National Academy Press, 1991); and Rebecca Cutter, *When Opposites Attract: Right Brain/Left Brain Relationships and How to Make Them Work* (New York: Dutton, 1994).

14. Satoshi Ishii and Tom Bruneau, "Silence and Silences in Cross-Cultural Perspective: Japan the United States," in *Intercultural Communication: A Reader*, 7th ed., ed. Larry A. Samovar and Richard E.

Porter (Belmont, CA: Wadsworth, 1991), 125.

15. Ibid.

16. Deborah Atwater, "Issues Facing Minorities in Speech Communication Education: Moving from the Melting Pot to a Tossed Salad," *Proceedings from the Future of Speech Communication Education, Speech Communication Association Flagstaff Conference Report* (Annandale, VA: Speech Communication Association, 1989), p. 41.

17. Ibid.

18. Ibid.

19. Carl R. Rogers and F. J. Roethlisberger, "Barriers and Gateways to Communication," *Harvard Business Review* 30 (July-August 1952): 46–52.

20. Harvey Mackay, "Listen Up!" *Successful Meetings*, July 1993.

21. Andrew D. Wolvin and Carolyn Gwynn Coakley, *Listening*, 5th ed. (Dubuque, IA: William C. Brown, 1996), Ch. 3, includes an analysis of the major variables affecting the listening process.

22. Ibid. See also Andrew D. Wolvin, Carolyn G. Coakley, and Kelby K. Halone, "A Preliminary Look at Listening Development Across the Life-Span," *International Journal of Listening* 9 (1995): 62–83.

23. The taxonomy is developed and detailed in Wolvin and Coakley, ibid., Part II.

24. Roy Berko and Carolyn Perry, ed., *Speaking, Listening, and Media Literacy Standards for K through 12 Education* (Annandale, VA: Speech Communication Association, 1996), p. 3.

25. Edward Addeo and Robert Burger, *Egospeak* (New York: Bantam Books, 1974), p. xiv.

26. Based on an instrument developed by Paul Torrance and Bernice McCarthy. The original instrument can be obtained from Excel, Inc., P. O. Box 6, Fox River Grove, IL.

Chapter 4

1. Diane Catellano Mader, "The Politically Correct Textbook: Trends

in Publishers' Guidelines for the Representation of Marginalized Groups," paper presented at the Eastern Communication Association Convention, Portland, ME, May 3, 1992, p. 4.

2. Ibid., p. 3.

3. B. L. Pearson, *Introduction to Linguistic Concepts* (New York: Knopf, 1977), p. 4.

4. Ibid.

5. For further discussion of this subject, see Charles F. Hockett, "The Origins of Speech," *Scientific American* 203 (September 1960): 89–96.

6. Gordon Heives, "How Language Began," *Current Anthropology* 14, no. 1 (1973): 1–2.

7. Jim Wise, "Word Game," *The Durham Herald-Sun*, September 6, 1992, p. 71–E9.

8. Norman Geschwind, "Language and the Brain," *Scientific American* 226 (April 1972): 76–83.

9. Norbert Wiener, *The Human Use of Human Beings* (New York: Anchor Books, 1950).

10. T. R. Tortoriello, *Communication in the Organization* (New York: McGraw-Hill, 1978), p. 13.

11. George Herbert Mead, *Mind, Self, and Society* (Chicago: University of Chicago Press, 1934).

12. Wise, p. 71–E9.

13. Barbara Warnick and Edward S. Inch, *Critical Thinking and Communication* (New York: Macmillan, 1989), pp. 257–259.

14. Mader, pp. 112–113.

15. Ibid.

16. Ibid.

17. Blaine Goss and Dan O'Hair, *Communication in Interpersonal Relationships* (New York: Macmillan, 1988), pp. 67–69.

18. For a complete discussion of double-speak, see William Lutz, *Doublespeak* (New York: Harper & Row, 1990).

19. National Council of Teachers of English Committee on Public Doublespeak, Urbana, IL; as reported in Lutz, p. 14.

20. Lutz, pp. xii, xiii.

21. Roger Brown, *Words and Things* (New York: Free Press, 1959), p. 22.

22. Howard A. Mims, "On Black English: A Language with Rules," *Cleveland Plain Dealer*, August 31, 1979, p. A–21.

23. Ibid.

24. Richard Stapleton, "You Say Grinder, I Say Hoagie," *USAir Magazine* (November 1993): 95.

25. Mims.

26. Randall L. Alford and Judith Strother, "A Southern Opinion of Regional Accents," *The Florida Communication Journal*, 21, 1992, p. 51.

27. Stapleton, p. 95.

28. Margaret Usdansky, "Census: Languages Not Foreign at Home," *USA Today*, April 28, 1993, p. 1-A.

29. Deborah Atwater, "Issues Facing Minorities in Speech Communication Education: Moving from the Melting Pot to a Tossed Salad," *Proceedings of the 1988 Speech Communication Association Flagstaff Conference Report* (Annandale, VA: Speech Communication Association, 1989), p. 42.

30. *The National Language Policy* (Washington, D.C.: English-Plus Information Clearinghouse, n.d.), p. 3.

31. *USA Today*, February 6, 1991, p. 6-A.

32. *National Language Policy*, p. 2.

33. Ibid., p. 4.

34. Material in this section is based on the work of W. Zelinsky, as discussed in Peter A. Andersen, Myron W. Lustig, and Janis F. Andersen, "Regional Patterns of Communication in the United States: A Theoretical Perspective," *Communication Monographs* 54 (June 1987): 128–144.

35. "People, Etc.," *Elyria (Ohio) Chronicle-Telegram Scene*, April 10, 1977, p. 2.

36. Deborah Work, "Who Call Like?" *Washington Post*, October 14, 1993, p. C-5.

37. Amy Reynolds, "Dudespeak: 'too cool'?" *The Towerlight* (Towson State University, Towson, MD), September 5, 1991, p. 29.

38. Work, p. C-5.

39. Ibid.

40. Ibid.

41. Sandy Banks, "Ebonics Is a Language with Its Own Set of Rules—An Interview with Orlando Taylor, Howard University," *Cleveland Plain Dealer*, January 14, 1986, p. B-2.

42. Robin Henry, " 'Black English' Causes Confusion in the Classroom—An Interview with Dr. Howard Mims, Associate Professor of Speech and Hearing, Cleveland State University," *Elyria (Ohio) Chronicle-Telegram*, July 26, 1987, p. G–2.

43. Anita Manning, "Schools to Recognize Black 'Ebonics'," *USA Today*, December 20, 1996, p. 3A; Michelle Locke, "School Board Oks Black English as 2nd language," Associated Press as reproduced in *Cleveland Plain Dealer*, December 20, 1996, pp. 1A, 19A; Jessee McKinley, "Critics Accuse Board of Double Talk," *New York Times* as printed in *Cleveland Plain Dealer*, December 21, 1996, p. 15A

44. Michael Hecht, Mary Jane Collier, and Sidney Ribeau, *African American Communication* (Newbury Park, CA: Sage, 1993), p. 85.

45. "Teaching Standard English: A Sociological Approach," unpublished handout based on the syllabus for the Basic Communication Strategies course at LaGuardia Community College, New York, Speech Communication Association Convention, Chicago, November, 1987.

46. "Teaching Standard English," with reference to Clarence Major, *Dictionary of Afro-American Slang* (New York: International Publishers, 1971).

47. Rachel L. Jones quoting black writer James Baldwin, "What's Wrong with Black English?" *Newsweek*, December 27, 1982, p. 7.

48. William Labov, "Allow Black English in Schools? Yes—The Most Important Thing Is to Encourage Children to Talk Freely," *U.S. News & World Report*, March 31, 1980, pp. 63–64.

49. Hecht, et al., p. 84.

50. Ibid.

51. For an in-depth discussion of the syntactic and phonological features of Black English, see Robert Hopper and Rita J. Naremore, *Children's Speech: A Practical Introduction to Communication Development*, 2nd ed. (New York: Harper & Row, 1978), pp. 161–164, 168–171.
52. Hecht, et al., p. 87.
53. Ibid., p. 88.
54. I. Sachdev and R. Y. Bourhis, *Language and Social Identification* (New York: Harvester Wheatsheaf, 1990).
55. Janice Castro, "Spanglish Spoken Here," *Time*, July 11, 1988, p. 53.
56. Ibid., as stated by Carmen Silva-Corvalan, University of Southern California.
57. Ibid.
58. Gary Althen, "The Americans Have to Say Everything," *Communication Quarterly* 40 (Fall 1992): 414.
59. Ibid.
60. Steven B. Pratt, "Razzing: Ritualized Uses of Humor as a Form of Identification among American Indians, paper presented at Central States Speech Association, Oklahoma City, April, 1994; also appears in H. B. Mokros, Ed., *Interaction and Identity: Information and Behavior* vol. 5 (New Brunswick, NJ: Transactions, 1994), p. 4.
61. Ibid.
62. Gerry Philipsen, "Navaho World View and Culture Patterns of Speech: A Case Study in Ethnorhetoric," *Speech Monographs* (June 1972): 134.
63. Ibid., p. 135.
64. Pratt, p. 2.
65. Ibid.
66. Hopper and Naremore, pp. 159–174; Naremore and Hopper, pp. 156–158; Labov, pp. 63–64; and the work of Howard A. Mims, Cleveland State University.
67. Based on research by Sandra Terrell and Francis Terrell.
68. Julie L. Nicklin, "'Switching' between Black and Standard English," *Chronicle of Higher Education*, April 20, 1994, p. A-6. For further information on this topic and an approach to alter pronun-

ciation and language usage, see Julie L. Nicklin, *Speak Standard, Too—Add Mainstream English to Your Talking Style* (Chicago: Orchard Books-Columbia College Chicago, n.d.).
69. "Black English, White Flag: Oakland Schools' Sell-Out to Street Slang Abandons Good Sense and Kids' Futures," *Cleveland Plain Dealer*, an editorial printed on December 23, 1996, p. 8-B.

Chapter 5

1. Janet Beavin Bavelas, "Redefining Language: Nonverbal Linguistic Acts in Face-to-Face Dialogue, a B. Aubrey Fisher Lecture," October 1992, Department of Psychology, University of Victoria, Victoria, B. C., Canada, p. 2. Also, an excellent learning aid for gaining awareness of intercultural characteristics is *Intercultural Communicating* (Provo, UT: Language Research Center, Brigham Young University); another is the Language Research Center's "Culturegram" series, which is intended to offer briefings to aid understanding of, feeling for, and communication with people around the world.
2. Judee K. Burgoon, David B. Buller, and W. Gill Woodall, *Nonverbal Communication: The Unspoken Dialogue,* 2nd ed. (New York: McGraw-Hill, 1996), p. 1.
3. Ibid.
4. Ibid.
5. Bavelas, pp. 2–3.
6. Burgoon, p. 136.
7. Ibid., p. 1
8. Ibid., p. 136.
9. Ibid.
10. Norbert Freedman, "You Have to Move to Think," report, Clinical Behavioral Research Unit, Downstate Medical Center, Brooklyn, NY, n.d.
11. Edward Hall and Mildred Hall, "The Sounds of Silence," *Playboy* 18 (June 1971): 148.
12. Edward Hall, as interviewed by Kenneth Freedman, "Learning the Arabs' Silent Language," *Psychology Today* 13 (August 1979): 53.

13. Discussion based on research reported by Paul Ekman, Wallace Friesen, and John Bear, "The International Language of Gestures," *Psychology Today* 18 (May 1984): 64–69.
14. Mark Knapp and Judith A. Hall, *Nonverbal Communication in Human Interaction,* 4th ed. (Ft. Worth: Harcourt Brace, 1997), pp. 13–20.
15. The statement is credited to having been said by Sigmund Freud.
16. Louise Sweeney, "Now Who's Telling Us the Truth about Lie Detectors," *Elyria (Ohio) Chronicle-Telegram*, October 30, 1983, "Sunday Scene," p. 10.
17. No specific identifying channels of nonverbal communication have been universally defined. The names used here are a compilation of those that have appeared in various communication textbooks.
18. Knapp, p. 9.
19. Ibid.
20. Ibid.
21. James T. Yenckel, "Fearless Traveler—Sorting through the Chaos of Culture," *Washington Post*, October 20, 1991, p. E10.
22. Burgoon, p. 41.
23. For an extended discussion of emotions and nonverbal communication, see Burgoon, Chapter 10.
24. Knapp, pp. 273–284.
25. For an extensive discussion of the face and eyes see Knapp, Chapter 10.
26. Knapp, pp. 43–45.
27. Edward Hall and Mildred Hall, "The Sounds of Silence," *Playboy 18* (June 1971): 148.
28. Knapp, pp. 386–390.
29. Hall, pp. 47–48.
30. Based on the theories of Milton Erickson presented by Ron Klein as part of the training units of the American Hypnosis Training Academy, Inc., June 1991; also see Knapp, pp. 375–376.
31. Mark L. Hickson III and Don W. Stacks, *Nonverbal Communication: Studies and Applications,* 3rd ed. (Madison, WI: Brown and Benchmark, 1993), p. 13.

32. Knapp, pp. 204–205.

33. For an extensive discussion of para-vocalics, see Knapp, Chapter 11.

34. Some research classifies touch separately as *tactile-cutaneous* rather than as part of proxemics. This discussion, although recognizing the distinction, includes touch within proxemics.

35. Hall and Hall, p. 148.

36. Burgoon, p. 224, referring to research by Edward Hall.

37. Ibid.

38. Burgoon, p. 224, based on the work of S. M. Jourjrard and N. M. Genley.

39. Diane Ackerman, "The Power of Touch," *Parade Magazine*, March 25, 1990, p. 3.

40. Roy Berko, Lawrence Rosenfeld, and Larry Samovar, *Connecting: A Culture-Sensitive Approach to Interpersonal Communication Competency* (Ft. Worth, TX: Harcourt Brace, 1997), p. 157.

41. Ibid., pp. 157–160.

42. Yenckel, p. E10.

43. Neal Roese, James Olson, Marianne Borenstein, Angela Martin, and Allison Shores, "Same-Sex Touching Behavior: The Moderating Role of Homophobic Attitudes," *Journal of Nonverbal Behavior* (Winter 1992): 250.

44. Ibid., p. 251.

45. Stephan Rechtschaffen, "Time-Shifting," *Psychology Today* (November/December 1993): 35.

46. Ibid.

47. Burgoon, p. 226.

48. Michael Argyle, "Inter-Cultural Communication," in *Cultures in Contact: Studies in Cross-Cultural Interaction*, ed. Stephen Bochner (New York: Pergamon Press, 1982), p. 35.

49. Edward T. Hall and Mildred Reed Hall, *Understanding Cultural Differences: Germans, French, and Americans* (Yarmouth, ME: Intercultural Press, 1990), p. 38.

50. R. Levine with E. Woolf, "Social Time: The Heartbeat of Culture," in *The Nonverbal Communication Reader* ed. J. A. DeVito and M. L. Hecht

(Prospect Heights, IL: Waveland, 1990), pp. 332–338.

51. For an extensive discussion on procrastination, see Albert Ellis and William Knaus, *Overcoming Procrastination* (New York: Signet 1979).

52. Diane Ackerman, "Our Most Mysterious Sense," *Parade Magazine*, June 10, 1990, p. 8.

53. Section based on Joseph DeVito, *Nonverbal Communication Workbook* (Prospect Heights, IL: Waveland Press, 1989), pp. 187–189.

54. Ackerman, p. 8.

55. Carol Austin Bridgewater, "Slow Music Sells," *Psychology Today* 17 (January 1983): 56.

56. Patricia McCormick, "Rock Music Can Weaken Muscles," *Elyria (Ohio) Chronicle-Telegram*, January 12, 1979, "Encore," p. 15.

57. Ibid.

58. Research provided by Muzak Corporation, unpublished materials.

59. Roxanne Washington, "Culture Weighs Body Image, *Cleveland Plain Dealer*, June 18, 1996, pp. 1E, 4E.

60. "The Eyes Have It," *Newsweek*, December 3, 1973, p. 85.

61. Ibid.

62. "Attractive Male Attorneys Earn More, Faster," *GW Hatchet* [George Washington University], January 18, 1996, p. 9.

63. Lynn Sherr, "Short Men," *20/20*, ABC-TV, December 27, 1996.

64. Ibid.

65. Ibid.

66. Mark Knapp, *Nonverbal Communication in Human Interaction*, 2nd ed. (Ft. Worth: Harcourt Brace, 1978), pp. 166–167.

67. Based on the concepts of Thomas T. Samaras in his to-be-published "The Truth About Your Height: Exploring the Myths and Realities of Human Size and Its Effect on Performance, Health, Pollution and Survival," n.d.

68. Jennifer Steinhauer, "It's 'The Gap' Once You're Hired, But Job Hunters Must Spiff It Up, " *The New York Times*, April 2, 1995, p. F13.

69. Ibid.

70. Ibid.

71. Ellen Neuborne, "Causal-Clothing Makers Make Pitch to Offices," *USA Today*, February 7, 1995, p. B1.

72. Elizabeth Snead, "Casual Look Suits Today's Businessmen," *USA Today*, August 13, 1993, p. 1D.

73. Mark Albright, "Menswear Sales on Upswing," *Elyria (Ohio) Chronicle-Telegram*, November 25, 1994, p. D8 as reprinted from the *St. Petersburg Times*.

74. Neuborne.

75. Pam Belluck, "Uniform Appeal," *The Baltimore Sun*, March 2, 1992, p. 5.

Chapter 6

1. Rebecca Cline, "Seminar in Interpersonal Communication," unpublished syllabus, Temple University, Philadelphia, n.d.

2. Roy Berko, Lawrence Rosenfeld, Larry Samovar, *Connecting: A Culture-Sensitive Approach to Interpersonal Communication Competency* (Ft. Worth, TX: Harcourt Brace College Publishers, 1997), p. 16.

3. Ibid., p. 303.

4. For further discussion of the "I," see Calvin S. Hall and Gardner Lindzey, *Theories of Personality* (New York: Wiley, 1957), p. 483.

5. For a discussion of left/right brain theory, see Betty Edwards, *Drawing on the Right Side of the Brain* (Los Angeles: Jeremy Tarcher, 1989); Constance Pechura and Joseph Martin, eds., *Mapping the Brain and Its Function* (Washington, DC: Institute of Medicine National Academy Press, 1991); and Rebecca Cutter, *When Opposites Attract: Right Brain/Left Brain Relationships and How to Make Them Work* (New York: Dutton, 1994).

6. A theory of Murray Banks.

7. For an extensive investigation of emotional expression see Berko, Rosenfeld, and Samovar, pp. 84–95.

8. Berko, Rosenfeld, and Samovar, p. 428

9. Lauri P. Arliss and Deborah J. Borisoff, *Women and Men Communicating:*

Challenge and Changes (Ft. Worth, TX: Harcourt Brace, 1993), p. 3.

10. Anne Moir and David Jessel, "Sex and Cerebellum: Thinking about the Real Difference between Men and Women," *Washington Post*, May 5, 1991, p. K3.

11. Ibid.

12. Arliss and Borisoff, p. 9.

13. Barbara Mathias, "Male Identity Crisis," *Washington Post*, May 3, 1993, p. C5.

14. John Gray, *Men Are from Mars, Women Are from Venus: A Practical Guide for Improving Communication and Getting What You Want in Your Relationships* (New York: HarperCollins, 1992), p. 16.

15. Mathias, p. C5.

16. Deborah Tannen, *You Just Don't Understand* (New York: Morrow, 1990), p. 14.

17. Moir and Jessel, p. K3.

18. Stephanie Gilbert, "Girl Talk, Boy Talk," [Washington, D.C.] *City Paper*, November 9, 1990, p. 20.

19. For a discussion on the differences between male and female communication, see Arliss and Borisoff; Tannen, and Gray. Also see Julia T. Wood, *Gendered Lives: Communication, Gender, and Culture* (Belmont, CA: Wadsworth, 1994) and Lea Stewart, Pamela Cooper, Alan Stewart, and Sheryl Friedley, *Communication and Gender*, 3rd ed. (Scottsdale, AZ: Gorsuch Scarisbrick, 1996).

20. "What's in a Word? A Job, Hood Senior's Study Says," *Washington Post*, June 6, 1991, p. MD8.

21. Tannen, pp. 43–44.

22. Based on research by H. G. Whittington, James P. Smith, Leonad Kriegel, Lillian Glass, and Hilary Lips.

23. For a discussion on interruptions, see Stewart, Cooper, Stewart, and Friedley, p. 54 and Wood, pp. 31, 144.

24. Based on the research of H. G. Whittington, James P. Smith, Leonard Kriegel, Lillian Glass, and Hilary Lips.

25. Ibid.

26. Ibid.

27. Gray, p. 26.

28. Ibid., p. 25.

29. Ibid., p. 15.

30. Patrick Fanning and Mathew McKay, *Being a Man, A Guide to the New Masculinity* (Oakland, CA: New Harbinger Publications, 1993), p. 13.

31. Gray, pp. 11–13.

32. Sharon Walsh, "Sexual Harassment Complaints Receiving Swift Investigation, *Washington Post*, April 7, 1991, p. H2.

33. Nelly Tucker, "Manhood: Hits and Myths," *Washington Post*, May 3, 1993, p. C5.

34. Judith Tingley, "Consider Using Genderflex," *Performance Instruction*, Washington DC, n.d., n.p.

35. Ibid.

36. Linda A. M. Perry, Phil Backland, and Lisa Merrill, "Sex Stereotypes and Expectations: Classroom and Campus Strategies for Change," syllabus of a short course presented at the Speech Communication Association Convention, October 29, 1992, Chicago, p. 1.

37. Tannen, p. 122.

38. Gary Kreps, *Sexual Harassment: Communication Implications* (Cresskill, NJ: Hampton Press, 1993), p. 11. For more information, see Mark Walsh, "Court Asked to Define Sex Harassment in the Workplace," *Education Week*, October 20, 1993, p. 37.

39. Kreps, p. 186.

40. Ibid., p. 15.

41. Toni Morrison, Nobel Prize for Literature acceptance speech, December, 1993, as reported on National Public Radio.

42. Kreps, p. 1.

43. Ibid., p. 107.

44. Ibid., p. 133.

45. Ibid., p. 13.

46. Ibid., p. 134.

47. Richard Morin, "Harassment Consensus Grows," *Washington Post*, 1992, p. A-22.

48. Based on the writings of Rebecca Ray.

49. Based on a theory of Jon Nussbaum.

50. Ibid.

51. For a discussion of the economic model of realtionships see: Berko, Rosenfeld, and Samovar, p. 289.

52. Based on the research of Anthony Brandt.

53. John Diekman, "How to Develop Intimate Conversations," *New Woman* 12 (November 1982): 70.

Chapter 7

1. Gary Althen, "The Americans Have to Say Everything," *Communication Quarterly* 40 (Fall 1992): 415.

2. Ibid, p. 414.

3. Roy Berko, Lawrence Rosenfeld, and Larry Samovar, *Connecting: A Culture-Sensitive Approach to Interpersonal Communication Competency*, 2nd ed. (Fort Worth, TX: Harcourt Brace, 1997), p. 372.

4. Ibid.

5. William A. Donohue with Robert Holt, *Managing Interpersonal Conflict* (Newbury Park, CA: Sage, 1992), p. 2.

6. Ibid., p. 3.

7. Ibid.

8. Diana Rowland, *Japanese Business Etiquette* (New York: Warner Books, 1985), p. 5.

9. Lennie Copeland and Lewis Griggs, *Going International* (New York: Random House, 1985), p. 109.

10. Berko, Rosenfeld, and Samovar, p. 374.

11. Donohue and Holt, pp. 12–17.

12. Based on the concepts of Marlene Arthur Penkstaff.

13. A theory of Susan Forward.

14. Ibid.

15. The principles are based on the theories of Sonya Friedman.

16. Roy Berko, "Dealing with Stress," an unpublished paper presented in a workshop to the counseling staff at the Alexandria (VA) Social Service Agency, December 1993.

17. This is a principle of Gestalt therapy, as explained by Les Wyman, Gestalt Institute, Cleveland, OH.

18. Discussion based on shyness-workshop materials prepared by Phyllis DeMark, Lorain County Community College, Elyria, OH, n.d.

19. Sharon Bower and Gordon Bower, *Asserting Yourself* (Reading, MA: Addison-Wesley, 1976), p. 87.

20. *Code of Virginia*, chapter 20.2, Section 8:01–576.4 (July 1993).
21. For information on mediation, see Jonathan G. Shailor, *Empowerment in Dispute Mediation: A Critical Analysis of Communication* (Westport, CN: London, 1994) and Dorothy J. Della Noce, *Mediation Fundamentals: A Training Manual* (Richmond, VA: The Better Business Bureau Foundation of Virginia, 1993).
22. Based on theories of Deborah Weider-Hatfield.

Chapter 8

1. Alan Gratch, "The Interview: Who Should Be Talking to Whom?" *Wall Street Journal*, February 29, 1988, p. A8.
2. Ibid.
3. Laura M. Graves and Ronald J. Karren, "The Employee Selection Interview: A Fresh Look at an Old Problem," *Human Resource Management* (Summer 1996): 163–180.
4. For an extensive review of employment interviews, see Jeanne Tessier Barone and Jo Young Switzer, *Interviewing Art and Skills* (Boston: Allyn and Bacon, 1995), Chapter 8.
5. Frank S. Endicott, *Making the Most of Your Job Interview* (New York: New York Life Insurance Company, n.d.).
6. "Executive Grooming 101," *Washington Post Magazine*, November 15, 1992, p. 16.
7. Robert McGarvey, "Tailoring an Image," *USAir Magazine*, May 1990, p. 76.
8. Ellen James Martin, "Making a Good First Impression," *Baltimore Sun*, May 27, 1991, p. 3.
9. McGarvey, p. 78.
10. Ibid., p. 80.
11. "Executive Grooming 101," p. 30.
12. McGarvey, p. 80.
13. "Executive Grooming 101," p. 30.
14. Charles J. Stewart and William B. Cash Jr., *Interviewing Principles and Practices* (Dubuque, IA: William C. Brown, 1997), p. 248.

15. U.S. Department of Labor, Employment and Training Administration, *Merchandising Your Job Talents* (Washington, DC: Government Printing Office, n.d.), pp. 7–8.
16. Anthony Medley, *Sweaty Palms: The Neglected Art of Being Interviewed* (Belmont, CA: Lifetime Learning Publications, 1978), excerpted in "Spring Job Market '81" *Washington Post*, May 3, 1981, pp. 11, 16.
17. Charles J. Stewart, *Teaching Interviewing for Career Preparation* (Urbana, IL: ERIC Clearinghouse on Reading and Communication Skills), p. 8.
18. Ronald P. Lovell, *The Newspaper* (Belmont, CA: Wadsworth, 1980), p. 229.
19. Sandra O'Connell, *The Manager as Communicator* (New York: Harper & Row, 1979), p. 21.
20. Norman C. Hill, *Counseling at the Workplace* (New York: McGraw-Hill, 1981), p. 10.
21. A psychological theory expressed on several broadcasts by Susan Forward, media psychologist, Talknet Radio Network.
22. Michael E. Stano and N. L. Reinsch, Jr., *Communication in Interviews* (Englewood Cliffs, NJ: Prentice-Hall, 1982), pp. 262–267.
23. These strategies are spelled out in detail in V. R. Buzzotta, R. E. Lefton, and Manuel Sherberg, *Effective Selling through Psychology* (Cambridge, MA: Ballinger, 1982), Ch. 5.
24. "Cold Feet," *Entrepreneur* (August 1996), p. 108.
25. Stano and Reinsch, p. 99.
26. Judi Brownell, "The Performance Appraisal Interview: A Multi-Purpose Communication Assignment," *The Bulletin of the Association for Business Communication* 57 (June, 1994): 11–21.
27. Paul Preston, *Communication for Managers* (Englewood Cliffs, NJ: Prentice-Hall, 1979), p. 254.
28. List based in part on Joan Linder, "Accepting Criticism Gracefully," *The Secretary* (May 1990): 29.
29. Walter R. Mahler, *How Effective Executives Interview* (Homewood, IL: Dow Jones-Irwin, 1976), p. 118.

30. "Delivering Bad News with the Good in Performance Reviews," *Washington Post*, May 26, 1996, p. H4.
31. Joseph P. Zima, *Effective Interviewing* (Palo Alto, CA: SRA, 1983), p. 281.
32. Ibid., p. 284.
33. Stewart and Cash, p. 286.
34. T. Richard Cheatham and Keith V. Erickson, *The Police Officer's Guide to Better Communication* (Glenview, IL: Scott, Foresman, 1984), p. 37.
35. Richard N. Bolles, *What Color Is Your Parachute?* (Berkeley, CA: Ten Speed Press, 1996).

Chapter 9

1. *Group Problem-Solving and Meeting Dynamics*, blind review manuscript (Cincinnati, OH: Southwestern Publishing, 1993), p. 2.
2. J. Dan Rothwell, *In Mixed Company* (Ft. Worth, TX: Harcourt Brace, 1992), p. 6.
3. *Group Problem-Solving and Meeting Dynamics*, p. 3.
4. Ernest Bormann, *Discussion and Group Methods* (New York: Harper & Row, 1969), p. 304.
5. Rothwell, p. 40.
6. Charles H. Kepner and Benjamin B. Tregoe, *The Rational Manager: A Systematic Approach to Problem Solving and Decision Making* (New York: McGraw-Hill, 1965).
7. Irving Janis, *Victims of Groupthink* (Boston: Houghton Mifflin, 1972).
8. For an extended discussion of groupthink, see I. Janis, *Groupthink: Psychological Studies of Policy Decisions and Fiascoes* (Boston: Houghton Mifflin, 1983).
9. *Group Problem-Solving and Meeting Dynamics*, p. 7.
10. Theory developed by Bibb Latane, Kipling Williams, and Stephen Harkins.
11. Charles C. Manz and Henry P. Sims Jr., *Business without Bosses* (New York: Wiley, 1993), p. 211.
12. Ibid., p. 2.
13. William Higgins, "Group Study: Strength in Numbers," *Commuter Connection* 4 (October, 1990): 1.

14. Marianne Schneider Corey and Harold Corey, *Groups: Process and Practice*, 3rd ed. (Monterey, CA: Brooks/Cole, 1987), p. 9.

15. Marilyn Elias, "Self-Help Groups," *Denver Post*, July 13, 1980, p. 38.

16. A theory of Susan Forward, media psychologist, Talknet Radio Network.

17. "How Cancer Patients Are Talking Their Way to a Longer Life," *Good Housekeeping* (June 1990): 251.

18. "Ann Landers," *Washington Post*, March 15, 1990, p. B12.

19. Gerald L. Wilson and Michael S. Hanna, *Groups in Context* (New York: McGraw-Hill, 1990), pp. 63–65.

20. Statistical study by Kathleen Wagoner and Mary Ruprecht.

21. Ron Zemke, "The Rediscovery of Videotape Teleconferencing," *Training* (September 1986): 46.

22. *Group Problem-Solving and Meeting Dynamics*, pp. 30–31.

23. For a discussion on the various definitions of a family, see Laurie Arliss, *Contemporary Family Communication: Meaning and Messages* (New York: St. Martin's Press, 1993); Judy Pearson, *Communicating in the Family: Seeking Satisfaction in Changing Times*, 2nd ed. (New York: HarperCollins, 1993); Janet Yerby, Nancy Buerkel-Rothfuss, and Arthur Bochner, *Understanding Family Communication*, 2nd ed. (Scottsdale, AZ: Gorsuch Publishers, 1995); and Kathleen Galvin and Bernard Brommel, *Family Communication: Cohesion and Change*, 4th ed. (New York: HarperCollins, 1996).

24. Rothwell, pp. 55–80.

25. Ibid., pp. 65–66.

26. Matt Helms, "License to Hate," *National College Magazine* (September 1992): 61.

27. Ibid., p. 64.

28. Henry M. Robert III and William J. Evans, *Robert's Rules of Order, Newly Revised* (Glenview, IL: Scott, Foresman, 1990).

29. In parliamentary procedure, the term consensus means "unanimous." In nonparliamentary use, the term is often assumed to mean "generally." For voting purposes, it is synonymous with "all." See Robert and Evans, pp. 52–55.

30. Robert and Evans, pp. 399–400.

31. Part-of-the-whole voting is sometimes referred to as two-thirds voting. For a discussion, see Robert and Evans, pp. 396–397.

32. Rothwell, p. 195.

33. Ibid.

34. Janis, p. 197.

35. The classic Dewey Inductive process was first discussed in John Dewey, *How to Think* (Boston: D. C. Heath, 1910), pp. 68–78.

36. Janis, p. 219.

37. Ibid., p. 203.

38. Rothwell, p. 221.

39. A process refined by Roy Berko from a concept of Eileen Breckenridge.

40. For a discussion on group meeting spaces see Dale Leathers, *Successful Nonverbal Communication*, 2nd ed. (New York: Macmillan, 1997), pp. 407–411.

41. Ibid.

42. Mark Knapp and Judith Hall, *Nonverbal Communication in Human Interaction*, 4th ed. (Ft. Worth, TX: Harcourt Brace, 1997), p. 175.

43. Leathers.

44. Ibid.

45. Mark Knapp and Judith Hall, *Nonverbal Communication in Human Interaction*, 3rd ed. (Ft. Worth, TX: Harcourt Brace, 1992), p. 168.

46. For a discussion of round and rectangular tables see: Knapp and Hall, 4th ed., pp. 177–179.

47. Leathers.

48. Knapp and Hall, 3rd ed., p. 168.

49. Ibid.

50. From the research of R. Sommer, as found in Knapp and Hall, 4th ed., pp. 116–118.

Chapter 10

1. George A. Borden, *Cultural Orientation: An Approach to Understanding Intercultural Communication* (Englewood Cliffs, NJ: Prentice-Hall, 1991), p. 133.

2. Larry Samovar and Richard Porter, *Intercultural Communication: A Reader* (Belmont, CA: Wadsworth, 1994), p. 79.

3. Gerry Philipsen, "Navaho World View and Culture Patterns of Speech: A Case Study in Ethnorhetoric," *Speech Monographs* (June 1972): 138.

4. Ibid.

5. Ibid.

6. Borden, p. 105.

7. Ibid.

8. Samovar and Porter, p. 79.

9. Ibid., p. 298.

10. Ibid., p. 291.

11. Ibid.

12. Ibid.

13. Ibid.

14. Ibid.

15. Ibid.

16. Ibid.

17. Ibid.

18. Janet Fox, "Changing Leadership Styles," *Amtrak Express* (May/June 1993).

19. Judith Pearson, Lynn Turner, and Todd-Mancillas, *Gender and Communication*, 3rd ed. (Madison, WI: Brown and Benchmark, 1995), p. 338.

20. Laurie Arliss and Deborah Borisoff, *Women and Men Communicating* (Ft. Worth, TX: Harcourt Brace, 1993), p. 168.

21. Lea Stewart, Alan Stewart, Sheryl Friedley, and Pam Cooper, *Communication between the Sexes* (Scottsdale, AZ: Gorsuch Scarisbrick, 1990), p. 162.

22. Ibid., p. 163.

23. Pearson, p. 338.

24. Barbara Bates, *Communication and the Sexes* (New York: Harper & Row, 1988), p. 155.

25. Arliss and Borisoff, p. 168.

26. Ibid.

27. Stewart et al., p. 159.

28. Ibid.

29. Julie Ann Wambach, *Group Problem Solving through Communication Styles* (Dubuque, IA: Kendall/Hunt, 1992), p. 150.

30. Based on the work of James E. Sikell, Florida Maxima Corporation.

31. Dorrine Turecamo, "Perfect Timing," *Successful Meetings* (October 1992): 119.

32. Kenneth D. Benne and Paul Sheets, "Functional Roles of Group Members," *Journal of Social Issues* 4 (Spring 1948): 41–49.

33. Dale Leathers, *Successful Nonverbal Communication* (New York: Macmillan, 1992), p. 376.

34. J. Dan Rothwell, *In Mixed Company* (Ft. Worth, TX: Harcourt Brace, 1992), pp. 116–119.

35. James MacGregor Burns, *Leadership* (New York: Harper & Row, 1978). For an analysis of leadership by noted social critics and leadership experts, see the March-April 1987 issue of *Liberal Education*. Also see Judy B. Rosener, "Ways Women Lead," *Harvard Business Review* (November-December 1990): 119–125.

36. Charles C. Manz and Henry P. Sims Jr., *Superleadership* (Englewood Cliffs, NJ: Prentice-Hall, 1989).

37. Ralph White and Ronald Lippitt, "Leader Behavior and Member Reactions in Three Social Climates," in D. Cartwright and A. Zander, eds., *Group Dynamics* (New York: Harper & Row, 1968), pp. 318–335.

38. Rothwell, p. 147.

39. For a discussion of leadership style, see Fred Fielder, *A Theory of Leadership Effectiveness* (New York: McGraw-Hill, 1967).

40. Arlene Schubert and George Schubert, "Leadership Emergence via Nonverbal Communication," a paper presented at the Central States Speech Association Convention, Chicago, April 13, 1978, p. 1.

41. Michael Hackman and Craig Johnson, "Teaching Leadership from a Communication Perspective," Department of Communication, University of Colorado, Colorado Springs, CO, unpublished paper, n.d., p. 6.

42. Hackman and Johnson, p. 2.

43. Schubert and Schubert, p. 3.

44. Based on a concept developed by Patricia Hayes, Indiana University-Bradley.

45. Wambach, pp. 168–169.

46. Contributed by Isa Engleberg, Prince George's Community College, Largo, MD. Used with permission.

Chapter 11

1. The study that discovered this concept is Kathleen Kendall, "Do Real People Ever Give Speeches?" *Central States Speech Journal* 25 (Fall 1974): 235. Other follow-up studies have affirmed the conclusion.

2. Kent Menzel and Lori Carrell, "The Relationship between Preparation and Performance in Public Speaking," *Communication Education* 43 (January 1994): 17.

3. For an extended discussion of demographics, see Andrew Wolvin, Roy Berko, and Darlyn Wolvin, *The Public Speaker/The Public Listener* (Boston: Houghton Mifflin, 1993), pp. 70–74.

4. For an extended discussion of speech outlining, see Wolvin, Berko, and Wolvin, pp. 173–177.

5. For an extended discussion of preparing the manuscript speech, see Wolvin, Berko, and Wolvin, pp. 178–182.

6. Based on the teachings and theory of Dorothy Sarnoff.

7. Stuart W. Hyde, *Television and Radio Announcing*, 4th ed. (Boston: Houghton Mifflin, 1995), p. 81.

8. For an extended discussion of pronunciation and articulation see Jon Eisenson, *Voice and Diction: A Program for Improvement*, 6th ed. (Needham, MA: Allyn and Bacon, 1992).

9. Hyde, pp. 83–85.

10. For a discussion on using gestures in a speech, see Wolvin, Berko, and Wolvin, pp. 194–195.

11. Joe Ayres and Tim Hopf, *Coping with Speech Anxiety* (Norwood, NJ: Ablex, 1993), p. xi.

12. Ayres and Hopf, p. 1.

13. Ibid., p. 5.

14. "Americas #1 Fear: Public Speaking," *Bruskin/Goldin Research Report* (February 1993), p. 4.

15. No definitive research is available to demonstrate that any of these activities are effective for everyone, but they have been used successfully by some people.

16. Discussion based on information given by Les Wyman, Gestalt Institute, Cleveland, OH.

17. This is a section of the Personal Report on Communication Apprehension (PRCA–24), from Virginia P. Richmond and James C. McCroskey, *Communication: Apprehension, Avoidance and Effectiveness*, 4th ed. (Scottsdale, AZ: Gorsuch Scarisbrick, 1995), pp. 129–130. For a more comprehensive public speaking apprehension test, students should take the PRPSA (Personal Report on Public Speaking Anxiety), which is reprinted in the Instructor's Manual accompanying this text.

Chapter 12

1. *Research on Digital Libraries* (Arlington, VA: National Science Foundation, 1993), p. 1.

2. For insight into the types of bias present in many different sources of information, see Robert Newman and Dale Newman, *Evidence* (Boston: Houghton Mifflin, 1969).

3. Pat Guy, "U.S. News to Be on Computer," *USA Today*, November 26, 1993, p. 5-B.

4. Deborah Tannen, *You Just Don't Understand* (New York: William Morrow, 1990), p. 122.

5. Norris McWhirter, *1984 Guinness Book of World Records* (New York: Sterling, 1984), p. 28.

6. Rob Rachowiecki, *Ecuador* (Berkeley, CA: Lonely Planet Publications, 1986), p. 13.

7. Darrell Huff, *How to Lie with Statistics* (New York: Norton, 1954), pp. 123–142.

8. For extended discussions of communication research, see Rebecca Rubin, Alan Rubin, and Linda Piele, *Communication Research: Strategies and Sources*, 3rd ed. (Belmont, CA:

Wadsworth, 1993) and James Watt and Sjef van den Berg, *Research Methods for Communication Science* (Needham Heights, MA: Allyn and Bacon, 1995).

9. The 3M Management Team with Jeannine Drew, *Mastering Meetings* (New York: McGraw-Hill, 1994), pp. 141–143.

10. *User's Guide Microsoft PowerPoint* (Microsoft Corporation, 1994) and Doug Lowe, *PowerPoint 4 for Windows for Dummies* (Foster City, CA: IDG Books Worldwide, 1994).

Chapter 13

1. Charles Petrie, "Informative Speaking: A Summary and Bibliography of Related Research," *Speech Monographs* 30 (June 1963): 79–91.

2. Jack E. Hulbert, "Planning and Delivering Effective Oral Presentations," *Business Education Forum* 50 (April 1996): 43.

3. Richard A. Lindeborg, "A Quick and Easy Strategy for Organizing a Speech," IEEE *Transactions on Professional Communication* 33 (September 1990): 133–134.

4. Morris Mandel, *Stories for Speakers* (New York: Jonathan David, 1964).

Chapter 14

1. Connie Koenenn, "The Future Is Now," *Washington Post*, February 3, 1989, p. B5.

2. Richard Wurman, *Information Anxiety* (Garden City, NY: Doubleday, 1989).

3. Michael F. Warlum, "Improving Oral Marketing Presentations in the

Technology-Based Company," IEEE *Transactions on Professional Communication* 31 (June 1988): 84.

4. Richard Hoehn, *The Art and Practice of Public Speaking* (New York: McGraw-Hill, 1988).

5. Categories based on those reported in James H. Byrns, *Speak for Yourself: An Introduction to Public Speaking* (New York: Random House, 1981), Chs. 14–17.

6. H. Lloyd Goodall and Christopher L. Waagen, *The Persuasive Presentation* (New York: Harper & Row, 1986), p. 105.

7. Suggestions for structuring a technical report are based on Richard Weigand, *Business Horizons,* School of Business, Indiana University, Bloomington, as reported in *Communicating Briefings* (January, 1986).

8. Hoehn.

9. G. H. Jamieson, *Communication and Persuasion* (London: Croom Helm, 1985), pp. 5–16.

10. Hoehn.

11. Ibid.

Chapter 15

1. Aristotle, *The Rhetoric of Aristotle,* trans. Lane Cooper (New York: Appleton-Century-Crofts, 1932).

2. Based on a speech given by an inmate of the Grafton Prison Farm, Grafton, OH. Name and setting withheld by request.

3. Robert B. Maxwell, "The 'Graying' of America," *Vital Speeches of the Day,* September 15, 1987, p. 710.

4. Jim Courter, "Step by Step," *Vital Speeches of the Day,* July 15, 1987, p. 581.

5. Donald M. Stewart, "Good Writing," *Vital Speeches of the Day,* August 1, 1987, p. 633.

6. James A. Baker III, "America and the Collapse of the Soviet Empire," speech presented at Princeton University, December 12, 1991, published in *Vital Speeches of the Day,* January 1, 1992, p. 167.

7. Duane A. Kullberg, "Accounting and Accountability," *Vital Speeches of the Day,* July 15, 1987, p. 608.

8. Abraham Maslow, *Motivation and Personality* (New York: Harper & Row, 1970), pp. 35–58. How Maslow's hierarchy is reflected in today's societal needs is demonstrated in M. Joseph Sirgy, "A Quality-of-Life Theory Derived from Maslow's Developmental Perspective," *American Journal of Economics and Sociology* 45 (July 1986): 329–342.

9. Discussion adapted from Bruce E. Gronbeck, Raymie E. McKerrow, Douglas Ehninger, and Alan H. Monroe, *Principles and Types of Speech Communication*, 12th ed. (Glenview, IL: Scott, Foresman/Little Brown, 1994).

10. A comprehensive summary of research on fear appeals is provided in James P. Dillard, "Rethinking the Study of Fear Appeals: An Emotional Perspective," *Communication Theory* 4 (November 1994): 295–323.

11. Eugene Finerman, "Humor and Speeches," *Vital Speeches of the Day,* March 1, 1996, p. 313.

12. Jonathan Alter and Pat Wingert, "The Return of SHAME," *Newsweek* February 6, 1995, p. 22.

GLOSSARY

Accent   The pronunciation and intonation used by a person that may cause some difficulty in understanding; sound is clearly identifiable, yet often not always understood by those outside that area, such as "southern accent."

Accenting relationship   The relationship of verbal and nonverbal communication in which the nonverbal message stresses the verbal one, such as turning the person to look at you while commanding, "When I speak to you, look at me!"

Action chain   A behavioral sequence with two or more participating organisms, in which there are standard steps for reaching a goal, such as the sequence of two businesspeople meeting and greeting each other.

Action-reaction principle   A theory which indicates that if someone acts in a particular way toward another person, the other person will react in a parallel manner, for example, when we smile, others are likely to smile back.

Ad hominem argument   Developing an argument that attacks the personal character of a source.

Ad ignorantium argument   An attempt to prove that a statement is true because it cannot be disproved.

Ad lib speaking   A speech given in which a speaker has no time to organize ideas and responds immediately when answering a question, volunteering an opinion, or interacting during an interpersonal experience.

Ad populum argument   An appeal to people's prejudices and passions rather than focusing on the issue at hand.

Adaptors   Movements that accompany boredom, show internal feelings, or regulate a situation; for example, those who are bored often tap their fingers on a table or bounce a crossed leg.

Adjourning   A group's temporarily or permanently going out of existence.

Aesthetics   The communication of a message or mood through color or music.

Affect displays   Facial gestures that show emotions and feelings such as sadness or happiness; pouting, winking, and raising or lowering the eyelids and eyebrows are examples of affect displays.

Agenda   The list of the topics to be discussed in a meeting or the problems that must be dealt with in the order in which they will be acted upon.

Aggressive behavior   Acting in a way to dominate, to get your own way at any cost.

Alphabetical language   A language system in which letters are combined to represent a single word; languages that are alphabetically based recognize the differences between vowels (e.g., in English, *a, e, i, o,* and *u,*) and consonants (e.g., in English, *r, b,* and *m*); English, Greek, and Hebrew are alphabetical languages.

Ambiguity   Vagueness caused by use of a word that has more than one interpretation.

Analogy   Information used to clarify a concept for listeners in which the speaker compares an unfamiliar concept to a familiar one.

Analytical thinking   Thought patterns emphasizing analysis, which dissects events and concepts into pieces that can be linked into chains and categorized; typical of Euro-American cultures and people descendant from those cultures.

Androgyny   The internalization of both masculine and feminine language and characteristics so that both men's and women's speech falls further from sex-type extremes and closer to some ground in between.

Anxiety   Excessive worry or concern; an important variable that may affect a person's perceptions and performance since negative anxiety causes stress.

Appraisal interview   An interview format that helps the interviewee to realize the strengths and weaknesses of his or her performance.

Appreciative listening   The attempt of a person to engage in enjoyment or sensory stimulation of a message, such as listening to humorous speakers, comedians, or music videos.

Arbitration   An attempt to solve a conflict by a third party to settle a dispute by hearing the evidence and making a decision on how the conflict will be resolved.

Artifacts   A person's clothing, makeup, eyeglasses, and jewelry, each of which carries distinct messages.

Asian-American dialect   English as spoken by immigrants who speak one of the Asian languages.

Asking   Seeking out information by inquiring in order to eliminate misunderstandings, aid in receipt of an intended message, and gain the proper information.

Assertive communication   Communication in which a person stands up for and tries to achieve personal rights without damaging others; centers on a person realizing that a person has the right to choose and control his or her life.

Assertiveness   When a person stands up for and tries to achieve personal rights without damaging others; centers on a person realizing that a person has the right to choose and control his or her life.

Assignment of meaning   The process of putting the stimulus received during listening into some predetermined category develops as we acquire our language system.

Attention (listening)   The focus on a specific stimulus selected from all the stimuli received at any given moment; listening phase in which the other stimuli recede so that the listener can concentrate on a specific heard word or visual symbol.

Attention span   The capacity of the short-term memory; rarely lasts more than 45 seconds at any one time.

Attitudes   A person's perspective and viewpoints.

Audience analysis   Assessing the demographic, psychographic, and rhetorographic characteristics of your prospective listeners.

Audio aids   A representation or the real duplication of a sound, such as a voice or music, which appeals to the listener's sense of hearing.

Audio-visual aids   A film, videotape, and/or tape-slide presentation that combines the dimensions of sight and sound.

Authoritarian leader   A leader who dominates and directs a group according to personal goals and objectives, regardless of how consistent these goals are with group members' goals.

Behavioral kinesiology   A theory that holds that particular kinds of food, clothes, thoughts, and music strengthen or weaken the muscles of the body.

Beliefs   A person's convictions.

Bipolar question   A closed question that requires a yes or no response, such as, "Would you like to work for this company?"

Black English   An alternative name for Ebonics; the primary language used by many African-Americans.

Body of a speech   The section of a speech that develops the major points as well as any subpoints pertaining to a speaker's central idea.

Brain dominance   The brain has two hemispheres by which a person processes information: the left (linear) and right (global) sides; brain dominance accounts for learning and listening in patterned ways based on which side of the brain is being used.

Brainstorming   The generating of possible solutions without evaluation of them at the time of their proposal.

Case method of organizational speech structure   A method for organizing a speech in which the speaker discusses the central idea without breaking it into subpoints.

Categorical syllogism   A type of deductive argument in which an argument is presented that contains premises and a conclusion.

Causal method of issue arrangement   A way of organizing the body of a speech that shows how two or more events are connected in such a way that if one occurs, the other will necessarily follow.

Centralized decision-making process   A decision-making process that views authority as being inherent within the individual, not his or her position; a technique used by many Mexicans.

Centralized group communication networks   A group communication pattern in which all information flows toward and through the leader of the group.

Channel/channels   The five senses by which messages are carried from and to the sender and receiver.

Charisma   The quality held by people who are compelling and have the ability to entice others.

Chart   A visual representation of statistical data that gives information in tabular or diagrammatic form.

Chronemics   The study of the way people handle and structure their use of time.

Circular time   A societal use of time in which there is no pressing need to achieve or create newness, or to insatiably produce more than is needed to survive; such societies, for example, many Native Americans, have successfully integrated the past and future into a peaceful sense of the present.

Clincher to a speech   The final statement made during a public speech that gives the speaker one more chance to reinforce the major ideas she or he has presented and then wraps up the presentation with a final message to clinch the selling of the central idea.

Closed question   A question that provides alternatives, narrows the possibilities for a response, and probes for opinions on opposite ends of a continuum, such as, "Do you think knowledge of a product or communication skills is the most important asset of a salesperson?"

Cluster   The grouping together of nonverbal signals such as gestures, posture, eye contact, and movement, in order to interpret the nonverbal message.

Code switchers   Individuals who can change the language/accent they use as is appropriate for a situation; selective use of Black English and mainstream American English depending on the situation.

Coercion   A leadership power method in which a selection of choices is given to solve a problem, all of which are undesirable.

Cognitive dissonance   The imbalance between a person's values, attitudes, beliefs, and actions.

Cognitive language   Language used to convey information; tends to be denotative.

Cognitive modification   A method that teaches people who have learned to think negatively to think positively; a useful tool to aid in overcoming communication anxiety.

Cognitive processing   The comprehending, organizing, and storing of ideas.

Committee   A small group that has been selected by a large group to be responsible for study, research, and recommendations about an issue.

Communication   Conscious or unconscious, intentional or unintentional, process in which feelings and ideas are expressed as verbal and/or nonverbal messages, sent, received, and comprehended. This process can be accidental (having no intent), expressive (resulting from the emotional state of the person), or rhetorical (resulting from specific goals of the communicator).

Communication apprehension   Speech anxiety that may be situation specific, in which a person is anxious about communicating in a specific setting (e.g., giving speeches) or general, in which a person is anxious about communication in all situations.

Communication stoppers   Phrases that put down the ideas of others in such a way that they stop participating; may cut off valuable input; "That will never work," "We've tried that before," or "That's ridiculous" are communication stoppers.

Communication system   A pattern of rules and methods set up in communicative relationships that describe how the relationship is functioning; a pattern of communication determined by who is participating, the setting, the purpose, and how they interact.

Comparative-advantage reasoning   A method of persuasion in which the speaker states possible solutions, then demonstrates how the proposal is the most workable, desirable, and practical.

Comparison method of issue organization   A way of organizing the body of a speech in which the speaker tells how two or more examples are alike.

Comparison-contrast method of issue arrangement   A method of organizing the main points of the body of a public speech by telling about both similarities and differences of two or more items.

Competitive turn-taking   Interrupting another speaker.

Complementing relationship   The relationship of verbal and nonverbal communication in which a nonverbal message accompanies a verbal message and adds further dimension to communication, such as nodding of the head vertically as a person says the word *yes*.

Comprehension listening   The attempt to recognize and retain the information in a message; to comprehend a message, the listener must first discriminate the message to recognize its auditory and visual components.

Conclusion of a speech   The section of the speech that summarizes, pulls thoughts together, or motivates listeners to take a prescribed action.

Conditional argument   A form of deductive argument that sets up an if/then proposition; the establishment of two conditions, one of which necessarily follows from the other.

Conflict   Any situation in which a person perceives another person, with whom they are interdependent, is frustrating or might frustrate the satisfaction of some concern, need, want, or desire.

Conflict accommodation   A conflict resolution style in which an individual puts the other person's needs ahead of his or her own, thereby giving in.

Conflict active societies   Societies in which conflict is accepted as an important part of life, which is common in most of the Middle Eastern, Mediterranean, Central and South American, and Arabic countries.

Conflict avoidance   Dealing with conflict by not confronting the conflict; putting up with the status quo, no matter how unpleasant, in order to avoid conflict.

Conflict avoidance societies   Societies that believe that face-to-face confrontations are to be avoided, which is common in many Asian societies.

Conflict competition   An attempt to resolve conflict by exerting power.

Conflict compromise   An attempt to resolve conflict by bringing concerns out into the open in an attempt to satisfy the needs of both parties.

Conflict integration   An attempt to resolve conflict by being concerned about the needs of all the participants; an attempt to resolve a conflict through a win-win solution.

Conflicting relationship   The relationship of verbal and nonverbal communication in which the verbal message and nonverbal message are in contrast, such as when a child says "I didn't steal the cookies," while he is looking at the floor and squirming.

Conflict smoothing over   An attempt to resolve conflict by preserving the image that everything is OK above all else.

Confucian principle of i   A principle that requires that a person be affiliated and identify with a small and tightly knit group of people over long periods of time, who aid and assist each other when there is a need, which leads to a mutually implied assistance pact among group members.

Congruency   The relationship between present and past patterns of behavior, in order to ascertain whether a person's present verbal and nonverbal patterns are parallel to his or her past patterns.

Connotative meanings   Understandings that are associated with certain words or to which an individual attaches particular implications (e.g., cat—referring to your love for your cat, rather than defining cats in general).

Connotative words   Words that have an implied or suggested meaning (e.g., love, hate, beautiful).

Consensus   A voting procedure in which every member of a group agrees on a proposal.

Contact culture   Those cultures characterized by tactile modes of communication which sanction touching, hugging, and close space proximity (e.g., Latin Americans, Mediterraneans, French, Arabs).

Context   Who is present, where the communication is taking place, and the general attitude of those assembled.

Contrast method of issue arrangement   A method of organizing the main points of the body of a public speech by giving specific examples of differences between the two or more subjects.

Counseling interview   An interview format designed to provide guidance and support to the interviewee; used by mental health professionals, friends, and family members, among others.

Conversation   An interaction with at least one other person.

Critical listening   An attempt to comprehend and evaluate the message that has been received; a critical listener assesses the arguments and the appeals in a message and then decides whether to accept or reject them.

Critical thinking   A process of reaching conclusions in which criteria are established and then solutions are matched with the criteria.

Criticism   The act of judging another person, decision, or process.

Cultural noise   Communication difficulty caused by preconceived, unyielding attitudes derived from a group or society on how members of that culture should act or in what they should or shouldn't believe.

Culture   A communication phenomenon because it is passed among its adherents by communication—written and oral, verbal and nonverbal.

Cutaway   A visual aid that allows the listener of a speech to see what he or she would normally have to imagine.

Cybernetic process   The theory that indicates that process of acquiring and using language functions much like a computer in that the cortex stores, computes, and eventually processes some of these incoming signals and puts forth the necessary information; starts to develop in humans at about the third month after birth.

Decentralized group communication networks   A group communication pattern in which ideas flow freely among all members of a group.

Decode   Translating of a received message.

Deductive argument   A system of reasoning which is based on logical necessity; a conclusion is stated in the form of a premise and proof is given to prove the premise is correct.

Democratic leader   A leader who directs a group according to the goals of its members and allows them to form their own conclusions.

Demographics   Factors which make the listeners of a speech unique based on their descriptions and backgrounds including such factors as their ages, genders, religions, ethnicity, educations, occupations, and race.

Denotative meanings   The interpretation of words which have direct, explicit meanings (e.g., *dog* carries the denotative meaning of a "four-legged, furry animal, canine").

Denotative words   Words that have direct, explicit meanings (e.g., book, dog).

DESC scripting A way of dealing with interpersonal conflicts that centers on the process of Describing, Expressing, Specifying, and stating Consequences.

Direct aggression The outward expression of dominating or humiliating communication.

Direct question A question that requires explicit and specific replies, for example, "Where did you last work?"

Directions Instructions for accomplishing a task, achieving an effect, or getting somewhere.

Directive intervention A method used by mental health professionals in which the counselor takes the stand that there should be active probing; that specific activities should be carried on outside the counseling session, that there should be role-playing and activities during counseling; and/or, that therapeutic hypnosis should be used in some cases to deal with certain types of problems.

Discriminative listening The listeners attempt to distinguish among auditory and visual stimuli.

Discussion question The issue or problem a group is to deal with at a meeting.

Disjunctive argument A type of deductive argument that is based on establishing an either/or argument in which true alternatives must be established.

Doublespeak A special form of language vagueness that is deceptive, evasive, and/or confusing; a conscious use of language as a weapon or tool by those in power to achieve their ends at the expense of others.

Dyad A pair of people, such as two persons engaged in a conversation.

Dysfunctional system A relational system that is not functioning due to the structure or roles being played by the participants.

Ebonics Ebony phonics; the primary language used by many African-Americans; sometimes referred to as Black English.

Economic model of relationships A theory that contends that people make judgments about interpersonal contacts by comparing relational rewards and costs. As long as rewards (are equal to or) exceed costs the relationship becomes more intimate; however, once costs exceed rewards the relationship begins to stagnate and eventually to dissolve.

Egospeak The art of boosting our own ego by speaking only about what we want to talk about.

Emblems Nonverbal acts that have a direct verbal translation or dictionary definition (e.g., making a circle with your thumb and pointing finger, while extending the other three fingers upward, signifying, "okay"); an emblem's meaning in one culture may not be the same as that same emblem's meaning in another.

Emotive language Language used to express the feelings, attitudes, and emotions of a speaker; employs emotional connotative words.

Empathic assertion A statement that may follow a simple assertion or be the first step in the assertive process that recognizes the other person's problems or rights.

Employment interview An interview that is used as a way of entering the job market or changing positions, getting promotions, and achieving salary increases, as well as admission to colleges and universities, internships or assistantships, and graduate and professional programs.

Encode Putting ideas into message form.

English-Only Movement A proposal to pass a constitutional amendment to make English the official language of the country.

English-Plus laws Proposals to allow the use of languages other than English and encourage the study of foreign languages.

Enthymeme A form of syllogism in which a premise is not directly stated because it is already shared by the communicators and therefore does not need to be verbalized.

Entry relational development phase The phase of a relationship in which biographical information and general attitudes are exchanged.

Environmental noise Outside interference that prevents the receiver from gaining the message.

Ethical communicators Those who conform to the moral standards a society establishes for its communicators.

Ethical value system The basis for a person's decision-making and understanding of why she/he will or will not take a particular stand or action; the basis for your communication ethics.

Ethics A systematic study of what should be the grounds and principles for right and wrong human behavior.

Ethnographers Researchers who study cultures.

Ethnographic Theory of Human Drives A theory that attempts to explain human needs, which indicates that survival of the species, pleasure-seeking, security, and territoriality must be satisfied.

Ethos Credibility; one of the three speaker components in the Western culture's system of persuasion.

Evidence   Proof that includes testimony from experts, statistics, and specific instances.

Exit relational stage   The phase of a relationship in which questions concerning the future of the relationship are raised and resolved.

Expert   A person who, through knowledge or skill in a specific field, gains respect for his or her opinions or expertise because knowledge has been acquired through personal experience, education, training, research, and observation.

Exposition   Information presented in a speech to give the necessary background to listeners so that they can understand the material being presented.

Extemporaneous speaking mode   The preparation method and reference aids in which a speaker develops a set of "talking points," such as notes or an outline to assist in presenting ideas.

Eye contact   A speaker looking into the eyes of the audience as he or she speaks.

Fair fighting   Conflict in which the participants are concerned with working toward an amicable solution to the problem.

Family   An assemblage of people who have legally been declared a group, or who have defined themselves as such; typical kinds of families include natural families, blended families, single-parent families, extended families, and self-declared families.

Faulty analogical reasoning   Reasoning that establishes that no analogy is ever totally "pure" because no two cases are ever identical.

Faulty causal reasoning   Occurs when a speaker claims, without qualification, that something caused something else.

Feedback   Response to a message.

Fight-or-flight   A neurological reaction to fear or endangerment which causes an individual to stay and battle it out, or run away.

Focus groups   A group designed to test reactions to a particular product, process, or service offered by an organization.

Follow-up assertion   A restatement of the simple or empathic assertion, then a statement of your own position, which may include a direct statement of the action you need or want.

Forecast   A statement that alerts the listeners of a speech to ideas that are coming.

Formal time   The way in which a culture divides its time, such as centuries, years, months, weeks, days, hours, and minutes.

Forum   An interaction during which questions are fielded by the participants from each other as well as from any audience present.

Frame of reference   A combination of factors that act as a perceptual screen, which allows for each communicator to understand the other's message from her/his unique perspective; the basis on which persons assign meaning to words, phrases, and sentences; contingent on a person's background, experiences, and perceptions.

Freedom of speech   The protected right to speak without restrictions; to be free to say what we want.

Functional system   A relational system that is operating to the general satisfaction of the participants.

Gender   One's psychological, social, and interactive characteristics; not the same as sex, which is one's biological or physical self.

Genderflex   The temporary use of communication behaviors typical of the other gender.

Generalization conclusion   A conclusion that is derived from predicting some future occurrence or explains a whole category of instances; the assumption that what holds true for specific instances will hold true for all instances in a given category.

Gestures   The use of hands, body movements, and facial expressions while speaking.

Global listeners/learners   The right hemisphere of the brain is responsible for intuitive, spatial, visual, and concrete matters; those with this listening/learning dominance prefer examples rather than technical explanations, prefer knowing the information can be useful and applied, are creative and rely on intuitive thinking, can follow visual/pictographic rather than written instructions, like to explore information without necessarily coming to a conclusion, and enjoy interaction rather than lecturing.

Goal of the speech   Terms that express the expected outcome of a speech, which usually include to inform or to persuade.

Group   An assemblage of persons who communicate, face to face, in order to fulfill a common purpose and achieve a goal.

Group cohesion   The interconnectedness of the members of a group.

Group communication networks   The patterns that are developed by members of groups to pass information between members.

Group conforming   The stage in group operation when there has been settlement of such things as norms, the group's purpose, and how to handle the role of power.

Group norm standards The habits of the thinking a particular group that may be used as a guide for persuasive speakers for developing their arguments.

Group norming The stage in group operation in which the group members come together and start a group, or welcoming new people into an existing group.

Group norms The rules by which a group operates.

Group performing The action stage of group process, when the group is working toward its goals with clearly established rules of operation.

Group storming The stage in group operations during which conflicts erupt, which most commonly takes place during the process of setting rules or working toward the group's goal.

Groupthink The mode of thinking by members of a group in which concurrence-seeking becomes so dominant that it tends to override realistic appraisal of alternative courses of action.

Guilty conscience The real or perceived fear by a person that she/he is going to get caught, get punished, or "found out."

Hasty generalization An unwarranted general conclusion from an insufficient number of instances.

Hearing A biological activity that involves reception of a message through sensory channels; the first action in the listening process.

Hidden agenda An objective or purpose that goes beyond the constructive interests of the group as a whole.

Hierarchy of Human Needs A theory of needs satisfaction; based on this view, a speaker must determine the level of need of a particular group of listeners and then select appeals aimed at that level.

High-prestige dialects Language and accents used by the mainstream members of a society.

Holistic thinking Thought pattern that doesn't dissect events or concepts but regards information in totality; a thought process typical in South American and Asian cultures and people descendant from those cultures.

Hypothesis conclusion A conclusion reached by taking into consideration all available evidence.

Ideal self Who a person would like to be or thinks he/she should be; the "perfect you."

Identifying language Language that names things, thus being able to clarify exactly what is being spoken about.

Ignoring the issue Reasoning fallacies that can result from using irrelevant arguments to obscure the real issue.

Illustrations Detailed stories used in a speech to clarify a point, not offer proof.

Illustrators Kinesic acts accompanying speech that are used to aid in the description of what is being said or trace the direction of speech.

Impromptu speaking A speech given with little or no preparation.

Inarticulates Sound, words, or phrases that have no meaning or do not help the listener gain a clear understanding of the message; fillers that cover up the speaker's inability to think of what to say or fill in thinking time or are bad vocal habits: "you know" and "stuff like that."

Individual norm standards A theory that states that certain people within any group influence the thinking of a group.

Inductive argument A reasoning system based on probability; a conclusion that is derived from the expected or believed from the available evidence.

Inferences Results when we interpret beyond available information, or jump to conclusions without using all of the information available.

Informal time Flexible use of time such as "soon," or "right away," which can cause communicative difficulty because they are arbitrary and mean different things to different people.

Information highway An assemblage of networks hooking primary and secondary schools, public and private institutions, commercial enterprises, individuals in their homes, and foreign institutions together for collaboration.

Information-gathering interview An interview that sets out to obtain information from a respondent; a format important to journalists, law enforcement authorities, health care workers, students, business people, and mental health professionals.

Informative briefing An information public speech that presents information to a specialized audience, followed by the exchange of data, ideas, and questions among participants.

Informative speaking A public speech that imparts new information, secures understanding, or reinforces accumulated information.

Innate neurological programs Those automatic nonverbal reactions to stimuli with which individuals are born.

Inner speech The acts of mumbling, daydreaming, dreaming, fantasizing, and feeling tension by which, awake or asleep, a person is constantly in touch with himself/herself; sometimes referred to as self-talk.

Interactional model of communication A process in which a source encodes and sends a message to a receiver (through one or more of the sensory channels); the receiver receives and decodes the message; encodes feedback and sends it back to the source, thus making the process two-directional; the source then decodes the feedback message; based on the original message sent and the feedback received, the source then encodes a new message that adapts to the feedback (adaptation).

Intercultural communication   When a person speaks to those with whom he/she has little or no cultural bond.

Internal or external listening response   An emotional or intellectual reaction to a message that has been received.

Internal summary   A short restatement of what just has been said in the section of a speech before proceeding to the next segment.

Interpersonal communication   Communication that takes place between two persons who establish a communicative relationship, which includes conversations, interviews, and small-group discussions.

Interrogation   An interviewing technique that uses leading questions in an attempt to discredit or incriminate an interviewee by asking questions that elicit information outside his or her factual knowledge; a technique used by law enforcement officers and trial attorneys.

Interrogation interview   An interview format designed to secure information from an interviewee through extensive use of probing techniques, used by lawyers, credit officers, tax specialists, and law enforcement officers.

Interview   A purposeful conversation between two or more persons that follows a basic question-and-answer format; interviewing is more formal than most conversations because the participants usually share a preset purpose and use a focused structure.

Interview format   An outline of the procedures that will be used to achieve the interaction's purpose.

Interviewee   The person who is being interviewed; should prepare for the session by knowing the purpose of the meeting and what his or her role and responsibilities are.

Interviewer   The person responsible for an interview's arrangements and takes the lead in conducting the activity; usually establishes the time, location, and purpose of the meeting.

Interview's conclusion   A summary of what has been accomplished during an interview, which may also indicate the next step to be taken after the interview has ended.

Intimate distance   The space varying from direct physical contact with another person to a distance of six to eighteen inches, which is used for our most private activities—caressing, making love, and sharing intimate ideas and emotions.

Intracultural communication   Communication in which a person interacts with those with whom she/he has a cultural bond.

Intrapersonal communication   Communicating with yourself, which includes thought-processing, personal decision-making, listening, and determination of self-concept.

Introduction to a speech   The beginning section of a speech that attempts to gain the listeners' attention and orient them to the material that will be presented.

Intuitive-affective decision-making approach   An approach to decision-making that attempts to develop a solution by using broad issues that do not appear to be directly related to the issue; these issues are linked together on the basis of whether or not the speaker likes the issues; a technique used in many Arabic cultures.

Inverted funnel schedule   A technique used in reprimanding that starts out with a clear, specific statement of the performance problem so that there is no question as to the problem and works toward a solution.

Johari window   A method of illustrating that allows a person to ascertain his or her willingness to disclose who he or she is and whether the person is interested in allowing someone else to disclose to her/him.

Kinesics   The study of communication through body movement.

Laissez-faire leader   A leader who uses a nondirective style and lets group members "do their own thing."

Language   A system of human communication based on speech sounds used as arbitrary symbols; does not remain static; it is constantly changing.

Language distortion   Confusion caused by language ambiguity, vagueness, or unclear inferences.

Language-Explosion Theory   Proposes that humans build communication skills from the core of language developed early in life.

Large groups   An assemblage of more than a dozen people who form to achieve a common purpose or goal.

Leaders   Those who guide a group.

Leadership   Those who influence a group to accomplish its goal.

Leadership power   An enforcing of obedience by the group leader through the ability to withhold benefits or to inflict punishment.

Leading questions   Questions that encourage a specific answer because they imply how the interviewee should answer the question, such as, "You wouldn't say you favor gun-control legislation, would you?"

Lecture   An information public speech that facilitates learning.

Lie detection/Lie detector   The attempt to read the body's nonverbal reactions by measuring changes in blood pressure, respiration, and skin response; attempting to detect a conflicting relationship between the verbal and the nonverbal.

Linear learners/listeners   The left hemisphere of the brain is most responsible for rational, logical, sequential, linear, and abstract thinking; people who tend to be left-brain dominant listen and learn best when materials are presented in structured ways and tend to like specifics and logic-based arguments.

Linear model of communication   A process in which a speaker encodes a message and sends it to a listener through one or more of the sensory channels.

Linear time   A societal use of time that is concerned primarily with the future; these societies focus on the factual and technical information needed to fulfill impending demands such as in most of Western Europe, North America, and Japan.

Linguist   A social scientist who studies the structures of various languages in order to provide concepts that describe languages.

Linguistics   The study of the structure of human language.

Listening   A process that involves reception, perception, attention, the assignment of meaning, and response by the listener to the message presented.

Litigation   Adversary communication in which a dispute is settled by presenting evidence to a judge or a jury who are given the responsibility of deciding who is right.

Loaded questions   A type of leading question that is designed to elicit an emotional response, such as asking a job applicant who was president of the union at a previous job to defend this company's policy of nonunion affiliation.

Logos   Logical arguments; one of the three speaker components in the Western culture's system of persuasion.

Lose-lose negotiation   A way of attempting to deal with problems, which centers on one person getting what he or she wants while the other comes up short; neither person is satisfied with the outcome.

Low-prestige dialects   Language and accents used by people who do not use mainstream language patterns; individuals who use nonstandard dialects.

Maintenance dimension of groups   The social responsibilities of a group, which center on meeting the interpersonal needs of the members.

Majority vote   A voting procedure in which the winner receive mores than half of the votes excluding those who do not vote or who abstain (i.e., do not want to vote).

Manuscript speech mode   The preparation method and reference aids in which the material for a speech is written out and delivered word for word.

Media conference   A technique that allows a group to conduct meetings via telephones, computers, or television.

Media interview   An interview which takes is broadcast on radio or television in which the interviewer asks questions of a guest.

Mediation   A process in which a neutral person, who has no vested interest in the outcome, facilitates communication between parties, and without imposing a solution on the parties, enables them to understand and resolve their dispute.

Meet while standing   A method of decision-making in which participants are forced to stand while making decisions so that they will work more rapidly because the participants get tired and want to finish their business and find someplace to sit.

Memorized speech mode   The preparation method and reference aids in which a speech is written out word for word and is then committed to memory.

Messages   The material/information that is communicated.

Method of issue arrangement for the body of a speech   A way of organizing the body of a speech, which usually takes one of six forms: spatial arrangement, chronological/time arrangement, topical arrangement, causal arrangement, comparison-contrast arrangement, or problem-solution arrangement; the sequencing of the body of a speech for listener clarity.

Method of speech development   The structure of a speech, which can be chronological, spatial, cause-effect, problem-solution, or topical.

Mirror question   A form of question that is intended to get a person to reflect on what he or she has said and expand on it; for example, the interviewee may say, "I've worked for this corporation for years, and I'm getting nowhere." The mirror question might be, "Do you feel you're not moving ahead in the corporation?"

Mockup   A visual aid that shows the building up or tearing down of a real object or model.

Modes of speech presentation   The preparation method and reference aids used during the speech; impromptu or ad lib, extemporaneous, manuscript, and memorized modes.

Monotone   A flat, boring oral sound resulting from constant pitch, volume, and rate.

Multiculturalism   A political and attitudinal movement to ensure cultural freedom, so as to eliminate the feeling among disfranchised groups such as people of color, gays and lesbians, and people from cultures other than the mainstream culture.

Multiculture   A society consisting of varied cultural groups.

Nationality   The nation in which one was born, now resides, or has lived in or studied for enough time to become familiar with the customs of the area.

Native American/American Indian language   Languages used by Native Americans/American Indians; there is no one language since Indian identity is not the same as tribal identity, as all tribes have differing languages and customs.

Negotiation   The act of bargaining to reach an agreement with at least two people working on a mutual problem.

Neurolinguistic programming   The theory that indicates that many nonverbal actions are inborn, part of the neurological system.

Noise   Any internal or external interference in the communication process including environmental obstacles, physiological impairment, semantic problems, syntactic problems, organizational confusion, cultural influences, or psychological problems.

Nominal Group Technique of Decision-Making   A group decision-making procedure that encourages generation of ideas from all individuals but avoids criticism, destructive conflict, and long-winded speeches.

Nonassertive behavior   Attempting to resolve conflict by avoiding conflict.

Noncontact cultures   Those cultures characterized by nontactile modes of communication, thus stressing little touching, hugging, or close space proxemity (Germans, English, North Americans).

Nondirective techniques   Counseling techniques in which the interviewer does not take an active role in a solution; can work only if the troubled person accepts that a problem exists, has the skills to identify what is wrong, and deals with it.

Nonstandard dialects   Pronunciation and intonation used by individuals who are not part of the mainstream society.

Nonverbal communication   All messages that people exchange besides the words themselves.

Olfactics   The study of smell.

1-3-6 Decision-Making Technique   A format for decision-making in which each participant works alone (1), then in a group of 3 and then in group of 6.

Open question   A question that specifies only the topic and invites the answerer to respond as he or she desires, such as, "What is your educational background?

Oral footnote   A statement that states the source of the material being presented in a speech.

Organizational noise   When the receiver fails to understand the message because the source failed to realize that certain ideas are best grasped when presented in a structured order.

Orienting material   The section of the introduction that gives the audience the background necessary to understand the basic material of the speech, often provides a historical background, defines terms that will be used in the presentation, ties the speaker's personal history to the subject, and illuminates the importance of the ideas to the listener.

Other-perceived Me   The person that others perceive you to be; it may be the same or different from your self-perceived I.

Paraphrases   Someone's ideas put into a speaker's own words.

Paraphrasing   The listener making a summary of the ideas she or he has just received.

Paravocalics   All the vocal effects made to accompany words, such as tone of voice—but not the words themselves, such as rate (speed), volume (power), pitch (such as soprano or bass), pause (stopping), and stress (intensity).

Participants   Those members of a group who interact to bring about the actions of the group.

Partitioning organizational speech structure   A method for organizing a speech in which the speaker starts with the introduction, leads into the central idea, then states the central idea, restates it, and divides it by listing the main issues to be covered in the order in which they will be covered, which divides a speech into topical section.

Partitioning step   The restatement made by a speaker who is using the partitioning organizational speech structure as she or he goes from one topical section to the other.

Part-of-the-whole voting   A voting procedure in which a specific number or percentage of those who are eligible to vote agree on an action to be taken.

Passive aggression   Pretending that nothing is wrong, but derailing any attempt to solve a problem that isn't to your liking in a way that doesn't appear to be aggressive, including using sarcasm or withholding; being sweet and polite, but, in fact, controlling what is being done.

Pathos   Psychological appeals; one of the three speaker components in the Western culture's system of persuasion.

Perceptions   The factors that combine to allow each individual to view the world, which are determined by a person's culture, communication skills, physical and emotional states, experiences, attitudes, memory, and expectations.

Perceptual filter   The device in the brain that strains the stimuli received and separates what makes sense from what doesn't based on a person's background, culture, experiences, roles, mental and physical state, beliefs, attitudes, and values.

Personal distance   An eighteen-inches to four-feet zone between people in which most North Americans feel most comfortable when talking with others.

Personal relational phase   The phase of a relationship in which information about central attitudes and values is exchanged.

Persuasion   The process of influencing attitudes and behaviors.

Persuasive interview   An interview format that attempts to change a person's beliefs or behavior.

Persuasive speech   A speech intended to influence the opinion or behavior of an audience.

Phatic language   Language used to reinforce the relationship between the participants in a communicative exchange; greetings, farewells, and small-talk exchanges such as "Hello, how are you?" and "Have a nice day."

Pictographical language   A language system, such as Chinese, in which symbols represent a single word; in contrast to alphabetical languages in which letters are combined into units called words.

Plurality   A voting procedure in which the winner received the most votes.

Pollyanna-Nietzsche effect   A group phenomena in which there is excessive optimism (*pollyannaism*) and an idealized belief (*nietzschism*) that the group is superhuman and can do no wrong.

Postspeech analysis   Information following a speech that enables a speaker to determine how a speech affected the audience.

Power   The ability to control what happens—to cause things you want to happen and to block things that you do not want to happen.

Power role   The ability to influence another's attainment of goal, which normally centers on controlling another person or persons, influencing the efforts of others, and accomplishing a goal.

Presentation graphics   A series of visuals that are projected via an overhead projector while the speaker is discussing each point; may be computer generated through such a program as Microsoft's PowerPoint.

Primary group tension   The normal jitters and feelings of uneasiness experienced when groups first congregate.

Primary signal system   The tools used to send and receive messages; the senses: seeing, hearing, tasting, smelling, and touching.

Primary sources of information   Sources of information that represent the original reports of the observations or research.

Prior to the speech analysis   The process of finding out the demographic, psychographic and rhetorgraphic characteristics of the prospective listeners before the speech is given.

Probe   A question that is used in interviews to elicit a more detailed response, such as, "Why do you feel that way?"

Problem-solution method of issue arrangement   A way of organizing the body of a speech in which a speaker attempts to identify what is wrong and to determine how to cure it or make a recommendation for its cure.

Problem-solving interview   An interview in which the interviewer and interviewee meet to solve a problem.

Process of the speech analysis   Observing the audience for feedback during a speech.

Proposal-counterproposal negotiating   Negotiation in which a plan or solution is presented and then a counteroffer made.

Proxemics   The study of how people use and perceive their social and personal space.

Psychographics   Attitudes and beliefs of the audience members are an important consideration. This profile can be determined by analyzing the listeners.

Psychological appeals   Enlists listeners' emotions as motivation for accepting persuasive arguments.

Psychological noise   Stress, frustration, or irritation causes us to either send or receive messages ineffectively.

Public communication   Characterized by a speaker sending a message to an audience, it may be direct, such as a face-to-face message delivered by a speaker to an audience; or indirect, such as a message relayed by radio or television.

Public distance A separation between individuals of as little as twelve feet but usually more than twenty-five.

Public meetings Assemblages of interested individuals attending a meeting in which there is no restricted membership.

Public self The image a person lets others know; based on the concept that "if others believe the right things about me, I can get them to like me; I can persuade them and generally get my way."

Public speaking anxiety A phobia, known as speechophobia, which is characterized by (1) persistent fear of a specific situation out of proportion to the reality of the danger, (2) a compelling desire to avoid and escape the situation, and (3) a recognition that the fear is unreasonable and excessive; it is not due to any other disorder. As with most phobias, it is curable.

Pupilometrics A theory that indicates that pupils dilate when the eyes are focused on a pleasurable object, and contract when focused on an unpleasurable one.

Purpose of the speech The speaker's expected outcomes for the presentation.

Question-and-answer session An on the spot set of unrehearsed answers that measures a speaker's knowledge, alerts a speaker to areas in a speech that were unclear or needed more development, and gives listeners a chance to probe for ideas.

Question of fact A proposal for action by a group in which something is established as true and to what extent.

Question of policy A question for action by a group of whether a specific course of action should be undertaken to solve a problem.

Question of value A question for action by a group of whether something is good or bad, right or wrong, and to what extent.

Quotations Material written or spoken by a person in the exact words in which it was originally presented

Razzing An American Indian/Native American storytelling form in which participants take some episode, humorous or not, from a present or past experience and relate it humorously to the others in attendance. The story, which is often lengthy, is then characteristically embellished and altered by others who are present.

Real self What a person thinks of herself/himself when being most honest about interests, thoughts, emotions, and needs.

Recalibrated A relational system that has been restructured.

Recalibration The process of restructuring a communicative system by altering the rules and methods by which the system is operating.

Receiver The recipient of a message.

Reception The initial step in the listening process includes receiving of both the auditory message and the visual message.

Red flag words Words or phrases that evoke emotional biases in a person based on her/his culture, religion, ethnic beliefs, and biases.

Reflexive actions Automatic nonverbal reactions caused by neurological drives, such as a person blinking her eyes when a pebble hits the windshield while she is driving.

Regulators Nonverbal acts that maintain and control the back-and-forth nature of speaking and listening between two or more people; nods of the head, eye movements, and body shifts are all regulators used to encourage or discourage conversation.

Relational costs An individual's investment of money, time, and emotion in a relationship; the investment as a part of the economic model of relationships.

Relational fusion When one partner defines, or attempts to define, reality for the other partner in a relationship.

Relational rewards An individual's profits from being involved in a relationships; the positive gains received as a part of the economic model of relationships.

Reprimanding interview An interview format that helps the interviewee to analyze his or her problems and develop techniques to correct them.

Requesting The process of expressing a desire for something.

Rhetorical language Using appropriate language based on the participants, setting, and purpose to accomplish the desired goal.

Rhetorical question A device used to gain the listener's attention at the start of a speech in which a question has no outward response.

Rhetorographics The place, time limit, time of day, and emotional climate for a speech.

Risky shift phenomenon A theory that holds that decisions reached after discussion by a group display more experimentation, are less conservative, and contain more risk than decisions reached by people working alone before any discussion is held.

Robert's Rules of Order The most commonly used a set of parliamentary guidelines for handling procedural agreements and disagreements.

Sales interview   An interview format that attempts to link the customer's needs and interests with a product or service.

Scale model   A representation of a real object that is in exact proportion to the dimensions of the original object.

Schema   Scripts a listener uses for processing information.

Schemata   Information that is shaped by the language categories and by the way our brains process information.

Secondary group tension   The stress and strain that occurs within a group later in its development.

Secondary sources of information   Sources of information that report, but did not generate, the original observations or research.

Selective communication   Choosing the symbol that best represents the idea or concept to be express, combining sounds into complicated structures so as to describe events and objects.

Selective perception   The process of a listener narrowing his or her attention on specific bits of pieces of information.

Self-concept   The view one has of oneself.

Self-disclosure   Intentionally letting another person know who you are by communicating self-revealing information which can be done through verbal or nonverbal messages.

Self-fulfilled person   The person who confidently chooses what to reveal and to whom; a self-fulfilled person is not intimidated into a negative self-concept and realizes that there will always be problems, frustrations, and failures in life.

Self-love   The acceptance of oneself as a worthy person.

Self-perceived I   The image a person projects; the way a person perceives herself/himself.

Self-talk   A nearly constant subconscious monologue or inner speech with ourselves; sometimes referred to as inner speech.

Semantic noise   Problems in coding or decoding a message caused by either source's understanding of the meaning of words.

Semantics   The study of the relationship of language and meaning.

Sex   One's biological or physical self; the sexes (male and female) are different because the brain is constructed differently in men and in women, which allows for the processing of information in a different way; not the same as gender, which is one's psychological, social, and interactive self.

Sexual harassment   Generalized sexist remarks or behavior; inappropriate and offensive, but essentially sanction-free, sexual advances; solicitation of sexual activity or other sex-linked behavior by promise of rewards; coercion of sexual activity by threat of punishment; and assaults.

Significant-Other Theory   Centers on the principle that our understanding of self is built by those who react to and comment on our language, actions, ideas, beliefs, and mannerisms.

Silent majority   Those members of a group who say nothing during the decision-making process.

Simple assertion   A statement in which a person states the facts relating to the existence of a problem.

Six-Step Standard Agenda for Decision-Making   A decision-making procedure that requires a reflective-thinking process, which stresses that a problem be identified and analyzed, solutions sought, and a solution selected and implemented.

Slang   Words that are related to a specific activity or incident and are immediately understood by members of a particular group.

Small groups   An assemblage of three to twelve persons who form to achieve a common purpose or goal.

Small-group ecology   The placement of chairs, the placement of the person conducting a meeting, and the setting for a small-group encounter.

Small talk   is an exchange of information with someone at a surface level and centers on biographics (name, occupation or college major, hometown, college attended or attending) or slightly more personal information (hobbies, interests, future plans, acquaintances).

Smell adaptation   When a person gradually loses the distinctiveness of a particular smell through repeated contact with it.

Smell blindness   When a person is unable to detect smells.

Smell discrimination   The ability to identify people, places, and things on the basis of their smell.

Smell memory   The ability to recall previous situations when encountering a particular smell associated when a person is exposed to the same or a similar smell.

Smell overload   Takes place when an exceptionally large number of odors or one extremely strong odor overpowers a person.

Social distance   A four- to twelve-foot zone that is used during business transactions and casual social exchanges.

Social loafing   Occurs when group membership leads people to work less than they would individually.

Source   The originator of a message.

Spanglish   A common linguistic currency used by Spanish Americans.

Spatial method of issue arrangement   A method of organizing the body of a speech in which the presenter sets a point of reference at a specific location, and then follows a geographic pattern in developing the material.

Speaker credibility   The reputation, prestige, and authority of a speaker as perceived by the listeners.

Speaking setting   Where the speech is given, what the time limit is, when the presentation is made, and the emotional attitude of the audience.

Specific instances   Condensed examples that are used to clarify or prove a point.

Speech of actuation   A persuasive speech whose objective is to move the members of the audience to take the desired action that the speaker has proposed.

Speech of conviction   A persuasive speech whose objective is to convince the listener to believe as the speaker does.

Speech of introduction   An information public speech that identifies the person who will be speaking to the audience and gives information that may spark listeners' interest in the speaker or the topic.

Speech participants   The speaker and the members of the audience.

Speech planning outline   A brief framework used to think through the process of the speech.

Speech presentation outline   A framework in which the speaker fleshes out the speech, planning outline details such as examples, illustrations, internal summaries, and forecasts.

Speeches about concepts   An information public speech that examines theories, beliefs, ideas, philosophies, or schools of thought.

Speeches about events   An information public speech that informs about something that has already happened, is happening, or is expected to happen.

Speeches about objects   An information public speech that describes a particular thing in detail such as a person, place, animal, structure, machine—anything that can be touched or seen.

Speeches about processes   An information public speech that instructs about how something works, is made, or is done.

Speech-independent gestures   Those gestures not tied to speech, but which carry their own meaning, such as holding up one finger when asked how many scoops of ice cream you want; emblems.

Speechophobia   The term used to define public speaking anxiety.

Speech-related gestures   Those gestures directly tied to, or accompanying the speech, including illustrators, affect displays, regulators, and adaptors.

Spiral form of explanation   A mode of organizing a speech in which a statement is made, then a story or analogy that deals with that statement is presented, and then it is often left up to the listener to apply the parallels and draw outcomes related to the original statement.

Spiral structure of argument   A narrative communication pattern, commonly used by Hispanics and Arabs in which stories are used to explain ideas; strikes many Standard American English speakers as abstract and imprecise because it does not set up a clear purpose and use evidence to clarify and prove.

Standard American English   The language generally recognized by linguists as representative of the general population of the United States.

Standard dialects   Pronunciation and intonation representative of the mainstream/high-prestige members of a society.

Standing-seated interaction   A communicative transaction in which the person in control stands and the other person sits, such as in teacher-pupil and police officer–arrestee transactions.

Statement of central idea   Defines the subject and develops the criteria by which to evaluate the material included in a speech; a statement that centers on what a speaker wants the audience to know, to be able to do, to believe.

Statement of the speech's central idea   The section of the speech that is intended to keep the speaker on course for developing a purposeful and well-organized speech; indicates the response the speaker wants from listeners.

Statistics   Any collection of numerical information arranged to indicate representations, trends, or theories.

Study groups   Small groups established to enable individuals to work together to study and learn with the assistance of others.

Study of language   The study of meaning, meaning based on words.

Substituting relationship   The relationship of verbal and nonverbal communication in which the nonverbal replaces the verbal. Such as performing the action meaning "yes" (nodding of the head vertically) for the spoken word *yes*.

Summary of a speech   The final segment of a speech in which the major points of the speech are restated.

Superleadership   A leadership style in which people are led to lead themselves and thereby release the self-leadership energy within each person.

Supplementary speech aids   Visual, audio, audio-visual, and computer-aided graphics that are intended to facilitate listener understanding.

Support group   A system that allows people to interact with others in order to increase people's knowledge of themselves and others, assist people to clarify the changes they most want to make in their life, and give people some of the tools necessary to make these changes.

Supporting speech material   Ideas whose purpose is to clarify a point being made in a speech.

Symposium   A group discussion format in which participants give prepared speeches with no interaction between each other or the audience.

Syntactical noise   Inappropriate grammatical usage; can interfere with clear communication.

Synthetic model   A representation of a real object that is not in proportion but nevertheless representative of the original object.

Systematic desensitization   A method used to aid people to overcome or control their communication apprehension in which they are taught to recognize tension in their bodies and then how to relax.

Tag questions   Question added onto the end of statements, such as "That movie was terrific, don't you think?" with the intent to get the partner to enter the conversation.

Task dimension of groups   The action responsibilities, which include decision-making, informing, appraising/examining, problem solving, and creating interest in staying on track.

Technical report   An information public speech that is a concise, clear statement explaining a process, explaining a technique, or discussing new elements, either to people within a business or industry or to people outside it.

Technical time   Precise time, as in the way some scientists look at how things happen in milliseconds.

Technobabble   Computer language used for other meaning.

Teleconferencing   A media conference conducted by television.

Testimony   A direct quotation or a paraphrase from an authority.

Theme statements   A device used to gain the listener's attention at the start of a speech that indicates exactly what the speaker is going to talk about.

Theory of field-related standards   A concept that proposes that not all people reach conclusions in the same way and thus may react differently to the same evidence or psychological material.

Therapeutic listening   The attempt to be an empathic listener, putting oneself in the emotional and intellectual place of the sender; requires a listener to learn when to ask questions, when to stimulate further discussion, and when, if ever, to give advice.

Time method of issue arrangement   A way of organizing the body of a speech, which orders information from a beginning point to an ending one, with all the steps developed in numerical or time sequence.

Topic of the speech   The subject to be covered in a speech.

Topical method of issue arrangement   A way of organizing the body of a speech in which a speaker explains an idea in terms of its component parts.

Touch   The placing of a hand on another's body.

Town meeting   A public meeting in which a presenter opens with some short, prepared statement that establishes the framework for the meeting, followed by individuals in the audience then engaging in a forum with the speaker.

Transactional model of communication   A process in which messages are processed simultaneously by the communicators. Communicator A encodes a message and sends it. Communicator B then encodes feedback and send it to A, who decodes it. These steps are not mutually exclusive; encoding and decoding may occur simultaneously.

Transformational leadership   A leadership style in which a leader serves as a transforming agent because he or she can change both the behavior and the outlook of his or her followers.

Transitions   Statements made during a speech that provide a connection between the points being made.

Two-valued orientation   The understanding that life is multidimensional and that meanings vary as the backgrounds and experiences of the communicators differ; the ability to classify ideas and contentions in an either/or orientation, rather than assuming everything is right or wrong.

Unfolding organizational speech structure   A method for organizing a speech in which the ideas bridge from one to another.

Vagueness   Ambiguousness that results from words or sentences lacking clarity.

Values   What a person perceives to be of positive or negative worth.

Vernacular Black English   Ebonics; the most common dialect used by African Americans.

Visual aids   Aids used in a speech that appeal to the listener's sense of sight.

Voting   A procedure that takes place when members are given an opportunity to indicate agreement, disagreement, or no opinion on an idea or candidate.

Win-lose negotiation   A way of attempting to deal with problems that centers on one person getting what he or she wants while the other comes up short.

Win-win negotiation   A way of attempting to deal with problems that centers on all participants satisfying their wants.

Work teams   Small groups of workers who function as teams to make and implement decisions about the work to be done.

Yes-response question   A form of leading question that is stated in such a way that the respondent is encouraged to agree with the interviewer, such as, "You would agree with me, wouldn't you, that this company's policies are fair?"

INDEX